International Relations

A Policymaker Focus

Second Edition

International Relations

A Policymaker Focus

Second Edition

Robert L. Wendzel
University of Maine

John Wiley & Sons
New York   Chichester   Brisbane   Toronto

Copyright © 1977, 1980 by John Wiley & Sons, Inc.

All rights reserved. Published simultaneously in Canada.

Reproduction or translation of any part of
this work beyond that permitted by Sections
107 and 108 of the 1976 United States Copyright
Act without the permission of the copyright
owner is unlawful. Requests for permission
or further information should be addressed to
the Permissions Department, John Wiley & Sons.

Library of Congress Cataloging in Publication Data:

Wendzel, Robert L., 1938–
  International relations.

  Includes index.
  1. International relations. I. Title.
JX1395.W45   1979   327   79-1215
ISBN 0-471-05261-2

Printed in the United States of America

10 9 8 7 6 5 4 3 2 1

TO DAD

Preface

This edition retains the central organizing feature of the first, the "policymaker focus." I am more than ever convinced of its value. As the first edition, this book is an analytic core text written primarily for students taking their initial course in the discipline. The book continually stresses the necessity of dealing with real world situations on a practical, specific basis.

The basic organizational structure of the first edition has been retained. In Chapter 1 the international environment within which the policymaker works is analyzed, Chapters 2 and 3 provide a discussion of policy formulation, Chapters 4 and 5 analyze the instruments of policy implementation, and Chapters 6 and 7 examine policymaking difficulties. This arrangement (along with the book's specific focus and small size) seems to optimize instructor flexibility because the various chapters can be interchanged according to the particular professor's classroom requirements. To take one example, whereas in my courses the chapters are studied in sequence, because I prefer to provide the student with the tools of and framework for analysis before discussing policymaking difficulties, others might be interested in discussing domestic constraints and common policymaking problems earlier and wish to use Chapters 6 and 7 (or either of them) immediately after Chapter 1. And there are other useful interchanges that could be made also. Given the multitude of teaching approaches in use today, this flexibility is a considerable asset.

As a result of the constructive suggestions of students and colleagues and certain developments in my own thinking, the second edition incorporates certain revisions. First, for obvious reasons, a degree of "updating" has occurred. Second, to increase student interest, I have used very recent examples to illustrate analytical points more frequently. Third, to the same end, more graphics have been employed in Chapter 3. Fourth, I have made a concerted effort to refine and clarify wherever feedback indicated this would be helpful. The most notable instance involved rewriting the orientation options section of Chapter 2. Finally, also in Chapter 2, additional material was essential to complete the discussion of alliance adjustments, so an examination of alliance prevention has been added.

Several colleagues made suggestions that were helpful in preparing the second edition. While the complete list is too long to be included here, I specifically thank Raymond D. Duvall of the University of Minnesota, Louis L. Ortmayer of Davidson College, David N. Farnsworth of Wichita State University, Hans Mair of Loyola College (Baltimore), Fred A. Sondermann of The

Colorado College, Austin F. Walter of Oregon State University, and Robert Bledsoe of Florida Technological University. Additionally, I acknowledge my enormous intellectual debt to Frederick H. Hartmann of the Naval War College, the man who over the years has done more to shape my thinking than any other single individual. I also owe much to my editor at Wiley, Wayne Anderson, who was both helpful and patient throughout. Finally, again the persistent and consistent help of my wife and typist, Karen, was invaluable. Without her the revision could not have been accomplished. Obviously, if errors exist they are mine alone.

Robert L. Wendzel

Preface to the First Edition

This book is a concise core text in international relations. It is written mainly for students who are taking their first course in the discipline, and it stresses the necessity of dealing with situations in the real world on a practical, specific basis.

The approach is primarily analytical, and its central organizing feature is the "policymaker focus." It has four parts.

1. It involves a concern for the policymaker's actual perceptions and actions. A considered effort is made to view things through the policymaker's eyes.
2. It includes an examination of the many factors that significantly affect the policymaker, whether he is aware of them (and correctly perceives them) or not. Thus it is broader than just the policymaker's perceptions.
3. My approach includes a continuing effort to induce the student to "put himself in the policymaker's shoes." Not only does this stimulate his interest but also it is the only way that he can appreciate the complexities and problems with which policymakers must deal.
4. The book contains a normative element. Frequently, there is an attempt to provide some guidelines as to how policymakers presumably "should" try to proceed in certain cases, what they probably "should" at least attempt to do, and so on.

Although the book is analytical, it will have eminent practical value. By focusing on the policymaker, it gives the student an understanding of the basic options that policymakers realistically might have available in concrete situations and the vast array of difficulties that they may encounter. Its pragmatic specificity also provides the student with a useful analytical foundation for his own examination of concrete situations.

Because this is a core text, some of the descriptive and historical material usually found in textbooks is not included. However, other works dealing with these areas can be used as a supplement according to the particular desires and needs of specific professors and students. This does not mean that no such material is used. On the contrary, I have included a variety of historical examples, many of which have considerable contemporary relevance. The key point is that historical and descriptive material is employed only for the purpose of illustrating analytical concepts.

My organizational approach is, first, to analyze the fundamental framework for the policymaker's activities—the basic features of the international environment within which he or she works. Second, in Chapters 2 and 3, I discuss the steps in formulating policy. Third, in Chapters 4 and 5, I analyze the instruments of policy implementation, the means of carrying out the policy previously decided upon. And fourth, in Chapters 6 and 7, I examine a variety of policymaking difficulties including domestic constraints.

I have tried to make this book as readable as possible, since it will be of little value to students unless they *can* and *will* read it. Therefore, jargon is avoided unless it is clearly necessary. Traditional concepts are used when their meaning is clear, but an effort is made to avoid ambiguous carry-overs from the past, no matter how venerable they may be. To add clarity and precision to the analysis, I have introduced, at some points, new common-sense terminology that specifically and accurately identifies the concepts being used.

This book is not a panacea. It does not attempt to provide a definitive description of all international relations; nor is it a prescription for the future of mankind. Furthermore, it is written in full knowledge that a myriad of methods for studying international relations already exists. But the book fills an important gap: it is a concise core analysis with a policymaker focus.

Many people made valuable contributions. Several of my academic colleagues at the University of Maine at Orono read portions of the book and made constructive suggestions. I thank them for their help. Wayne Anderson, Political Science Editor at Wiley, was patient and encouraging, and he had considerable impact on the volume. Finally, the persistent and consistent help of my wife and typist, Karen, was invaluable. Without her, the book could not have been written. Of course, if errors remain, they are mine alone.

Robert L. Wendzel

Contents

Three

Four

INDEX

International Relations

A Policymaker Focus

Second Edition

CHAPTER One

The International Environment

On January 14, 1975 a spokesman for the United States Department of State said that the United States was legally free to breach the Vietnam cease-fire agreements because of various violations previously committed by Hanoi.[1] At first glance one might assume that this statement meant that Washington was deeply concerned with these alleged violations of the law and that various legal considerations were important in determining the nature of the response. Some observers did make this assumption but others disagreed. Some felt that the reference to the law was just a "cover." According to this line of reasoning, policymakers were much more worried about what they perceived to be Hanoi's increasing power than about any legal niceties, and this statement was a warning not to go too far. In addition, some analysts speculated about the presumed unethical nature of such violations and wondered whether American policymakers were really responding for moral reasons, and still others believed that the statement was just a tactical move in what was perceived to be an ideological struggle against communism.

How important are such factors? Do policymakers generally pay any attention to law or ethics? Is power all that counts? What kind of world do we live in? What is international relations all about, anyway?

The answers to these questions are extremely important. Unfortunately, they are also terribly complicated and one usually cannot reach definitive conclusions. Some general understandings are possible, however, and are very necessary. If the policymaker does not understand the general nature of the international environment, he or she may formulate and seek to implement policies that are contrary to the usual "facts of life." To the extent that the policymaker does so, his or her policies will fail.

Although precise, totally verifiable answers cannot be forthcoming, one can gain a meaningful understanding of the basic nature of the international environment by answering these seven questions:

1. Who are the primary parties (actors, units, components) whose actions

---

[1]*New York Times,* January 15, 1975, p. 1.

and interactions comprise the essence of international relations, and what are their characteristics?

2. How are governmental functions performed in the international political system?

3. What impact do ethical and moral considerations have on policymakers as they formulate and implement policy?

4. What is the role of international law? Are policymakers significantly influenced and regulated by it in their activities?

5. Does ideology play a significant role in determining various aspects of policy? If so, what is it?

6. How important are power factors, how prevalent are considerations of capability? Is international relations really just a constant power struggle, with everything else of only minute importance?

7. Should the policymaker assume that most relations are conflictual in nature, or are other types of relationships also important?

THE PARTIES

There are two major types of parties in international relations: state and nonstate. Traditionally the former have received the lion's share of the attention, and justly so. As the analysis will show, however, nonstate actors are becoming increasingly important.

States

The primary parties (units, actors, entities) of international relations are the 150 or so states (also variously called nation-states, nations, or countries). They have been the primary unit of international action for over 300 years and are still so today despite the occasional importance of other entities (dealt with below).[2] States vary immensely in terms of size, population, social conditions, and so forth, but despite their differences they exhibit certain common attributes, and it is these that give them their "statehood." As seen from the policymaker's perspective, what are these characteristics?

The first and most prominent is *territoriality*.[3] The entire earth's surface is subject to the authority of political units with a territorial basis. A state exists within a more or less defined geographic area with vaguely or specifically delineated boundaries; without territory there is no state.

---

[2]The modern nation-state system developed in Europe with the breakdown of feudalism. In the fifteenth and sixteenth centuries feudal princes began to consolidate and enlarge their domains through conquest and marriage. Eventually this process culminated in the establishment of unified, centralized states organized on a national basis and ruled by absolute kings. These were the precursors of the states of today.

[3]For a different view that its importance may decrease see John Herz, *International Politics in the Atomic Age*, Columbia University Press, New York, 1959, Parts I and II.

This requisite of territoriality obviously has implications for the policymaker. Considerations of territorial defense or acquisition are pertinent in a wide range of situations and, in some cases, possess overriding importance. As we point out in depth in Chapter 2, the defense of one's home territory is a fundamental policy objective, one for which in all but the most unusual circumstances states would be willing to make a maximum expenditure of resources (including going to war). Governments exercise direct authority over population, resources and many other components of capability within a specific territorial area. Because these factors are of considerable significance as the foundation of international influence, the location and configuration of boundaries is critical.

Usually, international boundaries are clearly delineated on maps (and on the ground as well) by various indicators, and they are accepted as legitimate. This is not always true, however. In portions of the Arabian Peninsula, for example, there are no clearly defined frontiers. The lack of precise boundaries and the resulting uncertainty can easily lead to (and be used to justify) conflict. The lack of a definitive border delineation was a significant factor leading to the 1962 Sino-Indian war.[4] And particular boundaries are not always accepted as legitimate. Often there is a clearly drawn line but one party simply does not accept its validity and considers land on the other side of the demarcation to be its "home" territory (or simply desires to acquire territory to satisfy various other objectives).

A second attribute of statehood is the *right of internal control* and the means to achieving it. A state, because it is a "sovereign" (translate: "independent") political unit, is largely free to govern as it wishes within its own territory; there is no superior agency to which it owes allegiance.[5] Its governmental and economic systems may be organized in any manner it desires. Its government is the supreme lawmaker within its borders, and foreign political units cannot make and enforce rules or settle disputes on its territory without its consent. The state has the final authority over the people within its boundaries, literally holding the power of life and death.

Policymakers are highly resistant to any action they perceive as an infringement on this right, as the Russians demonstrated in early 1977 in their reaction to President Carter's human rights campaign. Mr. Carter, concerned over what he felt were serious violations of fundamental human rights, outspokenly condemned states he believed to be engaging in such violations, including the U.S.S.R. During this particular period Soviet dissidents were causing the Kremlin much grief; apparently oblivious of Russian sensitivity on the issue, the

---

[4] Also see pp. 78–151.

[5] The concept of sovereignty was originally developed by the French philosopher Jean Bodin. Writing amidst the near anarchy in sixteenth-century France following the Wars of Religion, he sought to strengthen internal control and promote national unity. His ideas of absolute power over citizens and subjects exerted vast influence on his contemporaries and have been influential to this day.

President even exchanged personal letters with one of the dissident leaders, physicist Andrei Sakharov, and invited former dissident Vladimir Bukovski to the White House. The Soviets were absolutely furious and stated that such attempts at "interference in our internal affairs" were categorically "rejected."[6] When soon thereafter Secretary of State Cyrus Vance went to Moscow for talks on limiting strategic weapons he found Washington's proposals summarily dismissed; if the United States wanted progress on arms limitations it would first have to cease its violation of the Soviet Union's right of internal control.

One might have thought Mr. Carter would have learned something from the 1974 Trade Reform Act episode. As part of their attempts to develop closer relationships in the early 1970s, the United States and the Soviet Union sought to increase trade. The 1972 Summit Agreements gave impetus to this desire. When the U.S. Congress passed the Trade Reform Act in December 1974 and made the granting of nondiscriminatory trade status to the Soviets contingent upon a Russian agreement to liberalize their Jewish emigration policy, the Soviets responded by nullifying their Summit trade pledge. They stated that such a provision was an unacceptable interference in their internal affairs; Jewish emigration from Russia was Moscow's business and no one else's.

The function of internal control is provided by the state's government (the existence of which, in practical terms, is also a requisite of statehood and could be treated separately). It is the body that is presumed to have the legitimate authority to exercise control, free from foreign interference, and it is presumed to possess effective command of the means of enforcing its decisions. If it does not, conflict will ensue, but at some point a *de facto* government will be established if the state continues to exist.

This description of the autonomy of internal control does not reflect the actual situation of some states today. Indeed, many states are highly permeable and the extent and types of penetration seem to be rapidly increasing.[7] Nevertheless, if one evaluated most states on a continuum from autonomous-controlled to penetrated-uncontrolled, he or she would find most were relatively autonomous-controlled. Generally speaking, policymakers at least begin with this assumption and make adjustments from there.

A third attribute is *external autonomy and equality,* that is, the right to international legal equality and the freedom to pursue whatever foreign policy one desires (although presumably this is to be done within the confines of international law). Every state is supposed to possess certain rights including those of self-defense, territorial integrity, and political indpendence. It can sign treaties, enter alliances, or exchange diplomats. It is presumed to be free from

[6]Very useful is U.S.S.R., Novosti Press Agency Publishing House. *L.I. Brezhnev: Speech at the 16th Congress of the Trade Unions of the U.S.S.R., March 21, 1977,* Moscow, 1977, pp. 27–31.

[7]See Andrew M. Scott, *The Revolution in Statecraft: Informal Penetration,* Random House, New York, 1965.

external interference in the choice of foreign policy objectives, orientations, and implements. It has the right to maintain armed forces and the ultimate authority to determine whether or not to wage war. In fact, a state is assumed to be free from any restraint on its external conduct except that which is self-imposed, mutually agreed to, results from prudent calculation, or is generally accepted international law (and even this can be debated).

Once again the presumed characteristics are not present in every case. States are clearly unequal in many respects and it is obvious that sometimes foreign parties do interfere with the formulation and implementation of policy. Respect for territorial integrity and political independence is sometimes nonexistent, dependencies may be created, and even direct intervention may be undertaken. But as was true with respect to the characteristic of the right of internal control, the attribute of external autonomy *is* generally assumed by policymakers to exist and it *is* honored more than violated. As such, it continues to have considerable operational validity.

The final requisites for statehood are a *permanent population* and an *economic system*. A state cannot exist without inhabitants. Although the composition of the population is in constant flux, the fact of its existence is permanent. Similarly, in all states there is some set of arrangements by which capital and labor are combined to produce and distribute goods and services. Both of these factors can vary tremendously from state to state as can their impact on policy, but they must exist for a political unit to be called a state.

Nonstate Parties

Although it is a fact that the primary parties in international relations are states, and one should always assume that states are involved unless otherwise specified, there are certain nonstate actors that occasionally play significant roles. These vary widely in terms of permanence, scope, and purpose.

Perhaps foremost among the nonstate parties is the *United Nations,* a universal membership, permanent, general purpose organization.[8] Theoretically competent to deal with any international issue anywhere in the world, its permanent institutionalization has forever changed the international scene. Procedures are different than before its existence, problems that might previously have been ignored now receive the glare of publicity, and new mechanisms are available to handle disputes. Small states are able to receive unprecedented status and have their grievances heard, sometimes wielding influence disproportionate to their economic and military strength. A wide range of functional activities are carried

---

[8]The most useful introduction is H. G. Nicholas, *The United Nations as a Political Institution,* Fifth Edition, Oxford University Press, New York, 1975.

out under its auspices. The style and tone of international relations, as well as the content, have been permanently altered. Because of these facts policymakers need to consider the role of the United Nations in a wide variety of situations.

But one must be careful not to overrate the United Nations' significance; in the most critical situations, those affecting peace and security, it is very seldom a major factor. And although many people do not realize it, it was never intended to be. The United Nations was set up so that any one of the Security Council's permanent members—the United States, the Soviet Union, France, Britain, and China—could prevent action from being taken against itself, its allies, or clients by using its veto, that is, by casting a negative vote on a substantive issue. This meant that the Security Council, which under the U.N. Charter was to have primary responsibility for peace and security, was *deliberately* precluded from operational capability in situations involving the Big Five or their friends. And the other major U.N. organ which might be significant in peace and security matters, the General Assembly, can only recommend action; compliance with its resolutions is purely voluntary.

Although the United Nations usually is not a decisive factor in matters policymakers believe vital to their security, it does provide certain capabilities that can be (and frequently have been) put to use. First, the United Nations can be employed as a *fact finder,* as a party external to a given situation that can impartially investigate issues and report its findings. Second, the United Nations, or one of its representatives, can act as a *mediator.* A third capability is *interposition.* U.N. representatives may be physically interposed between various parties to act as a shield and deterrent to hostile action; to observe, supervise, and report on a cease-fire; or to perform whatever other functions the parties so desire. Finally, the United Nations can be a *permanent forum for negotiations.* The constant contact and interaction of the various delegations provide innumerable opportunities for negotiations. Because these capabilities exist, policymakers know the United Nations is available to be used for constructive purposes. It is critically important to understand though, that whether policymakers decide to avail themselves of these capabilities *is up to them.*

Regardless of how valuable one thinks the Unted Nations has or has not been, it is essential to recognize that the organization is what the states have made it. The United Nations is state controlled, and as such is more a reflector than a determiner of policies; it will or will not be useful to the extent and in the manner that the states so desire. In consequence of the fact that it is without the independent capacity to make or enforce binding rules or to settle disputes between its constituent units, policymakers usually do not consider the United Nations to be an effective international party separate from its members.

A second nonstate party is the *limited purpose international organization.* There are a great number of these entities and they vary enormously in size and significance. Generally such organizations deal with economic or social problems and are not concerned with issues of peace and security. Some examples are the

International Labor Organization, Universal Postal Union, International Civil Aviation Organization, and the International Pacific Halibut Commission. Because such organizations have only limited influence apart from their membership and deal primarily with narrowly defined, functional problems, they seldom are of much political significance.[9]

Another type of international party is the *regional organization*, examples of which are the European Economic Community (EEC, the Common Market) and the Organization of American States (OAS). Although some of these actors may possess a degree of supranational authority and be competent to make and enforce decisions on a carefully limited range of issues without respect to their member states' desires, most of the time this is not the case. The EEC is the most "supranational" of all such organizations today and has developed many policies that its members accept as binding, but the vast majority of these have resulted from traditional governmental interaction within a regional arena and would not have occurred unless the members so willed. And, in most regional organizations, such as the OAS, there is no supranational authority.[10] Basically, regional organizations *at this time* lack the means to do much more than reflect the policies of their member states (although this conceivably could be changing in the case of the EEC).[11] Often they merely become the battleground in which traditional objectives are sought, and sometimes, as in the case of the Anglo-French controversy over Britain's admission to the Common Market in the 1960s, become a part of the issue.

Another type of nonstate actor is what might be called the *national liberation organization* (NLO). In the Vietnam conflict, for example, certainly the Viet Cong was a major party. Such organizations do not exercise legal authority over specific territory but often seek it. Indeed, their fundamental objective may be to acquire territory and create a state. One cannot generalize about the relationship of the other attributes of statehood and the NLOs because some or all of them may be possessed in varying degrees.

---

[9]For years there have been hopes and suggestions that growing international interdependence, recognition of common problems, and the advantage of multilateral solutions on a functional basis might lead the way to permanent peace. The definitive work in this area is David Mitrany, *A Working Peace System*, Royal Institute of International Affairs, London, 1943.

[10]Of course, the fact of membership may mean that protecting the organization and achieving its objectives become important to the members. The point still is though, that the *members* make the decisions based on *their* determination of *their* interests.

[11]There is considerable controversy over the cause, degree and probable future of European integration. See Karl W. Deutsch et al., *Political Community and the North Atlantic Area: International Organization in the Light of Historical Experience*, Princeton University Press, Princeton, 1957. Also very useful are Leon N. Lindberg and Stuart A. Scheingold, *Europe's Would-Be Polity: Patterns of Change in the European Community*, Prentice-Hall, Englewood Cliffs, N.J., 1970, Elliott R. Goodman, *The Fate of the Atlantic Community*, Praeger, New York, 1975, and John Paxton, *The Developing Common Market: The Structure of the EEC in Theory and Practice, 1957–1976*, Westview Press, Boulder, Colorado, 1976.

NLOs are very important in the Middle East. Various Arab guerilla organizations such as the Palestine Liberation Organization and its constituent subunits (particularly El Fatah) are primary actors in the Arab-Israeli conflict. Purporting to represent those Palestinians displaced by the four Arab-Israeli wars since World War II (a claim that many question), they may be in a position to prevent a stable Middle Eastern peace unless their interests are satisfied (or they are militarily crushed). Any policymaker considering a Middle Eastern problem must consider them in his or her calculations.

Finally, there are transnational parties, nongovernmental actors whose decisionmaking base is located in one state but whose operations cross international frontiers. The most prominent of these today are *multinational corporations* (MNC).[12] MNCs are business entities that operate in a variety of markets and employ management and labor of various nationalities as they seek to turn a profit. Logically enough, MNCs make decisions primarily on the basis of how they will affect the firm; the interests of the host (and the home) state are secondary.

A problem can easily arise because such enterprises often possess great economic and financial strength, sometimes superior to that of the host country. Because of this strength an MNC may significantly affect or even dominate the host's economy, especially its balance of payments and resource allocation sectors. This is particularly likely if the MNC is located in an underdeveloped country and is both one of the state's largest firms and is dominant in a key industry (a not uncommon situation).

The major problem here is one of control. MNCs possess no military strength and have no desire to determine a broad range of governmental policies. Naturally they are concerned with policies affecting their economic gain, however, and will attempt to influence them accordingly. The host country wishes to maintain control over its territory and not allow the MNC to become a "state within a state," yet sometimes it fears that a too restrictive policy will kill the goose that lays the golden egg. The policymaker needs to recognize that MNCs may play an important role in specific cases.[13] For example, the major multinational oil companies are a force to be reckoned with in terms of the stability of the Middle East.

This analysis of the actors in international relations began with the statement that the 150 or so states are the primary units of action. Despite the evidence indicating the existence of various other entities, the essential validity of this statement remains unimpaired. But as the analysis shows there are other pos-

---

[12]For a useful introduction, see Sidney E. Rolfe, *The Multinational Corporation,* Foreign Policy Association, New York, 1970 and Raymond Vernon, *Sovereignty At Bay: The Multinational Spread of U. S. Enterprises,* Basic Books, New York, 1971.

[13]There are those who suggest that the entire international system is undergoing a radical transformation and that MNCs exert more influence than many states. See Abdul A. Said and Luiz R. Simmons, eds., *The New Sovereigns: Multinational Corporations as World Powers,* Prentice-Hall, Englewood Cliffs, N.J., 1975.

sibilities and to neglect them would be a distortion. The policymaker must begin with the various states involved but be alert to the fact that nonstate parties could play a significant role in any given situation.

GOVERNMENTAL FUNCTIONS

What are the major characteristics of the international political world within which the policymaker works? One has already been noted, namely, that its primary components are states. The second major feature is that *there is no central institution or set of institutions to perform governmental functions*. Compare this to domestic political systems. Although they differ in terms of the particular form the institutions may take, all domestic systems have some centralized arrangements for making rules, interpreting and applying them, settling internal disputes, and enforcing decisions.

With respect to rulemaking, in democratic political systems there is a legislative process by which laws are passed; in authoritarian governments there are the commands of the leadership. The Communist Party of the Soviet Union determines the regulations under which Russians will live, while in Great Britain it is Parliamentary rule. No matter what the state or governmental system, there is some central apparatus for making the rules that authoritatively allocate the values for that society.[14] There is no central institution to perform this function in international politics.

The situation is similar with respect to executive functions. On the domestic political scene there is a central government that holds a preponderance of coercive power. It is charged with the responsibility of enforcement of the laws and decisions concerning their interpretation, and is responsible for enforcing the decisions made to settle internal conflicts. Because of its monopoly (or near monopoly) of the instruments of violence, it is able to carry out its enforcement duties. There is no comparable international agency, no "executive" with international military forces at its disposal.

Finally, in every political system disputes must be settled. Every domestic political system has some agency that is designed to perform this function. In the United States it is primarily the judicial branch of government. It is, in most cases, the ultimate arbiter of conflict. As was true with respect to rulemaking, application, and enforcement, the international political arena provides no central institution for discharging the function of conflict resolution.

The lack of central institutions, of "government" if you will, is only part of the problem. Another very important characteristic of international relations is what might be called *the absence of a sense of community*. Within most states there is usually some degree of consensus on political values. The general nature of the objectives to be sought and the types of means appropriate for their achievement are widely, if imperfectly, accepted. Over time, policymaking pro-

---

[14]This phrase is borrowed from David Easton, *The Political System: An Inquiry Into The State of Political Science*, Knopf, New York, 1953.

cedures become somewhat regularized and understood (at least by those in authority) and the norms of behavior and "rules of the game" are considered axiomatic. Transgressions of these factors tend to be viewed with disfavor and the assumption is that an effort will be made to apprehend and penalize the transgressor.

Within this framework of shared values and expectations, the rules made and applied by the central institutions tend to be followed as a matter of course. Usually obedience is not even an issue. The government, after all, has a "right" to perform these functions so long as it does so within the limits of the consensus, so the rules are expected to be followed. Even if obedience becomes an issue, the citizen will usually obey the law because he or she accepts the government's "legitimacy," its authoritative right to carry out governmental functions. If the citizen breaks the law and is caught and convicted, he or she expects to pay a price.

Because of this sense of community, most laws within domestic societies are obeyed voluntarily. It is considered both right and beneficial to behave in this fashion. Unfortunately there is no such sense of community in international relations. There is no shared network of values, no consensus on either means or ends. Whether to follow certain rules is an issue, indeed, so is the very content and determination of the rules. Similarly, value conflicts are often at the root of disputes. Because of these facts even if there were central institutions the problem would only be half solved. Without a sense of community even the appropriate apparatus would not be permanently successful.

Because there are no central institutions to make, apply, and enforce the rules, since there is no agency to resolve conflicts, and because there is no international sense of community, the policymaker acts within an environment that might be called *decentralized anarchy*.[15] Each party acts as its own legislator, executive, and judge. No state possesses the authority to make decisions for any other than itself. This being so each tends to look out for "number one" and seeks to influence others for its own benefit.

Because of this anarchical decentralization, and because policy differences will inevitably arise, conflicts must be settled by the states themselves. Because of the lack of centralized institutions and a sense of community there is little to indicate that a dispute will be settled to any party's satisfaction. Thus there is an ongoing process of attempting to demonstrate the benefits of acceding to "our" point of view.

Ultimately the only way one party may compel another to act in the desired fashion is through the threat or use of force. Otherwise it may just refuse and there is no institution capable of "persuading" it to change its mind. Similarly, only the possession of sufficient military strength and the will to use it can hope

[15]The term is adapted from John Spanier, *Games Nations Play: Analyzing International Politics*, Praeger, New York, 1972, pp. 51–56.

to guarantee survival (if even that can). Since there is no central authority with this capacity, the use of military might by the individual parties becomes the ultimate arbiter.

This brief analysis has shown that because of the lack of central institutions and a sense of community the policymaker operates within a decentralized anarchic system in which force is the ultimate test. This does not necessarily mean, however, that policymakers always perceive that force is all that really counts. Although they may in some cases, there are other factors that are often of considerable significance. It is to the first of these that we now turn, the role of ethics.

ROLE OF ETHICS

What role do ethical considerations play in the calculations of policymakers? To what extent do considerations of right and wrong, good and evil, influence their decisions? Are moral issues and value questions just raised for propaganda reasons, or do they really have an impact on the people who make policy?

Very often these questions are discussed in order to promote a particular point of view, and as such are couched in terms of a purported incompatibility between ethical considerations and what is called power politics.[16] It is sometimes assumed or postulated that ethical concerns and capability analysis based on self-interest are irreconcilable. It is suggested that policymakers perceive (or at least should perceive) a clear distinction between these contradictory factors. Furthermore, it is implied that policymakers have a clear choice in this matter; they can choose one or the other and which one is up to them.

Such a characterization is both oversimplified and inaccurate (as should become obvious by the end of this book). The analysis below demonstrates several instances in which ethics did play a role in policy calculations, thus underlining the point that ethics do count. But as will be shown later other considerations, including capability analysis, have sometimes been of similar or greater importance. In many cases it will be apparent that the process was very complex and several factors were involved, that there was no clear choice, and that different factors sometimes led to the same conclusion.

Types of Influence

Ethics are often important in the *formulation of long-range goals,* particularly those dealing with the kind of international system one hopes will develop.

---

[16]This purported incompatibility has led to much scholarly and public debate over what was called "Realism" and "Idealism." See in particular Edward H. Carr, *The Twenty Years' Crisis, 1919–1939,* Macmillan, London, 1939; Thomas I. Cook and Malcom Moos, *Power Through Purpose: The Realism of Idealism as a Basis for Foreign Policy,* Johns Hopkins Press, Baltimore, 1954; Hans J. Morgenthau, *In Defense of the National Interest,* Knopf, New York, 1951; and Hans J. Morgenthau, *Politics Among Nations,* Fifth Edition, Knopf, New York, 1973.

Ethical factors also may influence the selection of specific policies considered to be appropriate to achieving such objectives. Various policymakers have advocated and sought to achieve:

> a system of equal, free, and self-determining nationalities, each organized into its own state and living peacefully side by side.[17]

Former President Woodrow Wilson emphasized the necessity of self-determination and believed strongly that permanent peace could not be achieved without it; it was both the goal and the means. The principle of equality has sometimes possessed a similar status. The idea is that if all states have equal rights and obligations the major source of conflict (inequality) will be eliminated. According to this conception, security rests on cooperation and "real" cooperation is possible only among states who are equal politically and juridically.[18] Ethical considerations such as these may influence long-range desires and be in the back of policymakers' minds in their daily routines. As such they will be a persistent component in the policymaking process, although their impact will vary with time and circumstance.

Ethical concerns also *affect the self-image one possesses*. Many American policymakers apparently have come to assume that the United States is the repository of moral virtue and other states are just waiting in line to be enlightened. Somehow the conception arises that "our way" is ethically superior and other states will surely see this and request us to share our bounty. In such a situation the policymaker's approach to all situations will be conditioned by his or her ethical self-image.

Lest one misunderstand, however, it should be recognized that this phenomenon is not the province of any one state but instead it is rather common. Each party tends to see itself as the most virtuous, both in general terms and in the context of each particular situation. From the viewpoint of a Vietnamese Communist, for example, the Viet Cong were morally superior to Washington. As he saw things the United States had sabotaged the Geneva Agreements, prevented free elections, and thus prevented the unification of his country under popular leadership; he saw American assistance to Saigon as a process of penetration designed to turn Vietnam into an American colony. Aiding a repressive regime, Washington turned the Southern zone into a military base and eventually perpetrated outright aggression against the Vietnamese people by the most technologically destructive means. If one believed this way then he was ethically correct in opposing the United States and its "puppet." One reason the Viet

---

[17]John H. Herz, *Political Realism and Political Idealism,* University of Chicago Press, Chicago, 1951, p. 67.

[18]See Frank Tannenbaum, *The American Tradition in Foreign Policy,* University of Oklahoma Press, Norman, 1955, pp. 158–159.

Cong were so effective was that they believed they were in the right; ethical concerns did matter and influenced specific actions.

Ethical considerations may also *provide the catalyst for action or make the action undertaken much more militant*. This could be either because of the substance of what was done or because of the manner in which the actions were carried out. Both of these factors had an impact on American policymakers and their decision to enter World War I. When President Wilson said that the United States entered the war to "make the world safe for democracy," ethical concerns were critical in his mind. German violations of neutral rights, for example, were considered ungentlemanly. The sinking of merchant ships, particularly the *Lusitania,* and the eventual unrestricted submarine warfare, infuriated Americans; these things were just not done. Real resentment was aroused by:

> Germany's violations of American rights and the gentlemanly code of international ethics and decency . . . In their view German policy was deliberately, unalterably, and by the very nature of Germany's rulers inhumane, autocratic, militaristic, expansionist, and utterly barbaric in its standards of international conduct. On the other hand, they were convinced that the preservation of American ideals, American interests, and civilization itself depended on a British victory.[19]

Finally, and rather critically, ethical concerns *often act as a constraint*; certain objectives or means are modified or rejected for ethical reasons. In the Cuban Missile Crisis one of the alternatives considered for removing the Soviet missiles was what was called a surgical air strike (i.e., a surprise bombing raid). President Kennedy and his brother Robert (the Attorney-General) both rejected this option, partly on ethical grounds. It reminded them of an American-perpetrated Pearl Harbor. As the Attorney-General put it:

> I could not accept the idea that the United States would rain bombs on Cuba, killing thousands and thousands of civilians in a surprise attack. Maybe the alternatives were not very palatable, but I simply did not see how we could accept that course of action for our country.[20]

Certainly one method of weakening the adversary is to simply kill many of its leaders. In 1939, thousands of Polish officers were captured by the Russians and placed in prisoner-of-war camps. In early 1940 some 15,000 of them were murdered in the Katyn Forest massacre.[21] Thus, when Stalin suggested to Chur-

---

[19]Robert Osgood, *Ideals and Self-Interest in America's Foreign Relations,* University of Chicago Press, Chicago, 1953, p. 236.

[20]Robert F. Kennedy, *Thirteen Days: A Memoir of the Cuban Missile Crisis,* Norton, New York, 1971, p. 15. Certainly tactical and strategic considerations also entered the picture, however.

[21]The evidence is overwhelming on this point although the Russians have always denied it and charged Germany with perpetrating the act. The fact that Moscow even bothers to deny the charge shows that there is some concern over its implications.

chill in early 1944 that the way to resolve the German problem was to liquidate 50,000 German officers, he was taken very seriously. Churchill, however, found the suggestion reprehensible and made it plain he never would consider such action. Ethically he simply could not tolerate it.

The Rest of the Picture

The fact that policymakers often take ethical factors into account when formulating and implementing policy seems established beyond doubt. But this simple statement, while very important, does not give the whole picture. For one thing, there are cases where this does not occur, such as in the Katyn Forest massacre or the Nazi slaughter of six million Jews. One must also be aware of the fact that ethical statements are often deliberately used to rationalize and/or hide unethical behavior. It is also apparent that people seek to interpret their behavior in a way that seems just and correct, and are often able to manipulate facts and situations to this end.

Another difficulty is the natural tendency toward "psychologic," the tendency to interpret the same behavior as ethical if "we" do it but unethical if "they" do.[22] When the Japanese bombed Chinese cities in the 1930s killing many noncombatants, they were condemned for immoral behavior. Germany's massive attacks on Coventry, London, and Rotterdam received similar disapproval. By the end of World War II such raids were standard practice for all parties, however. The Allies presumed their activity was justifiable because the objective was presumed to be more ethical. In Vietnam, the Communist interpreted his presence to be ethical and the presence of American forces to be aggressive, and vice versa. Since (as noted above) there is no sense of community and no central set of governing institutions, each party is the definer and interpreter of the ethical factor in any situation. Given the differences in perspectives, objectives, and means it is obvious why so many differences arise.

Another problem for the policymaker is that *it is often terribly difficult to determine what is or is not ethical in a specific case.* In September 1938 British Prime Minister Chamberlain agreed to the surrender of certain German-inhabited strategic portions of Czechoslovakia to Germany at the Munich Conference. A man of impeccable principles, he believed he was acting ethically because he thought this agreement would ensure peace. World War II began a year later. His action was unwise, but was it unethical? Or take the Korean War, which began in June 1950. By mid-1951 the fighting had stabilized and armistice negotiations began. Most issues were resolved quickly but the question of returning war prisoners stalemated the talks. The U.N. Command insisted that no one should be forced to return to his country against his will, surely an ethical consideration,

[22]Charles E. Osgood, *An Alternative to War or Surrender,* University of Illinois Press, Urbana, 1962, pp. 26–30.

and the Chinese resisted.[23] Peking's position, traditional in international relations, was that everyone is returned regardless of individual wishes. While talks
were floundering because of the United Nations' ethical considerations, the
killing, wounding, and maiming went on. Was the United Nations' position more
ethical than if it had returned the prisoners and stopped the carnage?

Another facet of this problem arises because of the fact that *there is no
universal standard of ethics*. Different states have different cultures and social
structures, and different cultures and structures spawn different ethical systems.
Thus what is considered "good" or "bad" varies from one state to another.
Policymakers' conceptions of what is "just" are at least partly shaped by their
culture and social structure. Because of these facts policymakers from different
states will almost inevitably have different conceptions of what is or is not
ethical. It is hard enough to find agreement on what is ethical between people
from the same state. When cultural and structural variations are added the problem is compounded.[24]

An eternal ethical question is *to what extent does the end justify the means?*
Is it ethical for one to help a dictatorship survive if it will help him in turn? Was
Churchill's willingness to work with Stalin in order to defeat Hitler justifiably
ethical? To what extent are high-level bombing raids that kill innocent civilians
justifiable if one believes he is fighting a "just" war? The dropping of the atomic
bomb on Hiroshima resulted in over 70,000 Japanese deaths. Although more
than 100,000 lives were lost as a result of both bombs (the second landed on
Nagasaki on August 9, 1945), it is generally estimated that nearly one million
were saved, the anticipated cost of an invasion of the Japanese homeland. Was
the decision to drop the bombs ethical or not? And don't all parties believe their
cause is "just"?

How does one compare one act with another? Which was more ethical or
unethical, the starving to death of over a million Russians by Germany during the
World War II siege of Leningrad, or the British-American air raid on the German
city of Dresden in 1945, which killed about 135,000 Germans? Is high-altitude
bombing more ethical than the face-to-face gunning down of over 100 Vietnamese peasants by American soldiers at Songmy or the mass executions of
South Vietnamese by the Viet Cong around Hué in the 1968 Tet offensive?

Policymakers find themselves in confused and troubled waters where ethical
factors are concerned. It is clear enough that questions of right and wrong enter
into a wide range of calculations but it is also obvious that sometimes they do not
and sometimes ethics are deliberately used to rationalize or hide what is really
happening. Additionally, it is unfortunate but true that each party tends to think it
is the most ethical. Finally, very often it just is not clear what is or is not the most

[23]The UN Command also had other motivations, such as publicly humiliating the Chinese.
[24]A useful article in this regard is Henry A. Kissinger, "Domestic Sources of Foreign Policy,"
Daedalus, Spring, 1966, pp. 503–525.

ethical thing to do. This being so, all a policymaker can do is analyze the specific situation with these considerations in mind and attempt to ascertain what elements characterize the particular case.

THE ROLE OF LAW

What is the role of law for the policymaker? Often the subject of international law is "studied" in order to demonstrate either its great (or potentially great) impact or to show that it has little value. Neither approach is very helpful to the policymaker. He or she needs to determine the actual role that law plays, and understand the role it can play, without regard to proving its worth or limitation.

When speaking of international law one is referring to the rules and norms of conduct that states recognize as binding in their relations with other states. Such rules may prescribe certain actions, prohibit certain modes of behavior, or perhaps specify and define the conditions that lead to the operationalizing of various rights and/or obligations.

Modern international law developed with the transformation from feudalism to the modern state system in Europe. With the creation of the territorial state with its attributes of complete internal control and freedom from external authority, it became necessary to develop some rules for international intercourse. It was perceived to be necessary to provide for immunity for diplomatic agents, to define the nature and limits of national territorial jurisdiction, to create an acceptable body of regulations to handle the expansion of international economic relations, and to provide common rules for international maritime activities. Policymakers generally recognized their mutual self-interest in these and similar areas. Thus it was necessity and self-benefit that led to the creation of international law.

Sources of Law

What are the sources from which international law springs? The first is *custom*. Customary law comprises rules that states have come to consider as binding on themselves because of generally accepted usage over long periods of time. For reasons of self-benefit, habit or fear states will follow a certain course of action. As this becomes "the way things are done" it acquires some validity, until a time is reached when it is considered obligatory.[25] A good example is the variety of extraterritorial rights extended to foreign diplomats who are lawfully within one's borders. Policymakers are forced to be aware of international custom in their daily activities.

A second major source, considered by many today to be the most important,

---

[25]Technically, this should not be confused with mere frequency of conduct without obligation, which is known as comity. In practice, however, the distinction is difficult to make.

is the international *treaty*. Treaties may be bilateral or multilateral, and may simply codify or clarify existing custom or establish new rights and obligations.

From the policymaker's perspective there are two key points to remember about treaties. First, once a treaty is signed and ratified there is a recognized rights and obligations relationship. A party is bound to do or not do certain things, thus limiting its autonomy accordingly. Therefore, treaties must be entered into cautiously with careful attention given to their specific provisions.

Second, and equally important, no state is bound by a treaty it has not legally accepted. Thus the policymaker does not need to worry about being legally obligated by agreements between other states. This point is so obvious yet it is sometimes neglected. For example, the United States was not a party to the 1954 Geneva Agreements ending the first Indochina war. Thus all the later talk about American violations was misinformed because Washington could not violate an agreement to which it was not a party.[26]

These two factors lead one to realize that the rules binding on each state are different from those binding on any other. Because of this there is no universal or quasi-universal standard in many areas. Instead there may be a multitude of conflicting, confusing, and overlapping rules, or sometimes there may as yet not be any system of rules for a given type of activity. Obviously these situations allow the policymaker considerable flexibility of action, the freedom to interpret things to his or her own benefit without being charged with departing from the common standard.

In addition to custom and treaties, there are several less significant sources of international law, namely, *judicial decisions,* so-called *general principles,* and the *writings of scholars*. Occasionally states are parties to a controversy before an international court, in which case the policymaker would obviously be concerned with the judicial decision. This, however, is highly unusual. The reason is that the primary source of international judicial jurisdiction is the willingness of the states to submit their dispute for judicial determination, and states are simply unwilling to submit matters of major significance.[27] After all, in a judicial proceeding there is always a loser and no state wants an outsider (the court) to have the power to make it be that loser. The inevitable result is that policymakers usually consider judicial decisions to be a source of only secondary importance.

The same conclusion is true of general principles and the writings of schol-

---

[26]However, Washington unilaterally pledged that it would not use force to disrupt the settlement, and said it generally favored free elections for divided countries. Whether in fact it followed its own stated policy is obviously a matter of controversy. See U.S., Department of State, *Bulletin,* August 2, 1954, pp. 162–163.

[27]There is a provision (Article 36) in the Statute of the International Court of Justice (the United Nations Court) providing for compulsory jurisdiction. Only about 30 percent of UN members have availed themselves of this optional clause, however, and even they have so weakened it with restrictions and reservations that there is very little about it that remains "compulsory."

ars. The very generality of the principles means they are susceptible to widely varying interpretations, and policymakers will take advantage of this. Scholarly writing abounds with conflicting views and controversy thus providing a basis for determining what someone considers the law to be (or have been), but it also allows one considerable latitude in interpretation. Both of these sources may be consulted but neither will be considered binding.

It is essential to remember that the policymaker is seeking to ascertain "what the law is" within the international environment described earlier in the chapter. To reiterate, this means there is no central legislative organ to pass the laws, no executive to enforce them, and no judicial agency competent to settle disputes. Instead it is the individual states that perform these functions. Coupled with the lack of a sense of international community, this leads to a decentralized anarchic situation where force is the ultimate arbiter.

Why Law Is Obeyed

Since only the states can punish a lawbreaker, why is the law obeyed? *A point of immense significance is that it usually is obeyed.* The rules, guides, and norms of behavior accepted as binding by states in their mutual relations are in most instances scrupulously observed. In most of their activities policymakers are very concerned with acting in accordance with recognized legal procedures.

Why is this so?[28] We indicated above that international law originated because of perceived needs, the knowledge that it would be advantageous to all if there were certain accepted modes of operation in selected areas. This is still the most common reason for not violating the law; it is *simply to one's benefit to obey.*

In addition to the specific advantages that may flow from observing certain rules, there are two related considerations. First, there is the *expectation of reciprocity,* that is, the idea that other states will reciprocate by also undertaking certain obligations. It is hoped that this will lead to a situation of mutual self-advantage with each party having more to gain than lose by observing the law. The second related aspect is that *stability and predictability* are enhanced when actions are undertaken according to prescribed procedures. Without some regularization the ordinary relations among nations would be chaotic and it would be impossible to develop even a semirational policy. This, too, adds pressure to be law abiding.

Another reason law is obeyed is, simply, *habit.* Certain transactions are carried on routinely and little consideration is given to change. There is no reason not to follow the traditional pattern as long as things are going well. Furthermore, various parties develop a vested interest in the continuance of existing procedures, making change even less likely. Usually a crisis or an outside stimulus

[28]The author is particularly indebted to K. J. Holsti, *International Politics: A Framework for Analysis,* Second Edition, Prentice-Hall, Englewood Cliffs, N.J., 1973, pp. 417–420.

must intervene before the policymaker will react. Until that time, he or she will not question the existing order.

International law is also observed in order to enhance one's *prestige*. A state that develops a reputation for following the rules stands to receive certain benefits. Because there is no central agency for enforcing the laws it is up to the states to do it. Seldom will they enter agreements they assume will be broken and thus require enforcement. A state that constantly defaults on its obligations will simply not be trusted nor dealt with as openly as one that is law abiding.

The final reason for not violating the law, of course, is *fear of punishment*. It is in this area that international law is "weak" in comparison to domestic law. The lack of a central enforcement agency means that the only coercive sanctions available are those possessed by the states themselves. If none of the previously discussed reasons for observing the rules are appropriate, and no state is able and willing to enforce compliance, then the law can be broken without punishment being suffered.

When Law Is Usually Violated

We have seen that policymakers may and often do consult a wide range of sources to find out what the law is, and they usually attempt to formulate their policies in accordance with the generally accepted rules. The vast majority of international conduct occurs within regularized patterns of activity, and policymakers recognize that it usually is to their benefit to observe the law. Despite these facts, the law obviously *is* broken in certain cases, and often there is not much a state can do about it unless it is willing and able to compel compliance.

In what kind of situations do these violations readily occur? The answer is really quite clear: *in any case where one of the parties perceives a significant threat to its fundamental objectives it will quickly dispense with legal considerations that might inhibit their achievement.* What this means is that the policymaker does not consider legal factors to be of primary importance in a crisis, when there is a conflict that one thinks might endanger his or her state's survival, territorial integrity, belief system, or governmental-economic organization. These types of situations, while in the minority quantitatively, are clearly the most significant in terms of peace and security. And because there are no central mechanisms to force policymakers to consider international law in crisis situations, legal factors remain of secondary significance in determining policy and the outcome where peace and security are heavily involved.

Although they have little impact as a constraint or determinant of crisis policy, legal considerations often do play some role, however. First, even in a crisis policymakers seek to characterize their activities as being in accordance with international law. Sometimes this is not a deliberate manipulation of facts and principles but rather the employment of one of several possible legitimate interpretations. As was noted earlier, there is no universal standard in many areas so different interpretations often occur. Quite naturally policymakers will tend to interpret things to their benefit, and often they do so sincerely believing that they are not distorting things at all.

Second, policymakers may seek to use the law tactically to justify and support positions already taken. A decision may be made on the basis of capability considerations, for example, and then the policymaker will put together a legal argument to justify that decision. Cases in point would be the 1948–1949 Berlin Blockade and the Cuban Missile Crisis of 1962. Although elaborate legal justifications were developed in support of American policies there is little evidence to indicate that legal considerations significantly influenced the policymakers' decisions.[29]

THE ROLE OF IDEOLOGY

Another element that may influence the policymaker's calculations is ideology. Ideology has been defined as:

> The more or less coherent and consistent sum total of ideas and views on life and the world (belief system, doctrine, *Weltanschauung*) that guides the attitudes of actual or would-be power holders.[30]

This concept, the complex of ideas that supposedly explains past and present plus providing guidelines for the future, has also received other names such as belief system, social myth, or doctrine. Regardless of the label given to it, it roughly translates as one's world view.

Although one can argue terminology and definition, policymakers are not concerned with such activities.[31] Their interest is in the operational effects of the phenomenon. To what extent do these ideas and views on life and the world

---

[29]Lawrence Scheinman and David Wilkinson, eds., *International Law and Political Crisis: An Analytic Casebook,* Little, Brown, Boston, 1968. This was certainly not the first work to reach this and most of the other conclusions contained therein. However, it had special merit in that it examined a series of cases empirically and the findings substantiated much of what had been observed much less systematically before. It also is written and organized concisely so that the ordinary student can use it with relative facility, a rare quality.

[30]John H. Herz, "Ideological Aspects—International Relations," *International Encyclopedia of Social Sciences,* Cromwell-Collier-Macmillan, New York, 1968, p. 69. The term "Weltanschauung" roughly translates as "world view."

[31]Academics are, however, and the definitions are many. Those interested in pursuing this further should consult the standard work in the area, Karl Mannheim, *Ideology and Utopia: An Introduction to the Sociology of Knowledge,* Harcourt Brace, New York, 1936. For a useful concise discussion see Richard W. Sterling, *Macropolitics: International Relations in a Global Society,* Knopf, New York, 1974, Ch. 6.

influence the actual formulation and implementation of policy? Are they primarily general idea systems that affect only long-range goals or do they directly impinge upon specific detail? Are they more important than other considerations such as law, ethics and capability, or less so? These and similar questions may be critical as the policymaker tries to understand and anticipate the actions of his opposite numbers.[32] Unfortunately there seldom are clear-cut answers.

Let's examine two ideologies and their impact to see if we can get a better understanding of the phenomenon's operation. First we will briefly analyze the "liberal" American belief system, and then we will take a more detailed look at the role of communism in the conduct of Soviet foreign policy.[33]

The American Liberal Ideology

Ideology has played a significant role in American foreign relations.[34] Until the post-World War II era most twentieth century policymakers uncritically accepted certain beliefs as the "fundamental truths" of international relations. The developing Cold War brought much disillusionment, however, although some policymakers held to the original assumptions in the belief (or hope) that the conflict was an aberration and a new age of cooperation would develop once the Communists had been licked. Although the Vietnam war did much to destroy the remaining hopes, there are still those today who believe that Vietnam was just another aberration and the original beliefs are fundamentally sound.

The American liberal ideology begins with the assumption that *people are basically good*. Most of the time people will do what is right if just given the chance. There are no major national differences in this regard; although they may be in different stages of development and thus act somewhat differently at particular times, underneath, whether people are Ethiopians, Chinese, Americans, or Russians, they are all essentially good. This assumption has two very significant operational consequences. First, since most people are good it follows that if a certain individual, group, or government is bad, he or she (or it) is an aberration; presumably, therefore, his or her (or its) removal will restore "goodness" to its rightful position. Thus, World War I and World War II were fought to

---

[32]For a textbook that emphasizes the importance of seeing things from within different world views, see Steven J. Rosen and Walter S. Jones, *The Logic of International Relations*, Second Edition, Winthrop, Cambridge, Mass., 1977.

[33]This analysis must, of necessity, encompass a variety of generalizations. Naturally, not all American policymakers subscribed completely to the beliefs listed below. Similarly, communism does not perform precisely identical functions for all Soviet leaders.

[34]For a discussion of the basic beliefs, see Moos and Cook, Morgenthau (both works), Robert Osgood, and Tannenbaum, cited above. Also very useful are Frederick H. Hartmann, *The New Age of American Foreign Policy*, Macmillan, New York, 1970; George Kennan, *American Diplomacy, 1900–1950*, University of Chicago Press, Chicago, 1951; and Ernest W. Lefever, *Ethics and United States Foreign Policy*, Meridian, New York, 1957.

eliminate a certain few aberrants from the scene, the assumption being that their removal would lead to more normal (good) situations and peace would ensue.[35]

The second consequence is a belief that ethical concerns can provide a realistic basis for policy. Since people are essentially good, ethical factors often will be decisive in determining policymakers' choices, in all countries. Even when confronted with difficult decisions most policymakers will act ethically (as defined by Americans, of course). Therefore, deception, lying, breaking agreements, the deliberate use of force, and so on, are not the norm; one can reasonably expect that most foreign policymakers will conduct their relations in an aboveboard and honest manner, seeking international relationships based on trust and mutual benefit, and he or she can act accordingly. Leaders who do not play by these rules will "stand out like a sore thumb."

Another component of the American liberal ideology, one closely related to the belief in human goodness, is the idea that *people are essentially alike,* all having the same basic interests, desires, and fears (all people are created equal). And since states are governed by people, they too must have a *similarity of interests.* Because, as noted above, people are good and act ethically, these similar state interests must also be good and ethical. Therefore, since peace is more ethical than war, most states must be seeking peace most of the time.

In addition to these characteristics, people are also assumed to be fundamentally *rational.* With the proper guidance and education they can know what ought to be done, both generally and in specific cases. Since they are good, want peace, and generally act in a rational fashion, they will seek and learn how to manage international relations in a relatively peaceful manner. Therefore, if "they" are opposed to "us," it must be because they are misinformed or don't understand (or are held in the grip of an unscrupulous few). Once we "educate" them, once they understand the fact that we are "good" and they are "good," there should be no grounds for conflict. Being rational they will eventually comprehend this fact.[36]

None of this would mean much, however, if people were the prisoners of events. Americans have rejected this assumption, believing that *people are basically able to shape and control their destinies.* Events do not control people, people make events. After all, hadn't the United States seized its opportunities; hadn't it totally transformed the land and established continental, indeed, hemispheric political supremacy? And hadn't the United States achieved enormous

---

[35]The fact that the United States grew to "maturity" in the nineteenth century, which from the termination of the Napoleonic Wars to the early twentieth century was the most peaceful period in the history of the nation-state system, was highly significant in this regard; since America "grew up" in a time of peace its policymakers assumed that peace was the norm.

[36]Total rationality is impossible, of course, since one can never know all the information relevant to a particular subject, be aware of all the possible alternatives and their consequences, and so on. Here we simply mean that people do everything within their power to think and act on the basis of evidence and logic.

economic progress? Not realizing how much they had been aided by unique circumstances and the policies of other states, most Americans believed that they had gotten where they were solely by their own efforts. Therefore, (they believed) since Americans had determined their destiny, others could determine theirs.

Furthermore, at least according to the American liberal ideology, if states are willing to act decisively *problems can be solved*. As noted above, Americans looked back on their own history with a sense of pride; many problems *had* been solved. The ideal of "we shall overcome" was deeply rooted. Little children were told, only half in jest, that there is no such word as "can't." If there are problems, with good, rational individuals with similar interests working together they *can* be solved, so let's get at it. There is no reason things can't be better.

Finally, it has long been believed that *people in all states should have the right to choose their own form of government, and that if they have this right they surely will choose a Western-style democracy*. Such a governmental system (it is believed) allows the individual to achieve his or her fullest potential and provides the greatest degree of freedom consistent with public order, so obviously that is what people will choose. Furthermore, it is "clear" that most democratic governments will be controlled by good, reasonable people intent on, and capable of, solving problems. Given these facts, it is apparent that the more democratic a state's government the more peaceful will be its policies.

The concepts of the American liberal ideology lead to a very optimistic view of international relations. Because all people are basically alike and fundamentally good, they must want what "we" want, that is, a peaceful world of democratic governments. Because people are reasonable, able to control things, and solve whatever problems arise, what is there to prevent progress? Peace is the normal state of affairs, and cooperation is to be expected on most issues.[37] Conflict is unusual and the result of some particular aberration; eliminate the "bad apples" and conflict will disappear. Power and capability concerns are not usually very critical since most people are good and rational and war is bad and irrational. Whatever the trouble, let's take care of it and move on to a better world.

American optimism has often involved unrealistically high expectations, and the impact of specific events has sometimes brought frustration and disillusionment. Especially recently, confrontations with unyielding reality have led many to reassess these beliefs. In consequence, policymakers today are much more cognizant of the role that power plays than was the case previously. They also tend to be less optimistic; it no longer is "self-evident" that peace is the normal state of affairs, nor is it plain that all problems are soluble. Not all

---

[37]Since it would be eminently sensible to add order and stability via legal procedures and structures, as the United States had done internally, Americans have had great faith in the efficacy of international law in this regard.

Americans have undertaken such a reassessment, however; some, policymakers and observers alike, continue to embrace most aspects of the liberal ideology, with all the consequences that entails.

Soviet Communism: Functions

What about the impact of ideology on Soviet foreign policy? What functions does communism perform for Moscow's policymakers as they act on the international stage?[38] First, Communist ideology provides a *vision of things to come* (a function fulfilled by ethics for many nonCommunists). It is believed that, through the inexorable working of fundamental laws of history, class will struggle against class until capitalism perishes and the whole world comes to communism. The exploiters, the owners of the means of production (capitalists), will eventually be overthrown by the exploited, the workers (proletariat). Since the mode of production determines every aspect of societal life, the elimination of conflict over its control by means of the successful class struggle will eliminate conflict itself. The state will no longer be necessary and will just wither away, and each person will contribute according to his or her ability and receive according to his or her needs. This is the long-range goal, the future state of affairs that Communists seek to create.

Second, Communists believe that *conflict is unavoidable until their final triumph*. As indicated above, class struggle over control of the means of production is inevitable until only the workers are left. Through the dialectic process, history is the clash of economic contradictions, and change is continual.[39] The exhaustion of domestic profit possibilities will lead capitalist economies to seek foreign markets. This quest will inevitably lead to intercapitalist war. Furthermore, socialism (communism) and imperialism (capitalism) cannot exist side by side for an extended period of time, and any "coexistence" can only be temporary. Conflict (although not necessarily war) is inevitable here too, but com-

---

[38]A subject as complex as this is highly controversial and defies neat, categorical answers. Because of the complexity of Communist ideology we will not analyze its major components as such; such an effort is beyond the scope of this work. Instead, we will focus on certain *conclusions* about its general impact on policymaking for foreign affairs, touching only incidentally on the substance. Our analysis can only be taken as a set of interpretations, hopefully based on a reasonable degree of evidence. It is suggested that in addition to the various works of Soviet leaders, one consult Zbigniew Brzezinski, *Ideology and Power in Soviet Politics*, Praeger, New York, 1962; Elliot R. Goodman, *The Soviet Design for a World State*, Columbia University Press, New York, 1960; Richard F. Rosser, *An Introduction to Soviet Foreign Policy*, Prentice-Hall, Englewood Cliffs, N.J., 1969; Alvin Z. Rubinstein, ed., *The Foreign Policy of the Soviet Union, Third Edition*, Random House, New York, 1972; and Jan F. Triska and David D. Finley, *Soviet Foreign Policy*, Macmillan, New York, 1968.

[39]The dialectic process means that the outcome is determined by a clash of opposites. A given situation gives rise to tendencies for its destruction, and the result is a synthesis, a merging of the two to form a new situation. The process then begins anew and continues over and over until the final synthesis is achieved.

munism will eventually triumph.[40] Thus, a Communist sees no harmony of interests among states and no possibility of long-run peace or stability until that system emerges victorious. Until that day conflict and change are just in the nature of things.

Third, Communist ideology provides the *framework within which all international activity is analyzed.* It is the fundamental philosophy that provides standards for evaluating various policies. Whether something is "good" or "bad" will be determined by its place in the historical process and the degree to which it helps or hinders the inevitable ultimate result. Information will be interpreted through the lens of Communist thought and placed in various ideological categories.

Communism is the model through which reality is perceived and by which it is interpreted. For example, the landing of Allied troops in Russia near the end of World War I would be seen as a futile attempt by international capitalism to prevent its own inevitable destruction by destroying the Bolshevik regime, rather than as an effort by former allies to bring Russia back into the war against Germany. And World War II came about, according to Stalin:

> ...as an inevitable result of the development of international economic and political forces on the basis of modern monopoly capitalism. Marxists have repeatedly explained that the capitalist system of world economy contains the elements of a general crisis and armed conflicts, that consequently the development of international capitalism in our time takes place not peacefully and evenly but through crises and war catastrophes.[41]

Ideology also provides a *basis and method for analyzing specific problems.* For example, one might decide whether or not to provide assistance to a particular revolutionary group by determining the general stage of history in which she or he finds her- or himself, ascertaining the ownership of the means of production, discovering the particular phase of the dialectic process characterizing this situation, calculating the relative strength of the pertinent class forces, and finally determining whether or not these specific tactics will advance or hinder the revolutionary process.

Finally, communism provides the *vocabulary* within which Soviet strategy and tactics are hammered out. Decisions over relations with the United States are

---

[40]Disagreement over this point was an important factor in the development of the Sino-Soviet dispute. Whereas Lenin had spoken in terms of a series of terrible collisions inevitably occurring, in 1956 Khrushchev said that there was no fatal inevitability of war. He did not, however, say that conflict could be avoided, just that it might not be military; he also did not say that war was unlikely. Another point to note is that the Soviet leader did not alter the traditional Communist view of the inevitability of *intercapitalist* war.

[41]Quoted by Paul E. Zinner, "The Ideological Bases of Soviet Foreign Policy," *World Politics,* July 1952, p. 497.

debated in terms of the inevitability of war, the class struggle, the relative strength of socialism (communism) and capitalism, and so on. This linguistic factor is not trivial although it may seem so at first glance. The mere fact that Soviet and Chinese policymakers argue out their dispute in ideological terms indicates, unless one assumes them to be totally phony, that they consider ideological factors to have considerable importance. Furthermore, the constant use of concepts and terms tends to reinforce the speaker's beliefs and they may become internalized as unquestioned bases for action.

It is evident that Communist ideology provides Soviet policymakers with a vision of the state of affairs they believe will eventually develop, a belief in the inevitability of conflict and change until that time arrives, a framework within which to analyze all international activity, and the vocabulary within which to determine and execute policy. In terms of everyday policymaking it serves still another function by creating a certain sense of security.

Soviet policymakers can act with considerable *confidence* because they know that in the long run communism will triumph.[42] The fundamental laws of history are inexorable. Through the dialectical process class will struggle against class until the workers of the world emerge triumphant. There is simply no doubt; it is all scientifically determined. Because of this one can be patient. There is no need to hurry, no particular date by which objectives must be accomplished. This being so one can be flexible, adjusting tactics and strategy to the changing situation. If the situation is not ripe for revolution, then wait. If there seems to be a setback, it is only temporary. There is a certain ebb and flow to the historical process, and the wise policymaker will adjust his actions to it. Therefore, one need not be anxious or frustrated over specific incidents, because the ultimate outcome is clear.

Soviet Communism: Questions

Although communism does influence Soviet policymakers in the significant ways discussed, there are still some key questions to be answered. To what extent is ideology used as a tool to justify action taken on other grounds? To what extent is reality twisted to fit preconceived molds? Even when the general tenets are accepted by policymakers, to what extent are specific decisions determined?

These first two questions can be handled as a unit. The flexibility and inconsistencies in Communist ideology allow Soviet policymakers much leeway in "reinterpreting" and "updating" their ideas when necessity so requires. For example, when it became obvious shortly after World War I that the expected

---

[42]As Mr. Brezhnev put it in his report to the 25th Congress of the Communist Party of the Soviet Union on February 24, 1976, "capitalism is a society without a future." Compass Publications, Reprints from the Soviet Press, *L. I. Brezhnev: Report of the CPSU Central Committee to the 25th Party Congress*, 1976, p. 40.

worldwide revolution was not going to occur in the forseeable future, the Party leaders were able to speak in terms of socialism in one country (the Soviet Union) with that becoming the base for the eventual revolution. Thus, policies aimed at consolidating the regime's internal power were followed instead of those actively formenting revolution abroad, and were justified as necessary to solidify the "dictatorship of the proletariat." The imperialists would eventually be destroyed from this base. Lenin's original concepts provided no hint that only a portion of the world would be Communist, but when this occurred it proved necessary and possible in practice to rationalize the fact.

Another example involved Soviet relations with capitalist states. A strict interpretation of most Communist thought allows for little in the way of friendly relations with capitalists. In practice, however, Communist Russia has had to choose the lesser capitalist evil on many occasions just to protect itself (the revolutionary base). After the First World War she preferred Germany to the West; from 1933–1939 she continually warned against the Nazis; from 1939–1941 she was Germany's partner, yet from 1941–1945 she was the ally of Britain, France, and the United States against Germany. Today she is more friendly to the leading capitalist country, the United States, than to Communist China. None of this is to gainsay the specific decisions, each of which was designed to protect the Soviet Union. And each was explained ideologically as being part of the dialectic process, the struggle to resist fascism, protection of the revolutionary base, and so on. But clearly it is important to note that Communist thought could be and was used very "flexibly" in order to justify actions whose objective often was simple survival and whose major decision component was consideration of capability.

The fact that Communist ideology was so flexible brings up another point. Very often ideological factors reinforce other considerations such as power. The fact that one may be stressed does not automatically mean another is neglected, or indeed not benefited by the action undertaken. It has been reasonably argued that to even consider power and ideological factors separately involves a distortion because they are related, the latter providing the framework within which the former is considered. Much of Soviet history shows a process of mutual reinforcement, ideology and power considerations leading to the same result.[43]

Another key issue is the degree to which, even when general concepts are accepted as valid, a particular course of action is mandatory. Let's again take the example of world revolution.[44] Soviet policymakers have never denied that this is still one of their fundamental objectives, and indeed shall be achieved at some point in time as part of the inevitable historical process. But what does this mean

---

[43]Frederick H. Hartmann, *The Relations of Nations,* Fifth Edition, Macmillan, New York, 1978, Ch. 24.

[44]Ibid., raises many of these points.

in terms of particular cases? Are Soviet policymakers going to be actively fo-
menting revolution in all situations? Do all revolutionary groups deserve support
or just those that are Communist or Communist controlled? Should Communists
not seek immediate revolution but collaborate with nationalists whose policies
help to achieve Soviet national objectives? Should resources be expended to
support revolution abroad that could be used to shore up military defense at
home? Should one seek to overthrow all capitalist regimes as soon as possible,
even those that might provide assistance against common third party enemies?
Should revolution be sought with the same tactics and at the same pace in all
situations, or should they be adjusted to practical circumstances?

Each of these questions, and many others of a similar nature, have considerable practical importance and have received different answers at different times.
In each case the broad assertion gives no clue as to what to do in the particular
contingency. This lack of precision is a necessary concomitant of flexibility and
allows for the use of ideology as a tool, but this means that it seldom can provide
a blueprint for specific action. And this one case is representative of most of the
general facets of Communist ideology. Merely knowing that someone is a "true
believer" is often not particularly helpful in predicting his actions in a given
situation.

It has been shown that Soviet policymakers have often used ideology as a
tool and have acted on nonideological bases. Ideology has been twisted and
manipulated to support traditional capability-based decisions. It was also noted
that general concepts often give us little clue as to what specific policies may be
undertaken. But these facts should not lead one to underrate the significance of
the earlier analysis of the functions Communist ideology performs. The clear
vision of the future and the certainty of final victory provide for great strength,
tenacity, and patience. The fact that all acts are evaluated, all information is
interpreted and particular problems are analyzed within a given framework gives
the Russians a distinctive perspective, and an outsider must try to place himself
within that context if he is to understand Soviet policy at all. The fact that a
distinctive vocabulary is used and the same words have different implications for
different people makes it necessary for those dealing with the Soviets to be sure
that there are mutually accepted interpretations of all agreements. Finally, the
fact that conflict and change are considered inherent in the nature of the historical
process allows outsiders to know that the Soviets never expect a stable, non-
conflictual situation to develop until they emerge triumphant.

The brief examination of the American liberal ideology and the more detailed look at the role of communism in the conduct of Soviet policy have
demonstrated that ideology is often a significant factor in policymakers' calculations. But just as was true with respect to ethical and legal considerations, there
are many times when it is not decisive. There is another key input for policymakers, the consideration of capability or power factors, and it is to this that we now
direct our attention.

THE ROLE OF POWER

It is obvious to even the most casual observer that power (capability) plays some role in international relations.[45] Wars do occur, various degrees of force and/or coercion are used, and conflicts of all sorts are recurring elements in the news. But simply reporting this fact does not help us, or the policymaker, determine how important this factor really is. Are such developments typical or unusual? Do policymakers expect such things or are they surprised when they occur?

Many analysts and practitioners consider power to be the most crucial feature of international relations. The noted authority Hans Morgenthau writes:

> International politics, like all politics, is a struggle for power. Whatever the ultimate aims of international politics, power is always the immediate aim.[46]

According to Morgenthau, history and logic combine to support this conclusion. Policymakers are well aware of the importance of power, and they think and act in power terms. Many other analysts agree. Thus, it is said that the observer can understand international relations from the policymaker's perspective, in a sense be looking over his or her shoulder as he or she works, if the observer too thinks in those terms.[47]

Why is power so important to policymakers? Why is its attainment and maximization so critical? There are basically two schools of thought in this regard: (1) because of certain qualities of human nature, or (2) because of the characteristics of the system. The first, exemplified by Morgenthau but quantitatively in the minority, emphasizes what are said to be certain inherent features of human existence. It is argued that society is governed by objective immutable laws that have their roots in human nature, and human nature is fixed and unchangeable.[48] One of the facts of life is that people are not basically good, as many American policymakers have assumed. On the contrary, all peoples possess an insatiable desire for power. Furthermore, they are not rational either: "Reason, far from following its own inherent impulses, is driven toward its goals by the irrational forces which it serves."[49] Man's constant desire for power will bring about conflict, and he is not sufficiently rational to prevent it. Because of this the best a policymaker can do is expect and accept this fact and accommodate and adjust his own actions to these unalterable realities.[50]

[45]No definition of power or capability will be attempted at this point, leaving the student to his common-sense interpretation of what it really means. In Chapter 2 the policymaker's conception of this factor will be discussed.

[46]Morgenthau, *Politics Among Nations,* Fifth Edition, p.27.

[47]Ibid., p.5.

[48]Ibid., p. 4.

[49]Hans J. Morgenthau, *Scientific Man vs. Power Politics,* University of Chicago Press, Chicago, 1946, p. 154.

[50]My analysis of Morgenthau is drawn from a combination of his *Politics Among Nations, In Defense of the National Interest,* and *Scientific Man vs. Power Politics,* all cited above. Two points

The much more prevalent basis for the conclusion that policymakers are primarily seeking to maximize capability results from some of the characteristics of international relations discussed earlier. Because there is no set of central governing institutions to make rules, apply them, enforce decisions, and settle disputes, the states have to perform these functions themselves. Each state possesses the ability to make its own decisions, including the decision to use force. Each state can only rely on itself for survival. Because all states possess military strength and because there is no one else to rely on, self-help through the threat or use of force becomes the ultimate arbiter in all situations. For these reasons each state will automatically fear and distrust the others, and always be somewhat insecure. The more one state becomes secure by increasing its capability, the more others become insecure. It is a vicious circle as each state seeks to accumulate more and more. This is what leads to "power politics." As John Spanier puts it:

> The state system thus condemns each state to a continuing struggle for power because each faces a security dilemma. Nations seek power not because the maximization of power is their goal; they seek it because they wish to guard the security of their "core values," their territorial integrity and political independence. And they act aggressively because the system gives rise to mutual fear and suspicion; each state regards its brother state, so to speak, as a potential Cain.[51]

If power was as important and sought as constantly as these analyses seem to indicate, regardless of whether it was because of man's nature or the characteristics of the system, then what a jungle the policymaker would live in.[52] He or she would have to assume that everyone was constantly struggling, fearful, and

---

are important in this regard. First, because he has written so prolifically and covered so much ground, there are many different ways of interpreting and summarizing his work; this is mine alone. Second, one must remember that Mr. Morgenthau hit the scene like a cannon shell shortly after the Second World War and his work was revolutionary. He wrote to challenge the previously prevalent academic emphasis on ethics and law, and did so very successfully. A great academic debate followed. The student should consult the works listed in footnotes 16 to 19 and 34 above. Also useful in this regard are Hans J. Morgenthau, "Another 'Great Debate': The National Interest of the United States," *The American Political Science Review*, December, 1952, pp. 961–998, and Robert W. Tucker, "Professor Morgenthau's Theory of Political Realism," *The American Political Science Review*, March, 1952, pp. 214–224.

[51]Spanier, p. 56.

[52]We say "as these analyses seem to indicate" advisedly here. As indicated in footnote [50], Professor Morgenthau's work is very complex and allows much variation in analysis. Furthermore, although it is not always possible to tell precisely when he is describing "reality" and when he is proposing a theory that experience can never totally achieve, it is clear that *sometimes* he is describing only what he thinks the essence of politics *ought* to be, not what he thinks it is. See particularly his *Politics Among Nations*, Fifth Edition, pp. 4–10. In any event, the issue here is not the precise views of Morgenthau but the role of power, and that point *is* very clear.

suspicious of all. No one could be trusted. Conflict would be the usual order of things, and cooperation would be only a means of increasing one's capability. No one would be above suspicion and one would always have to expect the worst in order to protect him or herself. The only thing the policymaker would need to consider is power, because nothing else would really matter.

But is this really descriptive of the totality of international behavior? The answer is emphatically "NO!"[53] Were it true, the policymaker would have a much simpler (if somewhat more frightening) task than he or she actually does in terms of the types and categories of data involved.

But as was demonstrated in previous sections, law, ethics, and ideology do play some role in international relations. Policymakers in fact are often influenced by such factors and many times take them into account when making decisions. This is a fact and it alone demonstrates that power is not all that matters.[54] Thus, even if the concept of human nature has some validity, and modern research at least raises some doubt, even if it is fixed and unchangeable, an even more dubious assumption in light of much evidence pointing to the influence of one's environment, and even if it includes an insatiable desire for power, a debatable and unverifiable assumption, it is obvious that many other factors are involved and power is far from the only force determining the thoughts and actions of policymakers.

Similarly, it is also evident that regardless of system characteristics states are not always seeking to maximize power. Despite the arguments about the nature of the system condemning each state to a "continuing struggle for power," the evidence shows that in fact states don't always pursue such a policy. As we will see in Chapter 2, states choose from a wide range of objectives and these vary in their relationship to power, particularly in the sense of "struggling" for its "maximization."

In analyzing the actual behavior of various states one quickly sees that in some cases it would not only be incorrect but would also be a great distortion to say that power maximization was their goal or that they were constantly struggling for its attainment. Who would characterize modern American−British or American−Israeli relations in such a fashion? Would the creation of the World Bank be meaningfully described as part of a power struggle? How about ordinary international trade agreements or Canadian−American negotiations over navigation procedures on the Great Lakes? For some states almost no aspect of their activity seems usefully characterized in this way. Swedish neutrality would be an example. And, as George Quester has said:

---

[53]Both Morgenthau and Spanier might accept this. Even if they did they would still stress the overarching importance of power and suggest that all else is relatively insignificant.

[54]State practice is the most powerful evidence one could develop. For various academic arguments see the works cited in footnote [50] above.

Surely Iceland and Switzerland are nations, but they devote almost no effort to influencing the outside world politically, and thus are barely interested in power, much less deterministically dominated by it.[55]

If power is not all pervasive then how should one describe its role? Certainly it does have some degree of significance. The key point is that its significance can only be determined in light of the particular situation. Because of the system's characteristics it is true that there is always the possibility that power will be very important and may be decisive. Perhaps force will even be used. Since there is always this potential, policymakers must continually consider capability factors. For the same reason they must also be very careful, recognizing that they must act to protect their country and that conflicts can occur. On the other hand, they must also remember that other factors may enter into policy calculations and cooperation also might be possible; conflict is not the only type of relationship that can occur. Thus there are no *a priori* conclusions one can reach. It is essential to analyze the specific situation and the particular policymakers involved to see which factors are most pertinent in each case.

In this regard, as in so many, the factor of perception is terribly important. Policymakers must, of course, be aware of the role that ethics, law, ideology, and power usually play and then attempt to deduce the specific application from the generality. But they must go beyond a superficial analysis and take into account the fact that different individuals "see" things differently. They operate from different perspectives and seldom observe the situation in an objective manner. Although the world they perceive may be quite different from that which an objective outsider might see, *they will in fact act on the basis of their perception.* Thus policymakers must try to determine the particular perception of every other participant policymaker and, recognizing that each will act on the basis of his or her own subjective interpretation, act accordingly.

COOPERATION AND CONFLICT

The foregoing analysis has shown that law, ethics, ideology, and power are important in international relations, the role that each plays depending on many different factors. It is clear that although there are times that the policymaker must accord the highest priority to questions of capability there are times this is not so. Given these facts alone one would expect that there would be a wide variety of relations ensuing among states. In addition, one needs to recall that there are 150 or so states (plus nonstate actors) participating in international relations, each with its own history, geographic setting, political and economic system, and so forth. Each has its own policymakers and their differing percep-

---

[55]George H. Quester, *The Continuing Problem of International Politics,* Dryden Press, Hinsdale, Illinois, 1974, p. 13.

tions of and susceptibility to the general factors that have been analyzed, each seeking some of a wide range of possible objectives via a vast array of policy techniques (see Chapter 4 and 5), all of this occurring within a decentralized anarchical system allowing each immense latitude of choice. The end result is an amazingly complex system.

What does this mean in terms of conflict and/or cooperation? Do most of the relations in this complex world involve conflict or cooperation? Which should policymakers assume as they attempt to formulate and implement policy?

The answer is that they should *assume neither*. Because of the bewildering variety and immense quantity of international interactions policymakers deal with an unbelievably complex world. As the previous discussion has shown, even understanding the most basic concepts is an extraordinarily difficult task. It is clear enough, of course, that conflicts occur and do so for many reasons. Maybe states are simply seeking incompatible objectives. In such a situation if the objectives are sufficiently important, fundamentally opposed, cannot be adjusted, and neither side will give in, there will be conflict. Of course, there are many other causes, only a few of which can be mentioned here. Prestige may become involved and make compromise impossible; the snowballing phenomenon may set in until a conflict develops that no one anticipated; perhaps incorrect or inadequate information or certain preconceptions bring about unnecessary conflict; sometimes policy is conducted so ineptly that it leads to trouble, or perhaps there just was not adequate time to think things out. Maybe ethnic, racial, or religious differences cannot be reconciled. And the list could be extended. Not to belabor the point further, it is obvious that there are a wide variety of conflictual relations.

But some relations are only competitive, not conflictual, and many are cooperative. States seek some objectives that are divergent but not in conflict. For example, the United States may seek to provide economic assistance to India, the Soviet Union military aid. This relationship is competitive, not adversarial (although, of course, it could develop into that). Many times states seek complementary objectives. The United States and Pakistan wanted an alliance in the 1950s. Washington's main goal was to contain Communist China, Pakistan's to receive weapons for possible use against India. The resulting relationship was limited cooperation. Finally, states sometimes have a common objective and cooperate to seek its attainment. The United States and the Western European countries cooperated by forming NATO to attain their common objective of deterring a Soviet military attack.

Obviously too, the various "nonobjective" reasons for conflict mentioned above (and many that were not mentioned) do not always occur. Sometimes there is adequate time and information, prestige does not take over, snowballing does not occur, and so forth. Furthermore, sometimes objectives are modified so as to make them compatible once one realizes that the failure to do so will lead to conflict.

Not only are international relations in general a mixture of conflict and cooperation, but this is also true of the relations of any two parties. American–Soviet disagreements and confrontations since World War II have made headlines and rightly so as they have signified many areas of real conflict between the two most powerful countries in the world. Yet there have also been many areas of cooperation. The tacit consent to limit their competition to nonviolent means is one example. Another was the signing of the Limited Nuclear Test Ban and Non–Proliferation Treaties as the superpowers sought to limit the dangers of nuclear weaponry. Recently economic, medical, scientific, and cultural cooperation have increased, as have political–military concern and consultation over the growing capability of the People's Republic of China. And, of course, the Strategic Arms Limitation Agreements of May 1972 provide another example. Thus one sees a real mixture of conflict and cooperation even between Washington and Moscow.

As a policymaker one must avoid prejudging the issue. Things are just too complicated and unpredictable for one to make an *a priori* judgment. There may be either conflict or cooperation, or a mixture of the two, but a policymaker simply cannot know in advance. All one can do is analyze all aspects of the particular situation and try to determine which is the most probable in the specific case.

In this chapter the basic characteristics of the international environment within which the policymaker works have been analyzed. It is now time to move from the general to the specific, from general characteristics to the specific steps of policy formulation.

SELECTED BIBLIOGRAPHY

Black, Cyril, and Richard Falk, eds., *The Future of the International Legal Order,* Vol. I, Princeton University Press, Princeton, New Jersey, 1969.

Brzezinski, Zbigniew, *Ideology and Power in Soviet Politics,* Praeger, New York, 1962.

Carr, Edward H., *The Twenty Years' Crisis, 1919–1939,* Macmillan, London, 1939.

Claude, Inis L., Jr., *Swords into Plowshares: The Problems and Progress of International Organization,* Fourth Edition, Random House, New York, 1971.

Cook, Thomas I., and Malcom Moos, *Power Thru Purpose: The Realism of Idealism as a Basis for Foreign Policy,* Johns Hopkins Press, Baltimore, 1954.

Coplin, William D., *The Functions of International Law,* Rand McNally, Chicago, 1966.

Coulombis, Theodore A., and James H. Wolfe, *Introduction to International Relations: Power and Justice,* Prentice-Hall, Englewood Cliffs, New Jersey, 1978.

Duchacek, Ivo D., *Nations & Men: An Introduction to International Politics,* Third Edition, Dryden Press, Hinsdale, Illinois, 1975.

Goodman, Elliot R., *The Fate of the Atlantic Community,* Praeger, New York, 1975.

Haas, Ernst B., *Beyond the Nation-State,* Stanford University Press, Stanford, California, 1964.

Hartmann, Frederick H., *The Relations of Nations,* Fifth Edition, Macmillan, New York, 1978.

Herz, John, *International Politics in the Atomic Age*, Columbia University Press, New York, 1959.

Hoffman, Stanley, *Contemporary Theory in International Relations*, Prentice-Hall, Englewood Cliffs, New Jersey, 1960.

Holsti, K. J., *International Politics: A Framework for Analysis*, Third Edition, Prentice-Hall, Englewood Cliffs, New Jersey, 1977.

Kennan, George, *On Dealing with the Communist World*, Harper & Row, New York, 1964.

Keohane, Robert O., and Joseph S. Nye, "Transgovernmental Relations and International Organizations," *World Politics*, October, 1974, pp. 39-62.

Levi, Werner, "International Law in a Multicultural World," *International Studies Quarterly*, December, 1974, pp. 417-449.

Lindberg, Leon N., and Stuart A Scheingold, *Europe's Would-Be Polity: Patterns of Change in the European Community*, Prentice-Hall, Englewood Cliffs, New Jersey, 1970.

Mansbach, Richard W., Yale H. Ferguson, and Donald E. Lampert, *The Web of World Politics: Nonstate Actors in the Global System*, Prentice-Hall, Englewood Cliffs, New Jersey, 1976.

Meyer, Alfred G., *Communism*, Third Edition, Random House, New York, 1967.

Morgenthau, Hans J., *Politics Among Nations*, Fifth Edition, Alfred A. Knopf, New York, 1973.

Morgenthau, Hans J., *Scientific Man vs. Power Politics*, University of Chicago Press, Chicago, 1946.

Nicholas, H.G., *The United Nations as a Political Institution*, Fifth Edition, Oxford University Press, New York, 1975.

Osgood, Robert E., and Robert Tucker, *Force, Order, and Justice*, Johns Hopkins University Press, Baltimore, 1967.

Paxton, John, *The Developing Common Market: The Structure of the EEC in Theory and in Practice, 1957-1976*, Third Edition, Westview Press, Boulder, Colorado, 1976.

Puchala, Donald James, *International Politics Today*, Dodd Mead, New York, 1971.

Rosen, Steven J., and Walter S. Jones, *The Logic of International Relations*, Second Edition, Winthrop, Cambridge, Massachusetts, 1977.

Rosser, Richard F., *An Introduction to Soviet Foreign Policy*, Prentice-Hall, Englewood Cliffs, New Jersey, 1969.

Rubinstein, Alvin Z., ed., *The Foreign Policy of the Soviet Union*, Third Edition, Random House, New York, 1972.

Said, Abdul A., and Luiz R. Simmons, eds., *The New Sovereigns: Multinational Corporations as World Powers*, Prentice-Hall, Englewood Clifs, New Jersey, 1975.

Scheinman, Lawrence, and David Wilkinson, eds., *International Law and Political Crisis: An Analytical Casebook*, Little, Brown, Boston, 1968.

Spanier, John, *Games Nations Play: Analyzing International Politics*, Third Edition, Praeger, New York, 1978.

Stoessinger, John G., *The Might of Nations: World Politics in Our Time*, Fourth Edition, Random House, New York, 1973.

Tannenbaum, Frank, *The American Tradition in Foreign Policy*, University of Oklahoma Press, Norman, Oklahoma, 1955.

Vernon, Raymond, *Sovereignty at Bay: The Multinational Spread of U.S. Enterprises*, Basic Books, New York, 1971.

Two

Policy Formulation

Within the context of the major features of the international environment discussed in Chapter One, there are a series of steps that the policymaker *should attempt* to follow in formulating an optimum policy. This is an objective, not an accurate description of reality as the analyses of the problems the policymaker confronts and the constraints upon his or her actions (Chapters Six and Seven) will demonstrate. It also is an oversimplification because it involves a somewhat artificial separation of steps that are interrelated and that are often taken simultaneously. These facts, however, do not detract from the utility of examining what ought to be done and suggesting that one should try to come as close to the ideal as possible. That is the purpose of this chapter.[1]

STEP ONE: WHO IS INVOLVED?

The policymaker's first step is to ascertain who is involved in the particular situation being considered. How many parties are there, what are their relationships, and who will be critical in determining the outcome? It seems like this would be easy, but it is not, and very often differences in this analysis underlie severe disagreements over the policy to be adopted.

There are any number of situation configurations with which policymakers must deal but it is useful to think of them in terms of seven basic categories: (1) two primary parties, (2) a primary party and a coalition of equals, (3) a primary party and a coalition headed by a dominant party, (4) two or more coalitions of equals, (5) several primary parties, (6) two or more coalitions with each headed by a dominant party, and (7) any of the preceding with the addition of parties adopting any of the orientations described below that do not involve concern with the substance of the problem (such as neutral problem solver or balancer).

---

[1] The normative thrust of this chapter should be constantly kept in mind. Although policymakers often attempt to follow procedures of the nature described here, sometimes they do not, and many times things are much more complex and confusing than this analysis might imply (as shown in some depth in Chapters 6 and 7). Thus this chapter does not purport to perfectly describe reality but rather to provide the student with a conceptual framework that allows him to analyze situations from an ideal policymaker's point of view.

Policymakers must attempt to determine which configuration characterizes the situation in question and what this means in terms of the appropriate target for their policy. In each instance they are searching for the key party or parties, the one(s) who can wield decisive influence.

This task is always important but it can be critical in a crisis. In this situation the key question often is: Who is the "enemy"? Even this limited aspect of the problem can be exceedingly complex. Perhaps an example would be helpful: let's analyze the Vietnam conflict in the early and mid-1960s as it was (and might have been) perceived from Washington.

Who really was involved? Who was the "enemy"? Was this war fundamentally a domestic power struggle between two South Vietnamese factions, the Saigon Government and the Viet Cong (VC), later supplemented and expanded by outside forces? Was the VC the primary enemy of the Saigon Government, and was it essentially an organization of South Vietnamese dissidents? Or was the VC a front organization for the Democratic Republic of Vietnam (DRV), operating in accordance with instructions from the North? Or did the VC and DRV constitute a coalition of equals, neither dominating the other? Or were both the VC and DRV engaged in a war of national liberation largely controlled and directed by the People's Republic of China (PRC)? Or was this a three-way coalition? Or were these three, separate parties? Or were all three a part of a centrally directed Communist monolith seeking to communize the entire globe, with this being but one theater of that struggle? These were not mere hypothetical problems. On the contrary, they constantly confronted policymakers and received different answers at different times (although the policymakers were not always aware of their own confusion and the significance of the issue).

American conceptions shifted erratically among three possibilities. The enemy was: (1) a primary party, monolithic communism, (2) a primary party, Hanoi, and the VC was its creature, and (3) a primary party, China. Configuration number one was dominant (two primary parties) although the identity of the parties was a matter of dispute. On "our" side, at some point Washington took over the primary role from Saigon; as to "their" side, American policymakers never did reach a permanent conclusion concerning who the enemy really was (the complexity of the overall issue is demonstrated by the fact that even within a given configuration there can be wide differences of opinion).

Secretary of State Dean Rusk illustrated American confusion rather clearly in his testimony before the Senate Foreign Relations Committee on February 18, 1966.[2] At one point he said:

> We must view the problem in perspective. We must recognize that what we are seeking to achieve in South Vietnam is part of a process that has continued for a long

---

[2]For the text of his testimony, see U.S. Department of State, *Bulletin,* March 7, 1966, pp. 1−17.

time, a process of preventing the expansion and extension of Communist domination by the use of force against the weaker nations on the perimeter of Communist power . . . The Communist world has returned to its demand for what it calls a world revolution . . . So what we face in Vietnam is what we have faced on many occasions before. The need to check the extension of Communist power in order to maintain a reasonable stability in a precarious world.

This would seem to be clear enough. The enemy is Communist power and this is part of a gigantic effort to revolutionize the world. Yet later in the very same speech Secretary Rusk evidenced his lack of clarity when he referred to the act of aggression by *Hanoi*:

But the evidence is overwhelming that it is in fact something quite different. A systematic aggression by Hanoi against the people of South Vietnam.

Elsewhere he said:

These facts demonstrate beyond question that the war in Vietnam is as much an act of outside aggression as though the Hanoi regime had sent an army across the 17th parallel.[3]

When this conception was dominant, the Administration directed its activities toward Hanoi:

For months now we have done everything possible to make clear to the regime in Hanoi that a political solution is the proper course. This is the simple message that we have tried to convey to Hanoi through many channels. The regime in Hanoi has been unwilling to accept any of the possibilities open to it for discussion.

Clearly, if the enemy was the monolithic Communist bloc of Cold War fame the key would lie not in Hanoi but presumably in Moscow.[4]

Yet perhaps this was neither expansion by a Communist monolith nor an act of aggression by Hanoi. Rusk himself so indicated on October 12, 1967 when he opined that Communist China was the real instigator, or at least the underlying menace involved in the Vietnam war. At a press conference he said that it was really China that was testing Washington here, that ''Peking has nominated itself

---

[3]This seems to have been the more generally accepted American interpretation. See U.S., Department of State, *A Threat to Peace: North Viet-Nam's Effort to Conquer South Viet-Nam*, Publication 7308, 1961, and U.S., Department of State, *Aggression from the North: The Record of North Viet-Nam's Campaign to Conquer South Viet-Nam*, Publication 7839, 1965.

[4]If the real enemy was non-Vietnamese there would be no serious study of the history, culture, and politics of Vietnam because such subjects would be deemed essentially irrelevant to the outcome of the struggle. If the ''locals'' were mere pawns in the larger struggle one might feel that it made no difference that there had been a victorious anticolonial revolution led by Ho Chi Minh and that he was the most popular figure in the country.

by proclaiming a militant doctrine of the world revolution and doing something about it.''

This was not an abstract discussion divorced from policy implications. If China was the main enemy then all American policy had to be calculated on the basis of an expansionist China instigating a war of national liberation.

President Johnson seemed equally unclear. In his famous ''Patterns for Peace'' speech at Johns Hopkins University on April 7, 1965, he stated:

> The first reality is that North Viet-Nam has attacked the independent nation of South Viet-Nam.

Yet later he said:

> Over this war—and all Asia—is another reality: the deepening shadow of *Communist China*. The rulers in Hanoi are urged on by Peiping . . . *The contest in Viet-Nam is part of a wider pattern of aggressive purposes.*[5] (emphasis mine)

Other officials also demonstrated similar confusion but there is no need to further belabor the point. Much of Washington's difficulty in determining what should be done in Vietnam stemmed directly from this failure to determine with whom one should be (or was) dealing.

It should also be pointed out that the problem was even more complex than these ''official'' interpretations might indicate. Many nonpolicymakers held still another view. They also believed in the two primary parties configuration but felt that these primary parties were simply different South Vietnamese factions, the VC being essentially composed of southern insurgents. Two noted experts on Southeast Asia, George Kahin and John Lewis, put it this way:

> In sum, the insurrection is Southern rooted; it arose at Southern initiative in response to Southern demands . . . It gained drive under the stimulus of Southern Vietminh veterans who felt betrayed by the Geneva Conference and abandoned by Hanoi . . . They lost patience with the communist North and finally took matters into their own hands. Hanoi, despite its reluctance, was then obliged to sanction the Southerners' actions or risk forfeiting all chance of influence over the course of events in South Vietnam. Contrary to U.S. policy assumptions, all available evidence shows that the revival of the civil war in the South in 1958 was undertaken by Southerners at their own—not Hanoi's—initiative.[6]

Obviously, it is necessary to determine who is involved in order to know whom one should make as the target of his or her policies. This issue is not restricted to Vietnam, of course, but has relevance to many other situations. For

[5]See U.S., Department of State, *Bulletin,* April 26, 1965, pp. 606–610.

[6]See George McTurnan Kahin and John W. Lewis, *The United States in Vietnam: An Analysis in Depth of America's Involvement in Vietnam,* A Delta Book, New York, 1967, p. 119.

example, who really is involved in the various Middle East conflicts? Do the disputes revolve around an Arab coalition of equals and Israel? Is it Israel against an Arab coalition dominated by Egypt? Is it really Israel versus an implicit Egyptian-Syrian-Jordanian alliance? Is it a tacit Israeli-American coalition against an Arab coalition? What role does the Soviet Union play? Do the Soviets and Americans hold the trump cards? Are there really several primary parties but no cohesive alliances? Are the Palestinian Arabs really the key? If so, which Palestinian Arabs? Are the critical parties the Arab oil states, or the oil companies? Are inter-Arab disputes ultimately more important than Arab-Israeli conflicts?

Or switch to the problems of a divided Europe. Are there really just two primary parties, the Americans and Russians, with everyone else of minor importance? Or is the situation one involving two alliances headed by dominant partners in confrontation? Are opposing coalitions disintegrating and cross-alliance policies becoming more important? Is it really a case of several relatively independent parties all seeking their own objectives? What is the role of the Germans, West and East? Do they really hold the key?

The discussion could go on and on, but it would serve no purpose. It is clear that in all of these cases, Vietnam, the Middle East and Central Europe, determining who is involved is critical and difficult. Policymakers must deal with this problem in each situation they confront if they are to have any hope of formulating an effective policy.

STEP TWO: DETERMINATION OF OBJECTIVES

Once one has determined who is involved he or she must attempt to discover what each wants; what are their objectives?[7] At the same time the policymaker must be formulating his or her own.

All international actors have a wide range of objectives that they potentially may seek. These may vary in terms of breadth, the intensity with which they are sought, the time frame within which one hopes to achieve them, and the resources one is willing to allocate to their attainment. They may also differ in the extent to which a party really expects them to be attained, as well as the sources from which they come.

When speaking of "objectives" one is talking about the "ends" of policy. However, it should not be assumed that it is possible to neatly distinguish between "means" and "ends," and that the "ends" are definite and final. Few objectives are ends in themselves. Instead they are usually means to the achieve-

---

[7]At this point in the process the policymaker generally begins with the assumption that the policymakers of all states act in a unified, rational fashion, although he recognizes that this is an oversimplification and sometimes just plain wrong. However, one must begin here and make his adjustments and allowances later. See Chapters 6 and 7 for various qualifications.

ment of further ends (which in turn are often means to further ends, and so forth). What the situation really involves is a means-end chain of varying degrees of complexity.[8]

Fundamental Objectives

All states have certain fundamental objectives, a certain nucleus for the protection or achievement of which they would be willing to undertake a maximum expenditure of resources, including going to war, in all but the most unusual situations. The first of these, and the most fundamental, is pure *survival*. At rock bottom all of the policymaker's decisions must be based on their anticipated effect on the continued existence of his country. One must always ask, "is this helpful or harmful to security?" Survival is composed, at a minimum, of two parts: first, protecting the lives of a majority of the population, and second, defending the country's sovereignty or political independence (i.e. its capacity to make independent decisions concerning its internal affairs and external policies).

A second fundamental objective, and one that is often considered to be a matter of survival, is *territorial integrity*. In most cases the defense of one's home territory is critical. A state that loses its *entire* territory, of course, ceases to even be a state, as happened to Poland in the eighteenth century.[9] From 1795 until the end of World War I "Poland" did not exist. As this illustrates, there have been cases in which one's territory has just been relinquished, but this is highly unusual. Occasionally policymakers have "accepted" the loss of just a portion of their territory in the hope of preserving the remainder. Perhaps the most famous example of this was the "acceptance" by the Czechoslovakian Government of the loss of certain German inhabited strategic territories to the Nazis following the Munich Agreement in 1938.[10] In that case territorial integrity was violated but a certain territorial base was retained. But these two cases were extraordinary, very much the exception to the rule. The policymaker must assume that parties will consider preservation of their home territory to be a fundamental objective and will fight to protect it.

This does, however, raise another issue: what *is* one's home territory? It is not always clear where one state ends and another begins. It must be remembered

---

[8]See Keith R. Legg and James F. Morrison, *Politics and the International System: An Introduction,* Harper, New York, 1971, pp. 140–142.

[9]In a series of three partitions, in 1772, 1793 and 1795, Poland was divided among Prussia, Russia, and Austria (Austria was involved only in the first and third partitions).

[10]Of course the remainder was not preserved in this case. The best general account of the Munich Crisis is Sir John W. Wheeler-Bennett, *Munich—Prologue to Tragedy,* Second Edition, Macmillan, New York, 1963. A very useful and brief introduction replete with valuable documents, is Frances L. Lorwenheim, ed., *Peace or Appeasement? Hitler, Chamberlain and the Munich Crisis,* Houghton Mifflin, Boston, 1964. The best introduction to the Munich Era is still Winston S. Churchill, *The Second World War. Vol. I: The Gathering Storm,* Houghton Mifflin, Boston, 1948. Also see Chapter 1, p. 14.

that each state has its own conception of what is "home," and sometimes these conceptions are different. The People's Republic of China claims that 500,000 square miles of Soviet Asia actually "belongs" to China; the Soviets disagree.[11] Whose "home territory" is it? After World War II Germany was split into East and West, and the ancient citadels of Prussian (German) power were incorporated into Russia and Poland. What is, or is not, "Germany"? What about other divided nations (such as Korea)? Who "owns" land taken by conquest? These are pertinent, highly troublesome questions.

A third objective that has often been considered fundamental is the *preservation of a state's belief system from externally imposed change.*[12] States often consider the basic principles, beliefs, values, customs, and traditions by which they live to be of such importance that they would be willing to fight to maintain them. Certainly the United States would consider the protection of some democratic principles worth fighting for. Attempts by a foreign country to prevent the free exercise of religion or to prohibit freedom of association in the United States, for example, would not be tolerated. South Africa would not freely accept foreign-induced changes in its apartheid programs. The Soviet Union invaded Czechoslovakia in August of 1968 in part at least to prevent the danger to its own belief system that it perceived the Czech liberalization to pose.[13]

A fourth fundamental objective often is the *protection of the existing political or economic system from externally imposed change.* Obviously the Soviets would fight to preserve their existing governmental structure against the imposition of more democratic institutions, as would North Korea, Vietnam, China, and others. The leaders of Israel would not accept a change in the governmental structure that would allow true binational Arab-Israeli control. Washington would consider preservation of its mixed-capitalist economic system critical, and conversely the Soviets would certainly act to prevent the imposition of any system based on private ownership of property and the means of production.

Middle-Range Objectives

Fundamental objectives are essentially conservative, something to be defended or protected.[14] There are many other objectives states may seek which vary in

---

[11]See footnote 21 below.

[12]Both this and the following fundamental objective are directly related to the second attribute of statehood, the right of internal control. See Chapter 1, pp. 3–4.

[13]Philip Windsor and Adam Roberts, *Czechoslovakia: Reform, Repression and Resistance,* Columbia University Press, New York, 1969. For further discussion see Chapter 4, pp. 149–150.

[14]They are also more separable on paper than in practice. In most cases they are interrelated and often they compete with one another for limited resources. The policymaker is usually confronted with an uncertain choice among related alternatives none of which is totally acceptable or unacceptable. Although it is useful to analyze them separately, one must remember that in reality things are much more complicated.

significance depending on the situation. They may become exceptionally important and require the expenditure of considerable resources, or may receive lower priority. Generally their achievement is sought within a forseeable period of time, although not immediately. Such *middle-range objectives* sometimes resemble fundamental objectives, but there are salient differences in terms of their permanence, the perceived level of importance, and the intensity with which they are sought.

Middle-range objectives span the gamut of desires and a wide range of classification schemes are possible. For the policymaker, however, it is useful to divide them into political, material, ideological, and prestige objectives, even though he or she recognizes that there is considerable imprecision and overlapping here.

An example of a *political* objective would be the acquisition of additional territory, or the retention of that previously conquered. Another might be the creation of political dependencies as the Soviets did in Eastern Europe after World War II. Perhaps the objective is to negotiate a limitation of strategic weapons as the United States and Russia did in interim fashion in May, 1972. In other words, political objectives deal primarily with capability and security relationships.

Material objectives include anything affecting economic growth and development. In 1957, France, West Germany, Italy, the Netherlands, Belgium, and Luxembourg created the European Common Market in an attempt to break down nationalistic barriers to Europe's integrated economic growth. Less developed countries often seek a wide variety of economic assistance ranging from additional capital to applied technical instruction. The Soviet Union may purchase wheat from the United States while Washington buys oil from Persian Gulf states. Material objectives can become critically important and sometimes conflict over them leads to war.

Ideological objectives may include the spreading of a particular system of beliefs. Attempts by Communist leaders to "convince" their neighbors of the validity of Marxism-Leninism would be an example. When President Wilson took the United States into the First World War to "make the world safe for democracy," he was in part seeking an ideological victory.

Another ideological objective would be persuading another party that professes the same ideology as you to accept the "correct" (your) interpretation. Disagreement over the "correct" interpretation of Communism has been one of the major issues in the Sino-Soviet dispute.[15] In 1956 Nikita Khrushchev broke with orthodox Leninist and Stalinist doctrine by stating that there was no "fatal inevitability" of war between Socialists and capitalists. Because of the overwhelming strength of the camp of socialism, capitalist leaders might be deterred from going to war. The Chinese strongly disagreed; orthodox communism al-

---

[15]See pp. 76–78, for more on the Sino-Soviet dispute.

lowed no room for this capacity to avoid war; a series of terrible collisions was inevitable. Furthermore, if, in contrast to orthodox doctrine, some capitalists in some situations could choose to refrain from actions previously considered inevitable, if in some cases they avoid the inexorable laws of history, then why couldn't they in others?[16] Where would it stop? Persuading the other party of the correct interpretation clearly was a matter of some import.

The protection or enhancement of *prestige* is extremely important to policymakers. Even though the January, 1974 Israeli-Egyptian agreement to disengage forces along the Suez Canal fit in with Russian political objectives, the Kremlin let Washington know it was displeased because Dr. Kissinger had not consulted with the Soviets enough in the negotiation process; the Soviets wanted equal status with America. During these same negotiations Egyptian President Anwar Sadat said he could not accept an "Israeli" proposal, even if the substance of the proposal was to his liking. That being so, at Kissinger's suggestion an "American" proposal was formulated embodying many of the same provisions. Because he did not think his prestige would be harmed by working with Washington, Sadat found this acceptable.

A wise policymaker will recognize the importance of prestige and not place his or her counterpart's in jeopardy any more than necessary. President Kennedy heeded this maxim in the Cuban Missile Crisis by allowing Khrushchev a means of withdrawing the Soviet missiles that did not humiliate the Communist leader; the President did not want to provoke a spasm reaction. Failure to give sufficient weight to this element can be harmful to the pursuit of other goals. Hanoi's objective of eliminating American military forces from South Vietnam proved much more costly as a result of its massive conventional assault across the demilitarized zone in March of 1972. President Nixon responded by mining key North Vietnamese ports and initiating heavy bombing of the North. The President obviously felt that there was no need to kick Uncle Sam in the backside as he was leaving.

Specific Immediate Objectives

Finally, the policymaker needs to formulate the specific immediate objectives. After assessing the relationship of the particular situation to fundamental objectives and then considering what middle-range goals should be sought, it is necessary to ask "what is the immediate objective that fits in best with the overall plan?"

Suppose, for example, one has determined that his or her party's fundamental objective of survival is endangered because it is not sufficiently achieving the middle-range objective of economic growth. Perhaps what is required is a critical natural resource such as petroleum, and it has none in its possession. The

---

[16]Excellent is Hartmann, *The Relations of Nations,* Fifth Edition, pp. 478−483.

policymaker's specific immediate objective then might be to obtain the needed petroleum in the most feasible manner. After assessing the situation one would know whether to attempt to negotiate a trade agreement, seek to purchase oil, agree to adopt certain positions in the United Nations on certain issues, provide military assistance, use force, or whatever.[17]

To this point the picture that has been presented has been oversimplified because it concentrated only on "our" objectives. In actuality what the policymaker must do is make a *simultaneous comparative analysis* to determine the objectives of all of the parties. In each case the policymaker must ascertain the fundamental, middle-range and immediate goals, determine their relationships, and evaluate the significance of his conclusions. This is at best an imprecise activity and uncertainty about states' objectives is an ever-present fact of international politics.[18]

Sources of Objectives

In order to undertake this task with any degree of confidence it is very helpful to examine another issue: What are the sources of the objectives for the parties in question? From where do their objectives come?

Once again the task is complicated. Some objectives seem to spring from several sources while others seem to just develop. Furthermore, all attempts at classification distort reality somewhat. Policymakers, however, need to know where objectives come from if they are to understand them and perhaps influence future goal formation, and must attempt the task no matter how difficult.

There are several rather general sources of objectives. As noted in Chapter 1, *ideological and ethical factors* often influence goal formation. Communism provides the lens through which Soviet leaders see the world and the rationale for much of their action. American values condition the nature of United States objectives, so much so that many analysts have based much of their criticism of American policy on precisely this point.[19]

A second general source is *historical tradition and precedent*. The American objective of preventing significant European encroachment in the Western Hemisphere was enunciated in the Monroe Doctrine in 1823 and continues to this day.[20] For hundreds of years Britain sought specifically to prevent the domina-

---

[17]Although the classification scheme is different, an excellent example of this kind of analytical approach may be found in William D. Coplin, Patrick J. McGowan, and Michael K. O'Leary, *American Foreign Policy: An Introduction to Analysis and Evaluation,* Duxbury, North Scituate, Mass., Table 4.2, 1974, pp. 86–90.

[18]See Donald James Puchala, *International Politics Today,* Dodd Mead, New York, 1971, pp. 90–94.

[19]See footnote 34, Chapter 1.

[20]This concept had originally been proposed by the British as an Anglo-American venture. Washington was unwilling to cooperate, however, and proceeded on its own. In actuality the Doctrine's success in the nineteenth century was more a result of British naval strength and European concern elsewhere than it was due to American power.

tion of the Low Countries (Belgium, Netherlands) by a Continental Power to protect against a cross-Channel invasion, and generally to maintain a relatively equal Continental distribution of power. For much of its history (both before and since the advent of communism) Russia has sought to acquire additional territory, to create a buffer zone around its geographic heartland for defense in depth, and to break out of its landlocked position by acquiring ice free ports (particularly through the Dardanelles Strait to the Mediterranean). These and similar factors are often taken by policymakers as "givens," automatic and continual sources of objectives.

When analyzing historical factors, however, one should keep two points in mind. First, it is not just narrow precedent that is important but more generally a state's total historical experience. The Chinese belief that territory taken from them during periods of imperial weakness is rightfully Chinese will lead to concern with getting it back, even if they have not "traditionally" sought to do so.[21] A newly independent state with little tradition of any kind may well pursue objectives that are decidedly anti-colonial because of its experience.

A second point is that although historical factors are important they are not necessarily controlling. For centuries England supported the survival of the Ottoman Turk Empire for the purpose of protecting the British imperial lifeline through the Mediterranean to the East (and India, Singapore, Hong Kong, Australia, etc.). This often meant opposition to traditional Russian efforts indicated above. The altered circumstances of World War I, however, brought about an agreement with the Russians against the Turks. The point is this: although policymakers must look at a state's historical patterns and experience for clues to objectives, and recognize that it is an important source, they must avoid being mesmerized by the past and assume that nothing will change.

In addition to such general sources, *specific internal needs* may generate objectives. Population pressure on the food supply may bring about the goal of territorial expansion, and/or increased production, and/or population control. Economic necessities may require the purchase of strategic materials, creation of new trading arrangements, and procedures for obtaining new capital. Ethnic conflict may lead to a call for foreign intervention or preparation to repel it. The list is almost endless. Policymakers must examine the subject country's domestic conditions to ascertain what needs may spawn what specific objectives.

A wide range of external factors may also come into play. Policymakers *perceive threats to national security* and respond accordingly. The American objective of containment of communism arose in this fashion. Alliances are often formed for security reasons, as was true with NATO. Obviously, a major impetus to the quest for stronger armed forces is the perception that security is threatened.

Perception of a security threat is not the only external source of objectives,

---

[21]The Chinese list 19 specific territorial losses. A useful map reprinted from a 1954 Chinese textbook may be found in Hartmann, *The New Age of American Foreign Policy,* pp. 340–341.

however, although official statements may sometimes try to make it look that way. There are also *opportunities to take advantage of situations created by foreign events and conditions.* Domestic unrest provides great possibilities for penetration and intervention. The need for foreign assistance yields the opportunities for influence that go with giving such assistance. The disintegration of an alliance, such as the Sino-Soviet combine, may provide the opportunity to increase one's influence with both countries. A revolution that deposes an adversarial regime may put a more amenable one in its place.

Another external source is the *need to handle a common problem.* Of course, this could involve the two (external) sources discussed above, but it is much broader than that. The mutual Soviet-American recognition of a need to limit strategic weapons led to the SALT Agreements of May 26, 1972. Multilateral acceptance by six European countries of the need to break down nationalistic barriers to economic growth led to the creation of the Common Market in 1957. Concern over economic and environmental issues today is leading to international attempts to solve these difficulties.

It is necessary to explicitly point out a fact that has pervaded much of the previous discussion: *policymakers' perceptions of other states' objectives will significantly influence their own. This means that many times objectives will be primarily responsive in nature.* There is a constant interaction of events and perceptions and all states find many of their policies largely reactive. In fact, sometimes one may not even have been concerned with a given problem until conditions changed and others were perceived to be seeking certain things. For example, the United States paid little attention to the Mediterranean area until the post World War II era. It was only after Britain announced it was pulling out and Washington saw a Soviet threat that it responded with the Greek-Turkish Aid Program and the Truman Doctrine.[22]

Another source is the *needs of the leadership.* Any regime requires some degree of internal support if it is to stay in power. Given this fact, there is always the temptation to create incidents or proclaim possible threats to security in order to maintain this support. Throughout much of the 1950s and 1960s Red Chinese leaders were able to use the spectre of an American invasion to rally popular sentiment behind them. Today, charges of similar Soviet intentions serve the same purpose. Many leaders of newly independent, less developed countries are particularly prone to this activity. Prior to independence they often assumed that all of their troubles were caused by the colonialists. With the imperialists' departure, however, it has been discovered that significant problems (such as low economic growth) remain and that they are extremely difficult to solve. In order to divert attention from failures at home a dynamic, sometimes frenetic foreign policy may be undertaken.

---

[22]See Dean Acheson, *Present at the Creation: My Years in the State Department,* Norton, New York, 1970, Chs. 22, 24, 25. For further discussion see Chapter 4, p. 142.

It has also been said that "means determine the ends that may be sought."[23] In this type of case a state's capabilities are a "source" of objectives. Perhaps it would be more accurate, however, to say that policymakers *should* formulate their objectives within the framework of a realistic assessment of capabilities. It is obvious that this is not always what occurs. Ultimately, however, capabilities will determine the degree to which objectives will or will not be achieved.

To this point the sources examined have been limited in one critical respect: they are outside of the policymaking process itself. Each of these factors will compete for the policymaker's attention but they will "get through" in varying degrees with differing amounts of effectiveness. One also needs to examine a more proximate source of objectives: *the actual process by which the decisions concerning objectives will be made.* One must seek to determine the locus of decision and ascertain the identity of the key policy influencers. Are there key elites whose will shall prevail? Are there interest factions who control certain issues? Do some decisions really seem to be the product of bureaucratic conflicts? What effect do institutional and structural factors have? These and similar questions must be asked.[24]

This brings us to the final consideration, one that policymakers often respect more than observers: *it is human beings who make decisions.* In Chapter 3 the significant impact that individuals have on capability is analyzed; personal factors are equally important here. Whatever the objectives that are decided on, they are chosen by particular people with all their virtues and frailties.

In a brilliant little book *Why Nations Go To War,* John Stoessinger notes that many of the abstract forces often cited as causes of war (nationalism, militarism, alliance systems, economic factors, etc.), had less impact on the cases he studied than did individuals. His analysis indicated that "the personalities of leaders . . . have often been decisive."[25]

Whether a particular individual will be decisive in a given case cannot be prejudged, of course, but it is clear that some individuals will make the final determination of objectives. This being so, the final task with respect to sources is to determine who are the key individuals in any situation and analyze their characteristics.

STEP THREE: ASCERTAINING CAPABILITY

The third step in formulating an effective policy is ascertaining the capabilities of the participant parties. Terms like capability, power, and influence have given

---

[23]Howard H. Lentner, *Foreign Policy Analysis: A Comparative and Conceptual Approach,* Charles E. Merrill, Columbus, Ohio, 1974, p. 199.

[24]Many of these questions are analyzed in depth in Chapter 7.

[25]John G. Stoessinger, *Why Nations Go to War,* Second Edition, St. Martins, New York, 1978, p. 226. Obviously the jury is still out on the issue of the causes of war. For an excellent summary of many of the current theories see Rosen and Jones, Second Edition, Chapter 10.

rise to interminable and sometimes meaningless quibbling over definitions. Unfortunately, because policymakers so often deal in the currency of power and influence one cannot simply dismiss the issue as irrelevant. Rather than discussing the issue in abstract terms, however, our approach will be to view it from the policymaker's perspective. To him no single definition is sufficient because the concept is composed of several parts.

What then do policymakers mean when they speak of capability? *First, they are concerned with the identification and measurement of key elements that can provide the building blocks for the exercise of international influence.* Examples would be military capacity, economic strength, geographic factors, population characteristics, natural resources, and so forth. In this sense power is the sum of a set of components, a specific quantity of factors whose aggregate is directly related to the achievement of a state's objectives.

Usually this facet of the approach is closely connected with concern about the importance of force and war-making capacity.[26] It emphasizes the degree to which various components contribute to military effectiveness and those who stress this aspect tend to see international relations primarily in terms of conflict and coercion.[27]

It is essential that one go through this step and thoroughly analyze these raw materials of capability since they often do affect the success or failure of a state's policies. In fact policymakers usually do so and are influenced by their conclusions. For this reason, all of Chapter 3 is devoted to an examination of such components. However, any analysis that stops here is both oversimplified and inaccurate because capability is much more (or less) than such a sum of certain ingredients (a fact that has led some observers to go too far the other way and almost dismiss the components as irrelevant).

A second part of the policymaker's conception of capability is its relational quality. Capability involves a relationship between parties; policy actions and interactions occur as states affect other states. It makes no sense to speak of capability only in absolute terms because a useful analysis must include the relative and comparative aspects.

Operationally, policymakers are exercising capability when they are able to influence the behavior of another state at least partially in the way that they want to and in a direction that the target otherwise would not have gone. This may involve a modification of the target's activity by getting it to do something or stop doing something, or within each of these major categories to increase or decrease the scope and intensity of its actions. Capability also is exercised if the target is persuaded to continue an existing policy that it otherwise would have changed or to refrain from undertaking new actions it otherwise would have

---

[26]Although much of the literature today is placing less stress on this view occasionally a newer work gives it a reemphasis. See Rosen and Jones, Second Edition, Chapter 7.

[27]See Morgenthau, *Politics Among Nations,* Fifth Edition.

initiated. Thus, influence may continue after a target modifies behavior in the sense of reinforcing the new policy.

Because capability is not meaningful unless discussed in relation to other parties, abstract comments like China has such and such military capability or Egypt possesses X degree of economic strength have little utility in and of themselves. The question to ask is "compared to whom"? For example, although China's military strength might be immense compared to Nepal it certainly would not be relative to that of the Soviet Union.

Another point to remember is that *to some extent influence is mutual*. In other words, seldom is it exercised in one direction only; nearly always the target state will have some influence on the supposed influencer. Because situations often involve many parties the pattern of influence relationships may be very complicated. Each state is a target of signals and actions from many sources as well as being a sender. One should not make the mistake of assuming that influence will be equal in all directions, however. Quite the contrary; generally relationships are asymmetrical and certain states considerably more powerful than others. One must also remember that usually it is necessary to speak in terms of degrees of influence and not total dominance, although occasionally this may not be the case.

Another point to keep in mind is what is known as *feedback*. After the policymaker undertakes some action and responses occur, the situation is different from the original. Information concerning the differences soon begins to "feedback" to the initiator. As a result of the receipt of this data on situation changes, the initiator may have to modify policy to meet the new requirements.

The third facet of the policymaker's capability concept is that it is meaningful only within a specific policy context. Capability is really a means to an end, and can be most usefully operationalized in terms of a cost-benefit analysis concerning a state's achievement of its objectives. Capability is exercised via influencing other states in such a way as to increase the degree to which one achieves one's objectives without a corresponding increase in cost, maintains one's capacity to achieve one's objectives while decreasing the cost of so doing, or increases the degree of achievement and decreases the cost thereof.

As indicated earlier, one must define the problem at hand by identifying, and examining the number and importance of, the parties involved, and then proceed to an analysis of their objectives and the formulation of one's own. Capability becomes relevant only in relation to these parties and objectives.

It is this facet more than any other that shows that the raw ingredients approach to capability has its limitations. Certain combinations of ingredients cannot be directly applied to some situations. For example, the nuclear arsenal of the United States had very little direct impact on French policy toward Washington in the mid-1960s. A major objective of American policy was to maintain NATO diplomatic unity. When the French decided to pursue their own policies in certain areas the disparity of American and French nuclear striking power was irrelevant. Obviously Washington was not going to use nuclear force against its ally.

Similarly, one sees that American nuclear power has very little value in persuading nonaligned states to modify their behavior or objectives. In fact, its use is inappropriate to many military conflict situations such as guerilla warfare, various revolutionary activities, limited conventional wars, or even defense. It is pertinent primarily with respect to the objective of deterrence, and basically to situations involving possible Soviet attacks.[28]

When attempting to determine the significance of comparative capabilities in a given situation *the policymaker must also take into account the intentions of each party and their willingness to use whatever power they may have.* Sometimes there is a tendency to become too concerned with attempts to measure potential capability and one does not pay sufficient attention to the party's intentions. For example, whereas the United States possesses military strength far superior to that of Canada, it has no intention of using it against its northern neighbor. The mere existence of exercisable power, while creating the possibility of conflict and thus being a necessary part of any situation calculation, does not automatically lead to the conclusion that a conflict situation exists (if international relations were nothing but an unceasing power struggle, however, such might be the conclusion).

Even states with objectives directly contradictory to one's own may have no intention of using capability at a given time. The fact that a policymaker's adversary possesses a given weapons system is obviously more dangerous to one's security than if that system was possessed by his or her ally, but whether this adversary intends to use it or not is a critical factor.

A variation of this point concerns the willingness of a party to exercise power. The United States has nuclear strength available for the defense of Western Europe. It says it intends to use it if necessary. As the French have repeatedly questioned, however, is it really willing to do so? In other words, would Washington risk its own devastation to save Europe? Is its stated policy *credible*? The policymaker must always go beyond intentions and try to discover various parties' ultimate willingness to exercise capability.

A final facet of capability analysis is an examination of each party to determine its overall and specific susceptibility to influence. Susceptibility is in part a function of the factors we have discussed above: relational and comparative aspects in a given situation, and the intention and/or willingness of parties to use power. But it also is affected by the characteristics of the receiver, namely, its vulnerability and responsiveness to the type, quantity, and intensity of the capability states are attempting to use.[29] For example, a state that has immense oil reserves is not susceptible to use of an oil embargo. Similarly, a landlocked state is not vulnerable to an amphibious assault.

---

[28]See Chapter 4, pp. 157–162.
[29]This is discussed in more detail in Chapters 4 and 5.

Responsiveness also enters into the picture, that is, the degree to which a state allows itself to be influenced.[30] There are situations in which many factors seem to indicate that capability should be effectively exercised but in fact it is not. In effect, the target simply says "no!" When the United States dropped an immense tonnage of bombs on North Vietnam in the late 1960s many felt there was no way that Hanoi could refuse to come to the bargaining table on Washington's terms, but it did so refuse. It was terribly unresponsive, "unwilling" to be influenced. In such a situation the supposedly more powerful countries, if they are unwilling to militarily attack and conquer their adversaries, may actually be relatively powerless.

STEP FOUR: DETERMINING ORIENTATION

The fourth step is the determination of one's policy orientation toward the situation in question, that is, the degree and nature of involvement. Orientation will vary with time and circumstance, and because each state deals with many problems at once it may have several different orientations simultaneously. With respect to a given situation, however, usually only one orientation is possible (although there may be some that overlap, a factor that shall be considered in due course).

There are ten orientation options from which to choose, each with its own characteristics.[31] These can be usefully divided into three categories: (1) nonconcern options, those in which the policymaker is not really concerned with the outcome of the specific situation, (2) concerned nonissue options, those in which the party is concerned with the outcome but not because of his views on the substantive issues involved, and (3) issue options, those in which one is concerned with the outcome primarily in terms of substantive situational issues.

Nonconcern Options

The first of the nonconcern orientation options is simply *avoidance*; just do not become involved. As part of its general European policy from 1815 to 1917, for example, the United States studiously avoided involvement in European con-

[30]See Karl W. Deutsch et al., *Political Community and the North Atlantic Area,* Princeton University Press, Princeton, 1957.

[31]The purpose of this section is to get one to carefully think about the various choices a policymaker might have with respect to the degree and nature of his state's involvement in any situation. Thus it is a logical exercise designed to demonstrate the advantages and disadvantages of various possible choices rather than an attempt to describe what a policymaker necessarily does in a given case. On the other hand, one should not assume that this type of thinking does not occur. Although the procedures may not be identical and real life situations are more complex, policymakers inevitably concern themselves with their options for involvement and must engage in thinking similar to that described below.

flicts.[32] For centuries prior to the mid-1800s Japan refused to become involved in conflicts beyond her immediate geographical area, a course of action similar to that followed by China.

A rational choice of avoidance rests on the premise that noninvolvement will not be harmful to one's security (or at least less harmful than the projected consequences of involvement). This might be because the issues are perceived to be irrelevant or insignificant. For example, the resolution or nonresolution of the Arab-Israeli dispute is essentially irrelevant to Peruvian policymakers, so they have no reason to become involved. A second reason might be that one's noninvolvement would require or allow the involved parties to act in a way that inevitably benefits him. If the United States adopted an offshore deployment in Asia, one could argue that China's neighbors (including Russia) would be forced to take on whatever burden of containment was necessary.[33]

Of course, avoidance is not always wise. There are many situations in which issues are pertinent and/or only some type of option involving participation will advance one's interest, as the discussion below shows. The policymaker must evaluate each situation separately to see if avoidance would be useful or not. In addition to considering the *wisdom* of this orientation, one must also deal with the question of whether other parties will permit it. Geographical barriers such as high mountains and wide seas were major factors in allowing the United States, Japan, and China to be uninvolved for long periods of time, but modern technology has significantly reduced their impact. Furthermore, the parties of the modern world have become increasingly interdependent economically. In addition, a wide variety of policy instruments are available, and used, for purposes of penetration and subversion, and these may require a response.[34] Finally, a state may be drawn into a dispute by obligation (perhaps through an alliance), threat, or attack. Even though one may consider the issues irrelevant or insignificant, participation may be compelled by external factors.

A second orientation is *minimal nonalignment*. In this instance one does not avoid involvement but one's participation is low level and he does not take sides on whatever the issues may be. The policymaker determines that it is necessary to be minimally involved either in order to protect his or her party's interests or because some participation is forced on him or her. However, the policymaker also feels that a neutral stance on the issues is beneficial because the specific

---

[32]The term ''isolation'' has been used to describe a general foreign policy approach of noninvolvement. Because we are focusing on a given situation and recognize that a state may avoid one situation but be deeply involved in another the more limited terminology has been adopted. However, many of the same factors enter into considerations of the specific situation and the general approach. Holsti, Ch. 4, is particularly useful in this regard.

[33]See Hartmann, *The New Age of American Foreign Policy*. This is not to imply China is expansionist, but only to state that *if* it is her neighbors would, just to protect their own interests, shoulder the burden of containment.

[34]See Chapters 4 and 5.

situational issues are not pertinent to the achievement of his or her party's objectives, and/or one cannot significantly influence the outcome anyway, and/or an attempt to resolve the problem might require more resources than one is willing to commit, and/or any deviation from neutrality entails considerable risk.

Minimal nonalignment allows considerable independence and flexibility of action as well as minimization of any risk of antagonizing any of the parties by taking a conflicting position (although they might be unhappy because one did not support their view).[35] It allows a concentration of attention, effort, and resources on other issues in accordance with one's priorities. However, it suffers from many of the same potential drawbacks as avoidance including lack of direct influence on the parties and the issues (and thus the possible occurrence of actions detrimental to one's interest) as well as the possible difficulty of remaining unaligned and only lightly involved. Because there is a low level of participation the parties may well feel inclined to make one a target of their actions in order to alter one's involvement level and issue stance.

A third orientation possibility is *participatory nonalignment*. In this case the policymaker decides to be actively involved with the parties in this situation but involved in the pursuit of his state's objectives without respect to the situational issues. The parties will be dealt with not in terms of their positions on the problems at hand but instead on the basis of whether and how they affect the policymaker's nonsituation concerns; it is the policy not its source that is important.

The policymaker may thus consider the employment of a wide range of policy instruments with respect to the situational parties but does so without primary concern for their impact on the issues involved; this just is not his or her problem. The policymaker may attempt to play one party against another in order to optimize his or her influence and obtain maximum benefits from all. Sometimes this may prove successful. However, it can also cause considerable resentment on the part of the targets of such activity (as is indicated in Chapter 6 in the discussion of Egyptian President Nasser's relations with Washington 1955–1956).[36] This aspect of participatory nonalignment offers considerable potential for influencing the parties but involves correspondingly large risks.

Both minimal and participatory nonalignment are likely to become more feasible options in the 1980s. As fluidity increases and alliances become less cohesive, as economic and environmental interdependence increases, and as more power centers develop in the continued shift away from bipolarity, orientation options that maximize flexibility and conflict avoidance will likely have more appeal.

---

[35]The idea of freedom of choice, particularly for the newly independent countries of Asia and Africa, has been a matter of great importance. See Cecil V. Crabb, Jr., *The Elephants and the Grass: A Study of Nonalignment*, Praeger, New York, 1965.

[36]See Chapter 6, pp. 196–198.

Concerned Nonissue Options

In addition to nonconcern options the policymaker also has certain options from which to choose that demonstrate a concern for the situation's outcome, but it is a concern unrelated to the merits of the specific situational issues. The first of these is the *balancer*.[37] When exercising this option one agrees to commit his strength to the "weaker" side(s) in order to bring about a "balance," a relatively equal capability distribution. The catalyst for action is the previous inequality in capabilities and one's assessment of the consequences likely to flow therefrom.

It should be noted that this option is not chosen because of the nature of the issues, objectives, or parties involved, but because of an evaluation of the consequences presumed to result from perceived capability differentials. This being so, the balancer is not necessarily concerned with the resolution of issues per se, but with preserving situational stability and either deterring the outbreak of conflict or preventing the stronger side from winning. Such an option also precludes close association with one party or antagonism to another, because the needed flexibility could not be preserved in such a case.

The balancer option can be critically important because the balancer may hold the key to whether a situation is stabilized or deteriorating. To successfully employ it, one must have sufficient capability to be able to influence the outcome, be sufficiently flexible on issues and parties to be able to make the requisite adjustments, and be willing to actually commit enough resources to do the job. This is a combination that very few parties actually possess in today's world.[38]

The second concerned nonissue option is *neutral problem solver*. Here one is concerned with resolving the issues at hand, going beyond mere stabilization, restoration, or deterrence as in the balancer choice, actively seeking to settle whatever differences exist. One may or may not be particularly concerned about the precise substance of the resolution. Perhaps this option will be chosen only if it seems that a certain type of settlement is possible or maybe just solving the problem is enough.

There are two major facets of the problem solver: *mediator* and *compeller*.

---

[37]The literature on this topic is voluminous although it generally occurs within a different frame of reference, that is, what is termed the "balance of power." The student might begin with Inis L. Claude, Jr., *Power and International Relations*, Random House, New York, 1962, and Edward Vose Gulick, *Europe's Classical Balance of Power*, Cornell Press, Ithaca, 1955.

[38]It has often been said that Great Britain employed this option for lengthy periods prior to the twentieth century. Although it is clearly true that Britain often (but not always) acted to support the weaker side in Europe and changed positions rapidly, one can argue with some force that specific objectives such as preventing control of the Low Countries by a dominant Continental Power, etc. were the underlying reasons for her action, not any abstract concern with capability distribution or balance. In addition to Gulick, cited previously, it is suggested that one see A. J. Grant and H. Temperly, *Europe in the Nineteenth and Twentieth Centuries, 1789–1939*, Longmans, London, 1940, and Robert W. Seton-Watson, *Britain in Europe, 1789–1914*, Macmillan, New York, 1937.

Usually one thinks of the former. American Secretary of State Kissinger's shuttle diplomacy of 1974 and 1975 led to significant Israeli-Egyptian and Syrian-Israeli cease-fire and disengagement of forces agreements; President Theodore Roosevelt successfully mediated the end of the Russo-Japanese War of 1904; and the Soviet Union helped end Indo-Pakistani hostilities in the mid-1960s.[39] In each case the problem solver provided its good offices and clearly communicated between the parties, constituted a third party from whom suggestions could be taken without loss of prestige, made substantive suggestions as to reasonable compromises, attempted to clarify issues and positions, tried to get each party to see things from the other person's perspective, and attempted to demonstrate the advantages that would accrue from a settlement.

There are some dangers in this conciliatory facet of problem solver, however. A policymaker choosing this option risks meddling in affairs that the parties to the situation may prefer to keep private. Often states can exercise capability more effectively without the interference of a third party, and feel that an outsider will be a hindrance to settlement. Furthermore, an outsider sometimes allows the parties to avoid coming to grips with the real issues in the hope that an "easier out" may be found. A key point may be whether one is asked to participate or offers services on its own initiative. In the latter case the policymaker must be especially careful to anticipate the likely reaction of the parties. Even if the policymaker's assistance is requested, he or she must consider the probabilities of success and the possible consequences of failure.

An obvious danger is that of antagonizing one of the parties by what it perceives to be an inept handling of the job. Following the 1967 Arab-Israeli War, the United Nations Security Council appointed Gunnar Jarring as Special Representative to try to bring about a permanent peace based on Resolution 242 of November 22, 1967. His handling of his assignment so infuriated the Israelis, however, that by mid-1971 he had lost all credibility as a mediator. Israel felt that Dr. Jarring consistently violated any reasonable concept of neutrality. The crowning blow was the so-called "Jarring initiative" of February 8, 1971, an identical letter sent to both Israel and Egypt in which Jarring requested, as an "inevitable prerequisite" of peace, that Israel "give a commitment to withdraw its forces from occupied UAR territory to the former international boundary between Egypt and the British Mandate of Palestine" (in exchange for certain Egyptian concessions).[40] Of course, the determination of secure and recognized boundaries was a critical issue; to request this commitment in advance seemed clearly out of line for a neutral mediator.

Sometimes complete neutrality is not essential, however, as Secretary Kissinger's Middle East agreements showed. What is crucial, though, is the ability to act in a conciliatory credible fashion that demonstrates a grasp of the key issues,

---

[39]For further discussion of the Middle East disengagement agreements see pp. 45, 70, 147.
[40]For text see *New Middle East,* No. 31, April 1971, p. 44.

the role of prestige, the limits of realistic compromises, and the costs and benefits to all parties of various alternatives.

The second facet of problem solver is that of a compeller. Once again the policymaker is concerned with the outcome of the situation but not because of the substantive issues involved; the policymaker just wants things settled. Here, however, mediation has been judged to be ineffective and more coercive measures are required.

Why might a policymaker seek to compel an agreement if he or she is not greatly concerned with the substance? There are three basic reasons. First, one may perceive that other problems are more fundamental and this one is diverting attention, effort, and resources into low priority channels. Thus it is necessary to get things concluded one way or another and move on to more important matters.

Second, and more frequently, there is often a fear that unless a problem is solved now it will become more serious. More parties may be drawn into it meaning more points of view will need to be reconciled, positions may harden as public statements are made and interests become vested in certain policies (e.g., the United States in Vietnam under Lyndon Johnson), the level and intensity of disagreement may increase, prestige may become involved and make compromise more difficult, and eventually events may just seem to snowball out of control.[41] Thus the policymaker may decide that the problem should be solved now or else it may become insoluble.

Third, occasionally a party may previously have employed other orientations unsuccessfully, each failure incrementally damaging his or her prestige; in such situations policymakers sometimes conclude that they have little choice but to try and compel a settlement. In the 1975−1976 Lebanese civil war Syria first sought to mediate between the belligerents, but she was unsuccessful. Then Damascus tried to bring the hostilities to a "favorable" conclusion via an orientation of limited support, introducing certain Syrian-controlled Palestinian guerilla units to aid the anti-Christian coalition; this too was unproductive. Finally, his prestige and credibility deteriorating, President Hafez Assad acted as a compeller, sending in regular troops and armor. Subsequently a cease-fire was obtained, policed by forces of the Arab League (nearly all of whom were Syrian).

Another major orientation option is *exacerbater*, involvement in the situation in such a way as to prevent a settlement. Although one sometimes makes the hopeful assumption that parties always want problems solved, history shows that many times this simply is not so. Often policymakers seek to make trouble, to prevent any solution from being found, and to exacerbate existing difficulties. Chaos, confusion, and/or the persistence of difficult problems provide fertile ground for various kinds of penetrating or subversive activities, for example. Social disunity of various kinds may be desirable if one wishes to undertake guerilla warfare. The continuation or aggravation of a territorial dispute may be

---

[41]See Chapter 6, pp. 199−204, for an example of snowballing.

desirable because it allows an outsider to have his or her assistance sought; perhaps if the problem were solved the outsider would no longer be needed.

A recurrent hypothesis in this regard has been that the Soviet Union wishes to "keep the pot boiling" in the Middle East, to keep things stirred up so that some of the parties will turn to Moscow for assistance.[42] It is primarily the need for anti-Israeli weaponry and economic assistance, the argument goes, that prompts many Arabs to seek Russian aid. To what extent would the Soviets be needed if the Arabs and Israel were living together peacefully?

The obvious drawback to this option is that the parties to any situation want their objectives realized and will resent actions designed to prevent such achievement. If they perceive that one is trying to prolong or aggravate difficulties to serve his own purposes they may react strongly. In mid-June 1972 Egypt's President Sadat expelled several thousand Russian military advisers, condemning what he said was Moscow's no-war no-peace policy.

Issue Options

To this point our analysis has dealt with orientation options that varied in the degree of involvement and concern with the disposition of issues at hand, but none of them were primarily related to the substance of the problem and the various situational alignments. Now it is necessary to turn to substantive orientations. Although there are infinite variations and gradations of friendship and hostility and support or opposition, and any categorization is both somewhat arbitrary and a matter of degree, the policymaker still can usefully approach this matter in terms of four fundamental categories: (1) limited support or cooperation, (2) complete support or cooperation, (3) indirect opposition, and (4) confrontation.

It is necessary to point out that there can be some overlap in these categories. Limited support of party A may involve indirect opposition to party B and vice versa, and complete support of X may bring about confrontation with W and vice versa. However, it is also possible that indirect opposition can occur without supporting anyone, that complete support may not yield confrontation, and that confrontation can occur bilaterally. Although one may sometimes be looking at two sides of a coin, sometimes one is not.

If one is involved in a multilateral situation and calculates that certain parties and/or positions should be supported, he or she may choose to keep this support relatively *limited* and any relationship with like-minded parties loose and *informal*. There might be several reasons for this. First, this approach allows for considerable flexibility. Because there is no deep commitment it is possible to vary tactics and the degrees and types of support. If the situation should warrant one could always increase the support level. When in late 1975 the outcome of

---

[42]See the well-known authority Walter Laqueur, *The Struggle for the Mediterranean: The Soviet Union and the Middle East, 1958-68,* Macmillan, New York, 1969.

the war in Angola was still in doubt, the Soviets decisively escalated their military aid to the forces of the Popular Movement for the Liberation of Angola (MPLA) and Cuban combatants were introduced; in consequence, the tide of battle was turned. If the situation calls for a decrease in support this, too, is easily accomplished if the level is already low.

A second potential advantage is that the flexibility inherent in this option creates some degree of uncertainty, and this may be beneficial. For example, if a state is not sure whether or not another party will defend country X, it may hesitate to take the risk of attacking. If a potential adversary always knows what one will do it can plan its moves accordingly; sometimes it may help to keep the adversary guessing.

Another advantage is that this option is generally assumed to be less risky than full support (but may not be if it does not work). Because the level of support is low there is a relatively small allocation of resources; thus it is less costly. Also, one's prestige is not put on the line to the degree that it is when he is deeply committed. Finally, since many times this choice assumes that one's security is not directly involved (or else there would be a greater commitment), there tends to be less danger of being the primary target of hostile activity (although obviously there would be exceptions to this because one cannot always choose whether or not one is a target).

Sometimes a policymaker will choose this option simply because it is abundantly clear that certain common objectives exist and no stronger stand is necessary. For example, the United States does not need to make an explicit formal commitment to Israel in every phase of the Arab-Israeli conflict because it is obvious that Washington will not allow Tel Aviv's destruction.

Finally, a state may decide to give informal limited support because it feels compelled to do so. Perhaps it really would prefer to avoid this issue but because a strong ally, regional leader, or client is deeply involved the policymakers feel that they have no choice. Maybe this is an issue on which previous statements have been made that indicate a certain viewpoint, or a treaty relationship makes at least nominal support necessary.

There are also several possible disadvantages. First, the very flexibility involved can turn out to be detrimental. Since states seek to anticipate the actions of others, certainty is often a desired quality. The parties one is supporting want to be able to "count on" his actions and may well be resentful of what they feel is perfidy. Also, the lack of certainty may increase the likelihood of adversarial activity rather than decrease it. For example, if the Germans had been sure that the British would enter World War I (which they were not) they might have acted differently. American policymakers in much of the post World War II era assumed that uncertainty was an invitation to aggression and thus sought to construct a ring of alliances to deter potential Communist attack.

One's friends may also resent the fact that the support is so limited. In both the Korean and Vietnam conflicts the United States felt that its allies were not carrying their fair share of the load. Nominal or limited support may be considered to be phony, or an unwillingness to expend one's own resources when someone else will do it. This kind of feeling can easily spiral into mutual charges of bad faith and eventually have severe intracoalition repercussions.

Finally, although the costs and risks seem to be less, the opportunities for gain are also. In 1975 the United States was providing limited support (foreign aid) for the alliance of the National Front for the Liberation of Angola (FNLA) and the National Union for the Total Independence of Angola (UNITA) in their struggle against the Soviet-backed Popular Movement for the Liberation of Angola (MPLA). By late in the year, as Soviet assistance to the MPLA increased and Cuban combatants were introduced, it became increasingly apparent that the FNLA/UNITA alliance was losing. Washington was not willing to match the Soviet escalation, however, opting to keep its support very limited; shortly thereafter, when the MPLA emerged victorious, American influence in Angola virtually disappeared. If policymakers employ the orientation of limited support they need to recognize the fact that their self-imposed limitations may correspondingly limit their achievements.

The second half of this orientation is *limited bilateral cooperation on substantive situational issues.* There are a number of reasons one might opt to cooperate in no more than a limited fashion. First, it may be that in a given situation greater cooperation is simply not possible; in the 1972 American-Russian strategic arms limitation talks policymakers realized that broad agreements were out of the realm of possibility and limited their actions accordingly. Frequently there is a related consideration, a belief that it is useful to begin small; if cooperation cannot be achieved on the little things it cannot be achieved at all, and if it can, efforts can be stepped up. Another reason may be the flexibility such a low level of cooperation provides; not having invested great resources or prestige in a given situation one can alter (or even reverse) course without incurring significant loss. Finally, and often most importantly, policymakers may choose to keep cooperation limited because of third party concerns. Policymakers recognize full well that no situation is really just bilateral; all policies are conducted within a complex web of relationships, are themselves the product of a multitude of influences, and affect a number of different parties in varying ways.[43] Therefore, often one cannot "go overboard" in one situation because such action would cause major problems with third parties (and/or fourth, fifth, etc.). In an effort to preclude such developments, and since policymaking is an uncertain art at best, policymakers often feel it is wise to proceed in a very cautious, limited fashion.

In some situations of mutual interest, the limited support or cooperation option is insufficient to achieve one's objectives. If the issues in question are perceived to be of considerable importance, such as those affecting one's ability

---

[43]See Chapter 6, especially pp. 213–218.

to achieve fundamental objectives, the policymaker might feel it necessary to undertake a major expenditure of resources and be desirous of working closely with another party or parties toward the goal of a favorable substantive outcome. If so, the policymaker would likely choose the orientation of *complete support or cooperation* (support in a multilateral situation, cooperation in one that's deemed essentially bilateral).

Complete support inevitably produces certain results. Situational certainty is increased, a fact that can be either good or bad. Predictability will be appreciated by one's friends, as will the degree of support. No suspicions of failing to do one's share or sham participation will be in evidence. Similarly, adversaries will be aware of what is going on and be required to calculate accordingly. Presumably gains will not be made because of confusion or misperception about what one's country will do. In fact, the mere existence of such support may directly affect the situation's outcome. Finally, because of this deep involvement, the policymaker is in a position to consider bringing to bear all the state's options for increasing external capability and to make maximum use of the vast array of foreign policy tools available.

Complete support yields opportunities for considerable gain but also has certain potential drawbacks. For one thing, the very certainty eliminates much of one's flexibility and its accompanying advantages (noted above). Second, it is more costly in terms of resource expenditure. Because all states are limited in resources and because resources allocated to one situation are not available for others, the policymaker must husband his or her party's resources and distribute them on the basis of carefully determined priorities. The policymaker must be certain that this situation warrants a major commitment.

Another difficulty is that such a level of support automatically carries with it a substantial investment of prestige, making compromise more difficult. Particular groups and/or individuals have a vested interest in having the policy work. This being so there is a danger of being locked in, unable to adjust to changing circumstances. Furthermore, there may be a tendency to assume that just a little stronger and/or longer involvement will "solve" the problem. Because the commitment is so serious the policymaker may feel that failure (or anything that could be interpreted as failure) is simply not acceptable, and make his or her decisions accordingly.[44] Yet because no one can guarantee success, a high level of support may simply lead to a demonstration of ineptness rather than capacity. It is also possible that the certainty engendered will not yield the desired results; perhaps one's adversaries had already anticipated this position and had decided that confrontation was their best route. Finally, it is possible the adversary will

---

[44]Many analysts characterize the development of United States policy in the Vietnam War in this fashion. So much is written that one hardly knows what to recommend. Perhaps the most useful works to begin with are David Halberstam, *The Best and the Brightest,* Random House, New York, 1969, and New York Times, *The Pentagon Papers,* Bantam, New York, 1971.

interpret strong support of one party to mean that the policymaker will not support someone else. In 1950 when American Secretary of State Dean Acheson defined the U.S. defense perimeter in a way that did not include South Korea, some Communist leaders interpreted this to mean that support for South Korea was excluded and that country would not be defended by American forces.[45]

If a situation is perceived to be essentially bilateral the policymaker may opt to employ the second half of this orientation, *complete cooperation*.[46] There are some circumstances in which it is abundantly clear that the issues between two parties are important and the only way they can be solved is via full and complete cooperation. Cooperation of this sort occurs most frequently when parties have similar (or at least compatible) governmental structures, ideologies, and ethical systems, have common perceptions of the definition, causes, and possible solutions to the problems at hand, and neither party is perceived as a threat to the other's fundamental interests. The United States and Great Britain generally fit these criteria and employ this orientation in their mutual relations a great deal. It is evident though, that there are few situations in which all these conditions are present; complete cooperation is rare. Because of the decentralized, anarchical, complex nature of the international political world, policymakers seldom feel it prudent to cooperate too extensively with anyone, whether said party is purportedly friendly, neutral, or hostile; ultimately policymakers must base all decisions on the projected effect of any action on survival, and in that regard a party's only sure ally is itself.

A final comment with respect to the orientation of complete support or cooperation: the greater the level of support or cooperation one undertakes, the greater the adverse consequences of failure. When a major effort is made, if it is unsuccessful prestige may decline noticeably, influence significantly decrease, and so on. Given this rather obvious but enormously important fact, the wise policymaker will employ this orientation judiciously, doing so only when firmly convinced that the objective is worth the risk.

A third issue orientation is *indirect opposition* (which may involve limited support for certain parties in some cases).[47] The policymaker's analysis of the situation may indicate that if certain parties achieve their objectives his or her interests will be harmed, but he or she concludes that an orientation of confrontation would be unwise. There are several reasons why indirect opposition may be

---

[45]However, one should not jump to the conclusion that this exclusion was the sole basis of what has been called the "invitation" to attack. See John W. Spanier, *The Truman-MacArthur Controversy and the Korean War*, Norton, New York, 1965, Chapter 2. For the view that Acheson's omission was critical, see Robert T. Oliver, *Why War Came to Korea*, Fordham University Press, New York, 1950.

[46]To reiterate what was said earlier, we are speaking in terms of *gradations*, using the term "complete" only to make the point. Cooperation can never be absolutely "complete" in the sense that there would not be the slightest differences or disagreements.

[47]Much of the discussion in Chapters 4 and 5 is relevant here. See especially pp. 154–157, 165–168.

preferred. First, it may be that one wishes to have the opposition secret (or at least disguised). Obviously it was in Hitler's interest to camouflage his subversion of Czechoslovakia and Austria, for example.[48] American efforts to prevent Salvador Allende from gaining power in Chile and subsequent efforts to "destabilize" his regime, and the Somalian attack on Ethiopia in mid−1977 under the guise of support for the ethnic Somalians of the Western Somali Liberation Front, are additional cases in point.

A second advantage of this orientation is that generally the risks are lower than in a confrontation. Because the opposition is indirect one is less likely to be the target of direct retaliation. Similarly, it is usually easier to escape responsibility for the results if things do not go as planned. Because of this and because usually less prestige is involved, the consequences of failure tend to be less (however, this is not always the case as shown by the American experience following the Bay of Pigs episode in 1961).[49]

Another advantage of indirect opposition is that the policymaker can change the pace and intensity of effort if he desires more easily than if he were already at a confrontation level; it is easier to go up than down. (Even confrontations may involve degrees of effort, however, and thus illustrate this principle. For example, in the Cuban Missile Crisis, discussed in depth in Chapter 6, President Kennedy carefully managed to keep the level of dispute as low as possible at each step, knowing he could always escalate if necessary.)

Finally, it may be that the techniques most appropriate to one's objectives are those of indirect opposition. There are many situations today in which the traditional instruments of confrontation are ineffective or even counterproductive. Thus the policymaker may choose indirect opposition not out of a desire to avoid confrontation but simply because it is the most effective method of achieving his or her objectives.

The final orientation option is *confrontation*. There are some situations that the policymaker perceives to involve certain parties with considerable capability seeking objectives clearly contrary to his or her own, and he or she has no means to resolve the problem except to confront adversaries and "draw the line." (For many reasons, including the immense dangers of modern warfare and presumably a preference for the peaceful settlement of disputes, scholars sometimes fail to give sufficient emphasis to this option despite the obvious fact that it is often chosen.)

Confrontation is similar in some ways to complete support: it involves a judgment that the issues are important, it requires a willingness to take high risks,

[48]Fascinatingly described in William L. Shirer, *The Rise and Fall of the Third Reich*, Fawcett, New York, 1962, Chs. 9−13.

[49]On April 17, 1961 a small group of anti-Castro Cubans attempted to invade Cuba. Their force was liquidated within days. The group had been trained, directed, armed, and financed by the United States Central Intelligence Agency, and this fact was public knowledge. This being so, the result was a humiliating defeat for the new Kennedy Administration.

it requires the recognition that considerable resources may have to be expended, it will inevitably place one's prestige on the line, it obviously will result in antagonism from the adversary, and (if one is rational) it will only be employed in a situation in which success or failure matters immensely.

But confrontation differs importantly from complete support in two respects. First, it is an orientation the policymaker adopts as a result of his or her calculation of the probable impact on his or her state's fundamental objectives of certain anticipated actions by other party(ies), regardless of whether the policymaker's allies agree or not. The policymaker has determined that it is imperative that the source of the perceived threat to his or her state's objectives be "confronted" come what may, and whether his or her friends perceive the situation similarly and act in concert accordingly is of secondary importance. Confrontation is an orientation independent of other parties except the one(s) that is(are) the source of the threat, it is based on a judgment that one's security is significantly endangered, and it will be carried out with or without external assistance. The United States' decision to confront Russia in the 1962 Cuban Missile Crisis, for example, was not a matter of supporting someone else but was based on calculations about the impact of Soviet actions on American security.

A second difference, sometimes of great importance, is that since confrontation is unilateral in conception and implementation it is directly, specifically, and only concerned with one's own security, whereas complete support focuses initially, and perhaps primarily, on the security of the supported party, affecting the security of the policymaker's state only derivatively. To illustrate, if the United States employed the orientation of complete support with respect to helping Israel deter a military attack by an Arab state, the original focus would be on the survival of Israel; only derivatively would there be concern for American security. By way of contrast, if Washington again chose to directly confront the Soviet Union over what were judged to be unacceptable Soviet activities in Cuba it would be because of direct concern with the impact of those activities on American security.

Obviously there are circumstances in which complete support of one's ally is undertaken and one would have opted for confrontation had not the ally itself chosen to confront the adversary; when such a scenario exists the orientation calculations are reinforcing, the independent determination of the policymaker's own requirements blending with the desire to support his or her allies or friends. Nevertheless, knowing which orientation is the "real" source of a policy action is important; the intensity of activity, one's "staying power," and the willingness to expend resources are more likely to be at a maximum if policymakers have acted from a confrontation orientation. The reason for this, quite simply, is that usually a confrontation orientation is not chosen unless policymakers perceive that there is a major threat to fundamental objectives and they believe that ultimately there may be no one to count on but themselves. If such conditions obtain and the policymakers go ahead anyway, it is likely that they will do everything in their power to succeed; therefore, if they are opposed the probability of conflict is high.

STEP FIVE: EXTERNAL MEANS OF INCREASING CAPABILITY

To this point our analysis has focused on the four basic steps of policy formulation, steps that all policymakers should take to whatever extent they can. Many times, however, because of the pervasive importance of capability considerations, a fifth step is required, an analysis of various external means of increasing relative strength (internal capability components are discussed in Chapter 3).

Territorial Changes

The first category of such external techniques is territorial change. There are three basic changes a policymaker might seek: (1) territorial acquisition, (2) detaching territory from one's adversary without acquiring it, and (3) creating functional and/or spatial off limits zones.

The *acquisition of territory* affects capability because of its impact on the internal components of power. As a general rule adding land means adding strength (although, as is pointed out in Chapter 3, additional size does not always mean additional capability.)[50] By definition more land means the country is bigger. This simple geographical fact allows more room for the deployment and dispersal of critical facilities, forces and populace, provides room for additional growth, and makes a state more difficult to successfully attack, conquer, and occupy. Economically, too, it may be beneficial. Perhaps additional arable land will be obtained so agricultural output can be increased, or industrial complexes will be captured so manufacturing can increase, or a critical natural resource can be acquired to fuel the economy. Sometimes a particular strategic geographic advantage may be developed if a certain area is acquired. For example, when Israel captured Sharm al-Sheikh in the 1967 June War she gained the capacity to command the entrance to the Gulf of Aqaba.[51] New territory usually means additional population, which also may contribute to strength (although it could also be a drain if it is uncontrollable, there is not enough food, shelter, etc.). As discussed in the analysis of territorial integrity, sometimes territory is considered "ours" and its acquisition may greatly increase domestic political support. And one could give many more examples.

Although there are many possible advantages one could gain from territorial acquisition, the policymaker needs to carefully weigh the anticipated net benefits against the projected costs of acquisition. Except in highly unusual circumstances the days of relatively easy expansion are over. For example, although historically

---

[50]See pp. 87–88.

[51]Possession of Sharm al-Sheik allows one to effectively control the narrow Straits of Tiran at the entrance to the Gulf. For further discussion of the events leading to the 1967 war, see Chapter 6, pp. 199–204.

it was possible for Russia and the United States to expand continentally with little resistance, equivalent opportunities no longer exist (for them or anyone else). A similar feature of bygone days was colonial expansion, the acquisition and sub-jugation of nonadjacent areas populated by different and less technologically advanced peoples.[52]

Today, the policymaker seldom has the option of acquiring territory with little resistance. States consider defense of home territory to be a fundamental objective and will usually fight to protect it if necessary. There are no more open areas, and outright colonialism is no longer in fashion. Less developed countries have, or are able to get, powerful protectors who are unwilling to see anyone else acquire territory without a struggle, and major powers have their own strength (and that of their allies) on which to rely. Because of these facts acquisition of territory must be of singular importance in order for such action to be attempted.

Another point to remember is that it makes a difference from whom territory is sought. Obviously one reason for this is the level of resistance one will encounter; China would notice the difference between Russia and Nepal. It is also important because of the fact that the loser is weakened and in terms of one's basic security it is more significant if some states are weakened than others. For example, it clearly would make a difference to the United States whether the loser were China or Bhutan, even if the land acquired had the identical qualities. When Germany obtained the immensely valuable Skoda munitions works from Czechoslovakia as a result of the 1938 Munich capitulations the West also lost them. If they had been taken from a neutral country the West's absolute strength would not have decreased and the relative increase in German capability would have been considerably less.

A second type of territorial change involves *detaching territory from one's opponent although not acquiring it yourself.* One reason leaders of most Arab governments favor the creation of an independent Arab Palestine is because this would require the detachment of certain territory from Israel and weaken her accordingly. The Soviet Union has encouraged a separatist movement among the six million people of the Chinese province of Sinkiang as a means of weakening Peking's position in their border dispute. In the two World Wars Germany encouraged the Ukrainians to break away from Russia and set up their own state.

A recent successful use of this technique occurred in the India-Pakistan war of 1971 and the creation of Bangladesh.[53] Separated by more than 1000 miles of Indian territory, East and West Pakistan were very different culturally, econom-

---

[52]This fascinating topic has been the subject of innumerable studies. The beginning student might start with John A. Hobson, *Imperialism, A Study,* University of Michigan Press, Ann Arbor, 1965, and E. M. Winslow, *The Pattern of Imperialism,* Columbia University Press, New York, 1948.

[53]For an excellent concise introduction to this topic, see Rounaq Jahan, "India, Pakistan, and Bangladesh," in Gregory Henderson, Richard Ned Lebow, and John G. Stoessinger, eds., *Divided Nations in a Divided World,* David McKay, New York, 1974, pp. 299–336.

ically, and ethnically. The Bengali peoples of the East were understandably bitter over their subordination to the Western Punjabs; ethnic rancor and discrimination were apparent. A symbolic indication of this occurred in late 1970 when, after a devastating cyclone struck the Bengali coast, President Yahya Khan waited almost two weeks to visit the scene of the disaster. Politically, economically, and socially the Westerners ruled.

At the same time the intense antagonism between India and Pakistan resulting from the religious and territorial disputes that developed out of the partition of British India in 1947 continued unabated. The deep animosities that had led to the original fighting festered and it was clear that the 1965 war had settled nothing.[54]

In early 1971, following a domestic political struggle in which President Khan refused to open the National Assembly with its newly elected East Pakistani majority, East Pakistan rebelled and proclaimed that it was the new state of Bangladesh. At first the Indian authorities eyed the situation warily, limiting their assistance to handling millions of refugees fleeing from the conflict (and Pakistani atrocities). By midyear, however, Pakistani troops were chasing Bengalis across the Indian border and the Indian government began to assist guerilla activity. By late fall this assistance was semiopen. On December 1 India demanded that Pakistan withdraw her troops from the East. The response was a surprise (and futile) Pakistani air attack on December 3 and Indian troops invaded the East. The Pakistani army surrendered on December 16. The independence of Bangladesh was thus confirmed.

India had not initiated this problem although her long standing dispute with Pakistan had helped to create a volatile situation. By carefully taking advantage of developing events, however, she was able to intervene effectively with the result that territory was detached and her primary antagonist weakened accordingly.

The final territorial change a policymaker may seek is to make certain zones "off limits" either territorially or functionally. This may occur through mutual agreement, consent, or simply as a result of the policies of contending parties in competition but unwilling to push things to the point of conflict.[55] Usually such territories are considered too important to allow the other side to possess but not worth the price of acquisition. In such a case it is in the interest of all to remove them from the "game."

This has occurred many times. Afghanistan occupied such a position for centuries, separating the British in India from the Russian bear. In 1907 this status was confirmed by the Anglo-Russian agreement on the Middle East.

[54]The territory of Kashmir was divided between the two countries after the original partition. In 1965 warfare broke out over it anew, with neither side emerging victorious. See Russel Brines, *The Indo-Pakistan Conflict,* Pall Mall, London, 1969.

[55]The term "neutralization" is sometimes used to describe declaring a territory off-limits by mutual agreement, although it also has a wide range of other meanings.

Switzerland was permanently neutralized at the Congress of Vienna in 1815 and has had her neutrality respected. In more recent times, Austria was neutralized as a result of the 1955 peace treaty that "officially" ended World War II and brought about the withdrawal of Soviet troops.[56]

Sometimes areas become off limits without any official agreement. Policymakers may realize that all parties would benefit from eliminating these areas from competition but realize that it would not be feasible or necessary to seek a formalized arrangement. The result then may be a tacit consent to the situation. Siam (Thailand) and Abyssinia (Ethiopia) were "declared" off limits in this fashion for lengthy periods, as was Korea.

The number of areas permanently out of bounds is very small, however, for the obvious reason that such a status is dependent on outside parties for its continuance. Because of this fact policymakers do not often try to create such an arrangement. Even when it is sought, the rate of success is poor. Thailand, Ethiopia, and Korea, indicated above, are no longer "safe," nor is Tibet. Belgium was declared "perpetually neutral" in 1839 but, being the main highway from Germany into France, was trampled in World War I. Washington and Moscow sought to remove Laos as a bone of contention in 1962 but the agreements soon became relatively ineffectual.

Sometimes specific areas are declared off limits in a functional sense through some kind of limitation on militarization. There are many examples of demilitarization. According to the terms of the Versailles Treaty ending World War I, that part of Germany between the Rhine River and the border with France (Rhineland) was demilitarized; the 1954 Geneva Agreements ending the Indochina war established a demilitarized zone on either side of the provisional military demarcation line established in the area near the 17th parallel; as part of the Israeli-Syrian General Armistice Agreement that halted the fighting after the 1948–1949 Palestine War, demilitarized zones were established in those areas that were to go to Israel under the United Nations Partition Plan but that were occupied by the Syrians.

In each of these cases the parties recognized that making certain areas free of military activity would enhance their security. This is usually the purpose of such arrangements. This was particularly apparent in the El Auja case. When the Palestine war ended Israeli forces were occupying the little town of El Auja, a small desert village on a strategic road junction near the Egyptian border.[57] Cairo said it was the gateway to the Egyptian Sinai and could not remain in hostile hands; Israel said it was the logical invasion route into the Negev (Israel's southern desert) and a hostile force could launch an attack from there and cut her in

---

[56]See William B. Bader, *Austria Between East and West 1945–1955*, Stanford University Press, Stanford, California, 1966.

[57]This is concisely and perceptively discussed by Earl Berger, *The Covenant and the Sword: Arab-Israeli Relations 1948–1956*, University of Toronto Press, Toronto, 1965, Ch. 3.

half. When U.N. Mediator Ralph Bunche suggested demilitarization, both sides accepted, recognizing each other's security would be protected.

The May 1974 Israeli-Syrian disengagement agreements provide a good example of limited (de)militarization. In addition to the establishment of a U.N.-controlled area of separation, three zones of force restrictions were set up on each side of the no-man's-land. Within the first 10 kilometers each way only 6000 men, light artillery, and 75 tanks were allowed; in the next 10 kilometers no heavy artillery and a maximum of 500 tanks; and in the last 5 kilometers heavy artillery and missiles were prohibited.[58]

As was true with respect to declaring certain territories out of bounds, attempts to demilitarize various areas have not been very successful. Hitler reoccupied the Rhineland in 1936, the Vietnam DMZ was violated with alacrity, the Syrian-Israeli DMZs became foci of violence and antagonism, and Israel reoccupied El Auja prior to its Sinai assault in 1956.

Despite this fact, and fact it is, the policymaker still should consider this as a possible option. Certainly it is true that this approach has been unsuccessful but so have all others at one time or another. And the argument that parties will adhere to such arrangements only as long as it is in their interest to do so is similarly a straw man, because that is the case with every agreement.

It would be useful to conclude this topic by providing a representative list of the objectives a policymaker might be seeking if he or she tried to use external means of increasing his or her state's capability in this fashion:

1. Prevent one's adversary from increasing capability by denying it territory, particularly territory of special strategic significance.
2. Reduce general tension level between the parties by removing (or at least dampening) one source of conflict.
3. Reduce general tension level between the parties by demonstrating that agreements can be reached on at least some issues.
4. By eliminating one issue, be able to allocate more resources to other objectives.
5. Lower tensions and reduce probability and intensity of border incidents, aggravations, or accidents by reducing geographical proximity; especially important in terms of militarization limitations.

Alliance Adjustments

A second major category of maneuvers for increasing relative capability is alliance adjustment. There are three basic types, alliance formation, alliance prevention, and seeking to bring about the fragmentation of an opposition coalition.

The underlying rationale for *alliance formation* is simple. A policymaker

---

[58]*Jerusalem Post*, June 4, 1974, p. 4.

perceives that his state's objectives cannot be achieved, or achieved as efficiently, without outside help. Therefore an attempt is made to add the capabilities of one or more other states to his own in the pursuit of said objectives. The assumption is that collective, cooperative behavior backed by increased strength will maximize the attainment of specific goals at the minimum possible cost.

Sometimes it simply may not be possible to achieve one's goals without outside help. There was just no way that Britain could be victorious in World War II without the assistance of Washington and Moscow, for example. European economic cooperation could not be achieved unilaterally, so the Common Market was created in 1957.

There also may be situations in which one believes that an objective may be obtainable but the costs of unilateral activity would be excessive. In the early 1950s when NATO adopted its Forward Strategy (defending Western Europe against the Soviets at the Iron Curtain), it was evident to American policymakers that West Germany should help with its own defense. This led to Bonn's limited rearmament and inclusion in NATO in 1955.[59] President Roosevelt's objective of saving American lives was one major reason for the Far Eastern territorial concessions he made to the Russians at the 1945 Yalta Conference in exchange for their promise to enter the war against Japan.[60]

Whether a policymaker decides that an alliance should be formed or not is a decision of policy, not principle, and this means that there are many different types of alliances formed for many different purposes. There are relatively loose diplomatic coalitions, economic trading blocs, and bilateral or multilateral military arrangements. Alliances differ in terms of subject matter, parties, geographical scope, the nature of the commitments undertaken, duration, degree of integration, and commonality of interests.

Despite this range of possibilities policymakers are usually pretty clear about the reasons for a particular alliance. Often a perception of threat and the resulting insecurity is the prime driving force. It is clear, for example, that one of the major factors leading to the formation of NATO was the Western fear of a Soviet military assault on Western Europe.[61] Similarly, the December 2, 1954

---

[59]The French were greatly disturbed at the prospect of Germans with weapons, which, given the history of German-French relations in the preceding 100 years, was understandable. Also see Chapter 5, p. 174.

[60]The Russians were to enter the war within three months after Germany had surrendered. In return Moscow was to regain (fundamentally) the position she had held prior to her loss of the 1904 Russo-Japanese War.

[61]Seldom—if ever—is a policy undertaken because of a single factor. In most situations there are interrelated causes and each decision has a differential impact (as is pointed out in detail in Chapter 6). NATO, for example, was consummated only after it became obvious that World War II unity had disintegrated, several specific disputes had arisen, attempts to negotiate agreements had failed, and it seemed to many European and American policymakers that a unified strengthened Western bloc was a necessity. Despite the multitude of causal factors, however, the presumed major purpose of the alliance, to deter a Soviet military attack, was relatively specific.

Mutual Security Pact between the United States and the Republic of China (Taiwan) was the result of their mutually perceived threat to Taiwan from Red China. The consummation of such threat-perception alliances sometimes allows alliance members a freedom to pursue interests they could not have sought without some measure of security. The Western European states would not have followed the policies that led to the rapid economic growth of the 1950s without the protective shield of NATO.

Although it is sometimes assumed that military alliances are always defensive and deterrent in nature this is not necessarily so. The Tripartite Pact concluded by Germany, Italy, and Japan on September 27, 1940 prepared the way for their war against the United States, for example. Obviously, joint planning and execution is advantageous for offensive as well as for defensive actions.

There are times when alliances are concluded for less obvious reasons. Perhaps a particular regime decides that greater domestic support is needed for certain programs. The specter of an invasion is often created in order to rally the people behind their government, and concluding an alliance could be the consummation of this illusion.

Another reason would simply be to receive the tangible benefits of military and economic aid that often come with alliance agreements. This could be used to keep the local populace under control and prevent rebellion. Such aid also might be used for foreign policy objectives other than those anticipated by the supplying state. American weapons flowing to Pakistan were ''supposed'' to be used to restrain Red China, but the Pakistanis used them against India in 1965. It is obvious enough that Pakistan's reasons for receiving American assistance were different from Washington's reasons for giving it.

Finally, a policymaker may seek an alliance for nonalliance effects. Perhaps the situation is such that more important objectives may be sought in the future and it is hoped that an alliance will create a beneficial relationship that will be helpful in their achievement. Or it may be that not only more important objectives are sought but also a wider range of cooperative action, and this is to be just the start. Or lastly, perhaps an alliance may be concluded because of the anticipated impact on third parties (not third party ''targets''). As an example, take the Brussels Alliance of March 17, 1948, signed between Belgium, the Netherlands, Luxembourg, Great Britain, and France. Although complete in itself as a defensive military pact, a major purpose for its conclusion was to show Washington that these European countries would do what they could to prevent or combat a Russian attack; shortly thereafter NATO was formed.

It is generally assumed that alliances either make new commitments and/or add emphasis to existing ones. Another presumed effect of alliances is to add precision or clarity to the situation. While these characteristics are often present, such is not always the case and the point should not be overstressed. For example, in the Dual Alliance of Germany and Austria-Hungary signed in October 1879 each party agreed to support the other if Russia attacked. This was certainly precise and added a commitment to the previous situation. However, the Manila Pact of 1954 (that signified the creation of SEATO) required only that each party would act to meet the common danger in accordance with its constitutional processes.[62] The confusion over what this really meant was demonstrated by the fact that Washington said it was required to defend South Vietnam by the SEATO Treaty and Protocol whereas the other signatories said there was no such obligation (in that situation). A policymaker thus may add new commitments or emphasize old ones, and he or she may add certainty, stability, and precision to the situation, but the degree of change is dependent on the particular case.

When calculating whether to seek an alliance or not one must also recognize the possible disadvantages that might accrue. It must be remembered that states have a wide range of objectives only some of which are common. Others may be complementary, some are divergent, and some hostile. When joining an alliance either common or complementary objectives are sought and the alliance is presumed to help in their achievement. Noncommon objectives may be temporarily submerged or placed lower in priority, but they may reassert themselves later as conditions change. It is possible that a fall out among allies as noncommon objectives come to the fore may be more serious than if the alliance had never existed (witness the Sino-Soviet dispute).

Another problem is that alliances sometimes foster unrealistic hopes of the degree of cooperation that will ensue. The United States was chagrined at its NATO allies relatively unsympathetic view toward Israel in the October 1973 Arab-Israeli war, for example, but since each party views things in terms of its own objectives this was easy to understand. Whereas Washington was concerned with supporting Israel within the framework of a Soviet-American détente, its allies were worried about their oil supplies being shut off by the Arabs (plus being unhappy over America's lack of consultation with them concerning U.S. policy). Because of the differences in perspective, states also contribute different amounts to an alliance based on their assessment of its worth and the willingness of others to contribute, and this too can fuel differences among friends. A major issue today concerns the relative military and financial contribution of various members of NATO.

A final potential disadvantage is the lessening of autonomy which ensues following alliance formation. Sometimes states seek an alliance precisely for the reason of gaining greater influence over another country. The increased contacts, consultations, and commitments may provide opportunities for leverage which had not existed before. Such decreasing autonomy of alliance members was particularly evident in the first 15 years after World War II as alliances became more enduring, broad ranging, and structured than ever before. The policymaker must remember that once one joins an alliance one's options are more limited and

---

[62]For text, see U.S., Department of State, *Southeast Asia Treaty Organization,* Publication 6305, 1956.

one's obligations are increased. The policymaker may be under pressure from other members or even nonmembers to act in certain ways because the interests of alliance solidarity require it. This entanglement could conceivably even draw one into an unwanted conflict.

The second major category of alliance adjustment is *alliance prevention,* the effort to prevent one's adversary from gaining allies. Obviously, just as it is valuable for "us" to increase relative capability by forming alliances, it is similarly valuable for our opponents to do so; clearly it is in our interest to prevent this from occurring. The immediate objective in such a situation is to alter the calculus of costs and benefits made by the leaders of the sought-after state in such a way as to make it more advantageous for them *not* to become the ally of one's opponent than to do so. When states enter alliances they inevitably subordinate certain interests to interests the alliance is designed to serve. Given this fact, the policymaker seeking to prevent an alliance from being formed seeks to persuade his or her targets that their nonalliance interests should take priority, and then the policymaker acts in such a way as to help the target achieve those interests.

Adolf Hitler's policy toward the Soviet Union in 1939, persuading Moscow not to ally with Britain and France, provides us an excellent example. At the time conditions for alliance prevention hardly seemed promising. The Soviets were extremely apprehensive over the Nazis' advances and Hitler had long denounced both the Bolsheviks and the Russian people generally, labeling both subhumans only one step above the Jews. Stalin knew full well that at some point the Germans would attack the Soviet Union and had watched in dismay as the Western Europeans, seemingly paralyzed, had failed to make a concerted effort to stop Hitler. In 1936 Germany had remilitarized the Rhineland and early in 1938 Austria had been "peacefully" annexed; Britain and France had just watched. On September 30, 1938 the infamous Munich agreement had been signed, ceding the Sudetenland and giving the German army the important Skoda munitions works and some valuable mountain fortifications; the Russians, who had not even been invited to the conference, saw German armies move closer. Following the Munich agreement, Britain and France had pledged to guarantee Czechoslovakia's new frontiers, but when the Nazis annexed the rest of the country in 1939 London and Paris again had done nothing.

Stalin by now had concluded that the British and French (the capitalists) were seeking to embroil Germany and Russia in a mutually devastating war, the objective being the destruction of two menaces at once. This was when Hitler moved. Fully cognizant of Stalin's perception the German leader skillfully fanned Stalin's fears. Hitler also had another card to play. A very important but oft-overlooked result of World War I was the fact that Russia had suffered enormous territorial losses; Communist or not, states that lose territory usually want to get it back, and the Soviet Union was no exception. In hurried negotiations with Moscow Hitler agreed that the Soviets certainly ought to have a sphere of interest in Eastern Europe, regain a portion of Poland (lost in World War I), and recover Bessarabia from Rumania (similarly lost). These agreements soon were embodied in a secret protocol attached to the 1939 German-Russian Nonaggression Pact. Even though the situation in the late 1930s had hardly been propitious for Hitler's efforts at alliance prevention Hitler—admittedly aided and abetted by British and French ineptitude—had exploited the Soviets' nonalliance interests shrewdly, successfully preventing a Western-Soviet alliance from being formed. The strength of the opposition (Britain and France) had been rendered relatively smaller than it would have been had their alliance with Russia been consummated, and the Germans had reduced the number of their immediate antagonists by one.

Despite the complexities and problems of alliances and efforts to prevent their consummation, the formation of alliances has been and will continue to be a major means of increasing relative capability. Because parties have a wide range of objectives only some of which are served by a given alliance, however, policymakers may seek to counter this maneuver by *acting to bring about or encourage the fragmentation and possible disintegration of their adversary's alliance*.

Let's briefly examine the problem of NATO fragmentation and then look in more depth at an example with great relevance for today, the Sino-Soviet rift. The North Atlantic Treaty was signed when the world power distribution was bipolar, the Soviets and Americans being so superior in strength that no one else really mattered. There was a shared, intensely perceived threat of a Russian military attack in both Europe and Washington. Other interests were felt to be of less significance.

Over time many conditions changed.[63] Behind the NATO shield, and with Marshall Plan aid, Western Europe prospered. As states regained strength and became less dependent on Washington (even competing now in many areas) they began to assert their own independent conceptions of policy. A second alteration was in the area of threat perception. No longer did a Soviet attack appear imminent as a nuclear stalemate developed between the superpowers. Thus the major reason for NATO's existence seemed to be losing its significance. Third, this stalemate seemed to tie the hands of the superpowers and make it less probable that they would use force. This allowed the smaller alliance partners more flexibility of action. Fourth, as discussed earlier, France began to question the credibility of America's promise to automatically aid Europe against a Soviet attack now that Washington was also vulnerable. Fifth, a growing fragmentation in Eastern Europe encouraged cross-alliance relations with less fear of retaliation. Sixth, the general movement of the United States and Russia after 1962

---

[63]Useful in this regard are Francis A. Beer, *Integration and Disintegration in NATO*, Ohio State University Press, Columbus, 1969; Edwin H. Fedder, *NATO: The Dynamics of Alliance in the Postwar World*, Dodd Mead, New York, 1973; and Wolfram Hanrieder, *The United States and Western Europe*, Winthrop, Cambridge, 1974.

toward some kind of détente encouraged similar actions by the secondary allies. And seventh, intraalliance disagreements themselves, over both substance and coalition decision-making procedures, exacerbated the difficulties. These factors combined to produce a much less cohesive alliance.

Now let's examine the Sino-Soviet dispute. The Soviet Union and People's Republic of China signed a treaty of alliance and friendship on February 14, 1950, officially creating the Sino-Soviet axis. In the West this was presumed to be a mere formalization of the status quo within the Soviet bloc. Over most of the next decade, amid innumerable statements of the permanent fraternal friendship of all Communists, billions worth of economic aid and technical assistance flowed from Moscow to Peking as did considerable military assistance. In return, the Chinese followed the Soviet ideological and political line, and occasionally helped to bridge the differences between Moscow and her European satellites.[64]

Yet a conflict began to develop in the late 1950s and by the early 1960s a full-fledged rift had occurred. What had happened?[65] There seem to have been many contributing factors. First, there were several framework features. Number one, the mere increase in Chinese capability over the decade naturally led her to assert her own views. Second, the vast territorial claims that China makes against Moscow began to throb like an open wound.[66] This was more troublesome because of a third factor, namely, the Chinese view of their own history. Considering themselves to be the "Middle Kingdom" receiving tribute from inferiors around them, they traditionally considered non-Chinese to be barbarians. Russians were felt to be particularly uncivilized. Fourth, there were personal antagonisms. Contrary to the belief of many Westerners the Soviets had not always been particularly helpful to the Chinese Communists. In the 1920s they had forced the Chinese leadership to work with Chiang Kai-shek, for example, and after World War II Stalin had advised Mao (that "radish Communist") against fighting Chiang.[67] This resentment lingered on. Another personal element was Mao's belief (after Stalin's death) that he was the most authentic "revolutionary" left alive and the major strategic thinker within the Communist camp.

All of these framework features provided an explosive setting. As the years

[64]The Soviets assumed that a certain degree of "gratitude" would develop as a result of their aid; very little did, as is usually the case. See Chapter 4, pp. 140–142.

[65]There are a wealth of studies on this subject. Rather than footnote each point I will simply state that, in addition to the standard texts on Soviet and Chinese Foreign Policy, the following works have been especially helpful and I am indebted to all of them: Edward Crankshaw, *The New Cold War: Moscow v. Peking,* Penguin, Baltimore, 1963; William E. Griffith, *Sino-Soviet Relations, 1964–65,* M.I.T. Press, Cambridge, 1967; William E. Griffith, *The Sino-Soviet Rift,* M.I.T. Press, Cambridge, 1964; G. F. Hudson, Richard Lowenthal and Roderick MacFarquhar, *The Sino-Soviet Dispute,* Praeger, New York, 1961; Klaus Mehnert, *Peking and Moscow,* G. P. Putnam, New York, 1963; and Donald S. Zagoria, *The Sino-Soviet Conflict, 1956–1961,* Princeton University Press, Princeton, 1962.

[66]See Chapter 2, p. 47, and footnote 21.

[67]For further discussion of the Chinese Communist Revolution see Chapter 4, pp. 154–156.

went by Chinese leaders began to assert their own policy interests and their desire to have an equal share in decision making within the Communist camp. Perhaps these problems in themselves would have been sufficient to bring about the rift, but this will never be known since several specific policy issues also arose.[68]

In the mid-1950s a major dispute arose over the "correct" interpretation of Marxist-Leninist thought (and over who was the correct interpreter thereof). At the 20th Congress of the Soviet Communist Party in 1956 Nikita Khrushchev stated that there was no "fatal inevitability" of war between the Socialists (Communists) and capitalism because of the strength of the Socialist camp. This seemingly contradicted the orthodox Leninist position that communists and capitalists could not exist side by side for any length of time, and that a series of terrible collisions would inevitably occur. The Chinese stoutly defended Lenin's precepts and felt that Moscow was demonstrably incorrect as well as overly cautious. Furthermore, as we noted earlier, Peking was alarmed by the logical problem Khrushchev had created; if capitalists in some situations had the ability to avoid what previously were considered to be the inexorable laws of history, why couldn't they in others? Who could know what this might lead to?[69]

A second problem area concerned trade and aid. Despite the considerable assistance received Chinese policymakers felt that Moscow's efforts were insufficient. First, most of the economic assistance had to be paid for out of exports, instead of being free. Second, on a per capita basis it was less than other states such as Outer Mongolia received. It also seemed as if neutrals like Egypt were treated better. Finally, and of particular significance, the Soviets refused to help the Chinese develop their own nuclear capability despite a 1957 promise to give Peking a sample bomb and data on its manufacture. Many feel that this was a critical factor in the rising intensity of the dispute.[70]

There were several other specific disagreements: (1) the Chinese bitterly resented Russia's refusal to help in the liberation of Taiwan (Formosa), a fundamental objective of Peking's policy. They also were irritated by Moscow's lukewarm support in the 1955 and 1958 crises over the offshore islands;[71] (2)

---

[68]It is extremely difficult to ascertain cause and effect here, both with regard to the relationship between the framework features and the specific policy issues, and within each grouping. We truly have a case of interrelated events (see Chapter 6 for more examples) and make no attempt to single out or define specific relationships.

[69]See pp. 44–45.

[70]A particularly poignant example is the August 16, 1963 New York Times dispatch by Tad Szulc.

[71]Following their defeat by Communist forces in 1949 the Chinese Nationalists retreated to the island of Taiwan (Formosa). All Chinese consider Taiwan to be an integral part of China, and ever since their victory Communist leaders have announced their intention to liberate it. Nationalist forces, even after their loss, held onto some tiny islands between Taiwan and the mainland. In 1955, and again in 1958, the Communists shelled these islands heavily. In each instance American policymakers made it clear that they would participate in the islands' defense. The Russians, although condemning the American stance verbally, gave no indication they would do more than talk.

there was disagreement over how to deal with nonaligned countries. The Chinese believed in continuously working for revolution by aiding local Communist parties, whereas the Russians were willing to aid non-Communist nationalists who might weaken Western influence (such as Egypt's President Nasser); (3) in 1958 the Chinese sought to revitalize their economy in what was known as the Great Leap Forward. Moscow said it would not work, refused aid, and said "I told you so" when it was a failure; (4) by 1960 there was serious fragmentation within the Communist bloc. The open Chinese courtship of Albania and others obviously aggravated relations with Russia; (5) in October 1962, after several years of intermittent tension and disagreement over precise boundary locations, Chinese troops attacked certain Indian provinces. The Soviets not only failed to support Peking, they actually provided armaments to New Delhi (pursuant to previous agreements);[72] (6) when Khrushchev agreed to remove Soviet missiles from Cuba in 1962, China called it appeasement of the capitalists; and (7) the Soviet signature of the Limited Nuclear Test Ban Treaty in 1963 was directly in opposition to Chinese desires for a nuclear capability.

In both of the cases, NATO and Sino-Soviet, potentially incompatible objectives were originally subordinated in view of the bipolar distribution of capabilities and the common perceptions of threat. As time passed and the nonsuperpowers gained strength, however, they began to assert themselves. Perceptions of threat became less certain and specific intra-alliance policy differences arose. Particular incidents occurred that added to the fragmenting momentum, and a flexibility of approach became more evident. In the Sino-Soviet signature of the Limited Nuclear Test Ban Treaty in 1963 was directly in opposition to Chinese desires for a nuclear capability.
dispute (that has erupted into border violence several times).

A policymaker viewing such situations today may possess excellent opportunities for increasing relative capability, and it is likely that efforts to this end will be more frequent in the years ahead. By taking advantage of the different perceptions and objectives of the parties one may be able to induce greater fragmentation, appealing to those objectives served by nonalliance actions. But a key point to notice is this: *in neither of the cases cited above did an outsider create the alliance schism; in both cases it resulted from intra-alliance problems.* These developments began in spite of, not because of, the policies of others, although outsiders later began to take advantage and encourage them. One could even hypothesize that fragmentation would have occurred sooner if the opposite side had adopted a lower profile, been less of what was perceived to be a clear and present danger.

This is not to say that a policymaker should never seek to bring about alliance dissolution. If the opportunity presents itself certainly it should be considered. But one must always be aware that perceived attempts at divide and rule

---

[72]See Chapter 4, p. 151, for further discussion.

tactics may have the opposite effect, namely, driving the opponents together against a common enemy. Generally it seems to be more feasible to study the situation and seek to capitalize on trends already in existence.[73]

Autonomy Limitations

The final category of external techniques to increase relative capability is autonomy limitations. There are two basic types: (1) the creation of dependencies, and (2) manipulation of one's adversary's internal capability components. In each case the objective is to increase relative capability by decreasing the adversary's strength.

There are several possible types of dependencies but it is useful for the policymaker to think simply in terms of either economic or military dependence.[74] *Economic dependency* can be established in a wide range of circumstances.[75] Often a given country may have much of its economic health based on the production and sale of one particular product.[76] Not only is it the source of revenue for internal purposes, it is also the primary means of obtaining foreign exchange to purchase foreign goods. If a party is in the position of being the primary market for that product considerable leverage may be possible and one's decisions may have great impact. Of course, the availability of alternative markets, substitute products and so forth will affect this.

A similar possibility of foreign trade manipulation occurs if one's state is the primary supplier of necessary goods and services unobtainable domestically. If a party needs certain machine parts in order to develop its aircraft industry and must rely on foreign sources for them, its economic position is clearly weak. Also a state may be the primary supplier of critical resources, either natural or in

---

[73]Even the detachment of Italy from the Triple Alliance in World War I was possible only because of the existence of objectives that could only be accomplished at the expense of her alliance partner, Austria-Hungary, and objectives with which her alliance objectives directly conflicted.

[74]Historically another major type of dependency was the creation of the satellite states, the post-World War II establishment by the Soviet Union of complete political, military, economic, and ideological control over the nominally independent states of Eastern Europe. Relying on the presence of the Red Army, cooperation between secret police organizations, and a ruthless use of clandestine, economic and diplomatic policy tools, almost complete subordination was achieved. The creation of such a dependency today is hardly a feasible option for most policymakers, however. For an excellent introduction to the topic as well as the beginning of alliance fragmentation, see Zbigniew Brzezinski, *The Soviet Bloc: Unity and Conflict,* rev. ed., Praeger, New York, 1961.

[75]This analysis assumes that the policymaker is able to control and direct the personnel and institutions of his or her own state. This is obviously not always the case as the discussion in Chapter 7 demonstrates. Despite the fact that this assumption departs to some extent from reality, it is highly useful for the purpose here of showing various aspects of the creation of dependency. The student will simply have to recognize that in some ''real world'' situations policymakers have less autonomy and authority than these comments would indicate, and would have to adjust accordingly.

[76]Pertinent to the entire discussion of the creation of dependency is the analysis of the economic policy instrument in Chapter 4.

the form of capital. Perhaps the United States cannot run its industrial machine effectively without South African diamonds, or Israel's economy cannot develop without American economic assistance to cover its balance of payments deficits. In each case some degree of economic dependence is established.

Each of these variations has one facet in common, namely, an outside party plays a primary role because it is the major purchaser or supplier of an economic necessity. The degree of dependence will depend on many things including target vulnerability, alternative sources or markets, substitutability, bargaining skill, willpower, priority of objectives, relation to other issues, and the use of other instruments of policy.

But there is another kind of economic dependency one might seek to create, this one more insidious and deep seated. A very effective means of control occurs when one is able to manage or control the major economic enterprises within a given country. Control may be established by capital investment from governmental and/or private sources. Perhaps a given sector of the economy simply cannot develop and considerable outside financing is necessary. In this case particular outside sources may, via the quantity and terms of financing, take over effective control. The banking and financing institutions of all market economies play a key role in growth and development through their impact on credit and the money supply, and penetration of these institutions may give one a lock grip on local economic performance.

Many times outside parties establish new firms or take over the ownership of existing ones. In these cases much production and employment comes under the control of foreign entrepreneurs. This is particularly critical when such enterprises operate in key sectors of the economy such as Chilean copper mines or Bolivian tin mines. Sometimes top and middle management is either foreign or foreign selected, and again decisions are made based on foreign, not local interests. Today, as discussed in Chapter 1, various kinds of multinational corporations participate in international politics with an impact that is equal to or greater than that of many states, and indications are that their influence may well increase.[77]

A second type of dependency to be established is *military*. In the discussion of alliance formation it was stated that often a major motivating force is the desire to increase relative capability by combining strength. While this is sometimes true it often is not the whole story. Sometimes a powerful state will seek an alliance with a less powerful one in order to establish its dominance over the latter. Anytime a lesser power joins an alliance it runs this danger.

Military dependency may be established in specific ways. Perhaps an agreement has been reached to establish a military base. The presence of foreign troops on one's soil provides many opportunities for leverage. Maybe the dominating state is involved in training and directing local forces, or perhaps in

[77]See Chapter 1, p. 8, and the corresponding footnotes.

supplying their needs in terms of weapons systems and replacement parts. Obviously the recipient in this case is under some pressure to adhere to the wishes of the supplier. Many times various kinds of assistance programs have certain restrictions concomitant with them. Another point, sometimes overlooked, is that the constant contact provides innumerable opportunities for subtle influences, influences often unseen by outside observers.

But military dependence does not necessarily mean equivalent political influence. Dependency can arouse resentment and a policymaker in today's world must recognize that there are alternative sources for his recipient. While the dependent state has certain needs it also is trying to achieve its *own* objectives. Depending on its own analysis of the relationship between the assistance and its needs, in the context of supplier alternatives and its vulnerability it may suddenly seek to become less dependent. As indicated above, in the summer of 1972 when Egyptian President Sadat concluded that Soviet aid was prolonging rather than altering the territorial situation with Israel, Soviet advisers were peremptorily expelled.

A policymaker thus finds that the creation of economic or military dependencies does not automatically bring about a significant increase in relative capability. Because it sometimes does, however, it certainly is an option to consider. Furthermore, it has three characteristics that give it considerable appeal. First, generally the process begins on a voluntary, cooperative basis so one is not open to charges of imperialism (although this is still a question of degree). Second, given the nature of the process there is little likelihood that force will be used and thus the immediate danger to one's security is slight. And third, it is difficult to detect or "prove" that dependency is being created or exists, and so it is difficult to oppose or counter.

The second major type of autonomy limitation is the manipulation of the adversary's internal capability components.[78] The policymaker may be trying to limit his target's capacity to control his internal power factors and thereby decrease his relative strength, or perhaps to actually decrease the quality or quantity of the resources. Possibly one is even seeking to influence the composition or structure of the target government itself. Through a wide variety of possible actions one seeks to intervene in the affairs of another, interfering with (or penetrating) the internal processes of that country to its detriment and his or her state's resultant benefit.[79]

The list of potential methods is almost endless and we must content ourselves with a few brief examples (also see Chapters 4 and 5). A major component of capability involves the degree of support that a government re-

---

[78]The discussion here is restricted to means short of guerilla warfare. That topic will be considered in Chapter 4.

[79]While much ink has been used attempting to distinguish between intervention and interference, developing a precise definitional distinction is of little concern to policymakers. Here the terms are used interchangeably.

ceives from its populace, and a major objective may be to lessen that support. Perhaps there are ethnic, racial, or religious rivalries that can be exploited, or class differences containing the seeds of conflict that can be worsened. Maybe one can infiltrate the leading labor organizations, arouse or exacerbate their bitterness toward management and bring about disastrous strikes. Sometimes it is possible to infiltrate the media of communications and turn key representatives against the government. Perhaps there is a situation that may be used to create a scandal and bring down a certain official or administration, or maybe there is general unrest and one can help sponsor civil disturbances. Possibly, through covert propaganda facilities, the policymaker can deluge a receptive population with "news" about its government's failures and duplicity. Maybe a particular governmental official can be bribed and then exposed. Maybe false rumors can be started or stories "planted" in the press to create further disaffection. All of these and many other procedures affect the support a government receives.

Of course more tangible power components may be affected also. Governmental factors influence capability and perhaps it is possible to seriously impede the policymaking machinery or deliberately distort the information process on which it is based. Perhaps one can harm military capability by ferreting out defense secrets or by influencing training procedures or strategic conceptions so as to leave the adversary unprepared for the most likely contingencies. Perhaps equipment and facilities can be sabotaged. Possibly economic capacity can be harmed by infiltrating key organizations and then manipulating them in ways contrary to the state's objectives, or maybe one can contribute to an inflation psychology by various covert methods. Perhaps the policymaker can influence the outcome of internal power contests, including elections, and bring about a regime change. And so the list could be extended but to no good purpose at this time; the point is clear enough.

Increasing relative capability by manipulating the adversary's internal capability components is becoming more important, both quantitatively and qualitatively. The reasons seem clear enough. First, the use of techniques for this purpose is difficult to detect and prove. Second, the cost, in terms of personnel, equipment, finances, and prestige, is relatively small. This means that nearly all states can afford to use such techniques. Third, there is less risk of opposition retaliation or public condemnation if discovered than if more traditional means were used. Fourth, most states are vulnerable to some kind of manipulation, including the superpowers. Because of the dangers of modern general warfare, and the nuclear stalemate as well, even the superpowers are unlikely to use all out force unless grossly provoked. One may certainly expect to see a continuation of this trend throughout the decade.

This chapter has examined the major steps one ought to take as he is seeking to formulate his optimum foreign policy: determination of who is involved, the types and sources of objectives, characteristics of capability analysis, foreign policy orientation options, and procedures for increasing relative capability by manipulating external power influences. The analysis has not given sufficient attention to one key aspect of this process, however, the in-depth examination of the internal building blocks of capability. This is the task to which we now turn.

SELECTED BIBLIOGRAPHY

Beer, Francis A., *Integration and Disintegration in NATO*, Ohio State University Press, Columbus, Ohio, 1969.

Brzezinski, Zbigniew, *The Soviet Bloc: Unity and Conflict*, Revised Edition, Praeger, New York, 1961.

Churchill, Winston S., *The Second World War. Vol. I: The Gathering Storm*, Houghton Mifflin, Boston, 1948.

Claude, Inis L., Jr., *Power and International Relations*, Random House, New York, 1962.

Coplin, William D., Patrick J. McGowan, and Michael K. O'Leary, *American Foreign Policy: An Introduction to Analysis and Evaluation*, Duxbury Press, North Scituate, Massachusetts, 1974.

Crabb, Cecil V., Jr., *The Elephànts and the Grass: A Study of Nonalignment*, Praeger, New York, 1965.

Crankshaw, Edward, *The New Cold War: Moscow v. Peking*, Penguin Books, Baltimore, 1963.

Fedder, Edwin H., *NATO: The Dynamics of Alliance in the Postwar World*, Dodd Mead, New York, 1973.

Freedman, Robert O., *Soviet Policy Toward the Middle East Since 1970*, Praeger, New York, 1975.

Friedman, Julian R., Christopher Bladen, and Steven Rosen, eds., *Alliance in International Politics*, Allyn Bacon, Boston, 1970.

Griffith, William E., *The Sino-Soviet Rift*, MIT Press, Cambridge, Massachusetts, 1964.

Gulick, Edward Vose, *Europe's Classical Balance of Power*, Cornell University Press, Ithaca, New York, 1955.

Halberstam, David, *The Best and the Brightest*, Random House, New York, 1969.

Hartmann, Frederick H., *The New Age of American Foreign Policy*, Macmillan, New York, 1970.

Holsti, K. J., "National Role Conceptions in the Study of Foreign Policy", *International Studies Quarterly*, September, 1970, pp. 233–309.

Jordan, Robert S., ed., *Europe and the Superpowers: Perceptions of European International Politics*, Allyn Bacon, Boston, 1971.

Kahin, George McTurnan, and John W. Lewis, *The United States in Vietnam: An Analysis in Depth of America's Involvement in Vietnam*, a Delta Book, New York, 1967.

Kennedy, Robert F., *Thirteen Days: A Memoir of the Cuban Missile Crisis*, W. W. Norton, New York, 1971.

Laqueur, Walter, *The Struggle for the Mediterranean: The Soviet Union and the Middle East, 1958–68*, Macmillan, New York, 1969.

Legg, Keith R., and James R. Morrison, *Politics and the International System: An Introduction*, Harper & Row, New York, 1971.

Lentner, Howard H., *Foreign Policy Analysis: A Comparative and Conceptual Approach,* Charles E. Merrill, Columbus, Ohio, 1974.

Lerche, Charles O., Jr., and Abdul A. Said, *Concepts of International Politics,* Second Edition, Prentice-Hall, Englewood Cliffs, New Jersey, 1970.

Lovell, John P., *Foreign Policy in Perspective: Strategy, Adaptation, Decision Making,* Holt, Rinehart and Winston, New York, 1970.

Martin Lawrence W., ed., *Neutralism and Nonalignment,* Praeger, New York, 1962.

Neustadt, Richard E., *Alliance Politics,* Columbia University Press, New York, 1970.

New York Times, *The Pentagon Papers,* Bantam, New York, 1971.

Organski, A. F. K., *World Politics,* Second Edition, Alfred A. Knopf, New York, 1968.

Paul, David W., "Soviet Foreign Policy and the Invasion of Czechoslovakia: A Theory and a Case Study," *International Studies Quarterly,* June, 1971, pp. 159−202.

Pfaltzgraff, Robert L., Jr., *The Atlantic Community,* Van Nostrand Reinhold, New York, 1969.

Sayegh, Fayez A., ed., *The Dynamics of Neutralism in the Arab World: A Symposium,* Chandler, San Francisco, 1964.

Wilkinson, David O., *Comparative Foreign Relations: Framework and Methods,* Dickenson, Belmont, California, 1969.

Wolfers, Arnold, " 'National Security' as an Ambiguous Symbol," *The Political Science Quarterly,* December, 1952, pp. 481−502.

Young, Oran R., *The Intermediaries: Third Parties in International Crises,* Princeton University Press, Princeton, New Jersey, 1967.

Zagoria, Donald S., *The Sino-Soviet Conflict, 1956−1961,* Princeton University Press, Princeton, New Jersey, 1962.

Three

The Foundation of Capability

In Chapter 2 it was pointed out that capability analysis is a critically important part of the policy formulation process. As discussed therein, the policymaker must recognize the relational nature of power and the fact that capability analysis is relevant primarily when utilized in terms of specific policy situations. These facts are perfectly accurate and provide necessary warnings against simply compiling a list of a state's internal capability components and assuming that their sum equals "power." But one must not go too far in this regard. Although the mere possession of a given mix of components does not automatically guarantee influence, without strength in certain areas a state can not be influential. A state's capability is ultimately based on certain internal factors and in the long run they will in large part determine its influence potential. To put it another way, the internal capability components are the essential building blocks that comprise the foundation for international influence.

GEOGRAPHY

Geography is one of the most important factors affecting capability, its components being location, size, topography, climate, and shape.[1]

Location

The location of a state in relation to other states is a geographical fact of immense importance. Who is or is not one's neighbor has significant strategic implications and can have considerable impact on one's national security.

Let's look at a specific example. The continental United States is separated

---

[1]Another geographical factor is natural resources. Because of its scope and significance, however, we shall give it separate treatment.

from the Eurasian continent by bodies of water approximately 3000 miles wide to the East and 6000 miles wide to the West. For the 18th, 19th, and early 20th centuries this sea distance was an immense defensive asset as the oceans constituted significant barriers to invasion.[2] Because of changes in technology, of course, they are no longer as formidable as they once were since the high seas can act as highways as well as barriers and intercontinental missiles can cross them without difficulty. Nevertheless, the lack of proximity to one's potential adversaries is still a matter of some import because it is much more difficult to successfully attack and/or occupy across thousands of miles of ocean than across adjacent frontiers. Furthermore, because of the lack of proximity border incidents and disputes are much less likely to occur.

Consider this fact: only the United States, among the medium or great powers of the world, "grew up" in a location where it had no great power neighbors, and continues to exist in such a favorable position.[3] This lack of great power neighbors allowed a much wider range of policy orientation options than otherwise would have been possible, permitting, for example, Washington to choose an orientation of avoidance for most of the nineteenth century. Had it been located adjacent to a potential adversary this would not have been feasible.

In contrast, assume that one's country has several thousand miles of common border with a state that has great potential strength, and that the latter claims that over 500,000 square miles of its territory are being illegally occupied. Assume further that there is competition for the leadership of an ideological movement, disagreement over the correct ideological interpretation of certain elements within that movement, there are military forces of considerable strength arrayed against each other along the border, and that serious incidents occur. Furthermore, suppose that over the last 15 to 20 years there have been a series of disagreements over practical policy questions such as military assistance and economic programs, and that today there is a great power that is wooing both states and at the same time is a potential adversary. If one is a policymaker in this position the fact of geographical proximity combined with the factors previously mentioned obviously presents a policy situation very different from any faced by the United States. This, of course, represents a simplified and generalized thumbnail sketch of the Sino-Soviet border situation as seen from Moscow.[4] Quite clearly if Canada were hostile and powerful American-Canadian relations would be vastly different.

---

[2]Of course wide oceans do not, by themselves, provide an insuperable obstacle to attack and many lands were successfully invaded across wide oceans prior to, during, and after this period. Nevertheless, the seas *did* provide an immense defensive advantage in comparison to countries who were faced with the situation of a common land boundary with a potentially hostile, strong state.

[3]See Hartmann, *The New Age of American Foreign Policy*, Ch. 2.

[4]Also see Chapter 2, pp. 76–78.

Size

The second major geographical factor is size.[5] The Soviet Union is over two and one-half times as large as the United States and comprises nearly one-seventh of the land area of the earth. This territorial vastness has significantly contributed to the failure of all modern attempts to conquer her (as Napoleon, Hitler, and others found out when, in a sense, the country began to conquer them).

Size gives a nation's army room to retreat without surrender, room to hide to fight another day. It also allows the location and dispersal of critical population, economic, military, and governmental facilities and centers far from the borders, thus increasing their chances of survival in case of invasion or nuclear attack. Although this may be thought to have less significance today because of the advent of nuclear weapons, since most countries and most conflicts are nonnuclear, and since even the nuclear powers may participate in nonnuclear warfare, it is still of considerable importance.

A final military advantage of great size, if combined with a large population, is that a defeated large country would be very difficult to occupy and control. As A.F.K. Organski has stated, "The occupation of China would be formidable: it would require more soldiers and administrators than the United States possesses."[6]

A very small country possesses none of these advantages and is much more vulnerable to invasion, conquest, and occupation.[7] However, Japan's decisive defeat of China and Russia in 1894 and 1904, and Israel's four consecutive military victories over its Arab adversaries underline the fact that size alone is not determinative.

A large area is sometimes considered to confer the nonmilitary advantage of providing room for a substantial population, itself a major component of power. This is true, but in and of itself means little; mere space can just as easily be a source of weakness and a temptation to invasion as a source of strength. An area must be able to support a large population for it to be a positive element, and this capacity depends on factors other than size. For example, the Rub al Khali (the "Empty Quarter") in Saudi Arabia is useful only as a barrier to invasion because it is incapable of supporting human life on any scale.

---

[5]For analytical reasons our discussion considers each geographical factor separately. In reality they are related and the policymaker must analyze the impact of the particular "mix" on capability. For example, massive size plus proximity can easily be viewed by one's neighbors as "automatically" posing a security threat. See Alain-Gerard Marsot, "The Chinese Perspective," in Sudershan Chawla, Melvin Gurtov, and Alain-Gerard Marsot, eds., *Southeast Asia Under the New Balance of Power,* Praeger, New York, 1974, Ch. 4.

[6]A. F. K. Organski, *World Politics,* Second Edition, Knopf, New York, 1968, p. 129.

[7]This factor may contribute to an exceptional security consciousness and a marked tendency to act quickly and decisively when threats are perceived. This certainly has been one of the prime factors shaping Israel's political-military policy.

Great size can have other disadvantages. There is a point beyond which efficiency decreases. As has been true in Russia, for example, there can be difficulties in developing the efficient transportation and communication systems necessary to tie the country together. Sheer size can easily multiply the number and the complexity of the problems with which the government must deal, and this in turn may well lead to a burgeoning, overbearing governmental bureaucracy. If additional size means that various nationality groups will be incorporated within the borders, this too could lead to internal discontent.

Another point to be remembered is the obvious yet sometimes ignored fact that boundaries are made by people. This being so, people can change them. Witness the changes in Israel's geographic situation following the June War of 1967, changes that allowed her to occupy territory about seven times larger (in terms of square miles) than her pre-1967 area. One should not be mesmerized by current boundaries and assume a static situation.

Control of one's neighbors may have an effect similar to extension of size because it moves the area of potential border conflict closer to the enemy and further from the homeland. Certainly the activities of the Soviet Union after World War II in Central and Eastern Europe extended Soviet ''boundaries'' far into Europe. In case there would be an attack again from or by Germany, the attack would begin far from the heart of the fatherland.[8]

Climate

The third geographical feature is climate. There needs to be sufficient heat, a long enough growing season, sufficient rainfall (or irrigation possibilities), and soil of minimum quality in order for a country to produce crops. Otherwise it will be dependent on foreign sources to keep from starving.[9] Obviously there are areas of the world where these climatic conditions are not present: great portions of Canada, Alaska, Greenland, Soviet Union, western China, and Antarctica are too cold and their growing season is too short; desert areas in the Middle East, North Africa and the interior of Australia are too arid for cultivation, and there are many areas of the world where the soil is too low in nutrients or is so rocky it is nigh unto impossible to grow crops even with artificial fertilizers and modern technology.

Another climatic consideration is whether there are areas of the world that are so hot or so cold that human beings cannot function optimally with the result that these areas can never produce states with significant capability. It has been

[8]For a concise examination of this point as it figured in Soviet policymaking in the immediate post-war era, see Adam B. Ulam, *Expansion and Coexistence: The History of Soviet Foreign Policy, 1917−67*, Praeger, New York, 1968, Ch. 8.

[9]See pp. 101−102 for further discussion of agricultural capacity. Although ''soil'' might be discussed with reference to natural resources, because of its obvious relationship to the other conditions discussed it was felt that it made more sense to include it under this heading.

suggested that a great power cannot exist outside of the temperate zones.[10] It is certainly true that as one looks at history he sees that many of the great powers came from the temperate zones. But was this a cause and effect relationship or not? After all, many great civilizations of the past such as the Aztecs and the Mayans (and great African empires) flourished in relatively tropical or semitropical climates. Also, many powerful preindustrial empires such as the Romans, the Persians, the Arabs, the Greeks, and others operated in a climate considerably different, considerably less "comfortable" perhaps, than that of Western Europe or the United States.

Some observers seem to assume that the nontemperate areas of the world will never produce a great power simply because in industrial times they have not done so. It may be true that it is more difficult for Europeans and North Americans to work in such conditions than it is at home, but does it follow that people used to living in these conditions cannot function well? Perhaps even more important, is it not plausible to suggest that with changing technology it may become possible to increasingly control environmental conditions and thus greatly mitigate any possible energy inhibiting effects of climate? Although one cannot absolutely predict this will occur, a policymaker must not assume it cannot happen.

Topography

A fourth major geographical facet is topography. Topography, of course, has an impact on climate. Wind, temperature, rainfall, and soil conditions are influenced by the lay of the land, by the relative position of waterways within the country, by the height of mountains and valleys, and so forth. Topography also has important internal effects on the country. The location of plains, mountains, rivers, lakes, and valleys will have a considerable impact on both transportation and communication. These factors also have an extremely important effect on the location, density and unity of the population, the ease of moving military forces from one point to another, and on patterns of economic distribution and development.

Topographical factors also have an important strategic value vis-à-vis other nations and have sometimes set limits on expansion. Great mountain ranges like the Himalayas, the Alps, and the Pyrenees have served this function. A lack of natural barriers also is important. Consider, for example, that there are no natural barriers separating the Soviet Union from her western neighbors and that the north European plain from the Ural Mountains to Germany's Rhine River pro-

---

[10]As has been perceptively pointed out, however, "Until quite recently, prevailing ideas regarding the effects of climate on man came primarily from Europeans or from their descendants in other parts of the world. Many of these ideas appear to have originated simply as extensions of European ways of thinking and reacting." Harold Sprout and Margaret Sprout, *Toward a Politics of the Planet Earth,* Van Nostrand, New York, 1971, p. 278.

vides an easy avenue of attack. This fact inevitably conditions the intensity and nature of the response by the Soviet Union and the states of Western Europe to each other. This has considerable contemporary significance with the division of Germany and the impact (or potential impact) that a reduction of forces in central and Eastern Europe on the part of the United States and the Soviet Union might have.

One must always remember, however, that even barriers to attack can usually be overcome; they may make the job more difficult but not impossible. The mountains along the Syrian-Israeli border were an obstacle to Israeli advances but they *were* successfully assaulted in the 1967 war.

These same mountains, known as the Golan Heights, provide another illustration of the continuing importance of topography. Prior to 1967 the Syrians were able to lob mortar shells down upon the Israeli settlements below with relatively little opposition. Given this strategic fact it is extremely unlikely that Israel would ever be willing to completely give them up unless physically compelled to do so. They simply have too much strategic value to be considered an object of bargaining.

Shape

The final geographic factor is shape. In some cases this is critical. Pre-1967 Israel, very narrow with exceptionally long frontiers and very little depth, always faced the possibility of a knifelike attack cutting her in two. This was particularly true with respect to the territory known as the West Bank where Jordanian forces at some points were no more than ten miles from the Mediterranean Sea. Israel's 1967 victory gave her much more defensible boundaries by resting her eastern boundary on the Jordan River, greatly lessening the danger of divide and conquer tactics. The greater security afforded by the changed geographical configuration will certainly make Israeli policymakers hesitant to relinquish military control over the West Bank. Never again do they wish to be put into a position where a blitzkrieg might effectively partition the country.

Sometimes the implications of shape are altered by a change in neighbors. The country of Czechoslovakia was created from portions of the defeated Austro-Hungarian Empire after World War I. A long narrow state, she was bordered on the west by an unhappy Germany and shared more than one-half of her northern frontier with that same country. Germany had been stripped of many territories by the Allies after the war and her people were bitterly resentful.[11] It was very clear that most Germans wanted these territories back, and would be willing to make sacrifices to get them. In addition, there were significant German minorities in many non-German states, including nearly 3 million in the Sudeten-

---

[11]Germany lost Upper Silesia, the Polish Corridor, Danzig, Eupen-Malmedy, part of Schleswig-Holstein, and Alsace-Lorraine.

land region of Czechoslovakia, and the Nazis wanted them in an enlarged "Germany" also. In addition to having this potential enemy to the west and north, a considerable portion of Czechoslovakia's southern boundary was shared with the Germanic state of Austria, itself an object of Nazi expansion. Thus, when Hitler annexed Austria in March 1938 he flanked the Czechs on three sides and their defense problems became much more extreme (a not unimportant consideration at Munich in the fall).

POPULATION

A second major component of capability is population. To properly determine its role one must analyze questions of size, trends, ratios of productive to non-productive elements, educational levels, density, and spatial distribution.

Size

The first aspect to be investigated is sheer size. How many people are there in this particular country? It is sometimes said that the relationship of population size to capability is such that it is probably impossible to be a medium or great power without a relatively large population.[12] Why is this so? The reason usually given first is that a large population is necessary to have an effective military force.

It is true that there has been no modern military power with more than local influence that did not have a large population, and it is also true that despite advanced technology large masses of human beings still fight many wars. Furthermore, large modern armed forces require vast quantities of people to manufacture, supply, operate, and repair their highly sophisticated weapons and support systems. Finally, in a war of any length, a large population is necessary to keep the domestic economy in operation so it can contribute to the war effort.

Although these statements are accurate, if one stopped his analysis at this point he would get a very distorted picture. This argument deals primarily with one kind of military conflict, a conventional war over a considerable length of time between relatively equal modern adversaries. Although this is important, there are several types of conflict to which this concept is inappropriate. The development of a nuclear striking force does not necessarily require a large population, nor does the ability to launch a decisive first-strike attack with highly sophisticated forces against technologically inferior and less trained opponents. Perhaps even more critically, in today's world a wide range of guerilla and insurgent military activities may be successfully undertaken by states without

---

[12]Morgenthau, *Politics Among Nations,* Fifth Edition, p. 125. He states: "no country can remain or become a first-rate power which does not belong to the more populous nations of the earth."

large populations.[13] None of this is to gainsay the potential military advantage that a large population can yield, but only to point out that one must evaluate it in terms of the nature of the conflict and the parties involved.

A second reason that possessing a large population is usually important is its relation to economic strength. A large population is essential for the development of a modern economic system sufficiently powerful to be used to influence other states. Without sufficient personnel there cannot be the quantity of human talent necessary for the highly interdependent, specialized and technologically advanced systems of the industrialized world. It is also highly unlikely that a small population will yield the array of qualitative capabilities required for modern economic life. And although it is a truism, it is also a fact that a state without economic strength cannot exercise significant political influence for very long.

Another advantage of having a large population is that in case of military reverses one's country would be more difficult to occupy and control. Consider trying to control 800 million hostile Chinese, for example.

Finally, a large population is a potential market for the goods and services of others. Therefore, it can be useful in offering rewards and promises to those with whom one is dealing, or threatening to cut them off unless the appropriate policy changes are made.

Despite these advantages it is clear that merely possessing a large population does not automatically bring about significant power. It is also obvious that one cannot say that the larger the population the greater the capability, or else China would be the most powerful nation in the world with India second and so on (see Table 1). One cannot even say that size is always the most important aspect of the population factor. What other facets must be investigated?

Trends

One also needs to analyze population trends. Is the population increasing or decreasing, and how fast, in both absolute and comparative terms? From the Franco-Prussian war of 1871 until the beginning of World War II French population barely increased while Germany's grew rapidly. This signified a relative increase in German strength unless France could offset it in other areas (which she could not). The Germans, in turn, were worried about the growth of the Soviet Union. Today Russia and much of the rest of the world cast anxious eyes on the more than 800 million Chinese. The policymaker must not only ascertain the existing population relationship but also attempt to project current trends into the foreseeable future, an imprecise but necessary exercise.

---

[13]However, support or acquiescence of the population of the target country is helpful as was aptly demonstrated by the Viet Cong in the Vietnam War. For further discussion of guerilla warfare, see Chapter 4, pp. 154–157.

Table 1 Population of Selected States (Millions)

State	1970	1975	Annual Rate of Increase, 1970–1975 (%)
China	771	839	1.7
India	539	598	2.1
U.S.S.R.	243	254	0.9
United States	204	214	0.8
Indonesia	119	136	2.6
Japan	104	111	1.2
Brazil	92.5	107	3.0
Bangladesh	68	77	2.4
Nigeria	55	63	2.7
W. Germany	61	62	0.4
United Kingdom	55.4	55.9	0.2
Egypt	33	37	2.2
Poland	32.5	34	0.9
Zaire	21.6	24.9	2.8
Colombia	20.5	23.5	2.8
E. Germany	17.0	16.8	−0.2
Israel	2.9	3.4	3.1

SOURCE: *UN Statistical Yearbook, 1976,* pp. 67–73.

Productive Population Elements

Another task one must undertake is to determine the proportion of the population that is available for productive efforts. What percentage of the people are within the productive age brackets, in terms of both economic and military activity? Children and the elderly are basically nonproductive in these terms, constituting a net drain on a state's resources. Although the exact boundaries of the "productive years" vary with time, circumstance, and culture and so cannot be definitively determined, a good rule of thumb is to use 15 to 60 as the economically productive years and 18 to 35 for military service.[14]

Other questions are related to this facet of the productive population elements. In most countries men are the prime contributors to economic and military development, and therefore male-female ratios are important. Even though this is slowly changing in many states, it still should be investigated (but evaluated in light of altering conditions). Often particular racial, religious, or ethnic groups are not permitted to contribute fully, thus depriving the society of their resources. The extent and nature of this denial must be ascertained and its implications examined.

---

[14]The life expectancy of the population is an important part of this question. In many of the less developed countries people simply do not survive long enough to be within the productive years for very long.

These issues are important because they give us an indication of the proportions of the state's population that add to or detract from its capability. A nation with a large percentage of its people in the productive categories is doubly fortunate: it has more people who are productive as well as fewer who require their support.

Educational Level

The general educational level is very important. Education clearly affects the population's skills' levels, both in terms of quantity and quality. Without a reasonably literate population an industrial economy cannot begin to function. In fact, the differentiation, specialization, and interdependence of all modern governmental, social, and economic systems probably could not occur (at least not efficiently) without mass education. And certainly there cannot be significant technological development without advanced education.

Lack of educational quantity and quality also affects military capability. For example, armed forces with low skills levels simply cannot compete with highly sophisticated military machines if there is a direct, unrestricted confrontation.[15] A prime example of this was provided by the contrast in 1956 and 1967 between the highly mobile and exceptionally sophisticated Israeli armed forces and their numerically superior but less educated Arab neighbors. The Egyptians had excellent equipment but simply did not have the "know-how" to use it effectively. This was particularly significant in 1967 inasmuch as they had received intensive Soviet training and the result was still an Egyptian debacle.

This type of contrast is one that is difficult to significantly alter in a short time because one cannot change the educational level of a country overnight.[16] This lack of high grade educational performance has handicapped certain states with large populations that otherwise might be much more influential, such as India, Indonesia, and Brazil.

Density and Spatial Distribution

Population density and spatial distribution also need to be examined. Is the country densely populated, thus making it highly susceptible to nuclear devastation? Are there "too many" people on "too little" land, making it impossible to

---

[15]One must always remember that the United States imposed limitations on its activity in Vietnam in terms of the types of weapons used and the deployment of forces.

[16]The increased efficiency of the Egyptian armed forces in the October 1973 war with Israel does not disprove but rather confirms this argument. The intensive efforts to improve Egyptian quality after 1967 only partially succeeded. There was just too large a gap. Even the advantage of a surprise attack with sophisticated weaponry was not enough to overcome the deficiency.

raise enough food to support them? Is population growing rapidly, thus making things worse? Will these factors lead to demands on the government for territorial expansion? Even if the overall people per square mile figures are low, is the population concentrated in a few high density areas and thus susceptible to quick elimination? Are the major population centers near the frontiers? These and related questions need to be asked.

Finally, one must mention that for many countries the problem is too many people, and this *overpopulation* detracts from capability.[17] The stark reality is that this is the case in much of the world, and many policymakers must devote a great deal of attention to simply trying to keep their people fed.[18] The population explosion is very real. Between 1750 and 1900 world population doubled. It doubled again by 1950 and will double again before the year 2000. Starting from a different point but illustrating the same problem, whereas in 1970 there were about 3.5 billion people in the world, it has been projected that there will be 7.5 billion by the end of the century.[19]

The problem is severely compounded by the fact that the vast majority of this growth is occurring in the already "overpopulated" and relatively less developed countries in Asia, Africa, and Latin America (see Tables 1 and 2). Such states generally have relatively unproductive economic systems and have neither the economic infrastructure, the skills, nor the capital to remedy their deficiencies in the foreseeable future (as will be examined in more detail below). Although estimates vary, it is generally accepted that the "have-not" countries will possess at least 75 percent of the world's population by the turn of the century.

Excess population leads to chaos and bitterness and is a fertile ground for conflict. There are simply too many people relative to the economic, political, and social capacity of the country. Unless population growth is significantly slowed in these areas, and there is precious little to indicate that it will be, things are likely to get worse. Overpopulation will continue to be a drain on resources, preventing a state from achieving even moderate foreign policy objectives without excessive costs.[20]

---

[17]Many analysts feel that the entire future of mankind is endangered and that a new orientation and focus of study is necessary. For a general introduction to the subject see A. H. Ehrlich and P. R. Ehrlich, *Population, Resources, Environment: Issues in Human Ecology,* W. H. Freeman & Co., San Francisco, 1970, and Larry K. Y. Ng and Stuart Mudd, eds., *The Population Crisis,* Indiana University Press, Bloomington, 1965. There is also a trend in International Relations literature in this direction. See Sterling, and Sprout and Sprout, cited above.

[18]As Sterling says "The priority task of a poor country, almost by definition, is the attempt to feed its people." Sterling, p. 377.

[19]United Nations Association of the United States, *World Population,* New York, 1969, p. 10.

[20]Despite the fact that this problem may exist, population size still may have the positive attribute of making this country harder to conquer. Also, the mere existence of an overwhelming population disparity will yield the larger nation some influence because it could simply innundate the smaller with human waves if necessary.

Table 2   Population of Major Regions (Millions)

Region	1965	1974	Annual Rate of Increase, 1965–74 (%)
World	3288	3890	1.9
Africa	309	391	2.7
North America	214	235	1.0
Latin America	247	315	2.7
Asia	1824	2206	2.1
Europe	445	470	0.6
Oceania	17.5	20.9	2.0
U.S.S.R.	231	252	1.0

SOURCE: *UN Demographic Yearbook, 1974*, p. 105.

NATURAL RESOURCES

Natural resources are another component of capability. While no one would suggest that a nation that is richly endowed with natural resources will automatically become a great power, it is clear that the possession of large quantities of high quality resources provides a base on which capability can be built. A modern industrialized economy cannot function without critical resources including coal, iron, and petroleum as well as a wide variety of other minerals. Similarly, a modern military machine is dependent on certain strategic resources.

Six Basic Points

When analyzing the role of natural resources in capability determination the policymaker must keep six basic points in mind. First, it is necessary to distinguish between the mere possession of natural resources and their use. Resources contribute to economic and military strength primarily as they are developed. Minerals, for example, must be drawn from the earth and processed before they enter into the production process. If a state does not have this extracting, processing, and producing capacity its mineral resources contribute little to its usable strength.[21] One way around this problem is to grant development concessions to foreign countries or companies. In such a situation the country possessing the resource gains something in terms of political power and economic benefits, but also loses some resource benefits to the concessionaire. On the other hand, this is still a net gain because, by definition, without the concessionaire the resources would not be developed. A conflict situation can develop, however, as the possessing state learns to develop its own capacity or wishes to increase its share of the benefits.

A second point is that a country must also have political control over its own

---

[21] However, knowledge of their mere existence can sometimes provide bargaining leverage.

territory if it is to receive the optimum benefits from its resources. If it is a dependency of a foreign state, such as many Eastern European countries have been in relation to the Soviet Union in most of the post-World War II era, it obviously does not have full control over the use of its resources and therefore cannot reap all their benefits.

Third, it is very difficult to weigh the advantages of the possession of one resource against the possession of another. Since not all states possess equal quantities and qualities of resources, the situation is asymmetrical; iron is not equivalent to oil, and copper is not equivalent to manganese.

Fourth, resources reflect not only potentials but also limitations. The lack of resources will set (or at least should set) limits on the objectives one would formulate, and in point of fact *will* eventually set limitations on their achievement.

Diagram 1   U. S. Import Dependence and Import Sources (1977 estimates except where noted.)

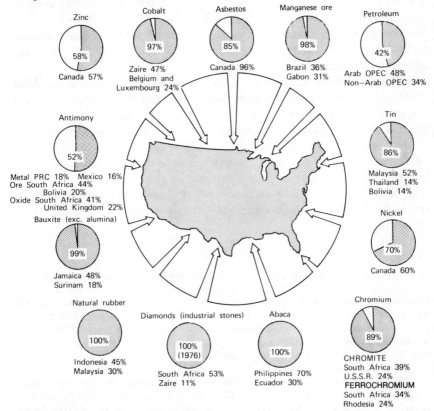

SOURCE: U. S., Department of State, *The Trade Debate*, Washington, D. C., May 1978.

Fifth, no major nation is self-sufficient. The United States, for example, imports over 90 percent of its industrial diamonds, manganese, cobalt, and bauxite, more than half its zinc, chromium, and nickel, nearly half its petroleum, and more than a quarter of its iron ore. All nations today have a certain degree of interdependence, although some are much more vulnerable than others.

Sixth, natural resources sometimes provide a nation or a group of nations with political power that they would not otherwise possess. An example today certainly is the possession of great petroleum resources by several Arab nations of the Middle East. However, possession of natural resources can also make a nation the object of political activities, which it would otherwise escape. One of the major concerns of the contending powers in the Congo crisis in the early 1960s was the fact that the Congo contained vast quantities of copper, uranium, and cobalt.[22]

Obtaining Resources

Because resources are so vital and no country is self-sufficient, the attainment of requisite resources often becomes a foreign policy objective. Historically, the necessity for resources was often a prime motivating force for territorial acquisition or colonialism. Today this direct method is much less fashionable and alternative techniques are usually used.

The most often used method is simply to negotiate a trade agreement. Most states must rely on trade to obtain resources since they need them, do not have them, and cannot get them any other way. Because there presumably are mutual benefits involved in any trade agreement each party has a stake in maintaining friendly relations. However, the degrees of dependence and vulnerability will affect the nature of this stake.[23] Sometimes, since the transportation facilities needed to bring the resources from a foreign country to one's own are so important, control of these facilities becomes critical. British and French dependency on the Suez Canal as a trade route was certainly a major factor in their 1956 decision to attack Egypt.[24]

---

[22]In mid-1960 Belgium began to withdraw from its African colony, the Belgian Congo. Immediately, civil war developed. Belgian paratroopers returned to restore order, and this led the Congolese "government" to request UN assistance. A United Nations Congo force was created to replace the Belgians but it was soon caught up in a civil conflict as several Congolese factions sought power. The situation was made worse as the Soviets and Americans turned it into a Cold War as well as a nationalist-colonialist issue. For a perceptive analysis see Ernest W. Lefever, *Uncertain Mandate: Politics of the UN Congo Operation,* Johns Hopkins, Baltimore, 1967.

[23]Trade can also be used as a weapon. See the discussion in Chapter 4, pp. 132–136.

[24]This was not the only reason, however. The British perceived Egypt's President Nasser to be a threat to British influence throughout the entire Middle East (which he was) and Prime Minister Eden called him another Hitler. The French saw Nasser as a threat to their interests not only in the Middle East but in North Africa as well.

Policymakers may strive to reduce interdependence and vulnerability via domestic programs. First, they may engage in extensive exploration of their own country hoping to discover heretofore untapped resources. Second, sometimes natural or synthetic substitutes can be devised. Third, various new processes are sought, perhaps increasing the yield of existing resources, using lower quality resources, or providing for a combination of resources into new materials.

Nations will vary widely in their ability to adjust to the rising demands for materials. They differ in the degree to which they possess the basic essentials, and in their capacity to develop and use them. They differ in their capacity to supplement whatever deficiencies they may have from foreign sources, and in their domestic ability to find alternatives. Finally, they differ in the degree to which they can make the resources which they do have, whether through possession or access, invulnerable to action by their adversaries. The policymaker must carefully analyze each of these factors.

The Big Three

Although it is not possible to discuss in detail the significance of all natural resources, it would be highly useful to analyze briefly the fundamental resources without which a country simply cannot become a strong economic power: coal, iron and petroleum.[25] For over 100 years *coal* has been by far the world's most important source of energy. Without abundant coal the Soviet Union's industrialization would have been much more difficult, and coal formed the bedrock of the industrial structure of modern Germany. Britain's industrial dominance in the 19th century rested upon a long lead in the utilization of good quality and relatively accessible coal, and the pace of American industrialization has been achievable partly because of its immense coal reserves.

Coal is important first because of the fact that it is the primary fuel for the production of various ores. Second, coal-fired boilers generate a large part of the world's electricity. Third, in many areas of the world its steam is still used to propel ships and railway locomotives. And fourth, in some areas it has become a primary raw material in a wide range of chemical industries. Because of the political problems involved in obtaining petroleum today it is quite possible that coal will become even more essential in the future.[26]

A second critical resource is *iron*. There is no way to develop a modern industrial society without great quantities of iron because without it one cannot develop a strong steel industry, and steel production is one of the major indicators of the overall strength of an economy. In addition to pure steel production, a wide variety of alloys (in which iron is combined with other metals) are

---

[25]This discussion is heavily influenced by Sprout and Sprout, pp. 286−290.

[26]Although petroleum limitations may hinder the use of coal since much of the machinery used in obtaining coal requires petroleum to function.

critically important today, alloys designed to increase the toughness, resiliency, and durability of the metals.

A third major natural resource is *petroleum*. A modern economy just cannot run without oil nor can a modern war machine with its concomitant mechanized weaponry and vehicles. The Middle East is the world's largest oil producing area and contains approximately 60 percent of the world's published proven oil reserves.[27] The dependence of the non-Communist world on Middle East petroleum is staggering. Japan, for example, obtains over 90 percent of its oil from there, Western Europe more than 60 percent. The United States, too, is a major importer of Middle Eastern petroleum, currently acquiring nearly one-fourth the oil it uses from that area.[28] Because petroleum is so crucial to modern economic life the Middle East is bound to be an area of immense importance in the coming decades.

Let us conclude this section by suggesting that one place an analysis of the particular situation within the general framework of our discussion, answering the following questions with respect to each party:

1. What resources does it need?
2. What does it possess, in terms of quantity, quality, variety, and accessibility?
3. Can it develop what it has?
4. Does it have control over its resources?
5. How vulnerable and dependent is it on foreign sources?
6. Can it find alternatives, internationally or domestically?
7. To what extent, and how, will resource deficiencies limit its immediate, middle-range, and long-run capability, particularly in the area of economic productivity?

ECONOMIC STRENGTH

A prime element of capability is economic strength. Traditionally, its importance has been explained by its close association with and influence on military capacity. In this respect the degree of industrialization is critical. The well-known authority, Hans Morgenthau, states:

> The technology of modern warfare and communications has made the overall development of heavy industries an indispensable element of national power. . . .
> Thus it is inevitable that the leading industrial nations should be identical with the great powers, and a change in industrial rank, for better or for worse, should be accompanied or followed by a corresponding change in the hierarchy of power.[29]

[27] See James A. Bill and Robert W. Stookey, *Politics and Petroleum: The Middle East and the United States,* King's Court Communications, Brunswick, Ohio, 1975, pp. 100–103.

[28] Derived from U.S., Department of State, *The Trade Debate,* Washington, D.C., May 1978.

[29] Morgenthau, *Politics Among Nations,* Fifth Edition, pp. 119–120.

This is an oversimplification, however. The military instrument of policy has a wide range of potential uses, only one of which is fighting a conventional war of considerable duration, the type of "modern" warfare scenario that he envisages. Granted, in this respect the argument is valid and is thus pertinent to many situations.

But there are others to which it is inappropriate. For the development of nuclear strength one could argue that the relative degree of industrialization is important but not determinative because a moderately developed economy with technological expertise and a solid financial base might be sufficient. Even more significant is the fact that many of the uses of the military instrument involve various types of limited or sublimited war.[30] These activities often do not require a high level of economic development. Thus although the concept of economic war-potential is relevant to some cases, it must be analyzed in light of the specific situation and evaluated accordingly.[31] None of this is to deny the relationship of economic and military power, but only to point out the complexity of the relationship.

Economic strength today is critically significant in its own right. First, the mere existence of a powerful economy exercises an influence because of its potential impact.[32] The United States economy's potential as a market, for example, will inevitably influence the policies of some states. Similarly, its immense productive capacity automatically makes it a potential threat to competitors or a possible source of goods, services, and capital.

Beyond mere existence, however, lies the realm of economic policy techniques (discussed more fully in Chapter 4). States often use economic tools to seek to achieve their objectives, and the stronger the economy the more varied and credible the options. One cannot effectively promise a program of technical or financial assistance if it cannot be given, nor can he threaten deprivation without the strength to deprive.

Agricultural Capacity

A major component of economic strength, and one that sometimes receives insufficient attention, is agricultural capacity. One can view the process of economic development as the shift from an agricultural to an industrial economy. This shift cannot be accomplished, however, unless and until each agricultural worker produces enough food to allow others to be set free to participate in the modernization process (unless one is dependent on foreign sources, a very risky situa-

---

[30]See Chapter 4, pp. 149−157.

[31]See Klaus Knorr, *Military Power and Potential,* D. C. Heath, Lexington, Mass., 1970, pp. 19−20.

[32]The performance of American industry in World War II and its potential for the postwar period had a significant impact on Stalin's policies. See Adam B. Ulam, *The Rivals: America and Russia Since World War II,* Viking, New York, 1971, Ch. 1.

tion). If a state is not self-sufficient or nearly so in food production, it is at a great disadvantage relative to those that are.

When a policymaker seeks to analyze agricultural capacity where does he begin? The first question one should ask is, can the state produce enough food to feed itself? Great Britain has been in serious jeopardy in wartime because she produces less than one half of the food she needs. Historically this required that she have a great navy to protect the sea lanes over which her vital food supplies were shipped. Today she must rely on NATO forces and Uncle Sam in time of peril.

The lack of self-sufficiency makes such countries very vulnerable. In many areas of the world people live close to subsistence and famines are common. Among the potentially great powers at this time both India and China must constantly face this threat.

The second major facet is agricultural productivity. Many states are able to produce enough food to feed their population but only through the overemployment of resources in agricultural activities. This is a major problem today in many of the "have not" nations of the world. Many times great powers are also confronted with this misutilization of resources. For example, approximately 30 percent of the Soviet Union's labor force is involved in agricultural production as compared to about 5 percent for the United States. If the Soviets were able to transfer this 25 percent differential to industrial, consumer, and service pursuits they would be able to vastly increase economic productivity.

In analyzing the questions of insufficient absolute production and low productivity one must also look at the probabilities of changes. To what extent is the soil of this particular country capable of producing much greater quantities and higher qualities of food? Is the climate such that this could occur? Through the use of various fertilizers, irrigation schemes, better qualities of seed and plant, better management, more efficient organization, and the application of higher levels of skill and knowledge, is it possible for these states with agricultural difficulties to overcome to some extent their agricultural problems?[33]

Economic Development

The real key to economic strength is encompassed by what is usually called economic "modernization" or economic "development."[34] Highly modernized or developed economies are characterized by a high degree of economic differentiation, a complex division of labor, highly organized and standardized

[33]One should note the fact that due to rapidly increasing population it is quite possible that even if food production and productivity are increased, in many of the most populaced parts of the world this may be insufficient to sustain what is already a very substandard level of existence.

[34]The processes of development and modernization are complex and composed of many interrelated factors only one of which is the economic. The most useful introduction to the general subject is Cyril E. Black, *The Dynamics of Modernization,* Harper, New York, 1966.

production systems, machinery being the major element of work energy, high levels of productivity, and high levels of total output.

How does a policymaker determine the degree to which a particular economy is developed? Unfortunately there are several indicators and there are serious difficulties associated with each. In addition, one runs into data problems. Many governments do not keep accurate national accounts and some hide or distort information that could be unfavorably construed. Despite these obstacles there is enough information to get a general idea of strength, and if one uses a combination of various economic indicators he can get a reasonably accurate picture.

The first standard is *gross national product* (GNP). GNP is an indicator of the total output of a given economy at market price, thus being a measure of production not potential. As such it reflects total output in all areas, and all changes in consumption, investment, and military or other governmental expenditures would be reflected. Relative GNPs provide a useful place to start any comparison because they indicate comparative magnitudes of strength and the limitations on a particular country's capability to support internal and external political commitments.[35]

There are, however, several difficulties with using GNP data. In the first place, unpaid labor such as occurs in households, and the value of goods exchanged via barter (which occurs to a great extent in less developed and some Socialist economies) are not included. Second, because GNP figures are based on monetary value they may not reflect the true contribution of any particular segment of the economy to that country's political commitments. For example, what is the true value of the motion picture industry to the capability of the United States? Another problem is that when one is comparing economies it is difficult to translate prices from one economic system to another because of the nature of the different systems and currencies. Prices may be artificially set and the official ratio between currencies may not reflect their actual value relationship. Despite all this, however, it is still useful to convert various country's GNPs to a common basis and make some comparisons.

An examination of current GNP data shows that the United States is by far the world's strongest economic power, alone accounting for nearly one-fourth of world GNP.[36] If United States' production is combined with that of its NATO allies the sum is a figure approaching 50 percent, and if Japan is added the proportion exceeds one-half. Looking at Western Europe as a whole, the coun-

[35]As always, identifying the parties in a situation is important. With respect to relative GNPs the question becomes "relative to whom?" Although Japan's GNP is of moderate size relative to that of the United States it is overwhelmingly larger than its regional competitors in East Asia. On the possible implications of this point see Donald C. Hellman, *Japan and East Asia: The New International Order*, Praeger, New York, 1972.

[36]Data for this and the succeeding paragraph are derived from U.S., Department of State, *Special Report: The Planetary Product "Back to Normalcy" in 1976–77*, June 1978.

Table 3   GNP, Selected States, 1976

State	GNP (in U.S. $billions)
United States	1,706.50
U.S.S.R.	857.00
Japan	538.65
W. Germany	422.03
France	335.63
China (PRC)	249.10
United Kingdom	215.13
Canada	159.18
Brazil	111.00
India	101.40
Poland	92.24
Australia	79.70
Iran	68.70
E. Germany	66.16
Sweden	64.98
Czechoslovakia	57.95
Saudi Arabia	48.90
Switzerland	46.32
Argentina	40.73
Indonesia	34.00
Denmark	32.82
Venezuela	32.20
South Africa	31.89
Nigeria	30.40
Norway	25.99
Libya	14.00
Egypt	13.00
Israel	12.20
Chile	10.40
Bangladesh	9.9
Cuba	8.9
Ghana	4.60
Zambia	3.00
Syria	2.60
Somalia	0.2

SOURCE: U.S. Department of State, *The Planetary Product "Back to Normalcy" in 1976–1977*, June 1978, pp. 30–36.

tries comprising the European Communities produce nearly 20 percent of the world GNP. The Communist states constitute another major economic force, accounting for about 22 percent. It is evident that the relatively few states included in the above categories produce an overwhelming percentage of the earth's goods and services; the converse is also true, that the vast majority of the countries produce only a miniscule proportion.

The policymaker must analyze not only current GNP but also trends and changes. Four features of today's world economy are especially interesting in this regard. First, the Soviet Union no longer is gaining on the United States, the GNP ratio having remained about 2 : 1 in Washington's favor since 1970. Second, the major oil-exporting states of OPEC (the Organization of Petroleum Exporting Countries) achieved almost unbelievable growth in the 1973–1976 period. Though this has now leveled off somewhat, their growth rates are still the world's highest. Third, Japan's GNP continues to expand more rapidly than that of any other industrialized state. And fourth, many of the poorer states are now growing more rapidly than some of the industrialized countries. There is an important caveat to be remembered here though. Because the base on which poor states build is very small, in many cases even though their rate of growth exceeds that of some of the developed countries their absolute deficit in GNP continues to increase.

A second major indicator of the degree of development is *gross national product per capita*. There are tremendous differences in this regard as Table 4 indicates. Two points are especially pertinent here. First, the immense gap between the rich and poor states is actually *increasing* despite the fact that the less developed countries (LDCs) are growing. Most of the LDCs are the same states that are suffering the pangs of overpopulation discussed earlier in the chapter, and the prospects for narrowing the gulf in the near future are not bright.[37] A second point is that even within the general category of the developed states there are significant disparities in GNP per capita; American GNP per capita is over twice that of the Soviet Union, for example.

The policymaker must remember, though, that production per capita figures do not automatically reflect economic strength for foreign policy objectives because different economies allocate economic resources differently and for a tightly controlled economy the precise per capita figures may not be that important. The Soviet Union, for example, was able to compete with the United States in a strategic arms race in the late 1950s despite the fact that its per capita production was considerably less than that of the United States.

A third major standard of economic development is *energy production and consumption* (see Table 5). This indicator includes all energy sources: coal, oil, nuclear power, solar energy, hydro-electric power, and natural gas. No nation can develop and operate a modern industrialized economy without a great supply of energy. It is useful in this regard again to consider gross as well as per capita figures. This is particularly true with regard to the People's Republic of China where per capita consumption is low but over the last few years total production has increased rapidly.

Another significant measure of economic development is *steel production*

---

[37]Some argue that this widening gap portends disasters that threaten to engulf not only the less developed states but the rich countries as well. See Charlotte Waterlow, *Superpowers and Victims: The Outlook for World Community,* Prentice-Hall, Englewood Cliffs, N.J., 1974.

Table 4   GNP Per Capita, Selected States, 1975, and Average Real Growth Rates, 1960–1975 and 1970–1975

State	P.C. GNP (in $)	Growth Rates % 1960–1975	Growth Rates % 1970–1975
Switzerland	8410	2.6	0.7
Sweden	8150	3.1	2.3
United States	7120	2.5	1.6
Canada	6930	3.6	3.3
Denmark	6810	3.5	1.7
Norway	6760	3.6	3.3
W. Germany	6670	3.5	1.9
France	5950	4.2	3.4
Australia	5700	3.1	2.4
Libya	5530	10.5	3.9
Japan	4450	7.7	4.0
Saudi Arabia	4010	6.6	4.1
E. Germany	3910	3.2	3.7
Israel	3790	5.2	4.0
United Kingdom	3780	2.2	2.0
Czechoslovakia	3610	2.7	3.0
Poland	2600	4.0	5.8
U.S.S.R.	2550	3.8	3.1
Venezuela	2280	2.2	1.5
Iran	1660	8.1	13.3
Argentina	1550	3.1	2.9
South Africa	1270	2.3	1.7
Brazil	1030	4.3	6.2
Chile	990	1.3	−2.7
Cuba	800	−0.6	1.0
Syria	720	2.2	1.8
Ghana	590	−0.2	−0.3
Zambia	420	2.0	0.9
China (PRC)	380	5.2	5.3
Nigeria	340	3.4	5.3
Egypt	260	1.5	1.3
Indonesia	220	2.4	3.5
India	140	1.3	0.5
Somalia	110	−0.3	−0.2
Bangladesh	90	−0.6	−2.3

SOURCE: World Bank, *World Bank Atlas: Population, Per Capita Product, and Growth Rates,* Washington, 1977, p. 6.

Table 5   Energy Production and Consumption, Selected States

	Production Total		Consumption Total		Consumption Per Capita	
	1972	1975	1972	1975	1972	1975
World	8031	8555	7477	8002	2000	2028
United States	2167	2037	2428	2350	11624	10999
U.S.S.R.	1386	1650	1205	1411	4870	5546
China	470	597	456	570	580	693
Saudi Arabia	448	530	7.5	12.5	912	1398
W. Germany	171	166	337	330	5461	5345
Nigeria	134	131	4	6	70	90
India	91	115	107	132	191	221
Indonesia	85	103	19	24	154	178
E. Germany	80	81	106	115	6220	6835
Japan	45	37	378	402	3568	3622
Brazil	21	25	53	72	546	670
Egypt	16	13	11	15	321	405
Bangladesh	0.82	0.69	2.02	2.18	28	28
Zaire	0.55	0.65	1.95	1.95	85	78

Quantities in million metric tons of coal equivalent and kilograms per capita

SOURCE: *UN Statistical Yearbook, 1976*, pp. 372−376.

(see Table 6). Steel is a basic ingredient in nearly all heavy industrial and military goods. To some extent steel production is a measure of flexibility because often it can be shifted relatively easily from civilian to military uses and vice versa. One must also remember that although steel in its simplest form is an alloy of iron and carbon, in the last 50 to 100 years scores of alloys have been developed in which steel is combined with other elements to produce materials that have a much greater strength, resistance to corrosion, hardness, or other desired properties. As Table 6 clearly demonstrates, there is a tremendous disparity between a very few states and the rest of the world in this area also.

A final indicator of economic development is the *percentage of the nation's labor force engaged in nonagricultural work*. As mentioned earlier, until a nation is able to produce sufficient food for its population and do so with reasonable efficiency it cannot release the resources necessary for modernization. If it is required to employ over half of its labor force in agricultural work it is unlikely to be very modernized and indeed, this is precisely what all the evidence shows.

Allocation of Resources

Another issue of primary importance is analyzing economic capability is the question of the allocation of resources. Who gets what part of the pie? Policymakers in all countries are faced with rising demands from a wide variety

Table 6   Crude Steel Production, Selected States

State	1966	1970	1975
World	475,700	593,900	643,000
U.S.S.R.	96,907	115,889	141,328
United States	121,655	119,309	105,817
Japan	47,784	93,322	102,313
W. Germany	35,315	45,040	40,414
China	16,000	18,000	29,000
France	19,585	23,773	21,528
United Kingdom	24,706	28,316	20,198
Brazil	3,782	5,390	8,306
India	6,660	6,286	7,884
E. Germany	4,485	5,053	6,480

Production figures in thousand metric tons

SOURCE: *UN Statistical Yearbook, 1976*, p. 320.

of sources and have insufficient resources to meet them. Therefore decisions must be made concerning which demands are to be met and which are not, and the degree to which those demands that are to be met will be satisfied. Although there are a wide variety of possible categories of allocation, for our purposes the most useful are personal consumption, capital formation, and government expenditures (subdivided into military and nonmilitary).

In all nations there is *a conflict between demands for a rapid improvement in the standard of living, that is, immediate personal consumption, and the necessity for new capital formation* (investment in productive capacity to bring about future economic development). States whose economies are primarily consumer oriented leave a smaller proportion of their resources available for economic growth and development. The significance of this fact depends, of course, partly on the degree of consumer orientation.

It also depends on the absolute level of development a state has already obtained. Although one cannot stipulate the relationship with mathematical certainty, it is essentially true that the higher the rate of investment in fixed capital the higher the rate of increase in gross national product. New capital can be obtained from domestic or external sources but most of it must come from savings in the domestic economy. In a highly developed economy the rate of capital investment need not be particularly high because there is already a high level of capital development. In other words, the rate of investment may be small but the absolute level of investment could still be considerable.

In a less developed country, however, a very high rate of capital investment as well as large absolute quantities will be required.[38] The problem is that there

_____

[38]For an excellent introduction to this problem of economic development in the less developed countries, see Lester B. Pearson, *Partners in Development,* Praeger, New York, 1969. A highly

simply are not sufficient domestic savings available to provide the necessary capital for rapid economic growth. How can the less developed countries save 10 to 15 percent of their national income per year when annual per capita income may be no more than a couple of hundred dollars (or even less)?

The problems of economic growth for less developed countries are magnified by the facts that these are usually the regions in which population pressure is the highest, where economic infrastructures are seldom adequate (marketing, distribution, transportation, and communications systems, etc.), technological levels are low, skills and technical talents are largely nonexistent, and the vast majority of the labor force is employed in subsistence agriculture. Often difficulties are compounded by the fact that such states are also dependent on foreign sources for their cash income, being primarily one-product economies.

In many of these countries the inhabitants have become aware of the advancements of technologically developed economies, have recently become independent, believe that they were unjustly held back by colonial powers, and demand the economic benefits that exist elsewhere. This is part of what is called the "revolution of rising expectations." Yet given the lack of domestic capital and these other economic handicaps, even with considerable external economic assistance it is highly doubtful that in the foreseeable future rapid economic progress can be made.

But the policymaker usually seeks external assistance because there is little alternative. The other presumed options are to increase production and/or reduce consumption. The reduction of consumption is hardly feasible since "by definition" one is talking about countries with extremely low per capita consumption. And one cannot simply wave a magic wand and increase production because that is the very problem, the problem that production cannot be increased. The problem is right at the beginning; capital begets capital but how does one get it in the first place?

Another allocation question concerns *government expenditures.* In analyzing this factor one is concerned with the relationship of government expenditure to national economic output, the role of the government in terms of controlling and directing production, the wisdom with which it participates in and/or manages the economy, the extent of participation and management, and the degree to which government expenditures are allocated to military purposes.

In all societies today governments play a major economic role. Policymakers are confronted with increasing demands for more and better social programs and services, and for protection of the environment as well as for a higher standard of living. One must balance these against demands for capital formation and for resources for external commitments, including those of military defense and military related activities.

---

useful anthology that focuses on the interrelated factors in development and the difficulty of ascertaining the most effective approach is Frank Tachau, ed., *The Developing Nations: What Path to Modernization,* Dodd Mead, New York, 1974.

The proportion of gross national product allocated to military purposes varies considerably from country to country and over time.[39] In terms of absolute dollar equivalents, in 1977 Saudi Arabia had the highest per capita expenditure for military purposes, nearly twice as much as the second-ranked state. With respect to the percentage of gross national product devoted to military expenditures, Israel led the way with nearly 30 percent followed by Syria at around 16.4 and Jordan at 15.5. Concerning expenditures by the superpowers the Soviet Union annually spends about 11 to 13 percent of its GNP on defense whereas the United States spends approximately 6 percent of American GNP. Turning to the European theater, most of the NATO countries spend in the 3 to 5 percent range as do their counterparts in the Warsaw Pact (excluding the Soviets). It should also be pointed out that there is a distinct upward trend in military expenditures in much of the Third World, resulting in the noneconomic use of scarce resources. This both diminishes current consumption and prevents the use of such resources for investment purposes and thus future economic development.

The statistics of military allocation provide some indication of the general scale of a country's military efforts. The rapidly increasing costs of not only direct participation in warfare but also the maintenance of large standing military forces, of research and development, of producing and testing highly sophisticated weapons, and perhaps of maintaining a military presence and supporting military forces overseas, may become so prohibitive that they will become increasingly unsupportable for many countries.

The discussion of economic strength can be closed with the reiteration of a couple of points made previously. First, while it is true that no single component of capability is the only determinant of national power, economic strength is obviously a critical element. Second, one must remember that economic capability is significant not only because of its impact on the states' potential for military activity, but also in its own right.

MILITARY STRENGTH

Another factor the policymaker must investigate is military strength, today perhaps the most controversial of all capability components. Nowhere is it more true that one must analyze capability with respect to the specific policy context in which he is operating, and assess capability in relation to the particular objectives and conditions thereof. There are many situations in which the utility of military power is much less than one would expect from mere assessment of its components.[40] Despite this fact and while not underestimating its importance, the policymaker must recognize that the essence of the existence of independent

---

[39]The data below is drawn from the International Institute for Strategic Studies, *The Military Balance, 1978–1979*, London, 1978, pp. 88–89.

[40]See Chapter 2, pp. 51–52.

states is their capacity to make their own decisions, and these decisioñs often involve judgments about the potential or actual use of military force. Wars of various kinds *do* occur and statesmen *do* sometimes decide to risk conflict or engage in violence. Thus the policymaker must always take into account the military potential of all of the parties to a given situation and the possibility that force will be used.

Quantitative and Distributive Aspects

Part of the policymaker's assessment of military strength involves a consideration of quantitative and distributive factors. In this regard he is concerned with such questions as the size of forces in being, the number of bases, the types and numbers of weapons, and so forth. A simple determination of the military manpower possessed by the Soviet Union, the United States, or the People's Republic of China gives some indication of military strength.[41] A comparison of such quantitative factors is often useful. Even if the Burmese army of 153,000 was well trained and equipped with extremely sophisticated weaponry, its relative size deficiency of nearly 2.8 million compared to the army of the People's Republic of China would be impossible to overcome in combat. This points out the fact that the policymaker is not concerned with absolute figures in the abstract but rather with comparing the strength of his or her country's forces (and those of its allies) with those of its potential adversary(ies).

But such gross figures are far from the whole story. When analyzing quantitative factors one must develop meaningful categories. As one gathers data on air forces, for example, it is not just how many bombers, but how many of what kind? Which fighters are designed primarily for offensive operations, and how many are interceptors? Not only how many missiles, but how many of what range, what payload, located where, how reliable, how vulnerable, and so on.

When examining forces in being one must also be concerned with the distribution among the various branches. How large, for example, is the army as compared to the navy or air force? The relevance of this distinction is illustrated by the case of China. Even a cursory examination shows that Peking's naval and air forces are clearly insufficient to allow it to be a conquest threat (at this point in time) to anyone other than its land neighbors.[42] A significant concentration of personnel in any branch has direct and obvious implications for capability and strategy.

When analyzing various states' armed forces the policymaker faces serious problems of comparability. Not only are there differences in the distribution of

---

[41]In 1978 the U.S. had 2,068,800 in its armed forces, the U.S.S.R. 3,638,000 and China 4,325,000. International Institute for Strategic Studies, *The Military Balance, 1978–1979,* pp. 5, 8, 56.

[42]See Ibid., pp. 55–57.

personnel and weapons among branches, the mix within each branch is considerably different. How does one compare bombers and missiles, or armored and infantry divisions? Even when trying to compare like categories one finds equivalence hard to determine. For example, if one is comparing infantry divisions, how does he take into account the fact that divisions are structured differently in different countries?[43] Despite these difficulties, of course, the policymaker must still attempt to assess quantitative and distributive factors.

Some observers have stated that military capabilities should be assessed on the basis of forces in being rather than in terms of estimates of potential.[44] This view seems to imply that any war will be over quickly, and thus the quantities of personnel and equipment only potentially available are largely irrelevent. Just as the assumption that most wars will be of considerable duration is an oversimplification, the assumption of decisively fought short wars, perhaps with nuclear weapons, also is too all-encompassing. Many wars occur between lesser powers and take on many of the aspects of a war of attrition, similar in some aspects to a conventional conflict like World War II. Also, it is possible for wars to occur between great powers and lesser powers in which the great power, for whatever reason, decides not to fully use its capability and becomes involved in a long standing conflict (Korea, Vietnam). Furthermore, it has been speculated that even confrontations among the great powers might be somewhat conventional. This was one basis for NATO's adoption of the doctrine of Flexible Response, attempting to provide some conventional options and not require an automatic response with nuclear weapons.[45] Finally, there are many conflict situations involving guerilla activities that involve the use of forces and resources for a considerable length of time; in these cases forces in being are not decisive at all.

To the extent that any of these longer contingencies are realistic another factor must enter the equation, namely, mobilization potential.[46] In analyzing this factor the policymaker must take into account several factors mentioned earlier: the military age structure of the population, its size, male-female ratios, and educational and skills levels. One must also examine the state's capacity to organize and allocate its resources effectively, and its morale and leadership qualities. Critically important in this regard is the economic base. In the discussion of economic capability it was stated that the relevance of economic strength to military capacity varies with the kind of conflict, and that in some situations the relationship may not be significant.[47] It is equally true, however, that in other cases it is. The question is: "Does this party have the overall capacity to support a sustained war?" The lack of such capacity has done much to influence Israel's

---

[43]The problem of establishing equivalence is at the crux of many disagreements about disarmament. The term "asymmetry" is often used to describe the lack of equivalence.

[44]See Legg and Morrison, p. 126.

[45]For further discussion of "flexible response" see Chapter 6, pp. 216–217.

[46]For an excellent introduction to the entire subject of military potential see Knorr, Ch. 2.

[47]See pp. 100–101.

military strategy. Tel Aviv's emphasis on firepower and mobility coupled with an offensive strategy is dictated by her presumed inability to sustain a war of attrition.

Qualitative Factors: Personnel

It should be obvious that the policymaker must go well beyond quantitative considerations into the general sphere of quality. Although the factors are somewhat overlapping, for purposes of analysis it is useful to subdivide qualitative considerations into the categories of personnel, the level of technological development, and leadership. The quality of the troops involved in a particular conflict may be decisive. In both 1967 and 1973 the superb quality and morale of the Israeli forces, fighting what they perceived to be wars for survival, more than offset the firepower of their Arab opponents. Perhaps even more to the point is the example of the success which the Viet Cong had against the immensely superior firepower of the United States in the Vietnam war. The Viet Cong's skill, their propensity to harmonize with the native population, their ability to make use of the geographical factors, their high morale and dedication, and their ability to gain critical information allowed them to neutralize Washington's vast technological advantages.[48]

Qualitative Factors: Technological

Another critically important component of military strength is the level of technological development. Wars have often been decided by the technological factor. Strategic breakthroughs are sought as states spend enormous sums for research and development.

All policymakers would like to have the technological advantage. When Israel purchased American F-4 Phantom jets and used them to counter Egyptian artillery in the war of attrition in 1969 and 1970, they achieved a technological advantage. This led to an Egyptian request for Soviet surface-to-air missiles and a later generation of MIG fighter interceptors to counter the Israeli edge.

Today the development of modern weaponry as a result of scientific and technological advances is enough to stagger the mind. The explosion of one nuclear warhead in the one megaton range would make a hole almost 300 feet deep and a half mile across.[49] Everything in the immediate area would be destroyed and a huge fireball would develop. Within four or five miles all combustibles would ignite and any humans that survived would be hideously burned. All

---

[48]One must always remember, however, that the United States acted within certain self-imposed limitations, such as the nonuse of nuclear weapons.

[49]A megaton (MT) is equivalent to one million tons of TNT. This is the size of the warhead carried by the American Minuteman II land-based intercontinental ballistic missile (ICBM). The Soviets have deployed the SS-9, which can carry a 25-MT warhead.

structures in this area would be destroyed and various materials would cut through the air like bullets. Windstorms of hurricane velocity would develop as would devastating soundwaves. Radiation would be horrendous and be spread over the miles by the wind. No one knows precisely what the genetic effects would be on the survivors nor what areas would remain uninhabitable due to radioactivity.[50]

This description is briefly illustrative of what might occur with only a single megaton blast. Suppose a larger attack occurred. An American submarine armed with Poseidon missiles today conveys more firepower (in terms of TNT equivalents) than was dropped by all of the Allied air forces on Germany in World War II. The noted defense analyst, Herman Kahn, speculates about deaths of 2 to 160 million, the continuing genetic impact of nuclear war, and then states that military planners should understand the importance of being able to accept retaliatory blows in the sense of being able to distinguish among 2 million, 5 million, 20 million, 50 million, and 100 million American or Soviet deaths.[51]

Today both the Soviet Union and the United States possess nuclear striking forces of frightening potential.[52] Diagrams 2 and 3 give a simple quantitative comparison of the number of missiles potentially available to each and the quantitative changes that have occurred since the early 1960s. Table 7 provides a more elaborate breakdown, presenting information on not only the quantity of missiles potentially available but also on other critical factors such as the number of deliverable warheads, equivalent megatonnage, and throw-weight.

It is obvious that determining equivalence is enormously difficult. Although the Soviets have more and bigger missiles that carry larger warheads, because of the fact that the United States has MIRVed all its Minuteman III ICBMs and many of its Poseidon SLBMs while the Soviets (at this stage) have most of their missiles deployed in either a single warhead or MRV mode, the United States has many more warheads.[53] And there are still more factors to consider. For example, it is a generally accepted fact that in terms of the capacity to destroy

---

[50]Experiences following the atomic blasts on Hiroshima and Nagasaki have not yielded many conclusive answers. Also, because those blasts were so "small," about one-fiftieth of the size of which our analysis speaks, one cannot know if the situations would be comparable anyway. For a useful discussion of the possible consequences of a major nuclear attack see National Academy of Sciences, *Proceedings of the Symposium on Postattack Recovery from Nuclear War*, Washington, D.C., 1967.

[51]Herman Kahn, *On Thermonuclear War*, The Free Press, New York, 1969, pp. 20 and 472. A key question in all this is, how much is too much? What is the unacceptable level of damage necessary to deter? See Chapter 4, pp. 157–162, for further discussion.

[52]Britain, France, and China have small nuclear forces and other states possess the potential for such. See Chapter 4, pp. 146–147, and corresponding footnotes.

[53]MIRV is an acronym for Multiple Independently Targeted Re-entry Vehicle. It refers to a system of several warheads on one launcher, each warhead capable of being independently directed to a separate target. MRV warheads are all launched in a pattern by one missile and cannot be individually directed to separate targets.

Diagram 2   U. S. and U. S. S. R. ICBM Launchers (Inventory)

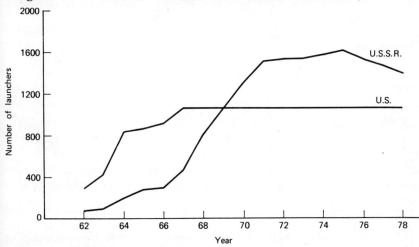

SOURCE: The International Institute for Strategic Studies, *The Military Balance, 1975—1976,* London, 1975, p. 73; *The Military Balance, 1976—1977,* London, 1976, p. 75; *The Military Balance, 1978—1979,* London, 1978, pp. 82–83.

Diagram 3   U. S. and U. S. S. R. SLBM Launchers (Inventory)

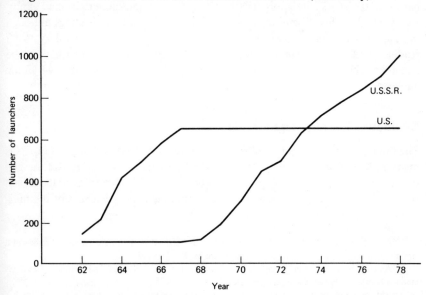

SOURCE: The International Institute for Strategic Studies, *The Military Balance, 1975—1976,* London, 1975, p. 73; *The Military Balance, 1976—1977,* London, 1976, p. 75; *The Military Balance, 1978—1979,* London, 1978, pp. 82–83.

Table 7   U.S.–U.S.S.R. Strategic Missile Balance, Mid–1976

	Number Deployed	Deliverable Warheads[a]	Equivalent Megatonnage[b]	Throw-Weight[c]
United States				
ICBM	1054	2154	1150	2.4
SLBM	656	5120	780	0.9
Total	1710	7274	1930	3.3
U.S.S.R.				
ICBM	1527	2195	2950	7.0
SLBM	845	845	845	1.3
Total	2372	3040	3795	8.3

SOURCE: The International Institute for Strategic Studies, *The Military Balance, 1976–1977,* London, 1976, pp. 73-77, 106-107. Details are solely the responsibility of the author, some modifications having been made.

[a] Individually targeted reentry vehicles; ICBM or SLBM with MRV are counted as having one warhead.

[b] This takes into account the fact that explosive force is exerted in all directions, some going up into the atmosphere and some "overdestroying" a very small area beneath. Equivalent megatonnage is a measure of area destroyed, usually expressed as two-thirds the power of its explosive yield.

[c] Throw-weight is the weight of the missile delivery package (warheads, guidance systems, penetration aids) at the end of the boost phase of flight. It is expressed in terms of millions of pounds at maximum range.

hardened targets (such as missile silos) accuracy is more important than explosive yield.[54] In this sphere the United States is believed to be leading, although the gap is narrowing. Other elements such as command and control systems, readiness, reliability, retargetability, target vulnerability, etc., also have to be taken into account.[55] When a policymaker seeks to analyze "capability" in the nuclear sphere he confronts a problem that almost defies comprehension.[56]

Qualitative Factors: Leadership

The final qualitative aspect of military capability is leadership. This encompasses many factors. It involves the degree to which leaders are able to bridge the gap between officers and regular soldiers and between various branches of the armed services as a whole. It concerns the quality and the appropriateness of the mili-

[54] Accuracy is usually measured in terms of Circular Error Probability, the estimated radius of a circle within which 50 percent of the warheads are expected to fall.

[55] And we have not even considered other weapons systems that might be involved such as manned bombers, shorter-range missiles, etc.

[56] Although it is reiteration, I again point out that what we are discussing here is the strength that a country could use if it should decide to do so. The question of its willingness to do so and the purposes for which its forces might be used will be handled in the analysis of the military instrument of policy. See Chapter 4, pp. 144–162.

tary training program. It includes the efficiency and the ability of the staff and command structure. It relates to the degree of receptivity toward innovation and change, the flexibility in military strategy and tactics, and the capacity to analyze and correctly assess military intelligence information. And finally, and critically, it involves correctly anticipating the type of conflict in which one is likely to be engaged, preparing one's forces adequately and appropriately to meet *that* kind of conflict, and following through with appropriate execution.[57]

There have been many failures in leadership strategy. Two quick examples will underline this point. First, the classic case of the Maginot line psychology of the French between World War I and World War II. The revolutionary effect of mobility on the tactics of war demonstrated at the end of World War I was not appreciated sufficiently by French policymakers. They therefore built a wall of steel and concrete between themselves and the Germans and neglected to develop their own mobile armored forces. The German General Staff, on the other hand, fully alive to the potentialities of armor, mobility, and heavy firepower, planned and later executed what became known as the lightning war (blitzkrieg). The onslaught of Hitler's Panzers and dive bombers against the French in World War II led to a devastating French defeat.

Another example occurred in the 1967 Arab-Israeli War. The Egyptian air force had a numerical superiority over Israel's. Unfortunately (for Cairo) its defensive strategy envisaged an Israeli attack from the East directly across the Sinai Peninsula and Egyptian radar was deployed accordingly. The Israelis circumvented this defense line with a series of strikes from the West, coming around behind the Egyptians and destroying nearly three-fourths of the Egyptian air force on the ground in the first two hours of the war. This defect in the Egyptian leadership cost them any possibility of winning. Of course, the reverse of the poor strategy is the good strategy. For examples one can simply point to the above cases, citing the brilliance of the German General Staff in the development of the blitzkrieg and the shrewdness of the Israeli air command in deciding on the routes of its attack on June 5, 1967.

The problem of the correct strategy is becoming more and more difficult to solve given the myriad of types of conflict that are possible and the fact that no country has unlimited resources. It is virtually impossible for a policymaker to be prepared to meet all contingencies and develop appropriate strategies to meet all possible types and levels of conflict. The best one can do is to analyze the likely possibilities, list them in terms of priorities, and develop appropriate strategies accordingly. Hopefully one anticipates correctly. If not, hopefully one has provided sufficient flexibility in his or her approach to at least partially counter unanticipated contingencies.

---

[57]One major difficulty of the American effort in Vietnam was that Washington trained the ARVN (SouthVietnamese) forces to fight a conventional war and thus they were ill-equipped to handle the guerilla tactics of the Viet Cong.

GOVERNMENTAL FUNCTIONS

Another major element of capability involves the forms, structures, and processes of government. The central concern in this regard is the degree to which the government can bring the country's potential capabilities to bear on the specific problem at hand, and the efficiency and dispatch with which this can be done. If policymakers cannot actualize potential capability, then such potential might as well not exist. If they can bring it to bear but only in a very inefficient manner, then they either will be less likely to achieve their objective, or do so only at a disproportionate cost. This is important at anytime but may be particularly crucial in short run crisis situations.[58]

Because no state possesses unlimited resources, allocation choices must be made. Decisions concerning the comparative merits of domestic and foreign policies are required, resulting in some resources being used for each type. Additionally, choices must be made among various external programs, which means that no single problem or project can be allocated more than a portion of the resources theoretically available for foreign affairs. How and to what extent does the organization and operation of the governmental system facilitate or hinder this decision-making?[59]

In examining these issues one must avoid oversimplified answers. It has sometimes been assumed that policymakers in authoritarian governments automatically possess major advantages compared to those in more democratic systems. It is postulated that they are not subject to public opinion constraints, are able to act with secrecy, speed, and decisiveness, are able to "shift gears" whenever appropriate, and are able to use whatever means they consider appropriate. Conversely, it is suggested that democracies fall short in these areas.

This argument has some degree of validity but entails major difficulties because it does not accurately describe the realities of the authoritarian policymaking process. It categorically assumes that the "advantages" noted above exist at all times but that is not so; sometimes they just are not there. Most of the time the differences between authoritarian and democratic systems in these areas are differences of *degree, not kind.*

All governments, for example, require some degree of acceptance by their populace to exist, and so policymakers are concerned with what people think. This may be less true in authoritarian systems than in democracies but it still is a

---

[58]Obviously the total of a state's resources is important as well as is their quality, as has been discussed in our analysis of the first five components of capability. But in the short run the governmental factor could be critical. It has been stated that, "in the short run, then, power differentials among·states in the international system stem much more from differential abilities to allocate resources to foreign policy pursuits than from differential endowments in basic resources." See Puchala, p. 181.

[59]Much of the analysis here is directly related to the problem of domestic constraints. For a more detailed analysis see Chapter 7 below.

factor of some importance. If an authoritarian government requires support from its people, then the "people's opinion" makes some difference. Sometimes an authoritarian rules by the sword, of course, but this is not common. And when he does it is only a mixed blessing because the more costs incurred in domestic political control the fewer resources available for foreign policy. It is true that sometimes resources *can* be allocated by fiat but if this is necessary it often leads to, or is a symptom of, considerable internal unrest.

Another point is that authoritarian governments as well as democracies are composed of congeries of people and interests that both compete and cooperate in the policymaking process, and this can lead to inefficiency, confusion, misdirected policies, and delays in both systems. Following the shooting down of an American U-2 spy plane by a Soviet rocket in May 1960, for example, there was great confusion in Moscow as to the appropriate response. An embarrassed public silence covered a variety of disagreements among various factions and decisions were postponed. It was not until the United States made a strong response almost inevitable by its public acknowledgement of guilt that Soviet policymakers reacted with vigor.[60]

Finally, the facade of unity that the outside world perceives often hides domestic power struggles. The mere existence of the Chinese Cultural Revolution of the mid-1960s was not apparent in the West until well after it had begun.[61] Similarly, most Americans were caught by surprise when Soviet Premier Khrushchev was ousted by comrades Brezhnev and Kosygin in 1964. In both of these cases foreign policy activity was hindered by domestic political struggles, just as domestic politics can hinder democratic foreign policy.

Despite these facts, however, it is still true that democratic policymakers are *relatively* less free to formulate and implement policy as they desire than are their authoritarian counterparts, and they often find it more difficult to act as rapidly. These difficulties have sometimes led to vast governmental efforts to deceive and mislead the populace, the obvious recent example being the contrast between the announced and actual American policies in Vietnam in most of the 1960s.[62]

---

[60]See Michael Tatu, *Power in the Kremlin: From Khrushchev to Kosygin,* Viking, New York, 1968, Ch. 2.

[61]In the mid-1960s a serious struggle for power developed in the Chinese Communist Party. Under Mao Tse-tung's leadership a great purge of Party and bureaucratic "reactionaries" was instituted. Thousands of youthful Red Guards spread Mao's slogans throughout the country, castigating the "imperialists" who were impeding the revolution. Unexpectedly strong resistance was encountered, however, and the entire party, military, and governmental structures were in turmoil. Serious fighting occurred in some areas and eventually the Red Guards themselves had to be curbed. Out of the chaos Mao emerged supreme but the Party was weakened and military interests became more important.

[62]We would again suggest starting with Halberstam and the Pentagon Papers. Also useful in this regard and generally with respect to the issue of American governmental deception, is Lincoln Bloomfield, *In Search of American Foreign Policy: The Humane Use of Power,* Oxford University Press, New York, 1974, pp. 99–112.

But this "difficulty" can also be an advantage if one assumes that a policy more responsive to the public will receive more support. Furthermore, more open systems tend to allow a greater interchange of concepts and data, presumably leading to more informed decisions. In addition, democratic structures supposedly tend to place more emphasis on individual initiative and creativity, which in turn should lead to more imaginative and innovative policies (although obviously it does not always work this way).

What conclusions can one draw so far? Perhaps only the negative one that no particular type of system is automatically more effective than any other. What this means for the policymaker is that he must get down to specific considerations and avoid *a priori* judgments resulting from mere system classification.

What are some of the key questions that need to be asked? *First, what are the actual components, formal and informal, of the political process in each target country?* It is obvious that the form of government alone does not dictate the nature of the political process, but it is also true that the particular structure does have an impact. Witness, for example, the United States system of checks and balances with an intermingling of functions. This means that no policymaker can ignore certain institutional features. The fact that foreign policy programs must be funded by Congressional appropriations means that an American policymaker must frame his policies with a wary eye on Capitol Hill.[63] All American treaties must be ratified by the United States Senate. Thus the President, if he is wise, will consult with the Senate and attempt to judiciously accommodate his policies to its views as President Carter did with respect to the Panama Canal Treaties. President Wilson's failure to do this led to the rejection of the Treaty of Versailles and the League of Nations at the end of World War I.[64]

Another question the policymaker must ask is *to what extent is this particular political system flexible, able to adjust to changing conditions?* Are there historical precedents that will eliminate or dictate certain options and objectives? Is there a prevailing ideology that is similarly rigidifying? Do the policymakers have their judgments largely determined by role perceptions that do not allow them freedom of activity, or by superior-subordinate relationships that prevent consideration of new ideas? Are the organizational processes such that particular groups have an inordinate influence over the policymaker to the extent that certain options will never be realistically considered? Do these and other considerations prevent or encourage innovation and creativity?

Another set of questions concerns the information gathering system. Is it such that adequate quantities of information can be obtained? Are the sources

---

[63]In 1973, after the signature of the Peace Agreements on Vietnam, the Congress voted to cut off funds for bombing in Cambodia. The President vetoed one bill, but under severe pressure for a further tightening of the purse strings agreed to end the bombing by August 15, 1973.

[64]Today, Presidents often resort to an "Executive Agreement" instead of a treaty since it has the same impact as a treaty but does not require Senatorial consent.

reliable? Is the data accurate and undistorted by misperception and incorrect interpretation? Can it be communicated effectively to the right people at the right time? Will it be used in an efficient manner so that a rational decision is likely to be made? Do bias and prejudice exist within the system that would prevent certain options from being realistically considered, and in some cases almost ensure that certain other factors will be taken as givens?

Finally, one must seek to determine if the government is organized in such a way that policymakers are able to provide the specific means of policy implementation that are appropriate for given objectives. In other words, to what extent are they able to translate potential into real power or prevented from doing so by the mere nonexistence of correct instrumentalities? For example, suppose a particular country has a highly diversified and highly differentiated modern economy with a strong industrial base. This mere existence gives this country a certain potential for action. If the economic strength cannot be utilized via its contribution to military and economic instruments of statecraft, however, instead being devoted to higher levels of domestic consumption, its contribution to that state's capability is limited.

There is no automatic answer to the question of governmental strength. Only by analyzing specific governmental components of the countries under consideration can one determine the degree to which policymakers may be organizationally able to translate capability potential into realizable power.

CHARACTERISTICS OF SOCIETY

Another component of capability is what one can call the characteristics of the domestic society: the degree of societal cohesiveness, and the degree of support that the government receives from its populace.

Degree of Cohesiveness

The degree of cohesiveness can have a significant impact on capability. Generally speaking, the more a society is fragmented the more attention, effort, and resources required to deal with this problem and the less available for foreign policy pursuits. Even when minorities are mercilessly crushed as in the case of the Nazi slaughter of six million Jews, the state is still diverting its attention and resources from foreign policy objectives.[65] Furthermore, the potential contribution of these groups is, of course, never actualized.

The causes and types of fragmentation are many and only a few can be discussed here. One is the existence of major *ethnic and racial differences;* these

---

[65]The Nazis argued that the result of the extermination of the Jews would be a strengthening of Germany, because the "backstabbers" would be removed. Although untrue in this instance, the principle could hold true in other cases.

often lead to conflict.[66] Whereas the United States became a "melting pot" and a variety of ethnic groups eventually melded into society (except for blacks and Indians), in the 1970s alone bloody civil wars based on ethnic disunity occurred in Chad, Pakistan, and the Sudan. In South Africa the minority white government continues to rule the black majority. In Iraq there are periodic violent conflicts between the majority Arabs and the Kurds as the latter seek independence. In World War II many Ukrainians joined the Nazis to fight against their Russian masters. Obviously these divisions are harmful to capability.

Religious differences too can cause disunity. In Lebanon the populace is about half Christian and half Islamic, and this factor has had a significant impact on Lebanese politics. In the 1958 crisis, for example, the country split largely along religious lines.[67] And the religious factor was very important in the 1975–1976 civil war. The original division of India and Pakistan, and the resulting wars, have been based on bitter Islamic-Hindu hostility. And we continue to witness the tragic dispute between Protestants and Catholics over the future of Northern Ireland.

In addition to subnational loyalties, groups may owe allegiance across national boundaries. Such *transnational attractions* can be terribly disruptive. The first example one thinks of is international communism, a world wide ideology, but there are others. Pan-Arabism was at the core of Egyptian President Gamal Nasser's policy in the mid and late 1950s, the idea that the Arabs are really all one people and existing territorial boundaries have no legitimate basis. The post World War II division of Germany and the development of Cold War blocs does not mean that all Germans have given up their desire for a unified country. Indeed, former West German Chancellor Brandt's phrase, "two German states within one German nation," shows the feeling of being one German people despite the political realities of the day. The division of Korea similarly does not eliminate a feeling of oneness and certain transnational attractions.

Despite the potentially disruptive effect of societal cleavages, one should not automatically assume that a severely fragmented society cannot have an effective foreign policy. Almost 45 percent of the Soviet Union is composed of ethnic minorities, many of whom bitterly dislike the majority Russians. Nevertheless, the U.S.S.R. is obviously a very powerful country.

Similarly, one cannot automatically assume that the existence of such cleavages will bring about the downfall of the government in times of crisis. In 1970 and 1971 there was violent civil conflict in Jordan between King Hussein's forces and various guerilla organizations. The population of Jordan was about two-thirds ex-Palestinian and many observers had assumed that if a crisis occurred the

---

[66]For a useful compilation of ethnic composition by continent and country see Sterling, Appendix D.

[67]On the religious issue see Michael C. Hudson, *The Precarious Republic: Political Modernization in Lebanon*, Random House, New York, 1968. The precise ratio is not known but non-Christians claim a majority.

Palestinians would revolt against the King. In actuality, when the conflict occurred the majority of the population simply ignored it.

The key questions the policymaker must ask in this regard are:

1. How much and what kind of disunity is there?
2. To what extent will its existence divert interest, attention, effort, and resources from foreign policy objectives?
3. How much would the country add to its capability if the problems were solved, and how much is it losing now?
4. Is the fragmentation likely to lead to policy alteration, regime change, or even civil war?
5. Is the country likely to "solve" the problem?
6. How vulnerable is the country to foreign penetration and influence because of this?
7. What should be the appropriate policy response?

Popular Support

The degree of unity is related to a larger issue, namely, the extent to which the populace supports the government and its policies. In analyzing this topic one must ask certain basic questions: First, and most obviously, is the general populace supportive, in opposition, or largely indifferent? Second, what is the attitude and strength of the various groups who are in a position to influence policymakers? Third, how intensely are the various opinions held, and how susceptible are they to change? Fourth, if there is compliance with the government's policies, is it largely voluntary or primarily the result of sanctions or fear? Fifth, if sanctions are being used, are they effective now and will they be in the future? Sixth, will the sanctions eventually drive the target groups into more concerted opposition to the government?

After analyzing these factors the policymaker turns to questions of time and relevancy. Is the present attitude one which is temporary or permanent? For example, is the American disenchantment with foreign policy and military entanglements flowing from the Vietnam War likely to continue beyond the early 1980s, or will it erode with the passage of time? Second, is this attitude one that applies to a broad range of issues or is it highly specific? Again using Vietnam as an example, is the American public inclined to adopt a "less involved" foreign policy as a general principle, or only to withdraw from involvement in Vietnam? Third, is this attitude directly pertinent to the specific problem under consideration?

The importance that popular support for governmental policies has sometimes had, and the difficulties when it has been lacking, can be amply documented. Certainly the disintegration of the support of the American people for continued involvement in Vietnam led to a weakening of the government's capability to achieve its stated objectives. The collapse of support by the Chinese people for Chiang Kai-shek's government was a significant contributor to Mao Tse-tung's rise to power.[68] The inability of the Saigon Government to obtain more than a modicum of public support was directly related to its inability to defeat its opponents despite massive American aid. Contrast these situations with the magnificent popular support that the English people gave their government in the Second World War, and the intense support of the Israeli populace against the Arabs in their various conflicts, and one can easily see how important it can be.

These, however, are dramatic and extreme cases. What about the more ordinary situation? Are there any guidelines one can follow that will help to answer the questions raised above? Perhaps there are. One should keep the following rules of thumb in mind:

1. Every government, to some extent, responds to domestic demands placed upon it by its populace. The more responsive it is, the more likely it is to be supported.
2. Every government has certain priorities among its objectives. The more important the objective, the more intensive will be the government's efforts to obtain popular support, and the more critical for that government that it be obtained.
3. The more the government's objectives and policies are consonant with the country's traditions, norms, belief system, and historical experience, the more likely they will receive support.
4. The smaller the discrepancy between the people's expectations of government and governmental achievement, the greater the support.

THE INDIVIDUAL POLICYMAKER

The final component of capability one must analyze is the impact of specific individual policymakers. It was said in Chapter 1 that the primary actor in international relations today is the nation-state. This is true. One must always remember, however, that when someone says that "Soviet Russia" is following such and such a policy, or "Egypt" reacted violently to this or that, he is speaking in metaphorical terms. In reality only human beings make decisions. The state does not take action; human beings act and make decisions in the name of the state. If one speaks then of the containment policy of the United States he is actually talking about a policy formulated by some specific individuals responsible for American foreign policy. What this means to the policymaker is that his analysis must include identification of the key personnel and an analysis of their specific characteristics.

---

[68]This is vividly described in U.S., Department of State, *United States Relations with China with Special Reference to the Period 1944−1949*, Washington, D.C., 1949. Also see Chapters 4 and 5, pp. 154−156, and 179−180.

Particular Characteristics

Ascertaining the particular characteristics of the individual decisionmaker is an important task because different individuals have different impacts upon a state's foreign policy. Obviously international politics is not just the interaction of so-called great men and women. It is also evident, however, that history shows that it *does* make a difference who occupies a position of influence at a particular time. It clearly made a difference when Hitler came to power in Germany, and no one doubts that Winston Churchill left a personal imprint on British foreign policy in World War II. Clearly Henry Kissinger's particular qualities significantly influenced the course of American policy.

One begins the process of identifying key policymakers by ascertaining the locus of the decision. Is there a key decisional unit, or is effective authority scattered among several agencies and groups? Then, within the context of his or her answers to these questions, the investigator must find out who are those particular human beings who are most influential in this area and whose authoritative acts are, for all intents and purposes, the acts of the state?[69] Obviously, one must obtain and accurately evaluate a great deal of information about the particular state under consideration in order to perform this task effectively.

The second step involves an assessment of the particular policymaker's basic personality structure.[70] What particular traits characterize his or her behavior and how relevant are they to his or her policymaking activities? Is the subject basically a trusting person or is he or she suspicious of everyone? Is he or she rational in most cases? How does this particular individual react to various kinds of stimuli? Are there certain patterns of behavior that characterize his or her actions in certain kinds of situations? Is this individual's personality such that everything must be interpreted in all-or-nothing terms in order for him or her to feel secure and confident, and are his or her fundamental beliefs therefore unshakable and absolute? Is the subject basically an insecure, outer-directed person? These and similar questions are particularly pertinent. Policymakers always make certain assumptions about the personalities of their counterparts, consciously or unconsciously, and such assumptions influence their behavior.[71]

Previous Experience

Another cluster of factors one must analyze can be combined under the label of previous experience. This could involve anything from childhood and teenage

[69]One of the most useful innovations in the study of political science is decisionmaking analysis. A particularly valuable introduction to this topic is, Richard C. Snyder, H. W. Bruck and Burton Sapin, eds., *Foreign Policy Decision Making,* Free Press of Glencoe, New York, 1963.

[70]The most useful introduction to this topic is Fred I. Greenstein, *Personality and Politics,* Markham, Chicago, 1969.

[71]One of the major factors determining Khrushchev's behavior in the early stages of the Cuban Missile Crisis was his perception of Kennedy as "weak." See John G. Stoessinger, *Nations in Darkness: China, Russia and America,* Third Edition, Random House, New York, 1978, Ch. 12.

experiences to social background and level of education, up through and including previous policymaking activity. Studies of Woodrow Wilson's childhood have argued, for example, that his later lack of perceptivity, his inability and/or unwillingness to compromise, and his messianic zeal were primarily the result of childhood influences, especially his relationship with his father.[72] If possible the policymaker should delve into his or her counterpart's early experiences to see if clues to his or her behavior can be discovered.

The simple fact of being alive in a certain time period and drawing certain "lessons" from the events of the day also can be important. Because the majority of American policymakers after World War II had lived through and "experienced" the results of the appeasement at Munich, there developed what has sometimes been thought of as the Munich complex, the idea that one cannot negotiate with an aggressor and a tough uncompromising approach must be taken against all who are perceived to threaten world peace.[73]

Finally, personal involvement in specific historical situations may do much to shape one's later outlook. As an Egyptian soldier in the 1948–1949 Arab-Israeli War, Gamal Nasser felt humiliated by the inadequacy, inefficiency, and corruption that characterized the Egyptian army's performance. He resolved that if he ever had the chance he would remedy these deficiencies. After he took over the government in the early 1950s he sought to build up Egyptian military strength and prevent any slights to Arab dignity. Thus when Israeli forces launched a successful attack into the Egyptian-administered Gaza Strip in early 1955, he was humiliated and intensified his existing quest for military assistance. When he was unable to obtain arms "without strings" from the West he was further humiliated, and reacted with a wounded sense of dignity by obtaining arms from those who attached no conditions, the Communists.[74]

Concept of Role

Another component of the policymaker's makeup is his or her concept of role. What does the policymaker think any person occupying a particular position is supposed to do, given the nature of the position? The policymaker's concept of role will be partly determined by what he or she thinks others expect the occupant to do. For example, even if one should desire to, no member of the Politburo of the People's Republic of 'China would be expected to advocate freedom of

---

[72]See Sigmund Freud and William C. Bullitt, *Thomas Woodrow Wilson: A Psychological Study,* Houghton Mifflin, Boston, 1967, and Alexander George and Juliette George, *Woodrow Wilson and Colonel House,* Day, New York, 1956. Most observers do not consider these studies to have *proven* such relationships, however, but only to have developed sufficient data to advance them as reasonable hypotheses.

[73]When President Truman was informed of the North Korean assault against South Korea in June of 1950, he specifically thought of the 1930s and the danger of history repeating itself. See Harry S. Truman, *Memoirs, Vol. II: Years of Trial and Hope,* Doubleday, New York, 1956, pp. 332–340.

[74]See Chapter 6, pp. 196–199, for further discussion.

political party organization. Similarly, since an American Secretary of State by the very nature of his role *is* the President's man, he is expected to advise and support the Chief Executive and not publicly advocate contradictory policies.

Role expectations tend to become more set as a person occupies a particular position for a considerable length of time. Precedents become established, procedures become routinized, and there seems to be less room for individual initiative.

Sometimes one may be forced to make some decisions that he would prefer not to make. This is a typical problem for the Vice-President in the United States. Hubert Humphrey was expected to support President Johnson's Vietnam policy, even though he did not always agree. Very often a man of differing experience and outlook than the President, the Vice-President is still a member of the team and because of his position is expected to support that team without reservation.

When one is dealing with a particular policymaker then, he or she must try to figure the extent to which, and in what ways, his or her opposite number will feel constrained to make or not make certain decisions simply because of the position that person occupies. To the extent that role perceptions determine one's decisions, individual personality characteristics will have less influence.

Physical and Mental Health

The final factors to be investigated are physical and mental health. Sometimes one forgets that it is people he or she is dealing with, and people have stresses and strains, get tired, have bad days, or get sick. The strain of responsible policymaking positions is great, and the physical deterioration of public leaders has often been significant. In the twentieth century both Presidents Eisenhower and Wilson became seriously ill while in office, President Roosevelt was seriously ill at Yalta and died shortly thereafter, Stalin died while still in power, as did Ho Chi Minh, Gamal Nasser, and others. What this means in a practical sense is that when one is dealing with someone it is important to look for signs of the degree to which that person may be unable physically and/or mentally to handle the complexity, the stresses, and the necessity for clear thinking that is required. To the extent that a policymaker is physically or mentally incapacitated he or she obviously is less able to do his or her job. In such situations there is considerable opportunity for one's opposite number to assert his or her own influence.

The first three chapters have examined the fundamental characteristics of the international environment within which the policymaker operates, analyzed the steps that should be undertaken to formulate an effective policy in a specific situation, and discussed the basic components of capability that provide the foundation for international influence. So far the discussion has focused on policy *formulation*. Now it is time to examine the instruments for *implementing* policy.

SELECTED BIBLIOGRAPHY

Adie, W. A. C., *Oil, Politics, and Seapower: The Indian Ocean Vortex,* Crane, Russak & Company, National Strategy Information Center, New York, 1975.

Aron, Raymond, *The Imperial Republic: The United States and the World, 1945 – 1973,* Winthrop, Cambridge, Massachusetts, 1974.

Bhagwati, Jagdish, ed., *Economics and World Order,* Macmillan, New York, 1972.

Black, Cyril E., *The Dynamics of Modernization,* Harper & Row, New York, 1966.

Calleo, David P., and Benjamin M. Rowland, *America and the World Political Economy: Atlantic Dreams and National Realities,* Indiana University Press, Bloomington, Indiana, 1973.

Cline, Ray S., *World Power Assessment 1977: A Calculus of Strategic Drift,* Westview Press, Boulder, Colorado, 1977.

Ehrlich, A. H., and P. R. Ehrlich, *Population, Resources, Environment: Issues in Human Ecology,* W. H. Freeman, San Francisco, 1970.

Finley, David J., and Thomas Hovet, Jr., *7304: International Relations on the Planet Earth,* Harper & Row, New York, 1975.

German, F. Clifford, "A Tentative Evaluation of World Power," *Journal of Conflict Resolution,* March, 1960, pp. 138 – 144.

Gray, Colin S., *The Geopolitics of the Nuclear Era: Heartlands, Rimlands, and the Technological Revolution,* Crane, Russak & Company, National Strategy Information Center, New York, 1977.

Greenstein, Fred I., *Personality and Politics,* Markham, Chicago, 1969.

Hopkins, Raymond F., and Richard W. Mansbach, *Structure and Process in International Politics,* Harper & Row, New York, 1973.

International Institute for Strategic Studies, *The Military Balance, 1978 – 1979,* London, 1978.

Jackson, W. A. Douglas, and Marwyn S. Samuels, eds., *Politics and Geographic Relationships: Toward A New Focus,* Prentice-Hall, Englewood Cliffs, New Jersey, 1971.

Knorr, Klaus, *Military Power and Potential,* D. C. Heath, Lexington, Massachusetts, 1970.

Pierre, Andrew J., "America Down, Russia Up: The Changing Political Role of Military Power," *Foreign Policy,* Fall, 1971, pp. 163 – 187.

Rostow, W. W., *The Stages of Economic Growth,* Cambridge University Press, New York, 1960.

Russet, Bruce M., *Trends in World Politics,* Macmillan, New York, 1965.

Russet, Bruce M., *What Price Vigilance? The Burdens of National Defense,* Yale University Press, New Haven, Connecticut, 1970.

Sawyer, Jack W., "Dimensions of Nations: Size, Wealth, and Politics," *American Journal of Sociology,* September, 1967, pp. 145 – 172.

Scott, Andrew M., *The Revolution in Statecraft: Informal Penetration,* Random House, New York, 1965.

Spiegel, Steven L., *Dominance and Diversity: The International Hierarchy,* Little Brown, Boston, 1972.

Sprout, Harold, and Margaret Sprout, *Toward A Politics of Planet Earth,* Van Nostrand, New York, 1971.

Sterling, Richard W., *Macropolitics: International Relations in a Global Society,* Alfred A. Knopf, New York, 1974.

Stookey, Robert W., and James A. Bill, *Politics and Petroleum: The Middle East and the United States,* King's Court Communications, Brunswick, Ohio, 1975.

Szyliowicz, Joseph S. and Bard E. O'Neill, eds., *The Energy Crisis and U.S. Foreign Policy,* Praeger, New York, 1975.

Tachau, Frank, ed., *The Developing Nations: What Path to Modernization?,* Dodd Mead, New York, 1974.

United Nations, *UN Demographic Yearbook, 1974,* New York, 1975.

United Nations, *UN Statistical Yearbook, 1976,* New York, 1977.

U.S., Congress, Joint Economic Committee, *Allocation of Resources in the Soviet Union and China—1977: Hearings Before the Subcommittee on Priorities and Economy in Government of the Joint Economic Committee,* 95th Cong., 1st Sess., June 23 and 30, and July 6, 1977, Part 3.

U.S., Department of State, *Special Report: The Planetary Product "Back to Normalcy" in 1976—77,* June, 1978.

Waterlow, Charlotte, *Superpowers and Victims: The Outlook for World Community,* Prentice-Hall, Englewood Cliffs, New Jersey, 1974.

Wicker, Tom, *JFK and LBJ: The Influence of Personality Upon Politics,* William Morrow, New York, 1968.

World Bank, *World Bank Atlas: Population, Per Capita Product, and Growth Rates,* Washington, D.C., 1977.

Four

Policy Implementation Instruments: Tangible

Once the policymaker has decided what the policy should be he or she must determine the most appropriate means of implementation. Since there are a wide variety of possible implementation instruments, it is not possible to discuss each one individually. Policymakers often break them down into two categories, however, those that are relatively tangible (such as economic and military activities) and those of a more intangible nature (such as communication and negotiation). We will follow the same pattern, the former providing the subject matter for this chapter, the latter for the next.

ECONOMIC

The first major instrument of policy implementation is the economic. Because of the essentiality of economic strength to capability and the complexity and interdependence of modern economic life, policymakers in all states must be alert to the potential influence of the economic tool and consider their options very carefully.

The number and variety of economic options might seem to be immense, since almost every facet of economic activity could conceivably be used as a weapon. In most cases, however, the policymaker's range of choice is much more limited for two simple reasons: (1) many times his or her state's economy is so weak that the options simply do not exist; and (2) sometimes domestic political pressures prevent the policymaker from using those he or she thinks would be most effective.[1]

Thus the policymaker's options may be greatly circumscribed by the conditions in his or her own state. Since this is so one must recognize that the following discussion will carry within it the critical assumptions of capability and freedom from constraints. To the extent that the components of capability

---

[1]As the analysis in Chapter 7 shows, however, domestic pressures are often relatively insignificant.

analyzed in Chapter 3 are insufficient or the domestic pressures examined in Chapter 7 prevent options from being utilized, the policy instrument is functionally nonexistent.

Trade Policy

International trade is a factor of major importance in policymakers' calculations. The volume of goods, services, resources, and capital exchanged internationally continues to grow and it becomes more and more apparent that various economic problems have world-wide implications. Because a host of economic interdependencies and vulnerabilities exist there are a great many situations in which there may be opportunities to exert influence.

The first major facet of trade policy involves the use of *tariffs* (taxes imposed on foreign-made goods coming into the country). Sometimes tariffs are imposed for domestic reasons: perhaps one is seeking to protect domestic production from foreign competition, wishes to discourage consumption, or is simply seeking to raise additional revenue.

But often a policymaker is seeking to apply economic pressure to a particular foreign state and is using tariff manipulation as the instrument. Even if this is not the policymaker's sole objective, a tariff automatically has an international impact. Usually, the higher the tariff, the higher the price. This means the foreign good is less competitive and fewer can be sold. The fear of this drop in sales may lead the foreign producer to modify its policy as the tariff imposer desires.

Sometimes it does not work that way, however. In August 1971 President Nixon imposed a "surcharge" of 10 percent on all imports into the United States not already subject to quota (quantity) restrictions. One objective of this tax was the provision of relief to American import-competing industries, another an improvement in Washington's balance of payments position.[2] The primary objective though was to bring about major policy modifications by the targets of that policy, America's trading partners in Europe and Japan, but this did not happen. Instead, the tariff simply created considerable ill will.

A policymaker may also manipulate his or her state's tariff structure in such a way as to reward the target of his or her actions. For years the United States has accorded Yugoslavia preferential treatment in order to help her maintain her economic independence of the Soviet Union. And as was indicated in Chapter 1, as part of its détente policy Washington recently sought to extend tariff benefits to the Soviets themselves (in early 1975 Moscow rejected that offer, however, because it contained a Congressionally imposed provision requiring freer Jewish emigration).[3]

---

[2] It was hoped that less money would go out as imports became more expensive. The United States continued to experience a balance of payments deficit, however.

[3] See Chapter 1, p. 4.

Quotas, quantitative restrictions, provide a second category of trade possibilities. The policymaker may simply limit the number of foreign goods his or her country can import. In this situation the foreign producer may sell goods under its own price arrangements but the quantity is limited. As measured by value, 6.4 percent of the manufactured products imported into the United States in 1977 were quota items.[4] Specifically (in the area of manufactured products), Washington maintained quota restrictions on imports of textiles, color television receivers from Japan, stainless and alloy tool steel, and nonrubber footwear from South Korea and the Republic of China.

The third category of trade manipulations involves the use of *boycotts* or *embargoes.* A boycott is a refusal to import. It may be selective, involving specified commodities, or be general, a refusal to purchase any commodities produced by a particular country. An embargo is a refusal by one country to sell its goods to another. This also may be specific or general.

The use of boycotts and embargoes is widespread. For example, in an attempt to prevent perceived enemies from obtaining goods that could increase their military strength, the NATO countries imposed a strategic embargo on both the Soviet Union and People's Republic of China. Similarly, following Fidel Castro's ascension to power in Cuba the United States used a wide range of restrictive economic instruments in an effort to compel him to modify his policy. These began with selective boycotts and quota reductions and eventually a complete economic and travel boycott developed.

More recently, shortly after the Middle East War broke out in 1973 the Arab oil states began to apply severe economic pressure on the industrialized countries. The price of oil jumped drastically and production was decreased. Soon a total embargo was imposed on oil supplies to the United States and the Netherlands, and production was decreased again (in effect a partial embargo on oil exports to Western Europe and Japan).

Suppose one is a policymaker looking at an exporting nation with a view to manipulating trade relations in some of the ways we have discussed. What are the questions he or she would need to ask? The first is, to what extent is the target's economy dependent on trade? This involves determining the percentage of the total economic activity that trade comprises, discovering if trade is critical in key economic areas, and so forth. Second, to what extent does the target rely on the export of one product for its trade revenues? And is our state in a position to materially affect the sale of that product? And third, to what extent is the target's trade conducted with one nation, either with ours or with someone's we can influence? [5]

Each of these questions helps the policymaker ascertain the *vulnerability* of the exporting country to trade manipulation. If a state depends heavily on foreign

---

[4]U.S., Department of State, Office of Special Trade Activities, August 1, 1978 (personal communication).

[5]As you, the reader, attempt to see things as the policymaker does, these are the questions *you* should ask.

trade for its economic development it needs to export goods in order to obtain the foreign exchange required to purchase the necessary imports.[6] If it cannot export enough or the prices it receives are too low, (such as has been the case with many developing nations that must rely primarily on the export of primary products) it must receive immense economic assistance or its economy will not progress. Similarly, to the extent that states rely primarily on the sale of one product, such as many Latin American states have had to do, any fluctuation in the quantity and price of the sales of that product can have a terrific impact. And if the situation is such that this one product is exported primarily to one country, also a typical situation, the policymakers of that importing state may be in a position to exercise overwhelming influence.

Of course, the policymaker needs to ask similar questions with regard to an importing nation. What proportion of its economy is dependent on imports? To what extent is a particular product an essential component of its economic system? And finally, to what extent is it dependent on one particular source for this particular import?

Despite the apparent logic of these statements, history shows that often manipulative policies have *not* yielded the benefits originally envisaged. Why might this be so? There are several possible explanations. First, threats of economic deprivation, and policies that attempt to bring this about, inevitably create immense feelings of hostility. Although hardship may occur, people learn to tolerate it, and the very resentment engendered by the hardship makes them more willing to stand the deprivation. Sometimes tolerating hardship becomes a goal in itself. People come to believe that it is their patriotic duty to show their willingness and capacity to suffer rather than give in to pressure.

Another point is that sometimes people simply learn to adapt. A restructuring of their domestic economic situation may occur as improvisation and innovation develop, and perhaps there will even be an underlying change in values. Third, some states possess relatively diversified economies and are just not very vulnerable. In these cases the interruption of normal economic relations is not critical (although it may be uncomfortable).

Finally, and critically, even if a product is of exceptional importance the policymaker usually will bend every effort to find an alternative rather than submit to the crude use of economic coercion. If one is the policymaker for an exporting country he or she will seek to find alternative markets. If one is the policymaker of an importing country he or she will seek to find alternative sources. Since in most situations the pressures applied are not universal but emanate from a particular source (or combination of sources) alternatives usually exist. Also, there usually are breaks in any system of sanctions. Finally, states seek to develop substitutes. Efforts are made to devise new products and methods to replace those that were taken away.

---

[6]Of course, one may be able to supplement one's capacity by other means for a while, but basically this statement is correct.

What were the actual results of the embargoes mentioned above? NATO's strategic embargo of the Soviet Union and Red China simply led the Communists to increase their efforts to produce necessary commodities, develop substitutes, and find alternative sources. The American embargo and boycott of Cuba, while isolating Cuba from her traditional trading partner, similarly forced Castro to find alternative markets and sources.[7] In neither case was policy modified nor were the targets prevented from obtaining the goods they desired. Actually, because of the activity that was stimulated the embargoes resulted in the strengthening of the targets.

On the other hand, the Arab oil offensive of late 1973 was partially successful. On November 6, 1973 the European Economic Community issued a declaration that recognized the "rights," (not just the "aspirations"), of the Palestinian people. And shortly thereafter Japan adopted a very pro-Arab stance with respect to the solution of the Arab-Israeli conflict. The United States, too, demonstrated an effort to adopt a more evenhanded approach to the problem, as witnessed by the American-instigated disengagement agreements of 1974 and 1975.[8]

Despite these "positive" accomplishments, the oil offensive was not as effective as some Arab policymakers had expected because the United States did not apply sufficient pressure to compel an immediate Israeli withdrawal, and Uncle Sam was able to "make do" through switches of supplies by the oil companies and some domestic conservation measures. In addition, Washington embarked on a program to develop alternative sources of supply, increase domestic production, and develop a common diplomatic posture with the oil-consuming nations.[9]

What conclusions can the policymaker draw? First, only in rare cases is trade manipulation effective, and sometimes it may even be harmful. Certainly it is an option to consider in certain situations but it should be approached cautiously. Still, in some cases moderate changes in the tariff and quota structure may bring about some policy adjustment. This is more likely to be true in cases where the product is of critical importance and where one is the primary source or market than in situations where there are a number of alternatives. In each case the degree of vulnerability, which is a reflection of the degree of need for trade in

[7]This is not to say that American measures did not have some economic effect, for they did. But in no way did they bring about a policy modification on the part of the Cuban government. On the contrary, their imposition simply reinforced Castro's existing predilection to the effect that he needed to ally himself tightly to the Communist bloc and develop Cuba's internal capability components as rapidly as possible.

[8]See Chapter 2, pp. 57, 70.

[9]In light of these facts, and because the Arab states were also hopeful that the United States would be more responsive to a persuasive-rewarding stance than it had been to one of coercive pressure, the boycott was eliminated in early 1974. For an excellent analysis of the oil weapon see Hanns Maull, "Oil and Influence: The Oil Weapon Examined," International Institute for Strategic Studies, Adelphi Papers, No. 117, 1975. With respect to Washington's "program," as of this writing it was largely ineffectual.

general, concentration with a single partner, and the significance of the particular product in question, must be weighed against the possibility of the development of substitutes and alternatives, the willingness to adapt, patriotic belt-tightening, and reciprocal action.

Before leaving the topic of trade manipulation three other options should be discussed briefly, options the policymaker may consider which, although not directly "trade manipulation," are of a related nature. The first is the *manipulation of currency exchange rates*. In order for country X to purchase goods from country Y, it needs to have its currency converted into that of country Y. Some ratio of currency exchange inevitably is established. If a state is able to manipulate this ratio it can affect the terms of trade between the two countries. For example, as discussed earlier, for most of the past several years the United States has had an "unfavorable balance of payments" (more money is flowing out of the country than is coming in). Twice since 1971 Washington has "devalued" the dollar, making it worth less in terms of foreign currencies. The purpose of this move has been to decrease imports and increase exports. Since it now takes more American dollars to purchase foreign currency, imports are more expensive, and American exports are cheaper. This and other types of currency manipulation may be options available to the policymaker. However, once again one must be aware of the fact that other states will not look kindly upon these activities and may react reciprocally.

A second type of trade effect-option is *preemptive buying*. This involves the purchase of particular goods or commodities so that the target of the activity will not have them available. During World War II the Allies often sought to outbid the Axis for materials that neutrals were willing to export to either side. *Dumping* is a third type of trade-effect maneuver. This involves the sale of goods at an artifically depressed price to drive the price of this particular good down on the world market so as to make it less profitable for other countries having to sell it. This obviously would have an inhibiting effect on the trade of the country or countries in question.

The general record here is the same as with trade manipulation. Although occasionally, in a specific case over the short run, the activity yields the desired result, often the long run impact is either negligible or harmful to the manipulator.

Foreign Aid

The second major economic instrument is foreign aid, the transfer of cash, credit, goods, or technical advice from one nation to another. Foreign aid has long been an accepted technique of policy. In the eighteenth and nineteenth centuries, for example, European states often provided loans to "backward peoples" as a means of gaining a colonial foothold. Subsidies of equipment and money were regularly a part of military alliances. After World War I the United States made large loans to some twenty countries.

It was not until after World War II, however, that foreign aid was used extensively and systematically. The United States led the way. Responding to the perceived threat of a Soviet takeover of Europe, American policymakers responded with a variety of assistance programs (see below). This was the beginning of a global effort that to this point has cost more than $135 billion.

Although Washington has provided more than twice as much aid as everyone else combined, many other states have significant programs.[10] After Stalin's death the new Soviet leaders embarked on a large but selective assistance program, and today foreign aid is an important policy instrument for Japan, West Germany, Australia, Italy, France, Sweden, Canada, and China.[11]

What are the major categories of foreign aid programs? The first is *development assistance*: foreign aid is provided on the grounds that it contributes significantly to economic development.[12] These programs may involve cash grants, the presumed purpose of which would be to enable countries to obtain capital necessary for rapid development, or favorable credit arrangements such as long term low interest loans, the procedure favored by the Soviet Union during most of the 1950s and 1960s.[13]

A second major category is *military assistance,* the supplying of money and material for military uses (including aid for defense support programs). These transfers are considered a part of foreign aid because of the fact that when the recipient's military is being aided he is able to divert his own resources from its support to a heavier investment in economic projects.

American military assistance programs developed after World War II in connection with the policy of containment. They constituted the largest part of the United States effort until the early 1960s when the economic sector became

[10]It should be pointed out that a state can have a relatively small program but that program can be highly significant if it is concentrated in a few selected areas. For example, although the overall magnitude of the Japanese effort is small compared to that of the United States, it is very important in the politics of East Asia. As early as 1967 Japan extended a greater absolute amount of assistance to the region (excluding Vietnam) than did the United States. See Hellman, p. 109.

[11]Obviously not all states have the economic strength to extensively employ this instrument. Thus this analysis is primarily concerned with what is basically an instrument of the policymakers of major powers. It should be noted, however, that even states with little strength occasionally may use foreign aid, though they must do so on a highly specific and selective basis.

[12] This has been the rationale for much of the American effort. The best analysis of American aid programs, although the statistics are somewhat dated, is still Joan M. Nelson, *Aid, Influence and Foreign Policy,* Macmillan, New York, 1968.

[13]In the 1950s and 1960s there was much controversy concerning whether the American approach (emphasizing grants) was inferior to the Soviet approach, which emphasized credits and loans. American policymakers assumed that grants, because they were outright gifts, would bring about greater gratitude than a loan which had to be repaid, and in some cases this seemed to be true. On the other hand, in certain situations grants apparently had a tendency to make the recipient feel as if he were accepting charity and made him resentful of that fact. Thus in some cases the more "expensive method," that is the loan, was politically more palatable to the recipient nation than the cheaper gift. A useful discussion of the advantages and disadvantages of each may be found in Joseph S. Berliner, *Soviet Economic Aid,* Praeger, New York, 1958.

pre-eminent. Following the 1973 Arab-Israeli War the military portion once again became dominant as American policymakers sought to resupply Israel and construct more "cooperative" relationships with the oil-rich states of the Persian Gulf.

Many other states are actively involved in arms traffic. The Soviet Union has had an extensive military assistance program for years, and France, Britain, West Germany, Italy, and the People's Republic of China also have made significant efforts in this sphere.[14]

The third main type of foreign aid is *technical assistance,* the transfer of knowledge and skills from one country to another. Relatively inexpensive, technical assistance programs allow personnel from industrialized countries to advise and cooperate with recipients in a coordinated attack on such practical problems as fishery development, control of malaria, the construction of roads, educational advancement, and so forth, and do so on more of a personal level than is generally true with regard to economic development assistance. Technical assistance efforts have been a very small portion of total foreign aid activities since the Second World War. Because of difficulties in other areas, however, they seem to be becoming increasingly significant and probably will continue to grow in importance.

What have policymakers providing foreign aid sought to achieve with these three types of programs? *What have been their objectives?*[15] Although sometimes cloaking other goals in the language of economic development, policymakers have really sought to assist *economic development* in many cases.[16] For many Americans the objective of economic growth has a certain ethical content. It is believed that all human beings deserve a certain minimum standard of living and those who are more fortunate have an obligation to help bring this about.

More often, however, American policymakers have sought to assist in economic development because of what its achievement was presumed to lead to in turn, namely, democratic government, the development of a capitalist economic system, and a more open society on the part of the recipients. These in turn, some have assumed, lead to peaceful foreign policies. Some policymakers also assume that with more economic development states become more stable and this will reduce the probability of internal unrest. This in turn reduces the possibility of external exploitation. It is also argued that development will enable the recipients

[14]From July 1977 through June 1978 there were more than 130 major *identified* arms agreements in the world. See International Institute for Strategic Studies, *The Military Balance, 1978–1979,* Table 12, pp. 104-107. Of course, this understates the arms traffic considerably since it does not include various unidentified agreements.

[15]One must be careful to distinguish between the stated objectives and the "real" ones. Sometimes they are the same, but sometimes they bear little relation to each other. A useful classification of "real" objectives may be found in Hans J. Morgenthau, "A Political Theory of Foreign Aid," *American Political Science Review,* June, 1962, pp. 301–309.

[16]Naturally this has often been a major objective of the *recipients.*

to remain independent and avoid becoming dependent on outsiders for their security and survival. Thus, some policymakers have believed that economic development and technical assistance have great potential for bringing about peace and stability in a system of states based on the principles of western democracy and economic capitalism.[17]

What does the record show in this regard? Obviously, as the cases of Germany and Japan in the 1930s and the Soviet Union today demonstrate, there is no automatic relationship between economic development and democracy.[18] If one looks at the recipient states since the Second World War one finds that many are not concerned with democracy at all, and those that are concerned define it only in terms that are consonant with their own particular traditions and objectives. Those who had or sought a governmental system Americans might consider democratic prior to receiving aid, mostly the Western Europeans, have continued to do so. Those who previously had not, mostly leaders of non-Western less developed countries, did not start. Thus there is little historical evidence to indicate that economic development necessarily leads to Western-style democracy.

Even less promising conclusions appear with regard to the relationship between economic development and capitalism. In many less developed countries capitalism has been equated with the exploitation of the masses by the private privileged classes, both colonialist and native. Capitalism is an anathema, and economic development is hardly likely to increase the use of capitalistic devices within the system. Actually the evidence indicates that there is more of a tendency to move in the direction of less private enterprise and ownership of the means of production and a greater degree of state control, than vice versa.

Similarly, one cannot predict with confidence that development will be stabilizing; it depends on the characteristics of the recipient and the relationship of the level and type of performance to the demands and expectations of key groups. The process of economic development is uncertain and complex and there are times when it may be disruptive rather than stabilizing. In many of the less developed countries order has been maintained for generations only through the ruthless use of force by the ruling classes. If economic development occurs and if new groups arise to challenge the control of the privileged, a potentially revolutionary system develops. Generally it is the groups that have already begun to rise who are the most revolutionary in their expectations. Economic development, instead of increasing stability, may increase instability and create precisely the opposite of the stable situation that the policymakers had hoped to create.

---

[17]Naturally there are exceptions to this generalization.

[18]On the other hand, it may be that a certain *minimum* level of economic development is a prerequisite to the establishment of a successful democracy. There is much to indicate that where abject poverty exists and there is no hope for the future, freedom with responsibility also will be absent.

The idea that development will increase the likelihood of a peaceful foreign policy also is unsubstantiated. Both rich countries and poor countries have attacked and been attacked, and there is little hard evidence to indicate that simply because a country is economically developed (or developing) it will pursue a peaceful foreign policy.

In addition to recognizing the lack of necessary correlation of these elements, the policymaker must also ascertain whether or not economic development is really possible in a given case. The extreme difficulties facing the less developed countries as they seek to modernize and grow were discussed earlier.[19] Development is a task of immense proportions, one that economic assistance in and of itself often cannot influence significantly. Many times the amount of capital required is so large, the development of the economic infrastructure so complicated and time-consuming, thè upgrading of educational and skills levels such a gargantuan undertaking, and the changing of human and cultural traits such a laborious and uncertain process that the odds against any significant growth are overwhelming.

What this means for the potential provider as well as the recipient is that expectations must be kept at a relatively low level or else considerable disenchantment may set in with each side blaming the other. The parties, assuming they both sincerely desire economic development, must face this situation realistically so as not to be overly disappointed if rapid progress does not occur. If it is decided that the odds are favorable, they each must be prepared for a long term program of a fairly significant size.

The policymaker of a potential providing state also needs to ask whether or not economic development is a "good" objective in a particular case. Since development presumably means the recipient will be "stronger," one must ask whether or not that would be to the state's interest. This is not the kind of judgment one can make *a priori*. If the recipient is more friendly toward one's adversaries than toward oneself then presumably it would be better if that state were weaker rather than stronger.

A second major objective of many policymakers of providing states is what might be termed the achievement of *sufficient gratitude*. The providing policymaker expects the recipient, in return for the economic assistance, to have enough gratitude to at least be sympathetic toward the assisting state's foreign policies and perhaps sustain or modify his or her own behavior according to the giving state's desires. It is the idea that I help you, and out of gratitude for that help I expect you to be sympathetic to me or to continue or change what you are doing in the way I want you to. This has been, and continues to be, a major objective of aid programs.

Much to their chagrin, both the Soviet Union and the United States have discovered that the objective of sufficient gratitude is seldom achieved. When

---

[19]See Chapter 3, pp. 108–109.

President Kennedy took office in 1961 he determined to set the United States on a new course with respect to Egypt. As a part of his program nearly a billion dollars worth of food was given to Cairo over the next three years. In return Washington wanted President Nasser to cease his anti-American outbursts, become more moderate with respect to the Arab-Israeli issue, cease supporting the Algerian rebels, and perhaps accept a position of favorable neutrality with regard to American policy in the Congo. None of these changes occurred.

As part of its price for extensive economic aid to the People's Republic of China, the Soviet Union expected Mao Tse-tung to follow Soviet dictates on several issues in the late 1950s, but instead the Sino-Soviet conflict developed.[20] If the Soviets had received "sufficient gratitude" from Peking the Chinese would have been willing to do as they were bidden. Soviet threats to reduce this assistance, and then its actual reduction, instead of compelling a modification of Chinese policies simply increased Peking's hostility.

For two decades prior to the 1975–1976 civil war in Lebanon the Soviet Union had been Syria's primary arms supplier. When Syria's President Assad was considering becoming involved in the Lebanese conflict the Soviets, recognizing the dispute's unpredictability and worried that action by Damascus might damage radical Arab unity and/or provoke Israeli counteraction, counseled against such a maneuver. To back up their "advice," the Russians threatened to slow down the weapons supply if their counsel was ignored. Assad's "gratitude" was not sufficient to enable Moscow to persuade him, however, and (as we discussed in Chapter 2) Syria did intervene, beginning with mediation and eventually escalating to the point of dispatching thousands of troops to compel a cease-fire. The Soviets responded as they had said they would and sharply reduced the flow of arms, but Assad did not alter course.

Gratitude means very little in international relations. Recipient policymakers know that assistance is provided on the basis of self-interest, and they take it in the same way. Their reasons may be very different from the provider's, and they may put the aid to unexpected uses. They may seek aid only for prestige or simply for purposes of maintaining themselves in power, for example, or even use it against one of their provider's other friends. Seldom do they feel they "owe" anyone any gratitude for aid. And for the same reasons discussed in connection with the effectiveness of trade manipulation, recipients are seldom amenable to foreign aid pressures. They adapt themselves to get along without, they resent efforts at coercion and fight it, there are alternative sources and they know it, and so forth.

Most policymakers today are concluding that assistance agreements seem to follow policy change rather than bring it about. The United States agreement to help Egypt reopen the Suez Canal in early 1974 came only *after* Egypt had adopted a more neutral position between Washington and the Soviet Union.

[30]See Chapter 2, pp. 76–78.

Upon close investigation one discovers that this has often been the case. The Soviet offer to finance the Egyptian High Dam came after the Egyptians had been rebuffed by the United States. Soviet aid to Iraq was begun only after the July 1958 coup; it did not lead to it. Generally speaking foreign aid does not itself cause a major modification of policy. Instead, the opportunities for developing and cementing new relationships occur first and then foreign aid may be an effective instrument to achieve that limited objective.

A third major objective of foreign aid is *providing support for the recipient state*. In this situation the policymaker does not attempt to have the recipient modify its policy. If the policies and objectives of the recipient are not in accord with the wishes of the provider they can at least be tolerated. The problem here is the recipient's ability to effectively carry out these policies and the purpose of the assistance is to help provide such capability.

Some support assistance has been of an emergency short term nature. In the immediate post World War II era the Communists put severe pressure on Turkey and Greece. From Turkey Moscow demanded territorial concessions, a favorable revision of the Montreaux Convention governing the Dardanelles Straits, the conclusion of a defense treaty similar to that which the Russians had concluded with their Balkan satellites, and leases for military bases. In Greece, Communist-led rebels had been fighting government forces since the latter stages of World War II, and had intensified their activities following the British evacuation.

Faced with this situation American policymakers felt compelled to act. One of the major moves was the passage of the Greek-Turkish Aid Program. This measure was signed into law on May 22, 1947 and provided some $400 million worth of economic and military assistance.[21] The quick dispensation of emergency funds was a major force in thwarting Communist efforts.[22]

Sometimes support may be provided in an emergency situation but on a longer term (though not indefinite) basis. During the same period that the Greek-Turkish Aid Program was developed it became painfully obvious to American policymakers that Western Europe, devastated by World War II, was in a state of economic disintegration. Perceiving a major Soviet threat and afraid that such chaos was an open invitation to mischief, and recognizing that the Western European states could not help themselves, the Truman Administration decided to act. If the Western Europeans would take some initiative and provide the United States with a comprehensive plan for European economic reconstruc-

---

[21]For a fascinating brief discussion of the background and objectives of this program, see Acheson, pp. 262–271, 290–301. One should also note that Truman's speech requesting Congressional action led to a relatively open-ended commitment of American strength. See Hartmann, *The New Age of American Foreign Policy*, pp. 126–128.

[22]Washington also used the military instrument in a limited, nonviolent way via a series of demonstrations of force, and coupled this with some diplomatic (and not so "diplomatic") threats. It was this *combination* of instruments that turned the tide.

tion, Washington would help in developing the final details and provide the necessary financial help. The Europeans did provide such a blueprint and this led to the European Recovery Program (Marshall Plan). Over the next four years Washington gave more than $13 billion in economic assistance. The aid was enormously successful and the result was a startling economic recovery. By the end of the program production had either reached or exceeded prewar levels in nearly all areas.

In neither the Greek-Turkish Program nor the Marshall Plan did American policymakers seek to bring about major policy modifications because the recipients already had objectives that were compatible with American desires. The problem was that they did not have the capability to achieve those objectives. The assistance programs provided this capability.[23]

A third type of supportive assistance is a little different. Sometimes there is a more or less continuing program that purposely is not of a quantity or quality sufficient to enable the recipient to totally achieve that which it may desire. For example, although the Soviet Union has often supplied the government of Syria with economic and military assistance, it has always made sure that the quantity and quality of this assistance was not sufficient to allow Damascus to be in a position to militarily threaten Israel because such an occurrence might lead to a confrontation with the United States. There is much supportive assistance of this third type, more or less continuous but limited, Chinese assistance to the guerillas of Dhofar in the Arabian Peninsula and Soviet assistance to Iraq being two more examples.

This type of assistance can give the policymaker many problems. Generally the provider in such cases is attempting to do two things. First, it wants to provide enough support to allow the recipient some hope of achieving his objectives but not enough to really help him do it. And second, it seeks to develop sufficient gratitude in the recipient so that the latter's policies will reflect the provider's interests. But this is a very risky operation and the recipients can easily become very disenchanted with the provider if it refuses to give the quantity and quality of aid desired (as was indicated earlier with respect to the expulsion of Soviet "advisors" from Egypt in July 1972).

Finally, sometimes the provider may have a program of continuous, nearly unlimited, support. It is probably incorrect to say that any providing state will just give whatever is sought, but it is certainly clear that there are cases in which the recipient is assured of having its legitimate needs met on a continuing basis. Although Israel does not automatically receive everything it asks Washington to provide, American policymakers make absolutely sure that she receives everything necessary to maintain a first-class military machine, and make sure that the

---

[23]In both of these cases the recipients had the will and capacity to carry through to success. No amount of external assistance will be sufficient if these ingredients are missing. The United States provision of over $2 billion worth of futile aid to the Nationalists in the Chinese civil war is eloquent testimony to that fact.

rest of the world understands that this is a permanent, firm commitment (as permanent and firm as anything can be).

In this kind of relationship the recipient is as influential as the provider. Although Israel is dependent on the United States for assistance, because of its commitment Washington is not in a position to apply as much pressure as it might appear.[24] It is true that, given her policies and the potential strength of the Arab forces surrounding her, Israel might have trouble finding alternative arms sources (although this might not be true) and thus the United States would presumably have some leverage. But if Washington decreases its aid all that happens is that Israel is weaker, and this is not Washington's objective. If American policymakers desire a militarily secure Israel they must provide aid. If they must, and Israel knows they must, then in a sense the Israelis are "in the driver's seat."

Before leaving this section a few concluding remarks are in order. First, policymakers have learned that the economic instrument is considerably less effective than many assumed in the 1950s and 1960s. Seldom can it be used in such a way that the recipient will modify its policy under the threat or actual use of economic deprivation. Second, seldom does much gratitude develop in return for assistance. Third, seldom is the economic tool particularly effective by itself. Instead, it is useful primarily as a part of a coordinated package of policy instruments. Fourth, often it has been successfully used to help sustain or support recipients whose interests and policies are already favorable. And fifth, in some cases its use has actually been counterproductive, creating conditions that were harmful to the provider.

Because of the importance of economic strength as a component of capability, the growing interdependence of the world economy, the fact that economic development itself is a goal of most states, because there are continuing demands for assistance, and because sometimes economic tools *are* effective and other states are using them and may gain an edge if one does not compete, economic policy instruments will continue to be of considerable importance. But if and when policymakers use these tools they should do so with a cautiously realistic appreciation of what can and cannot be accomplished.

MILITARY

The second major instrument of policy is the military. Because policymakers operate in an international environment of "decentralized anarchy" they continually must make judgments concerning the potential or actual use of military force. This requirement is nothing new. As Lerche and Said have pointed out:

---

[24]Of course, if maintaining Israel's strength was not deemed so critical, the situation would be different and the United States would be in a position to use its leverage.

"Reconciling policy considerations to the threat, initiation, conduct or avoidance of war has long been one of the major concerns of the statesman."[25]

But there have been some dramatic changes in the nineteenth and twentieth centuries that make the current policymaker's task much more difficult. Due to many factors including an intensification of nationalism, the industrial, scientific, and technological revolutions, and changes in international morality, wars today have a tendency to become total. Entire populations sometimes become involved, both as participants and targets. Objectives tend to be universalized and conflicts become struggles between "Good" and "Evil." It is no exaggeration to say that we are living in an age of unmatched carnage.[26]

The problem has been compounded by the nuclear revolution. The immense destructive potential of today's weapons systems almost defies comprehension.[27] The wrong move might literally be a matter of life and death for millions. And with ballistic missiles, supersonic aircraft, and who knows what other scientific marvels, such horrible destruction can be efficiently and accurately delivered in a very few minutes. When one analyzes these facts (in the context of the tendency toward total war) he sees why it is imperative that the policymaker be ever so careful when contemplating actions involving the threat or actual use of the military tool.[28]

Because of the intensity of emotion that war arouses, it is not surprising that at times policymakers lose sight of the critical fact that a military victory must not be the ultimate objective of war. One must remember that the world goes on after the war is over (hopefully), so wars should be fought to obtain some rational political purpose.

The requirement of political rationality applies across the entire spectrum of uses of the military, and indeed there are many. Although there are various classification possibilities, a useful approach, and one that policymakers often employ, is to analyze one's options in terms of the level of activity and amount of violence anticipated, threatened, or undertaken.[29] This will be our approach also.[30]

---

[25]Charles O. Lerche, Jr., and Abdul A. Said, *Concepts of International Politics*, Second Edition, Prentice-Hall, Englewood Cliffs, New Jersey, 1970, p. 92.

[26]The introductory student could usefully consult Morgenthau, *Politics Among Nations*, Fifth Edition, Chs. 20 and 22, and Hartmann, *The Relations of Nations*, Fifth Edition, Ch. 8. Also very helpful is Raymond Aron, *The Century of Total War*, Beacon, Boston, 1954.

[27]Also see Chapter 3, pp. 113–114.

[28]This very problem is one of the reasons that some policymakers increasingly resort to the careful *nonuse* of the military instrument in their policies.

[29]Different national perceptions are important in this regard. Our analysis focuses on the activity and violence levels as seen by the policymaker of the country considering the use of the military. What are low levels for one country may be very high for another.

[30]This analysis does not specifically deal with a situation of total combat, either offensively or defensively. The military aspects of such activity are beyond the scope of this work, and the pertinent political points have already been covered, namely, total victory must not be the ultimate aim and political rationality must govern the conduct of the conflict.

Before considering these different levels specifically one additional point needs to be made, namely, that the degree to which a policymaker can effectively use the military instrument is greatly affected by his own state's military capability. Obviously a policymaker cannot employ a tool if he has no tool to use. Thus the particular purposes for which the military instrument may be used by the policymaker in question must be determined in light of the quantitative, distributive, and qualitative components of military capability discussed earlier.[31]

Nonactivity—Prestige

Because of the importance of military capability historically, the possession of a strong military force has often been a mark of international status. This fact has long been accepted by policymakers and is a point not lost on the leaders of the less developed countries. One of the first goals of Egypt's President Nasser on gaining power in the early 1950s, for example, was the development of a strong military. When a small South African country receives jet fighters and other modern weapons its policymakers are often interested primarily in attempting to increase their prestige. Seldom can one find a legitimate military objective that would be served by the acquisition of such weapons.[32]

The acquisition of nuclear striking capacity is a particularly significant means of increasing prestige because of the vast qualitative difference between nuclear and nonnuclear weapons. Given the immense destructive potential of even a few nuclear warheads, possession of even minimal nuclear striking ability is a matter of considerable political prestige, a fact recognized by policymakers in all countries.

Today five countries have deliverable nuclear capacity: the United States, Russia, Great Britain, France, and the People's Republic of China. In addition, India has exploded an atomic device and is moving in the direction of obtaining nuclear striking capacity, and many other states have the potential for such acquisition.[33] The spread of nuclear knowledge, reactors, and materials has made the problem of nuclear development much less formidable than it was just a few years ago. There is no doubt that at least an additional 20 states today could develop nuclear strength if they desired, including West Germany, East Germany, Japan, Egypt, and Israel. For better or worse, the decision whether or not

---

[31]See Chapter 3, pp. 110–117.

[32]This is a case of bolstering internal as well as external prestige.

[33]This problem of nuclear proliferation (the spread of nuclear weapons) is of immense importance to the superpowers. Their fear of the likely consequences of such an activity led to the negotiation of a Non-Proliferation Treaty (which came into force in 1970). The NPT provided primarily that nations possessing nuclear weapons would not transfer them to nonnuclear states and the nonnuclear signatories would not acquire or build them. Although signed by the United States, Russia, and Great Britain, the other states currently possessing nuclear forces, China and France, did not sign the treaty, and many of the near-nuclear nations have either not signed it, or if they have they have not ratified it.

to acquire nuclear weapons now lies largely beyond the control of the super-powers.[34]

In the situations discussed above, policymakers have gained (or sought) increased prestige through the mere possession of a strong military force. They have not actually employed the instrument in any active way, but sometimes even nonactivity can be beneficial.

Nonviolent Activity

Military forces are sometimes effectively used in a nonviolent manner.[35] Usually this occurs within some kind of negotiating context with each move designed to communicate a particular capability and possible intent to a specific party.[36]

Let's look at some brief examples. In the analysis of territorial changes in Chapter 2 the May 1974 Israeli-Syrian Disengagement Agreement was briefly discussed.[37] This agreement was to run for six months and expire November 30, 1974. Syrian policymakers, in order to maximize uncertainty in the hope that this would persuade their Israeli counterparts to make substantial concessions, refused to indicate publicly whether or not they would agree to an extension of the United Nations Disengagement of Forces (UNDOF) mandate.

Throughout much of 1974 the Israelis had been building extensive fortifications on the occupied Golan Heights.[38] As the time drew near for a decision on extension, construction was speeded up. When this did not bring about any assurance from the Syrians, the Israelis decided to begin large scale military maneuvers on their side of the neutral zone. These maneuvers simulated various types of combat using both reservist and regular army troops. Particular emphasis was placed on those types of warfare most likely to occur between the Syrians and the Israelis, and the Israeli armed forces publicly emphasized maneuvers of an offensive character. Israeli policymakers did not engage in violence. Their use of the military, however, was very effective and played some role in the resultant Syrian decision to extend the UNDOF mandate.

Another example of the effective use of the deployment of military force occurred in mid-1934. In July the Nazis staged a coup in Vienna, Austria, and

---

[34]Holsti, Second Edition, p. 311.

[35]One of the most effective instances of this occurred in the Cuban Missile Crisis. See Chapter 6, pp. 219–221.

[36]This statement is true of nearly all usages of the military instrument. It should also be pointed out that whether violence erupts is not determined solely by the policymaker of the initiating country. The analysis here is concerned with uses of the military instrument which the policymaker does not intend to have result in violence. Of course, if a certain reaction ensues on the part of the target violence may develop.

[37]See Chapter 2, p. 70.

[38]*Jerusalem Post,* October 22, 1974, p. 1. In 1974 there was more construction than during the entire period between the June 1967 War and the Yom Kippur War of October 1973.

murdered Chancellor Dollfuss. In response, Italy, under the leadership of Mussolini, concentrated heavy troop formations on the border (at this time Mussolini had not yet decided to join with Hitler). Upon seeing this troop deployment Germany disavowed the coup; the Italian nonviolent activity had been successful.

Another example occurred in early 1957. Following the Suez crisis of 1956 (in which Britain, France, and Israel had unsuccessfully attacked Egypt), the popularity of Egypt's President Nasser rose dramatically and seemed to pose a threat to many Western-oriented Arab policymakers.[39] One such leader, Jordan's King Hussein, was under immense internal pressure to reorient both his domestic and foreign policies to bring them into line with Nasser's. Strikes and riots occurred as he resisted, and a series of incidents developed that seemed to be leading to a full scale civil war. The United States, interested in supporting Hussein as a Middle Eastern counterweight to Nasser, announced that it considered the independence and integrity of Jordan to be vital to American interests, and dispatched the Sixth Fleet to the Eastern Mediterranean.[40] Such gunboat diplomacy proved to be very effective, and the crisis soon abated. Privately administration officials left no doubt that this was a calculated show of force.[41]

Sometimes a nonviolent show of force is not effective, however. Such activity is designed to threaten the target, to warn that unless the desired modification of behavior occurs some harm will be perpetrated. If the threatener does not have the capability or will to carry out its threat, or if the target at least perceives this to be the case, the threat (by itself) will not be effective.[42]

In August 1957 the Syrian Government uncovered an alleged American plot to overthrow the existing regime. Because of Syria's increasingly close relations with Russia, her "leftist" domestic structure, her rabidly anti-Israeli attitude, and her antagonism to Western-supported Arab leaders like Jordan's King Hussein, it was clear that Washington would oppose her on many issues.

Whether there was a CIA-engineered plot is not clear from the evidence but the Syrian policymakers certainly thought there was.[43] They expelled three American diplomats and Washington retaliated by declaring the Syrian Ambassador unwelcome. Remembering the success of its military demonstrations in the Jordanian crisis a few months earlier, Washington had the Sixth Fleet ostentatiously engage in maneuvers in the Eastern Mediterranean.

This time, however, it backfired. Instead of being cowed, Syrian

---

[39]Also see Chapter 6, pp. 211–213.

[40]This occurred so suddenly that 150 sailors were left in port. *New York Times,* April 25, 1957, p. 1.

[41]Ibid., p. 2.

[42]See Chapter 5, pp. 184–186, for a further discussion of threats.

[43]This point is very interesting although irrelevant to our concern. For an interesting discussion see Patrick Seale, *The Struggle for Syria: A Study of Post-War Arab Politics 1945–1958,* Oxford University Press, London and New York, 1965, Ch. 21.

policymakers stepped up their anti-American campaign and stated that such gunboat diplomacy substantiated their charge that the United States was the real imperialist in the region, a major enemy of all Arabs.[44]

In the Syrian case the military maneuvers were mere bluff. Not so in Czechoslovakia in 1968. For many months the Czechoslovakian Government had been steadily moving toward a more democratic government, and this was perceived by Moscow as a threat to its system. In the spring of the year the Warsaw Pact states held scheduled military maneuvers inside Czechoslovakia, but when it came time to withdraw they were especially slow. This implied threat brought no appreciable alteration in Czech policies. Then the Soviets staged some war games near the frontier. Once again Czech policymakers refused to bend. As is discussed below, in August the Russians (with the "assistance" of other Warsaw Pact states) invaded; they were not fooling. Here the Czechs guessed wrong, but the point for our discussion is that the nonviolent use of the military was again ineffective.

Limited Isolated Violence

Moving up the scale, the policymaker may conclude that some degree of force or violence would be useful but warfare should be avoided. Thus the operation should remain limited in terms of objectives, targets, and duration, and probably would involve a particular incident (or series of incidents) or a one-shot military operation.[45]

The Israeli Government has long made use of limited isolated violence. As discussed above, in late 1974 the Syrian Government had not given any public indication concerning whether or not it would approve an extension of the UNDOF mandate. About the same time the Palestinian question put Israel on the diplomatic defensive. At the Rabat Conference in October Arab leaders agreed that the Palestine Liberation Organization (an organization Israeli policymakers characterized as gangsters and murderers) was the sole legitimate representative of the Palestinian people. It was further agreed that any portions of the old Palestine Mandate recovered from Israel would be the responsibility of the PLO. In late November the United Nations General Assembly voted to affirm the

---

[44]Their case was not harmed when Secretary Dulles said he hoped that "the people of Syria would act to allay the anxiety caused by recent events." That looked like an invitation for a coup. The quote is from U.S., Department of State, *American Foreign Policy: Current Documents, 1957*, p. 1038.

[45]Just as was true with respect to whether or not an activity remained nonviolent, whether or not the violence remains limited and isolated also is to a great extent dependent on the reaction of the target. Our classification is dependent on the policymaker's own objectives and his perception of the likelihood of the target's reaction being such that the violence would remain limited and isolated. This involves a great deal of subjective judgment, of course, and sometimes mistakes are made. What is planned as a limited operation may escalate into a much less limited conflict (and occasionally into warfare of considerable duration).

Palestinians' "right to national independence and sovereignty" after listening to PLO leader, Yasir Arafat, state his case.

In order to emphasize its own military strength and the fact that it would not be pressured into negotiating with the PLO, Israeli military units undertook a wide variety of attacks against PLO supported facilities in Lebanon. These attacks included several small infantry forays that destroyed installations and equipment as well as inflicting minor casualties, and air sorties as far into Lebanon as Beirut. In each case the operation was specific, its military objective was clear, and its political objective was to demonstrate that Israel had the military strength and political willpower to make its own decisions concerning with whom it would negotiate over land it controlled.

Another example of limited military operations occurred on the night of August 20, 1968 as troops from the Soviet Union, East Germany, Poland, Hungary, and Bulgaria crossed the Czechoslovakian border and proceeded to occupy their "ally." In this case the objective was primarily to eliminate a regime that was becoming too "liberal" (read: "capitalist" and "democratic") for Soviet policymakers' tastes. The Soviets did not expect much military resistance, and they did not get it. As a result their limited violence proved successful.

Although there are many other examples, it would be superfluous to give them. It is clear that policymakers often decide to engage in the limited use of violence, and sometimes it works. But many times it does not. Sometimes reciprocal escalation develops as in Vietnam, and a limited war occurs. The policymaker must recognize this possibility. Unless one is in a situation where his target is either clearly inferior in capability and has no potential for external assistance, or else it has no intention of resisting anyway, he runs an immense risk that what begins as an exercise in limited violence will actually turn into some type of warfare. If this is acceptable, all fine and good; if not, one must engage in limited violence with a great deal of caution.

Limited War

Sometimes it appears that one can achieve his objectives only with the sustained but limited application of force. Limited wars are not new, of course, but with the tendencies toward total war and the appalling destructiveness of modern weaponry the necessity of keeping conflicts limited has gained a new urgency.[46]

In some senses, of course, nearly all wars are limited. Although there are exceptions, it is highly unusual for a party to seek the annihilation of its adversary with every means at its disposal. Even in World War II some types of weapons were not used and some methods were not employed. Despite this fact,

---

[46]The best introductory books on this topic are still Henry Kissinger, *Nuclear Weapons and Foreign Policy,* Harper, New York, 1957, and Robert Osgood, *Limited War: The Challenge to American Strategy,* University of Chicago Press, Chicago, 1957.

there is still an important distinction to be made here. The concept of limited war implies a conscious effort to use the military instrument for rationally defined political purposes, and to keep the conflict under control by definitely limiting or excluding certain factors. A point of some significance in this regard is that because different parties have different perceptions, orientations, and objectives the same conflict can be quite limited for one participant but relatively unlimited for another. For example, although Washington saw the Vietnam war as a limited conflict, for Viet Cong policymakers it was a struggle for survival.

What are the major limitations one may seek to impose? The first lies in the area of *objectives*. The policymaker may seek only a set of specific narrowly defined goals. Rather than territorial conquest and the subjugation of an adversary, for example, he or she may attempt only a limited gain.

One of the greatest practitioners of limited war was the nineteenth-century Prussian, Prince Otto Von Bismarck. After decisively defeating Austria in the Seven Weeks' War (June to August, 1866), for example, he refused to annex many of the territories that he had captured. His purpose had been to demonstrate Prussian superiority in North Germany, and make some limited territorial gains. This he had accomplished. By going no further he avoided incurring permanent Austrian hostility.[47]

Another example was provided by the Sino-Indian conflict. In conjunction with a festering boundary dispute and the political contest for Asian supremacy, Communist Chinese forces attacked India's Himalayan provinces in late 1962. The Chinese easily overran their opposition and demonstrated that they had the capacity to conquer the entire subcontinent if they should desire, but they did not.[48] This attack accomplished two carefully limited objectives. First, it clearly established Peking's military superiority. Second, it reaffirmed China's position on borders, namely, that the existing frontiers were artificially imposed and had no legitimacy; the true borders of China were those of the Middle Kingdom.[49]

A very important factor in achieving limited objectives via the limited application of force is clear communication. The policymaker must make sure that other parties *know* his or her objectives are limited or else he or she is inviting counter action. Bismarck and Mao were able to succeed because outsiders who might have intervened did not do so because they accurately assessed the conflict's objectives.

As mentioned in Chapter 2, however, ascertaining the objectives of one's counterparts is a critical but terribly uncertain task. What *are* his objectives, and *are* they limited? Chamberlain thought Hitler's objectives were limited, but he was wrong. Doubly frustrating is the fact that sometimes the policymakers them-

---

[47]Useful is Hartmann, *The Relations of Nations,* Fifth Edition, pp. 336–337.

[48]Because the Cuban Missile Crisis was occurring simultaneously it is unlikely that any outside power capable of preventing this would have done so. They had their own troubles.

[49]See Chapter 2, p. 47, and footnote 21.

selves are not sure what they are after, or they may start out with one goal but change as the situation changes. The original American objective in Korea was simply to prevent a North Korean conquest but Washington opted for territorial unification when battlefield conditions improved (and later changed again in the light of battlefield reverses).

Policymakers also may seek to *limit the means employed* and deliberately exclude the use of certain weapons systems.[50] As has been mentioned previously, the United States deliberately excluded the use of nuclear weapons in the Vietnamese conflict. Although there have been minor exceptions, generally speaking chemical and biological weapons have not been extensively used in warfare. The assumption behind weapons exclusion is that the situation can be more easily controlled and escalation can be prevented if certain parts of one's arsenal are not used. Presumably the adversary will recognize that mere destruction is not desired and that survival is not the issue. Hopefully nonparticipants will also be cognizant of these facts, will avoid participation, and will recognize that some measure of praise should be forthcoming.

One may also seek to *limit the number of participants*. Indeed, a major reason for limiting objectives and/or means is to avoid provoking others into participation. Sometimes one has one's eye on a specific nonparticipant. American policymakers in the Vietnam conflict were constantly looking toward Peking and stating that various military raids were in no way a threat to Chinese security.

The concern also may be more general. Although one cannot say there is a precise relationship between the intensity of warfare and the number of combatants, it is usually true that, other things being equal, the fewer the number of participants the more controllable the situation becomes. For example, suppose in the next Middle East war (assuming there is a next Middle East war) all of the Arab states become heavily involved against Israel (one must remember that this never has occurred in previous conflicts). If such were to happen it is quite possible that, for those participants, the war would become unlimited and someone's survival would be at stake. Should that occur the conflict would be very difficult to control.

Another way a policymaker may seek to control a conflict is by *limiting the targets* of his or her activity. The less vital a particular target is to a state's survival the more the policymaker for that state can tolerate its being attacked, and vice versa. This type of limitation may refer simply to declaring (tacitly or explicitly) certain geographical areas off limits. In the Korean War, for example, the Chinese enjoyed what become known as a "privileged sanctuary" in that the United States did not (except for minor incidents) attack the territory of the Chinese state itself. Similarly, the United States was allowed its "privileged

---

[50]The reference here is to the nonuse of weapon systems that a state possesses. Obviously a state cannot employ weapons it does not have but that type of "limitation" is not meaningful for our purposes.

sanctuary'' in the sense that many of its troops and supplies came from Japan and Peking made no effort to attack her.

Sometimes the participants seek to make use of the question of targeting in order to apply pressure to another belligerent. In the Vietnam conflict it was not until early 1965 that the United States began to bomb Hanoi's "privileged sanctuary" in the north, and then it began in terms of areas near the demilitarized zone. When Washington was not able to bring Hanoi to the bargaining table on the terms it desired it increasingly chose targets that were more vital to the North Vietnamese war effort such as port facilities in Haiphong, steel complexes, electrical facilities, and so forth. As we know, however, the gradual escalation did not prove successful.

A very successful recent use of limited warfare occurred in October 1973. After his ascension to power in 1970 Egyptian President Sadat sought to bring about some progress toward the "removal of the consequences of Israeli aggression," that is, some Israeli movement away from the Suez Canal and the return of some of the territories taken by her in the 1967 war. By late 1973, despite all his efforts, no progress had been made. Because of this on October 6, 1973 Egypt launched a military assault across the Suez Canal, and began the Yom Kippur War.

The Egyptian attack clearly was only a limited warfare maneuver. The Egyptians did not have the military capability to defeat Israel, and knew it. Instead they hoped to make a good military showing, which in fact they did, and thus improve their bargaining position. This would compel Israel to think very seriously about negotiating some type of compromise agreement, forcing her to recognize that merely digging in on the banks of the Canal was not a sufficient policy.[51] Sadat made it clear that he would not accept this indefinitely and that such a policy would prevent any possibility of a peace settlement.

Sadat also was seeking to demonstrate to the remainder of the world that the Arabs were developing a military capability of some note and other states (particularly the United States) should recognize that no longer was Israel guaranteed of a sure military victory. He hoped that, once outsiders recognized this fact, they would make more of an effort to help bring about a settlement. As mentioned earlier, in 1974 and 1975 the United States did act as a problem solver and helped bring about the Israeli-Syrian and (two) Israeli-Egyptian disengagement agreements.

In concluding this discussion of limited war activities it should be emphasized again that when a policymaker decides to engage in combat he is undertaking a very risky course of action. While it sounds fine in the abstract to talk about controlling warfare, when war occurs intense emotions are aroused. The time pressure, the problem of adequate information, problems of communi-

---

[51]This statement is not meant to imply that the Israelis actually *were* following such a policy. These comments refer only to *Egyptian perceptions* and objectives.

cation, the snowballing effect, domestic political pressures, as well as problems of interaction and perception between the parties, make the situation very difficult to control. If one can maintain control by limitation as the Egyptians were able to do in the 1973 conflict (with the assistance of outside powers) then perhaps limited war can be effective, but one must always recognize that it may not be possible to keep a "limited" conflict limited.

Guerilla Warfare

There is one type of limited war that deserves special treatment because of its importance today: guerilla war.[52] The term "guerilla war" covers a wide variety of conflicts and situations but two elements are always present: there is some type of revolutionary activity against the existing government, and the tactics of the conflict are unconventional with an emphasis on mobility, harassment, and infiltration.

The "book" on guerilla war was "written" by Mao Tse-tung in the Chinese Communist revolution.[53] The Chinese Communist Party was established in 1921 at the instigation of the Communist International in Moscow, and took its place among the series of revolutionary factions competing for power in the wake of the collapse of the Manchu Empire.[54] Under Soviet direction the Chinese were compelled to collaborate with the Kuomintang (the Chinese Nationalist Party). This uneasy partnership was dissolved in 1926 and 1927 as the Nationalists, under the leadership of the Moscow trained General Chiang Kai-shek, launched a military campaign aimed at gaining control over all of China. Although that objective was never totally achieved, Chiang did inflict a series of military defeats upon his rivals and emerged as the most powerful force in the country. When a series of Communist insurrections failed in the late 1920s the Party was driven from the cities into the north west provinces.

Until this time Mao had been only one among several leading Communists. After it became clear that the Russian-dominated policy had failed and the existing leadership was inept, however, Mao and his associates were able to take over. Taking advantage of Kuomintang incompetence and the beginning of the Japanese onslaught he began a guerilla campaign.

---

[52]Also variously called sublimited war, war of national liberation, people's war, ambiguous conflict, or unconventional war.

[53]Mao actually did much writing, but the comments here are referring to his example and the fact that many later revolutionaries adopted his methods. For an understanding of his basic ideas in this sphere see Mao Tse-tung, *On Guerilla Warfare*, Praeger, New York, 1961.

[54]The Manchus lost power in 1911. The succeeding years were characterized by governmental impotence and warlord rule. The country was divided into a series of military fiefdoms, each controlled by a regional warlord or military leader, and the central government became little more than a puppet of whichever warlord happened to be in control of the region at the time. Soon two "central governments" competed for control, one in the imperial capital of Peking, the other at Canton.

Mao recognized that traditional Marxist doctrine predicting the revolution of the industrial proletariat was inappropriate to the Chinese situation because no industrial proletariat existed. Showing the flexibility of good leadership, he placed *his* emphasis on the peasants and capitalized on their disaffection with the Kuomintang. Alternately fighting and collaborating with the Nationalists (as they continued their efforts against the Japanese) he built both a highly disciplined political party and a very effective military machine. Tactically he used the difficult terrain for evasive tactics, avoiding direct combat situations that might drain his military strength. Mobility and surprise were his assets and when it looked like he might lose a battle he quickly retreated.

When World War II ended China was still in turmoil. There was no effective military or political control, transport and communication facilities were disrupted, inflation was rampant, and corruption continued unabated. Full scale civil war developed. Mao continued to avoid massive confrontations and harassed and frustrated his opposition. He made use of captured or abandoned equipment plus some weapons turned over by the Russians in Manchuria. Mao was not concerned with defending or obtaining particular pieces of territory or lines. In reality there are no front lines in this kind of activity. His forces concentrated on small scale operations against communications lines and supply depots, ambushed convoys, and generally used hit and run tactics.

In an effort to cut their losses the Nationalist forces retreated to the cities (a traditional Chinese defense technique) thus leaving the countryside to the Communists (which was precisely what the latter desired as they continued to build their strength on the peasantry). Eventually the cities became isolated and supplies were cut off. Counter thrusts became nearly impossible and the civilian population (at least most of it) just stood back and watched, ready to join whichever side seemed to be winning.[55] It was not so much that the government was despised by the people as it was that the public was indifferent. Early in 1948 the Communists took the offensive as morale among even the best Nationalist formations began to crack. Chiang's demoralized troops simply lost the will to fight. With Nationalist strength dissipating the Communists were now able to engage in direct confrontation and usually emerged victorious. In early 1949 Peking fell to Mao's forces. Before the year was out Chiang retreated from the mainland to Formosa and Mao was in control. In October he proclaimed the People's Republic of China with its capital in the old imperial city of Peking.

Since the time of Mao's successful revolution others have followed his example. Some states have provided outside assistance for such activities. China and (North) Vietnam, for example, have played major roles in supporting national liberation movements throughout Asia, and scores of other "people's" forces have been aided by states as they have employed guerilla tactics throughout much of the less developed world.

---

[55]This often is the situation in successful revolutions. Seldom do the masses rise up and overthrow their government. Instead, they simply fail to give it support.

Guerilla warfare can be primarily an internal operation, like Mao's, or the insurgents can receive extensive external assistance. Various covert means of infiltration and penetration are potentially available if one seeks to use them to assist guerilla activities: economic and military assistance, infiltration of key organizations, bribery, propaganda activities of many types, and so on.

Despite the many techniques available a foreign policymaker usually cannot instigate and direct successful guerilla warfare on his own; revolution is not exportable. Instead, his role is one of assisting, facilitating the insurgents' activities, and exacerbating the problems of the existing government. The reason for this limitation is that guerilla activity cannot be effective without some degree of popular support, and this will be forthcoming only if the populace is somewhat alienated from the government to begin with.[56] Although an outsider may be able to magnify discontent and provide the discontented with certain capabilities, seldom can he create the situation in the first place.

It must be remembered that effective guerilla warfare is more than a military operation. It employs a wide range of techniques that affect the psychological and political attitudes of the populace, and it relies on a certain degree of popular cooperation for its continuance. For this reason it cannot be successfully countered by solely military means, although obviously military capability is important.[57] The Saigon Government could not defeat the Viet Cong even though it received immense military assistance from Washington. It is only a combination of military strength and a government responsive to its people's needs that will be successful.

Foreign policymakers can be expected to continue and perhaps increase their participation in guerilla warfare activities in the years ahead. There are several reasons for this.[58] First, it is often possible for one to keep one's participation relatively disguised (or maybe even secret), thus minimizing the risks of a direct confrontation. Second, the consequences of failure tend to be relatively small due to the relatively small commitment. Third, such operations are relatively inexpensive. The weapons and supplies required are comparatively meager and thus are within the capability of nearly all parties.[59] Fourth, only a small number of men is required to start and never does the personnel requirement become excessively large. Fifth, because of the dangers of nuclear warfare policymakers are actively seeking alternative uses of force. Sixth, states are much more permeable than in the past and it is difficult to prevent penetration.

---

[56]See Chalmers A. Johnson, "Civilian Loyalties and Guerilla Conflict," *World Politics,* July, 1962, pp. 646–661.

[57]Statements such as this are sometimes misinterpreted. No one is saying that military strength is not important. It is, and is a necessary part of effective counterinsurgency strategy. But one must recognize that it is only a *part* of the answer and is not sufficient by itself.

[58]Also see Chapter 2, pp. 63–64, 81–82.

[59] This, of course, can change. If the guerilla forces alter their tactics to engage in confrontations, their needs will drastically increase. At this time external aid may be decisive.

And seventh, conditions in many countries are ripe for revolutionary activities, and many of the problems seem unlikely to be remedied in the forseeable future.

Deterrence

Finally, the policymaker may seek to use the military for purposes of deterrence.[60] The approach here will be twofold: first, an attempt will be made to define and analyze what appear to be the basic components of sound deterrence, and second, many of the factors involved will be examined through an analysis of the evolution of American strategic policy.

Basically, deterrence means that policymaker A seeks to prevent policymaker B from doing something by threatening B with unacceptable costs if he or she does. By posing this threat A is seeking to preclude certain types of activity (usually activities involving military attack). Deterrence involves a critical psychological relationship between the "deterrer" and "deterree," and when successful is characterized by the effective nonuse of military force.

What are the requirements for effective deterrence?[61] *First, the policymakers must act as rationally as possible.*[62] There must be accurate evaluations of the capabilities and intentions of the relevant parties, different national perceptions must be taken into account, careful precautions must be taken so as to prevent organizational inefficiency from disrupting planned policy, and the costs and benefits from each potential decision must be accurately calculated and balanced. If rationality is not present no system of deterrence can be guaranteed to be effective.[63] If states are headed by people who are "trigger happy," careless, power hungry, unstable, or whatever, or if there is not careful control over subordinates and they undertake senseless activities, deterrence may be unworkable.

---

[60]The subject of deterrence is so complicated and amorphous that one hardly knows where to begin. Volumes have been written and an entirely new area of specialization, deterrent theory, has emerged. Unfortunately there is little agreement among scholars or policymakers. As John Raser has said, "what looked like a forest to early deterrent scholars is now seen to be a tractless jungle and its explorers are unable to set up any guideposts reading 'this way to safety'." John R. Raser, "International Deterrence," in Michael Haas, ed., *International Systems: A Behavioral Approach*, Chandler, New York, 1974, p. 320.

[61]Though for reasons of analytical clarity our discussion is focused on a bilateral relationship in which military considerations and the perceptions thereof are dominant, it is essential to remember that in the "real world" events are interrelated and multilateral relationships, third-party influences, and nonmilitary factors all may be relevant.

[62]Total rationality is impossible, of course, since one can never know all the information relevant to a particular subject, be aware of all the possible alternatives and their consequences, and so on. Here we simply mean that the policymakers do everything within their power to think and act on the basis of evidence and logic.

[63]There may be some situations in which deterrence is ineffective even if rationality *is* present. For example, if one has the capacity to completely destroy the enemy's retaliatory forces in a preemptive strike, such an attack may be very rational and deterrence may fail.

The second component of deterrence is *credibility*. This involves several elements. First, in order for credibility to be established one must have the military capability to inflict what is considered by the deterree to be an unacceptable level of damage. Second, credibility requires the capacity to communicate the extent of one's capability to the deterree. Obviously a state will not be deterred on the basis of the second state's military strength if it is not aware that the second state has this strength. Usually such communication is relatively easy.

A third component of credibility is the willingness to use power. One's threat to carry out an activity that will bring about unacceptable damage must be believed by the target of that threat; otherwise, there will not be a deterrent effect. The target must think that the threatener is willing to do what it said it would. Simply because a party has a certain level of military strength does not necessarily mean that it is willing to use it. Once again communication, in this case communication of willingness, is terribly important.

A critically important fact to note is that *credibility depends on the beliefs and perceptions of the target of the deterrent policy, that is, the deterree*. It is not what the deterre*er* thinks is important that will be decisive, but the thoughts and ideas of the deterre*e*. When analyzing the question of what is an unacceptable level of damage to Russia, it is not important what would be unacceptable to *American* policymakers but rather what level of damage is unacceptable to *Soviet* leaders.

The final component of effective deterrence is *stability*. It must be clear that one is not attempting to create a first strike capability, a capacity to destroy its opponent. If it looks as if first strike capability *is* one's objective, the target policymaker may be provoked into a preemptive strike in order to avoid the perceived possible strike against his or her state. When such terrible weapons are available, the one who strikes first may possibly be able to destroy the other side's forces and thus escape retaliation.

An analysis of the development of American strategic policy will help illustrate some of these points. Following World War II American policymakers assumed that if there was to be another war it would be general, the result of a Soviet attack on Europe.[64] The resulting American posture was a basic reliance on the *threat of atomic retaliation*. Since the United States was the only state to possess nuclear weapons at this time this was a first strike/counter city strategy.[65] If the Soviets launched an attack the United States would retaliate with a nuclear response on the major cities of the Soviet Union. From the Soviet point of view, in light of the American atomic monopoly, this kind of policy was credible but it also was threatening and destabilizing.[66]

[64]See Chapter 6 for further comments on American postwar perceptions.

[65]First strike in the sense that the United States would be the first to launch a nuclear attack. The trigger for such a strike was presumed to be a prior Soviet assault.

[66]Although there was no Soviet attack on Western Europe at this time, and thus one can argue that deterrence was effective, one could argue that this deterrent policy was designed to prevent a war

The testing of a Soviet atomic bomb in 1949 and the development of the Korean War helped bring about some changes.[67] The United States began to place somewhat more emphasis on the danger of local warfare and President Truman called for a substantial increase in American defense spending.

When the Eisenhower Administration took office in 1953 it decided to take a new look at military strategy. The main policy was called *massive retaliation*. The Administration was worried about the spiraling costs of defense. It felt that reliance on a more unified strategy emphasizing the role of one of the services (Air Force) would be both less expensive and more effective. The strategic policy was enunciated by the secretary in early January 1954 when he said that henceforth the United States would respond to provocations with massive retaliatory power by means and at places of its own choosing.[68]

Massive retaliation was not really very different from the first-strike/counter city policy of the Truman Administration. It could not help but be destabilizing and threatening to Soviet policymakers. The Russians were busily engaged in building their own nuclear force, testing thermonuclear devices, and developing delivery systems that could threaten the United States. Because of this the policy of massive retaliation came to resemble a mutual suicide pact. Since there was no defense against nuclear attack it was as if Mr. Dulles was saying, "if you destroy us I will make sure we take you with us when we go."

Many came to believe that this policy had severe deficiencies. It implied in all cases the threat of (and perhaps preparation for) total war, regardless of the extent and type of provocation.[69] Although the secretary was vague in terms of precisely what would happen if the Soviets provoked Uncle Sam, the possibility of massive response was there. Apparently he assumed this would be sufficient to deter both general and localized wars.

Both logic and a spate of local conflicts convinced many, observers and policymakers alike, that massive retaliation *by itself* was insufficient as a strategic doctrine. It allowed policymakers no flexibility of response. Since American strategic forces were vulnerable and might be destroyed in a surprise first strike, Washington's response would have to be automatic. This led to a

---

that the Soviets themselves never contemplated. If that is so the Soviets could only see it as a potentially aggressive accumulation of power.

[67]Although the Korean War was important in this regard, it only gave additional momentum to changes already in motion. A defense posture study known as NSC 68 had been adopted prior to the North Korean attack.

[68]John Foster Dulles, "The Evolution of Foreign Policy," U.S. Department of State, *Bulletin*, January 25, 1954, pp. 107–110.

[69]Extensive reliance on massive retaliation seemed to mean that, when faced with low level or limited provocation, one's options were limited to massive response or acquiescence. This dilemma had much to do with the development of limited war capacity, discussed above, and the doctrine of flexible response, discussed in Chapter 6. For the view that nuclear weapons make huge conventional forces obsolete see Bernard Brodie, *War and Politics*, Macmillan, New York, 1973, Ch. 9.

greater concern for the development of invulnerable retaliatory forces (second strike capability). If a state is committed to not launching a first strike, and if its adversary can launch a surprise attack and wipe out one's nuclear forces, then the situation is very unstable. Stability requires that states possess weapons that can survive a surprise attack and be capable of delivering a retaliatory blow of unacceptable proportions.

When the Kennedy Administration took over the beginnings of change that occurred in the latter Eisenhower years received further impetus. Greater emphasis was placed on the development of mobile Polaris missile submarines in order to decrease vulnerability. There was an effort to develop a greater mix of retaliatory forces (a combination of strategic air command forces and land and sea based missiles) so that there would always be at least one retaliatory force available. And as land based missiles began to be deployed in underground concrete silos there were efforts to "harden" these shelters to provide the greatest possible resistance to an attack.

In 1962 a shift in strategic doctrine occurred. In a major speech in Ann Arbor, Michigan, Secretary of Defense McNamara announced what became known as the *doctrine of counterforce*.[70] The basic idea of counterforce is deterrence by threatening to destroy military targets (instead of population centers). Under this operation cities would be spared and every effort made to minimize casualties among civilians.

Counterforce was also an intrawar deterrent doctrine. The idea here was that should war-preventing deterrence fail, a counterforce strategy would be the least immoral method of fighting a war because it would involve the least number of noncombatant casualties. In this sense it was hoped that deterrence would operate within the framework of a nuclear war, and that a nuclear war could be a limited war.

It was also assumed that counterforce targeting would give one's opponents an incentive to avoid striking cities. As Professor Rosi put it, "by retaliating in a controlled manner against military targets in the USSR, while avoiding Russian cities, the United States would seek to negotiate a truce before an all-out, city-destroying attack was launched by either side."[71]

The difficulty with a counterforce strategy is that it inevitably has first strike implications. Obviously attacks against an adversary's forces are more effective if launched before the latter's weapons have been fired. Although a party might say that its posture was second strike counterforce, and mean it, opposition policymakers would be compelled to consider the contrary. This is precisely what the Russians did, and the result was the addition of considerable impetus to

---

[70]See U.S. Department of State, *Bulletin,* July 9, 1962, pp. 64–69.

[71]Eugene J. Rosi, ed., *American Defense and Détente: Readings in National Security Policy,* Dodd Mead, New York, 1973, p. 98.

the arms race.[72] The more one sought to make counterforce credible, to increase its capability to destroy the opponent's forces, the more destabilizing it became. And neither side really believed the other would avoid its cities anyway.

McNamara never made it quite clear if Washington was shifting completely to counterforce or not, and by the mid-1960s some changes were apparent. The new policy was the *doctrine of assured destruction*. This was the second strike/counter value strategy. Although the precise terms varied from time to time, the doctrine's essential postulate was that the United States should, after absorbing a Soviet attack, have the retaliatory capacity to destroy an unacceptably large portion of Russia's population and industrial capacity (usually the proportions stipulated were one-third and two-thirds respectively.)[73] Developing a force of this capacity required both an increase in offensive strength and a decrease in vulnerability. Washington increased its emphasis on hardening of missile silos, and began testing the MIRV. The Soviets, too, stepped up their efforts.

When Richard Nixon became President American superiority in missile launchers was decreasing.[74] In light of this fact, the immense costs of the arms race, domestic political factors inhibiting new missile programs, and the recognition that the most stable deterrent situation seems to involve mutually invulnerable retaliatory forces, the President adopted the *strategy of sufficiency*. While maintaining the assured destruction capacity discussed above, he sought to stabilize the situation and prevent the Russians from gaining superiority. These efforts led to the Strategic Arms Limitation Agreements of 1972 in which overall quantitative limits were placed on the strategic missiles each side could possess.

But the SALT Agreements and perceptions of parity did not prevent the arms race from continuing, nor did they stop the growth of strategic doctrine. On February 5, 1974 Defense Secretary Schlesinger proposed a refinement of the sufficiency-assured destruction posture.[75] Within this framework Mr. Schlesinger advocated *"selective targeting options."* In language that seemed to

---

[72]Useful in this regard is Edgar M. Bottome, *The Balance of Terror: A Guide to the Arms Race,* Beacon, Boston, 1971. Another very important stimulant was the adverse (as the Soviets saw it) outcome of the Cuban Missile Crisis, the Kremlin believing it was forced to accept a humiliating defeat because of its strategic inferiority. See Chapter 3 above, Diagrams 2 and 3.

[73]According to Morton Halperin, however, the original figures were 25 percent in both cases. See Morton H. Halperin, *Defense Strategies for the Seventies,* Little Brown, Boston, 1971, p. 73.

[74]See Chapter 3, Diagrams 2 and 3 for an examination of the trends.

[75]See the secretary's testimony before the Senate Armed Services Committee. U.S., Congress, Senate, Committee on Armed Services, *Fiscal Year 1975 Authorization for Military Procurement, Research and Development, and Active Duty, Selected Reserve and Civilian Personnel Strengths,* Hearings, 93rd Congress, Second Session, February 5, 1974, pp. 1–163. With respect to the current status of American assured destruction capability the secretary testified that the United States could retaliate, even after an attack ''more brilliantly executed and devastating'' than he thought the Soviets could deliver, and destroy more than 30 percent of Soviet population and 75 percent of Russian industry (and still have something left for the Chinese).

combine counterforce and flexible response concepts, he indicated that Washington intended to "shore up deterrence across the entire spectrum of risk," providing selective options for "measured responses" against a wide range of military targets. This facet of the approach clearly was concerned with intrawar deterrence. The old question of course arises, namely, is the increased capability required to accomplish this objective a stabilizing or destabilizing factor?

With these developments American strategic doctrine seemed to stabilize. When the Carter Administration assumed office it quickly adopted the posture of its predecessor. Policymakers stated that a rough strategic equivalence existed between Washington and Moscow and that American retaliatory forces could withstand a major Soviet attack in sufficient numbers to strike back with devastating power against the appropriate target system; to the extent that control, selectivity, and deliberation were useful, they too could be provided.[76] For better or worse, there seemed to be considerable agreement in the United States on both what America's strategic doctrine was, and on what it should be.

After all this discussion what conclusions does one reach concerning deterrence? Unfortunately there is little of which one can be sure. Observer and policymaker alike must make their most informed judgments on the components of effective deterrence, each hoping that policymakers are correct (or that, if not, no one will launch a nuclear war anyway), and then pray that they are right.

The analysis in this chapter has made it clear that policymakers have a variety of economic and military options potentially available as instruments of policy implementation. But this is only half the picture. In addition to (or in combination with) such tangible tools, one also has a variety of less tangible options in the spheres of communication and negotiation, and it is to these that we now turn.

SELECTED BIBLIOGRAPHY

Art, Robert J., and Kenneth N. Waltz eds., *The Use of Force: International Politics and Foreign Policy,* Little Brown, Boston, 1971

Baldwin, Robert E., *Nontariff Distortions of International Trade,* Brookings, Washington, D.C., 1970.

Berliner, Joseph S., *Soviet Economic Aid,* Praeger, New York, 1958.

Bottome, Edgar M., *The Balance of Terror: A Guide to the Arms Race,* Beacon, Boston, 1971.

Brodie, Bernard, *Strategy in the Missile Age,* Princeton University Press, Princeton, New Jersey, 1959.

Brodie, Bernard, *War and Politics,* Macmillan, New York, 1973.

---

[76]See the testimony of various officials before the House Defense Appropriations Subcommittee early in 1977. U.S., Congress, House of Representatives, Subcommittee of the Committee on Appropriations, *Department of Defense Appropriations for 1978,* Hearings, 95th Congress, First Session, 1977, Part 2.

Galtung, Johan, "The Effects of Economic Sanctions, with Examples from the Case of Rhodesia," *World Politics,* April, 1967, pp.378—416.

Giap, Vo Nguyen, *Banner of People's War: The Party's Military Line,* Praeger, New York, 1970.

Halperin, Morton H., *Defense Strategies for the Seventies,* Little Brown, Boston, 1971.

Hanrieder, Wolfram, ed., *The United States and Western Europe,* Winthrop, Cambridge, Massachusetts, 1974.

Huntington, Samuel P., "Foreign Aid, for What and for Whom," *Foreign Policy,* Spring, 1971, pp. 114—134.

Johnson, Chalmers A., "Civilian Loyalties and Guerilla Conflict," *World Politics,* July, 1962, pp. 646—661.

Kahn, Herman, *On Thermonuclear War,* Second Edition, Free Press, New York, 1969.

Kaufmann, William W., *The McNamara Strategy,* Harper & Row, New York, 1964.

Kindleberger, Charles P., *Power and Money: The Economics of International Politics and the Politics of International Economics,* Basic Books, New York, 1970.

Kissinger, Henry, *Nuclear Weapons and Foreign Policy,* Harper & Row, New York, 1957.

Knorr, Klaus, *On the Uses of Military Power in the Nuclear Age.,* Princeton University Press, Princeton, New Jersey, 1966.

Knorr, Klaus, *The Power of Nations: The Political Economy of International Relations,* Basic Books, New York, 1975.

Laqueur, Walter, *Confrontation: The Middle East and World Politics,* Bantam, New York, 1974.

Mack, Andrew, J.R., "Why Big Nations Lose Small Wars: The Politics of Asymmetric Conflict," *World Politics,* January, 1975, pp. 175—200.

Mao Tse-tung, *On Guerilla Warfar,* Praeger, New York, 1961.

Montgomery, John, *Foreign Aid in International Politics,* Prentice-Hall, Englewood Cliffs, New Jersey, 1967.

Morgenthau, Hans, J., "A Political Theory of Foreign Aid," *American Political Science Review,* June, 1962, pp. 301—309.

National Planning Association, *U.S. Foreign Economic Policy for the 1970s: A New Approach to New Realities,* Washington, November, 1971.

Nelson, Joan M., *Aid, Influence and Foreign Policy,* Macmillan, New York, 1968.

Orbis, Fall, 1974, pp. 655—790.

Osgood, Robert, *Limited War: The Challenge to American Strategy,* University of Chicago Press, Chicago, 1957.

Pranger, Robert J., and Roger P. Labrie, eds., *Nuclear Strategy and National Security: Points of View,* American Enterprise Institute for Public Policy Research, Washington, D.C., 1977.

Pryor, F.L., *The Communist Foreign Trade System,* Allen & Unwin, London, 1963.

Quester, George H., *Nuclear Diplomacy: The First Twenty-five Years,* Dunellen, New York, 1970.

Raser, John R., "International Deterrence," in Michael Haas, ed., *International Systems: A Behavioral Approach,* Chandler, New York, 1974, pp. 301—324.

Rosi, Eugene J., ed., *American Defense and Détente: Readings in National Security Policy,* Dodd Mead, New York, 1973.

Schelling, Thomas C., *Arms and Influence,* Yale University Press, New Haven, Connecticut, 1966.

Snyder, Glenn H., *Deterrence and Defense,* Princeton University Press, Princeton, New Jersey, 1961.

Spero, Joan Edelman, *The Politics of International Economic Relations,* St. Martin's Press, New York, 1977.

Strange, Susan, "The Politics of International Currencies," *World Politics,* January, 1971, pp. 215−232.

Strausz-Hupé, Robert, and Stefan T. Possony, "Economics and Statecraft," in Robert L. Pfaltzgraff, Jr., ed., *Politics and the International System,* Second Edition, J.B. Lippincott, Philadelphia, 1972, pp. 308−318.

Thayer, Charles W., *Guerilla,* New American Library, New York, 1963.

Trager, Frank N., "Wars of National Liberation: Implications for U.S. Policy and Planning," *Orbis,* Spring, 1974, pp. 50−105.

U.S. Congress, Senate, Committee on Armed Services, *Fiscal Year 1975 Authorization for Military Procurement, Research and Development, and Active Duty, Selected Reserve and Civilian Personnel Strengths,* Hearings, 93rd Congress, Second Session, 1974.

Windsor, Philip, and Adam Roberts, *Czechoslovakia: Reform, Repression and Resistance,* Columbia University Press, New York, 1969.

Young, Oran, *The Politics of Force,* Princeton University Press, Princeton, New Jersey, 1968.

Zoppo, Ciro Elliot, "Nuclear Technology, Multipolarity, and International Stability," *World Politics,* July, 1966, pp. 579−606.

Five

Policy Implementation Instruments: Intangible

Policymakers sometimes seek to achieve their goals via means that are relatively intangible. These means may include actions that are designed to communicate with and influence the masses in another country, or involve various communications designed to signal one's policymaking counterparts. Often a negotiating situation develops and one seeks either to solve a problem via an agreement or just to gain certain benefits from the negotiating process itself. Occasionally one may negotiate an agreement for some reason other than solving a problem. These intangible implementation instruments provide the subject matter for this chapter.

COMMUNICATION

Almost all political activity involves communication of some sort.[1] Some communications are directed toward the masses and are termed "propaganda." Others are aimed at foreign policymakers, themselves. These are called "signals."

Propaganda

The twentieth century communication revolution has had a significant impact on the conduct of international relations. Because of the information explosion and rapid technological progress it is feasible for policymakers to seek to influence the attitudes and behavior of foreign populations. The term given to these activities is propaganda, the deliberate attempt to alter the attitudes and behavior of

---

[1] Richard N. Fagen, *Politics and Communication,* Little, Brown, Boston, 1966, p. 17. Also see footnote 11 later in the chapter.

foreign groups with the hope that the reaction of these targets will be that desired by the propagandist.[2] All governments have propaganda programs today.

Americans do not like the term "propaganda." They believe that propaganda is just another word for the lies of one's enemies and that such activities should not be engaged in by any self-respecting policymaker. This conception of propaganda is inaccurate and oversimplified, however. It is inaccurate because it assumes that only lies are used and that is not so; it is oversimplified because propaganda includes various mixtures and types of truth and falsity.

Since it is obvious that the propagandist does not attempt to present an unbiased argument based on clearly established facts, what *does* he or she do? Generally, *the propagandist approaches a particular problem with a set of carefully selected facts, many of which are accurate, and seeks to arrange them in such a way as to create the maximum favorable impact on his or her target.* In this process one is not making an objective report. Thus the entire picture may not be presented, attempts are made to manipulate emotions, distortion and exaggeration occur, and certain facts are omitted. Despite this, history indicates that the composite message must have some basis in reality or else it will eventually fail, and thus most propaganda contains some degree of truthfulness.[3]

The *weapons* of propaganda are many: radio broadcasts, television programs, films, pamphlets, newspaper articles and editorials, cultural exchanges, seminars, magazine articles, leaks of information, and a host of other activities. The mechanisms seem to be limited only by the imagination of the policymaker.

Propaganda objectives are as varied as the objectives of all policy. They may be general, involving an attempt to create a general receptivity to one's policy, or specific, such as the creation of dissatisfaction among particular groups. Perhaps one is seeking to exploit existing racial hatreds and fan a smoldering discontent into the flames of rebellion. Maybe it is an attempt to convince the masses that their government is inept or inefficient and thus create a climate for subversion. No matter what the particular purpose, the policymaker is seeking to influence the attitudes and behavior of the target state's people in a way favorable to his or her state.

In developing a propaganda program one of the policymaker's first tasks is to determine precisely *who should be the target* of the communication. It is usually not feasible to consider an entire population as one's target.[4] Seldom are the masses as a whole susceptible to foreign influence (and most people usually

---

[2]Terence H. Qualter, *Propaganda and Psychological Warfare,* Random House, New York, 1962, p. 27.

[3]We are speaking in terms of conscious actions by the policymaker. Different people have different perceptions of "the truth," information may be inaccurate, and many other factors can prevent a "truthful" presentation. Such problems are not our concern here, although they are very important. Our analysis is concerned with the degree of *deliberate* truthfulness.

[4]The failure to recognize this fact was a distinct defect in American propaganda in the early years of the Cold War.

are not very interested in international affairs anyway). Furthermore, only certain component groups are in a position to significantly influence policymakers no matter what the governmental system. The propagandist needs to find out who these key policy-influencers are, determine which of them may be susceptible to propaganda, and concentrate his or her efforts accordingly.[5]

A second task is *to ascertain the types and depth of the attitudes held by the various groups.* This is essential because some kinds of attitudes are quite susceptible to manipulation but others are not. Two rules of thumb are appropriate here. First, propaganda that reinforces existing attitudes or activates latent favorable predispositions is more effective than that which attempts to alter hostility. Second, deeply ingrained attitudes of any type are seldom amenable to change. People resist and selectively reject information that does not fit their existing notions. Furthermore, host governments are often able to counter one's efforts with their own programs.

These facts lead to the conclusion that propaganda is more effective with respect to one's allies than in changing the views of the populace of one's enemies. And the historical record substantiates this point. But propaganda may be useful with respect to an adversarial target group: (1) if its attitudes are only weakly held; (2) if the object of the attitude is new and opinions have not yet formed and/or solidified; and (3) if there are several different attitudes about a given subject and they tend to offset each other.[6]

In attempting to influence certain attitudes within the target groups the policymaker engages in what is called "image projection." The policymaker recognizes that people make judgments and take actions on the basis of the mental images they possess, not in terms of objective reality. Consequently one seeks to project the best possible image of his or her state in the hope of influencing the images of his target.

How does one project the best image? What kinds of messages condition the audience most effectively? What type of communications make the target most receptive to one's policies in general, and respond as desired in the particular situation?

There are no guarantees of success but an effective message usually seems to contain the following elements.[7] First, it must be *simple.* People are not interested in detailed, sophisticated explanations or proposals. They want something that is direct and to the point. Second, effective propaganda *plays on the emotions.* A simple slogan such as "ban the bomb" or the use of emotion-laden terms like "peace loving people" or "imperialist warmongers" usually affects peoples' images more than reasoned arguments. Third, the communication must

[5]For a useful discussion of this problem see W. Phillips Davison, *International Political Communication,* Praeger, New York, 1965.

[6]This would hold true for nonadversaries as well.

[7]Useful is Norman J. Padelford and George A. Lincoln, *The Dynamics of International Politics,* Third Edition, Macmillan, New York, 1976, pp. 354–356.

be of some *direct interest* to the recipient. If it does not deal with a problem that is of personal concern then at best it will be ignored and at worst it will be considered to be an attempt at deception. Fourth, the message must be *credible, believable*. If it is ludicrous, or at least appears to be, once again the best one could hope is that the reaction would be neutral, and more than likely it would be counterproductive. Purported American concern for a supposed Soviet military threat to the Middle East in 1957 was considered to be an obvious "red herring" by the Arabs since they had just been attacked by Britain, France, and Israel and defended (diplomatically) by the Soviets.[8] Fifth, to be credible it must be *visible*. There must be something tangible that makes this message "real" in the eyes of the target. After the Soviets launched Sputnik in 1957, their professions of technological progress seemed much more real. And finally, the message must *sympathetically identify* with the local experiences of the people. American attempts to promote a capitalist economic system in many of the less developed countries, where a history of private exploitation by large landowners often exists, hardly identifies with local experience in a favorable way.

It is difficult to evaluate the effectiveness of propaganda. It has been stated that "we might liken the process of propaganda . . . to that of 'retouching' a photograph: Within limits, individuals engaged in both activities can do much to improve the image with which they are concerned, but the results are also fundamentally determined by the nature of the original picture.'"[9] In other words, a favorable image can be maintained only if policy actions have a favorable impact.

Mass communication can alter the degree and intensity of reaction, and might be very influential for a short time, but eventually the acts of the state will be more important than the pictures of those acts portrayed by the propagandist. Observer and policymaker alike must remember this point. All state actions influence attitudes to some extent and they all have propaganda connotations. As Lerche and Said pointed out, "effective propaganda may increase the policy impact of diplomatic, economic, or even military moves, but it can rarely accomplish a specific end by itself.'"[10]

Signals

A second kind of international communication is signalling, that is, the transmission of messages or cues from the policymakers of one country to their counterparts in another.[11] Once again one is tempted to say that actions speak louder than

---

[8]See the discussion of the Suez crisis in Chapter 6, pp. 196−198.

[9]Cecil V. Crabb, Jr., *American Foreign Policy in the Nuclear Age,* Third Edition, Harper, New York, 1972, p. 400.

[10]Lerche and Said, Second Edition, p. 89.

[11]As mentioned earlier, communication is involved in all political activity in some way. The discussion of the economic and military instruments above, and negotiation in the next section, continually highlight its importance.

words. The American precautionary military alert to the perceived threat of unilateral Soviet intervention in the 1973 Middle East war, for example, clearly signalled Washington's determination not to allow any Soviet intervention to go unchallenged. Israeli raids on suspected guerilla bases in southern Lebanon in mid-November 1974 immediately prior to the appearance of the Palestinian guerilla leader, Yasir Arafat, at the United Nations signalled Tel Aviv's determination not to allow its future to be determined by UN resolutions. The maneuvers of the American Sixth Fleet in the Eastern Mediterranean at the time of the 1970 Jordanian Civil War signified Washington's unwillingness to allow the situation in Jordan to deteriorate too far.[12]

Other examples are less obvious but not necessarily less important. If negotiations should be decided on in a particular case the location of those negotiations might be a signal as to the importance attached to them by the respective parties. The diplomatic rank of the representatives to the negotiations might have similar significance.[13]

Sometimes signals may be unintentional, and occasionally the absence of expected activities also "communicates." During the 1968 Czechoslovakian crisis there was no official statement, either on behalf of the Soviet Government or the CPSU, about the invasion. Also, there was a lack of the usual signatures of the Soviet leadership (Brezhnev, Kosygin and Podgorny) on all official documents in the days immediately following the assault. These facts were an unintentional but clear signal that there was great confusion and disagreement within the Politburo.[14]

In reality, "every act of international behavior involves communication in either an implicit or explicit sense insofar as it provides information to other nations."[15] Unfortunately, acts may be interpreted in many different ways. There is no automatic guarantee that the receiver will "get the message" in precisely the manner and to the extent that the sender desired.[16] Here one must deal not only with the structure and content of communications but also with the elusive quality of intentions. What does the sender of a message "really" mean? Did the Soviet construction and testing of four new intercontinental ballistic missiles in 1974 mean that they were simply trying to gain a better bargaining position for the SALT II Talks, that they were only trying to upgrade their deterrent force, that they were trying to develop a first-strike capability, or what?

If the policymaker is seeking to communicate accurately it is necessary to take pains to prevent the "message" from being misinterpreted. A good example

---

[12]This was particularly important because of the 1958 landing of Marines in Lebanon discussed in Chapter 6.

[13]See pp. 180–182.

[14]Windsor, p. 67. See Chapter 7, pp. 149, 150 for further comments on the crisis.

[15]Warren R. Phillips, "International Communications," in Michael Haas, ed., *International Systems: A Behavioral Approach,* Chandler, New York, 1974, p. 178.

[16]Once again the problem of perception rears its ugly head. In addition to the relevance of many earlier examples, much of the analysis in Chapter 6 is pertinent here.

of such an effort occurred at the end of November 1974 when President Ford went to Russia for a summit meeting with Soviet Communist Party Secretary, Leonid Brezhnev. The conference was held in Vladivostok. The choice of this location could have been misinterpreted by the Chinese as signalling an American "tilt" toward Moscow in the Sino-Soviet dispute, since that city was a part of the territory taken from the Chinese by the Tsar in the mid-1800s. As discussed earlier this land is considered by Peking to be inescapably Chinese. In order to reassure the People's Republic of China that the site did not signify an American "tilt," Secretary of State Kissinger continued on to Peking after the Vladivostok meetings concluded.

Before dispensing with the discussion of the importance of actions in communications, the question as to whether or not the supposed dichotomy between actions and words really means very much ought to be raised. Professor Stanley Hoffman doubts it. He wrote: "the distinction between acts and verbal policies is losing its usefulness."[17] And as Frank and Weisband have pointed out, words define action.[18] In this sense words really are verbal weapons and may be as important as concrete acts.

This is not nit-picking. Statesmen act (partially at least) on the basis of the communications they receive, and these involve the use of words. Words that paint a picture directly contrary to actions undertaken will have little impact, but these are seldom used. In most cases the policymaker receives a composite set of signals, a composite containing *both* words and actions. This being so, perhaps one should consider words and actions together as an entire communications system rather than attempting to separate one from the other.

In diplomatic communication generally great care is taken to choose precisely the right word. There is often a great difference in this regard between the observer and the participant. Many times the former fails to appreciate the fact that the policymaker usually labors to select a particular word or phrase that conveys a specific meaning. If an observer attempts to read documents rapidly just to get a general sense of what is being said he may well fail to grasp the essence of the "message."

On April 7, 1965, in his famous Johns Hopkins speech, President Johnson said that the United States was prepared to discuss the Vietnam conflict with all governments concerned.[19] While this may have seemed to indicate a willingness to talk with all interested *parties,* it did not. The key word here was "governments" and since the Viet Cong was not a "government" it was not included. This phraseology was specifically designed to exclude the possibility of talking to them.

---

[17]Stanley Hoffman, *Gulliver's Troubles or the Setting of American Foreign Policy,* McGraw-Hill, New York, 1968, p. 63.

[18]An excellent development of this may be found in Thomas M. Frank and Edward Weisband, *Word Politics: Verbal Strategy Among the Superpowers,* Oxford University Press, New York, 1972.

[19]See U.S., Department of State, *Bulletin,* April 26, 1965, pp. 606–610.

The same kind of problem has been reflected in the Middle East conflict. For several years after the passage of Resolution 242 by the United Nations Security Council on November 22, 1967, various Arab policymakers said they would be willing to make provisions for the security of all "states" in the area. Some people might have assumed that such comments promised a measure of security for Israel, but they did not. Many Arabs did not consider Israel to be a "state." Today when Israel talks of negotiating with "states" or "governments" it is excluding the possibility of negotiations with the Palestine Liberation Organization since the PLO is neither.

Policymakers need to, and usually do, *study* language very closely. Early in 1968 radio Hanoi broadcast a statement concerning the effect that a complete unconditional bombing halt would have with regard to negotiations. This statement changed only one word from previous formulations but it was a critical change. Whereas previously most DRV statements had said that a bombing halt *could* bring negotiations, now it was said that it *would* bring negotiations.

Of course, while the particular terminology must be examined carefully, it must be analyzed in context. On October 1, 1977 Washington and Moscow issued a joint communique containing mutually acceptable principles for settling the Arab-Israeli dispute.[20] One of the agreed upon phrases provided that any settlement should insure the "legitimate rights of the Palestinian people." Previously, the United States had judiciously avoided employing the phrase "legitimate rights," because many thought that such terminology at least implied an endorsement of the concept of an independent Palestinian state, a concept Washington had opposed. Certainly this turnabout meant something, but did it signify a major policy change or, given the other provisions of the document and the circumstances of its issuance, was it simply an indicator of a minor alteration? After studying the rest of the communique intensively, policymakers concluded that, because of the context, the latter was the correct interpretation.

A critical but often underrated task of the policymaker is determining the significance of *what was not said*. One must be very careful in generalizing about the meanings of a particular message and not automatically infer that certain things were meant even though they were not said. Sometimes one discovers that what is *not* said is the most critical "message" involved in a particular communication. For example, UN Security Council Resolution 242 provides that Israel shall withdraw from territories occupied in the recent conflict (referring to the 1967 Arab-Israeli War). It does *not* provide that Israel shall withdraw from *all* such territories or from *the* territories. This omission was deliberate. The Resolution's framers did not intend that the Resolution should automatically mean a total Israeli withdrawal, and the omission of either "all" or "the" was very significant.

In 1971 and early 1972 there were three Egyptian-Soviet meetings concern-

---

[20]For the full text see U.S., Department of State, *Bulletin,* November 7, 1977, pp, 639–640.

ing the continuation and/or increase of Soviet military assistance to Cairo. Each time the Egyptians sought to receive offensive weapons, aircraft that was equivalent in firepower to the Phantom jets that Washington was supplying to Israel. Each time they were turned down. The communiqués that followed the meetings, while reiterating general Soviet support for whatever means were necessary to eliminate the "consequences of aggression," never mentioned the provision of offensive weaponry designed to achieve that objective. This omission was significant.

In 1976, in his speech to the 25th Party Congress of the Soviet Communist Party, Party Secretary Leonid Brezhnev said that in its relations with the Socialist countries the CPSU followed the rule of dealing in a spirit of true equality.[21] If problems arose, they would be resolved in a spirit of friendship, unity, and cooperation. That, in fact, *was* how the Soviets shaped their relations with the "fraternal socialist states—Bulgaria, Hungary, Vietnam, the German Democratic Republic, the Korean People's Democratic Republic, Cuba, Mongolia, Poland, Rumania, Czechoslovakia and Yugoslavia." Notice the omission of China (and Albania) from Brezhnev's list of "fraternal socialist states"! This was a clear signal that relations between Moscow and Peking had in no way improved.

Sometimes, of course, omissions may have unintended consequences. Secretary of State Dean Acheson's famous speech of January 12, 1950 excluding Korea from the United States defense perimeter may have led the Communists to assume that the United States would not react to defend South Korea against a military invasion.[22]

Communications are an important part of the policymaker's arsenal. Seldom are messages successfully employed separately from the other policy instruments, however; they are most effective as part of a package. We now turn to one of the key components of such a package, negotiation.

NEGOTIATION

The final instrument of policy implementation is negotiation. There is a tendency for observers to assume that policymakers always enter the negotiating process for the purpose of reaching an agreement, and that the sought-after agreement is designed to solve some problem. Although sometimes this is the policymaker's goal, often it is not. A policymaker may decide to enter the negotiating process to achieve one of a variety of nonagreement objectives. In these situations the negotiating process is simply a means to attaining other objectives and no agreement of any kind is expected. Another variation occurs when the policymaker seeks an agreement but the agreement itself if not designed to "solve" the

---

[21] See Compass Publications, Reprints from the Soviet Press, *L. I. Brezhnev: Report of the CPSU Central Committee and the Party's Immediate Objectives in Domestic and Foreign Policy: 25th Congress of the CPSU, February 24, 1976,* White Plains, New York, 1976.

[22] Also see Chapter 2, p. 63, and footnote 45.

problem. One must not assume anything with respect to the policymaker's objectives in negotiations, but instead analyze the particular case in order to discover what those objectives might be.

Nonagreement Objectives

A policymaker may enter the negotiating process for many reasons unrelated to an agreement.[23] Sometimes for example, he may just be *stalling*. In mid-1956 the United States withdrew an offer to help Egypt's President Nasser finance the High Aswan Dam and did so in a calculatedly offensive manner.[24] Responding to this diplomatic slap Nasser nationalized the Suez Canal Company and took over this strategic Canal's operation. Britain and France, the Company's major stockholders and states at odds with Nasser over many other issues, immediately began considering the use of force to remove him from control.

Secretary of State Dulles urged negotiation. In this regard he developed two different plans for the "nonpolitical" operation of the Canal. His efforts led to the convening of two international conferences, and each of these yielded proposals for a form of international control. If either had been implemented, of course, Nasser would have had to give back what he had won. Most observers doubted that he would do so and they were right. Apparently Dulles did not think he would either, as former diplomat Robert Murphy has succinctly pointed out.[25]

If Dulles did not think Nasser would agree, what *was* he trying to do? To a great extent he was just stalling in the hope that something would "turn up" and the problem would be solved. Problems sometimes do just seem to slowly die a natural death. This attempt to buy time also had the objective of keeping British and French eyes on the possibility of a peaceful settlement so that they would not resort to force. Dulles did not enter these negotiations with much hope that they would solve the problem; he was just stalling.

Another reason one may engage in negotiations was illustrated by British and French actions in the same crisis. As they saw things they were getting nowhere. Washington was using delaying tactics as it erratically shifted course between incompatible objectives, and Nasser was still in control of the Canal and seemingly on his way to an immense political victory.[26] Seeing no peaceful way of removing him London and Paris began to plan a military attack. But they wanted to appear reasonable. They therefore decided it would be useful to take the case to the United Nations before launching the assault.

[23]This section owes much to the work of Fred Charles Iklé, *How Nations Negotiate,* Praeger, New York, 1967, Ch. 4.

[24]Washington was very anti-Nasser because of his recent arms deals with the Russians. See Chapter 6 for a more detailed analysis of this crisis.

[25]Robert Murphy, *Diplomat Among Warriors,* Doubleday, Garden City, New York, 1964, p. 386.

[26]For further analysis of the incompatible objectives see Chapter 6, pp. 194–199.

They introduced a resolution which, for all practical purposes, just endorsed the proposals for international control that had been developed at the previous international conferences. There was no possibility such a resolution would be acceptable to Egypt (nor to the Soviet Union), and the sponsors knew it. The real purpose of entering these negotiations was to be on the record as having exhausted every means of peaceful redress so that when the attack was undertaken they could say they had no choice but to engage in a military operation. As this example shows *sometimes policymakers embark on negotiations recognizing no agreement can be reached, doing so only in an attempt to provide themselves with an excuse for undertaking other types of activities when the negotiations fail.*

American and Russian policymakers entered negotiations at the 1954 Berlin Conference for still other nonagreement reasons. No real negotiations had occurred on the German problem since before the Berlin blockade of 1948−1949, and there was nothing to indicate that any would be successful now. The West's position of forming a unified government via free elections, and allowing it to ally with anyone it desired, was clearly unacceptable to Moscow (since both sides agreed that a free Germany would be anti-Russian). The Soviet plan advocated the creation of a provisional All-German coalition government formed on the basis of parity between Communists and non-Communists (despite the latter's vast numerical majority). This "government" would then supervise "democratic elections," but the resulting creature would not be able to ally against any of the World War II victors. This proposal was not acceptable to Washington.

Why then did the Soviets and Americans want the Conference? Each knew the other would not accept its proposals. First, each party was seeking to have a *particular impact on third parties.* In 1953 there had been serious riots in East Berlin that the Soviets had forcefully suppressed. This suppression had hurt the Russian image and the Soviets were seeking to show their Communist allies that Moscow "really" was interested in solving the German problem. Also, the Soviets were seeking to signal French leaders that perhaps the only way to prevent a resurgence of the hated Germans was through a deal with the Kremlin.

It was this latter problem, French antagonism and discouragement, that prompted Washington. At the same time that she was being humiliated by impending defeat in Indochina Paris was also being asked to consider the rearmament of her traditional enemy, Germany. The United States felt that NATO's strength had to be increased and this was feasible only with German participation. Since German armies had defeated the French three times in the last 100 years, Paris was understandably apprehensive. Thus American policymakers tried to use the Berlin Conference to reassure Paris that Washington *did* want to solve the German problem but only in a way that would prevent any possibility of German militarism developing independently. Therefore constant consultations occurred in the negotiating process and unified positions, strategy, and tactics resulted. It was made clear that a reunified German state would be acceptable only if it was carefully controlled by the Western states, including France.

In addition to having an impact on third parties each policymaker in this case was trying to appear to be the one who was the most "reasonable." And this is another nonagreement objective. Because negotiations are considered by many people to be inherently "good," *policymakers may negotiate simply to reap the possible psychological and prestige advantages that result from being considered the "good guy."* In the Berlin Conference each side wanted to appear to be the most dedicated to a "just" solution to the German problem and demonstrate that its proposals were the more ethical and practical.

Policymakers often seek such propaganda objectives. As an attempt to give the illusion or appearance of seeking an agreement and to reap the benefits therefrom, policymakers may engage in "posturing," assuming a public posture that conveys an attitude of reasonableness regardless of one's real positions. Both American and Chinese negotiators employed this device extensively in their various talks in the 1953–1967 period.[27]

Finally, a policymaker may enter into negotiations for the purpose of *gaining information*. Perhaps one is trying to more accurately assess military strength or determine the degree to which a particular policy is supported by all alliance members. Maybe he is seeking a more precise understanding of the views of a given policymaker and feel that a face to face meeting would be most helpful. Maybe he is seeking to more clearly define the issues or to understand different national perceptions of a given problem.

Policymakers often approach arms limitation talks with the idea of gaining information.[28] Certainly this was a major objective of Washington in the SALT I negotiations. American policymakers were continually seeking to discover what the Soviets considered to be the components of stable deterrence. Although the United States was desirous of obtaining an agreement (and did so, as noted earlier), this nonagreement objective was also of critical importance. As pointed out in the discussion of deterrence, it is not what the deterrer believes to be an unacceptable level of destructive damage that is important, but what the deterree believes.

Nonsolution Agreements

Policymakers not only may enter the negotiating process with no idea of reaching an agreement, they also may do so to reach an agreement that in no way is intended to "solve" a problem. Since this is so one must always seek to determine the "real" purpose of any agreement and not assume it is designed to settle anything.

What are some of these nonsolution objectives? One *is to gain time while*

---

[27]See Kenneth T. Young, *Negotiating with the Chinese Communists: The United States Experience, 1953–1967*, McGraw-Hill, New York, 1968, Ch. 13.

[28]Of course, this may not be the *only* objective.

preparing for further activity. In this case the policymaker recognizes that the particular agreement does not solve the problem; its purpose is to provide a breathing space during which preparations can be made for later action. Throughout the Vietnam war policymakers of the Democratic Republic of Vietnam made it clear that they considered Vietnam to be one country that was only temporarily divided into two zones; at some point in the future it would be reunified. Hanoi knew the United States would not be a party to an agreement that explicitly provided for reunification under DRV control. Therefore, after its negotiators had extracted all the concessions they could, Hanoi signed the 1973 Paris Peace Agreement. By its terms American forces would withdraw and the people of South Vietnam would be able to exercise their right of national self-determination. The agreement did not reunify Vietnam under the DRV, of course, but it did "ratify" the elimination of the major obstacle thereto, the United States. A little more than two years later Hanoi's military forcibly reunified Vietnam.

Another example of buying time occurred with the Nazi-Soviet Nonaggression Pact of 1939. Following the remilitarization of the Rhineland in 1936 and the annexation of Austria in 1938, Hitler turned his efforts toward Czechoslovakia. Any movement in that direction had to be perceived by Soviet policymakers as a threat to the Fatherland. When the Czechs were scuttled at Munich and in early 1939 the remainder of the country was absorbed by the Nazis, Stalin intensified his existing efforts for an alliance with the British. Because of his ideological preconceptions and the series of Western capitulations to Hitler, however, he was deeply suspicious of their ultimate intentions and also began to negotiate with the Germans. As talks with the West deadlocked the Soviets began to turn more and more toward Hitler, and on August 23, 1939 the Nonaggression Pact was signed. One week later Germany attacked Poland.

Stalin did not believe that this agreement eliminated the Nazi threat. He constantly assumed that Hitler would eventually move against Russia.[29] But the agreement gave the Soviets time to prepare to make the conditions under which the battle would occur much more favorable.[30] Additional forces could be trained and equipped, and the home front readied for the struggle. Because the Pact contained a provision allowing the Russians to occupy eastern Poland after the Germans defeated the Polish army, the Soviet defense line was moved that much

---

[29]An interesting footnote here is that Hitler was very fearful that the Soviets would attack Germany. Shortly after the conclusion of the Pact he warned his generals that Moscow would adhere to the Pact "only as long as Russia considers it to be to her benefit." Shirer, p. 657. And it has been suggested that Stalin "seems to have contemplated opening hostilities himself in 1942, if the Nazis did not start sooner." Wesson, p. 158.

[30]Despite this the Soviets were incredibly unprepared. There were no orders or plans, no mobilization, and Stalin was nearly in a state of nervous collapse. Apparently the Russians did not feel that Hitler would launch an attack without at least presenting some prior demands, or that he would move before crushing the British. Since neither of these conditions were present Stalin felt no urgency and believed there was plenty of time to make the necessary arrangements.

further west. Besides, Hitler's attack would test British and French promises to defend Poland.

Sometimes a policymaker will sign an agreement in order to *deceive*. A good example of this occurred in Indochina shortly after the Second World War. For over half a century prior to the Second World War Indochina had been a French colony.[31] A series of nationalist groups had sought national independence, the most effective being the Indochinese Communist Party headed by Ho Chi Minh. Following the Nazi invasion of France, French authority in Indochina collapsed. Shortly thereafter the Japanese served a series of ultimata upon the French and for all practical purposes took control.[32]

As the war progressed the Communists expanded their base of support and became the primary nationalist organization, changing their name to the Vietnamese Independence League or Vietminh. As the war drew to a close confusion reigned supreme. At the Potsdam Conference in July 1945 the Allies agreed that when the war ended British forces should occupy the southern half of Vietnam and Chiang Kai-shek's Chinese Nationalists the north.

The Vietminh had assumed they would receive Allied support after the war ended but this was not to be. France was determined to reassert control, and maintaining good relations with her was deemed by the other Allies more important than recognizing the role of the Vietminh.

When the war ended the appropriate occupation forces entered Vietnam, and Ho Chi Minh began guerilla operations. At the same time the French moved in, hoping to replace the occupation troops and reassert their authority. In late 1945 and early 1946 a series of military skirmishes occurred between the French and the Vietminh. Negotiations began and an agreement was signed on March 6, 1946.

The agreement provided that Ho's Democratic Republic of Vietnam would become a free state with its own government, parliament, army, and treasury, and that it would be a part of the Indochinese Federation and French Union. The French also agreed that there should be a referendum in Cochinchina (the southern portion of Vietnam) to determine whether or not its inhabitants wished to be united with the remainder of the country. Ho agreed to allow the French to introduce 15,000 troops into the north to relieve the departing Chinese, but with the understanding that each year thereafter 3000 men would be withdrawn until all were gone.

Ho thought he was signing an agreement that would bring him nearly complete independence, but the French had no intention of allowing this to occur. Almost immediately they set up a puppet government in Cochinchina in open violation of the terms of the agreement, and quickly made it clear they

[31]The colony of Indochina included the states we know today as Vietnam, Cambodia, and Laos. This discussion is concerned primarily with Vietnam.

[32]The French did retain some local administrative control, however.

intended to keep considerable administrative control over the remainder of the country. French policymakers had sought to deceive Ho, and they did.[33] Shortly thereafter war broke out anew, and this time it would last for many years.

Another purpose of reaching an agreement that one recognizes is not a final solution is to use it as a *stepping stone toward a final settlement.* In this case it is usually hoped that some momentum toward resolution will develop, and it is believed that something is better than nothing.

A useful example of this would be the passage of United Nations Security Council Resolution 242 of November 22, 1967 following the 1967 Arab-Israeli War.[34] In the atmosphere of intense bitterness that followed the decisive Israeli victory, and with a number of interrelated issues each of which was dependent to some extent on the others but each of which in and of itself was immensely difficult to solve, it simply was not possible to reach a final definitive agreement in the months after the conflict. Most of the parties recognized this fact and a wide variety of draft resolutions were introduced and debated.[35]

Some type of compromise had to be reached if there was to be any agreement. The phraseology had to be sufficiently general to be acceptable to all parties. If this could be accomplished each party could interpret the various provisions as it saw fit. Differences had to be glossed over in an effort to reach some type of general statement on which all parties could agree and that could be used as a basis for a final settlement. This indeed, is precisely what occurred.

In this situation the policymakers recognized that the problem was not "solved." However, the policymakers did feel as if some start had been made toward a final resolution. They were not simply signing an agreement in order to gain time necessary to prepare for further military action.

A policymaker must always recognize that agreements may be sought for these nonsolution reasons, and handle himself accordingly. The mere signing of an agreement indicates nothing other than that an agreement has been signed. In each case one must seek to accurately determine the reasons why each policymaker agreed, what he believes he agreed to, and what he hoped to achieve by his actions.

Negotiating to Reach an Agreement

Despite everything said above, it is still true that many times policymakers enter the negotiating process with the objective of seeking an agreement that will solve

[33]Much has been written on this topic. I would suggest that the introductory student consult appropriate portions of the following works. Joseph Buttinger, *Vietnam: A Political History,* New York, Praeger, 1968; Bernard Fall, *The Vietminh Regime,* Ithaca, Cornell University Press, 1956; Ellen J. Hammer, *The Struggle for Indochina, 1940–1955,* Stanford, California, Stanford University Press, 1966; and Donald Lancaster, *The Emancipation of French Indochina,* London and New York, Oxford University Press, 1961.

[34]Also see p. 171.

[35]See Arthur Lall, *The U.N. and the Middle East Crisis of 1967,* New York, Columbia University Press, 1968.

a problem. Achieving such an accord, of course, is not easy. The following *four conditions* must be present if it is to be accomplished:

1. The parties must truly desire such an agreement.[36]
2. The substantive interests involved and the objectives that the parties seek must be reconcilable.
3. Both the process and the outcome of the negotiations must be such that none of the parties' prestige is unduly harmed.
4. The negotiators must have sufficient skill in the use of bargaining tactics to achieve their objectives.[37]

In some cases negotiations would be of no value because some of the essential conditions would not be present. It is useless to negotiate if the parties do not really want an agreement or simply have irreconcilable positions. An example of this situation occurred during the Chinese Civil War following World War II.[38] The United States was anxious to bring about a negotiated settlement of the conflict and sent General George Marshall to China to act as a mediator; and on February 25, 1946 an agreement was actually signed. It provided a basis for the reorganization of the military, the integration of forces, and the creation of procedures to bring about a common government. Almost immediately, however, both sides violated both the terms and spirit of the agreement, and each accused the other of doing so first. As Mr. Acheson later pointed out, the United States had been too optimistic. Neither side wanted an agreement and neither was willing to make any reasonable concessions.[39]

The only type of agreement that could have lasted in this case would have been one that involved someone's surrender.[40] And this points out another situation in which it is futile (and often harmful) to try to achieve an agreement: one cannot solve the problem of aggression against oneself by negotiating with an aggressor bent on conquest.[41] Such an aggressor will make no meaningful com-

---

[36]Of course, this "desire" may be a result of threats or coercion by one's adversary, and not be solely the result of one's own wishes.

[37]Much literature today focuses on this last factor. Obviously it is important as the discussion below indicates. But it must be remembered that if the first three conditions are not present no amount of bargaining skill will induce an agreement.

[38]See Chapter 4, pp. 154–155 and corresponding footnotes for further comments on the Chinese Civil War.

[39]Acheson, Chs. 16 and 23. The most useful introductions to American-Chinese relations in this period are Tang Tsou, *America's Failure in China 1941–1950*, University of Chicago Press, Chicago, 1963, and U.S., Department of State, *United States Relations with China with Special Reference to the Period 1944–1949*, Washington, D.C., 1949.

[40]The Communists and Nationalists were each using the agreement for purposes of deception and stalling.

[41]This does not mean one should never enter the negotiating process with such a party, however. First, one may seek nonagreement objectives or nonsolution agreements. Second, there may be *other* issues on which meaningful agreements can be reached.

promise. Any concession he makes will be temporary and will be utilized to prepare the way for further action.[42]

Negotiating: Preliminaries

Once the policymaker has determined that he is in a situation in which there is a reasonable possibility that negotiations might prove fruitful, he must deal with certain preliminary factors. The first issue is simply *who should be involved in the negotiations?* This question is deceptively difficult and involves two major considerations. First, most conflicts are multilateral rather than bilateral; that is, they involve several parties rather than just two. As a result the conflict can be definitively settled only when many viewpoints and objectives are reconciled. This does not automatically mean that all of the parties should be simultaneously involved in the negotiating process, however. Generally speaking, the more parties involved the more disagreement because there are more issues, more different perspectives, and more opportunity for tactics that are designed to serve purposes other than reaching an agreement. One might prefer to negotiate only a small part of the issue with a smaller number of parties and hope to build momentum toward a more comprehensive settlement.[43] Of course, the disadvantage with the smaller group is that not enough viewpoints are considered and one cannot resolve the problem until all the parties have their objectives sufficiently reconciled. The policymaker does not always know in advance which approach would be better; he can only try to make an intelligent judgment based on the facts of the particular situation.

The second consideration is that participation and the conditions thereof are often intimately related to prestige. This is particularly true when one of the parties either has no formal diplomatic status or at least is not recognized by some of the other participants. In the Middle East today one of the major questions concerning negotiations concerns what role the Palestine Liberation Organization should play. The same kind of question arose in the 1950s when the United States and her European allies were negotiating with the Soviets over Germany. Since the Western powers did not recognize the German Democratic Republic it was always a question as to whether or not policymakers from that party should be invited. In the early stages of negotiations concerning Vietnam the issue of Viet Cong representation was similarly critical.

Often the bargaining over such procedural matters is as intense as the bargaining that later occurs on substance. However, if the parties are really

---

[42]The tragic concessions made to Hitler and his reiteration that each demand was the last Germany would make in Europe stand as vivid reminders of this fact.

[43]This was the rationale for the Kissinger approach of a step by step settlement of the Middle East conflict: the negotiation of small disengagement agreements first in the hope that these would, if they were observed, create conditions of trust that would then lead to, or create momentum toward, a final settlement.

desirous of moving on to substantive negotiations ways can be found to handle the prestige element. At the 1959 Geneva Foreign Ministers Meeting, for example, West Germany and East Germany participated in the form of advisor groups and each was given a position at a small table on the circumference of the larger table at which the delegations of the major powers sat. In the Paris negotiations on Vietnam a round table was used with a line down the middle and each party could interpret it as he saw fit, namely, that there were two sides and thus only two delegations, or that there were four separate delegations.

Although the issue of who should be involved sometimes seems petty and foolish to the general public, it is not; it reflects factors of basic importance such as bargaining strength and prestige. Furthermore, because each of the "questionable" parties is seeking to attain a certain degree of legitimacy, often legitimacy as a co-contender for the right to rule the particular land in question, if they participate on an equal footing there might be some degree of tacit inference that in reality they had already achieved their objective of co-contender legitimacy.

The policymaker is also concerned with the *location of the talks*. This is important because of the prestige and bargaining strength factors that it reflects. If the negotiations occur on the home ground of one of the parties, or on the ground of one of its major allies, that party automatically appears to have gained the upper hand. Consequently, in conflicting issues of major importance usually either a neutral site will be selected, such as Geneva, or there will be an alternation from a site favoring one party to a location favoring another.[44]

Yet another preliminary issue for the policymaker concerns *the diplomatic rank of the negotiators* attending the conference. The decision on this matter is a reflection of the importance that the particular parties attach to the negotiations (or at least to this particular stage of the negotiations). Generally speaking, the higher the rank the more significance attached. The rank also may reflect the "distance" one is from an agreement. On very technical matters it may be necessary to begin at a relatively low diplomatic level because so many technical factors are involved. As one approaches agreement on technical issues and the political issues become more paramount, however, the level of diplomatic rank will increase (assuming the parties at this point want to reach an agreement).

The policymaker (and the observer) must always remember that negotiation is a means to an end, not an end in itself. Presumably one has gone through the various steps in policy formulation, made some choices, and decided that negotiation is the most appropriate means of achieving certain objectives. As always, the policymaker is seeking to influence the policymakers of other countries in a manner such that they will make certain beneficial decisions.[45] To accomplish

---

[44]The SALT I negotiations so alternated between Helsinki and Vienna.

[45]This point is not new but it is often understressed. See Roger Fisher, *International Conflict for Beginners,* Harper, New York, 1969, Ch. 1.

this one must try to see things from one's counterpart's perspective, understand that person's perceptions of the situation, determine what decisions it would be useful to have that person make, ascertain what decisions may be possible, and act accordingly. In each case the policymaker is trying to persuade his or her opposite numbers that the cluster of consequences resulting from the decisions the policymaker would like them to make would be more beneficial than the consequences resulting from other decisions or no decision at all.

Negotiating: Openers and Style

The negotiating process itself usually begins with policymakers stating their maximum positions. Different policymakers have different negotiating styles. Most Western European diplomats, for example, and Americans as well, have tended to assume that one should begin with a presentation of his most rational argument, couch it in very reasonable terms, and try to demonstrate why it is the most "ethical" solution possible. What "should" develop then is some degree of mutual accommodation and the result should be a compromise solution.[46]

Negotiators from authoritarian revolutionary states such as the Soviet Union, the People's Republic of China, and Nazi Germany, however, have frequently operated in a different fashion. To a considerable extent this seems to have been the result of their view of the purpose of negotiations. Policymakers in authoritarian revolutionary states have typically conceived of negotiation as simply a part of the overall struggle, as but one aspect of a much broader conflict. Because of this they have not assumed that any agreement they might reach would necessarily be lasting; this being so, of course, negotiations have often been undertaken for nonagreement reasons or in an attempt to achieve nonsolution agreements. If they really do want an agreement that will "solve" the problem, they want one that will do so (only) in a way that is one-sidedly beneficial. Negotiators who perceive the negotiating process in this light frequently use highly intemperate language, sometimes seek to simply outlast an adversary in sort of a contest of stamina (often by the endless reiteration of irrelevant points), are exceedingly inflexible, and tirelessly repeat propagandistic and/or ideological generalizations.[47] Such tactics are not the most conducive to reasonable compromise, of course, but usually that is not the object; the goal is victory.

---

[46] "The negotiator, therefore, must begin with demands that are nicely calculated in their excessiveness to match what is considered excessive in the position of his opponent while making it clear that concessions may be expected." See Hartmann, *The Relations of Nations,* Fifth Edition, p. 102.

[47] In recent years the Soviets and Chinese have made slight changes in their negotiating styles on those occasions when they have determined it to be essential that an agreement with the West be obtained. Whether such changes are a reflection of an altered view of the purpose of negotiations, however, remains an open question.

Negotiating: Rational Arguments

To many it would seem logical that negotiators would employ rational arguments in the negotiating process, and that such arguments would be tactically effective. It is a fact that rational arguments are employed, but how effective are they as a bargaining tactic? The answer is "not very," either in terms of their intrinsic merits or appeals to abstract goals. Given the nature of the international system (described in Chapter 1) most policymakers assume that each party is seeking only to achieve its own objectives as it defines them, and a rational argument is simply a tool being used for that purpose.

This is not to say that arguments have no value. They do. They are one means by which each party attempts to communicate. They are a vehicle for expressing the intensity with which one holds a particular point of view and the degree of firmness that is involved. Arguments can also help clarify positions and provide an informational base for further negotiations. But mere rationality, reasonableness, and appeals to morality do not do much influencing.

After the presentation of opening statements the negotiating process continues as parties either restate previous positions or make new proposals, offers or counterproposals. Each policymaker now must analyze the opposition's position very carefully: what is it that the opposition seeks precisely, what is the minimum position that the opposition will accept, and so forth. One's next move hinges on the answers to these critical questions.

Negotiating: Promises

What are the policymaker's other possible tactics? One is the promise of reward. A promise is in many ways like a bribe. A party pledges that it will do thus and so which will be beneficial to you if in return you will do thus and so which it desires. The types of promises vary immensely, ranging from a purported willingness to perform minor diplomatic services to the assurance of long term economic assistance or military support.

Sometimes promises are made tacitly rather than explicitly. One advantage of a tacit promise is that if it is not accepted no one loses prestige because its existence was not public knowledge. Also, a tacit promise by its very nature is somewhat vague and commits the promising policymaker less than an explicit statement. For this very reason, however, tacit promises often are not effective.

In order for a promise to have any effect it must fulfill two elementary conditions. *First, it must be credible;* the target state must believe you. As mentioned in the analysis of deterrence, credibility involves the perception of the target state with respect to a party's capacity to do what it said it would do, and one's willingness to do it.[48] Does one have the capability to fulfill one's promise,

---

[48]See Chapter 4, p. 158.

does the target know it, and is there some reason for believing that the promise will, in fact, be kept? In this latter regard a policymaker's reputation for performance will be particularly important. If a policymaker has a reputation of not carrying out promises, his or her current promise probably will lack credibility.

The second thing the policymaker must do is *convince his or her counterpart that the value delivered in return for the requested concession will be worth the trade.* In other words, the promisor must promise to do something that the promisee considers important enough for the promisee to do whatever the promisor has requested. For example, one of the major questions in the Middle East has been, ''Would prospective Arab political concessions, such as the granting of diplomatic recognition, be sufficiently important to Israel to induce Tel Aviv to make geographical concessions such as the withdrawal of military forces and return of previously conquered territory?''

Negotiating: Threats

In addition to presenting arguments and making promises, the policymaker may also employ various ''coercive'' tactics such as warnings or threats. In a general way warnings and threats are the opposite of rewards. The policymaker announces to his target that unless it does Y (or does not do Y) the policymaker will be forced to do Z and this will be harmful to the target.[49]

Whether a threat will be effective depends to a great extent on its *credibility.* Once again it is necessary to view things from the point of view of the policymaker being threatened. He or she must believe that the threatener has the capability to carry out the threat and the willingness to do so.[50] What makes a threat credible? First, as discussed earlier, capability. Presumably some equivalence between the level of the threat and the objective to be obtained is also important.[51]

Another important factor is the degree of commitment. Commitment may be established by public statements that involve the prestige and position of the policymaker's state (and perhaps his personal position or that of his regime as

[49]Many writers make a distinction between warnings and threats. Usually the idea is that a warning means that if one's opposite number does not comply with his wishes then certain consequences will naturally occur. On the other hand, a threat is conceived to be a situation in which, if the opposite number does not do what is desired, the threatening party will make a special effort to harm him. See Iklé, pp. 62−63, and Thomas C. Schelling, *Strategy of Conflict,* Oxford University Press, London and New York, 1960, pp. 123ff.

[50]Weakness does not always detract from credibility as long as some capability is present. If a policymaker has little to lose because of weak political support or seems to have no other real choice but to carry out a threat that is made, he might be willing to take much greater risks than would be ''reasonable'' given his capability situation. William D. Coplin, *Introduction to International Politics: A Theoretical Overview,* Second Edition, Rand McNally, Chicago, 1974, p. 307.

[51]Kenneth E. Boulding, *Conflict and Defense: A General Theory,* Harper, New York, 1962, p. 255.

well). Also, one's reputation is a factor that has an impact on the credibility and the appearance of commitment. The United States partial mobilization and movement of the Sixth Fleet to the eastern end of the Mediterranean Sea at the time of the 1970 Jordanian Civil War was seen by many as a harbinger of possible intervention considering the fact that American Marines had landed in Lebanon in 1958.[52] Specific actions also may add to or detract from the level of commitment. The stationing of American military forces in West Berlin where they would inevitably become involved in any European conflict gives some credence to the idea that the United States would never allow Soviet forces to occupy Europe.

Despite these particular means of establishing commitment, *the only real way of guaranteeing credibility is to leave as little room as possible for judgment or discretion in carrying out the threat.*[53] If a party puts itself in a position of having no choice but to carry out its threat, either in the sense that it will automatically follow or that there are no reasonable alternatives, then it has established a commitment and its threats will have maximum credibility (assuming one is able to communicate these facts to the target state and its policymaker's perceptions of them are accurate).

To this point the discussion has proceeded as if establishing maximum credibility was necessarily a good thing. But this is not always so. One may not always desire maximum commitment for the reason that, by definition, the greater the commitment the less the flexibility. In other words, as a policymaker proceeds to tie his or her own hands in order to establish maximum credibility he or she loses a certain amount of flexibility, flexibility that may be necessary in order to negotiate effectively. This cuts down the possibility of changing and reformulating positions or perhaps retreating in case the target of the threat simply says "go ahead." In that case the threat may not induce an agreement but may in fact create a situation that prevents any possibility of an agreement and forces the policymaker to either carry out the threat or surrender.

This raises the entire question of *whether or not making a threat is a useful bargaining tactic.* Obviously, in some cases it is. The threatened policymaker believes that the threatener has the capacity and intention to carry out the threat and that if the threat is carried out the consequences will be much worse than making the desired decision. But there are other cases in which a threat may not be so valuable to the threatening state. As mentioned above, the establishment of maximum credibility ties the policymaker's hands. This means that one has relinquished the initiative and the outcome now depends solely on the other party's choice.

A second difficulty with employing threats is that presumably the opposition anticipated some costs when it began its actions, and it may have anticipated this

---

[52]See Chapter 6, pp. 211–213, 215–216, 217, for further discussion of the Lebanese crisis.
[53]Schelling, p. 40.

threat. If a party acts as it was expected it would, such action will hardly get an opponent to change his behavior.

Furthermore, as indicated above in the discussion of the economic and military instruments of policy, people adapt quite rapidly and resent pressure being applied to them. Rather than submit to a threat they may believe that the costs of enduring an executed threat are preferable to the costs of giving in. Also, they may already have gone so far in the particular line of action that they feel that they have no choice but to continue.

Another set of reasons that mitigate against the use of threat involve the costs of actually carrying it out. Suppose, for example, A has threatened to withdraw economic assistance from B unless a certain political course of action is followed. Suppose B says "go ahead", either because B does not believe A will do it or because B simply reacts negatively. Is it to A's benefit to actually do it? In some ways, yes, because if A does not it will look as if A was bluffing and A's reputation will suffer. On the other hand, if A does, it will lose the opportunity of gaining influence that giving economic assistance would have provided. Sometimes a party gets into a situation where it ends up doing something it would prefer not to do for no reason other than that it said it would, and this may not be beneficial.

Finally, perhaps the idea of executing the threat is that it will teach one's adversaries a lesson. But this may or may not be the case. They may find alternatives, for example, if we cut off economic assistance. It could be that rather than *them* learning *their* lesson, the adversaries may have concluded that the policymaker has learned his or hers as he or she suffers from the execution of the threat. They may believe that the policymaker will learn that such actions are not effective and he or she will not repeat them again.[54]

Negotiating: Bluffs

The final bargaining tactic is the bluff, claiming that one can and will do something that in fact one either cannot or will not do. This is a very dangerous tactic and one that must be handled with care. The policymaker must always try to anticipate what his or her action will be if the bluff is called. Whether or not a bluff will be effective will, of course, depend on the perceptions of the parties involved, the degree to which the proposed action seems to be feasible, and the reputation of the policymaker. In 1936 Adolph Hitler ordered his troops to remilitarize the Rhineland, that area of Germany between the Rhine River and the border of France. This action was a direct violation of the Treaty of Versailles. Hitler was actually bluffing. His generals had orders to retreat if fired upon. He was successful, however, because of the desire of the British to accommodate him to prevent the outbreak of a new war, the impression that the

[54]Fisher, Ch. 3.

Western powers mistakenly had of German military readiness at the time, and the fact that the territory being remilitarized was "after all" German. In this case the successful execution of a bluff added greatly to Hitler's reputation and thus the credibility of future threats.

An opposite result occurred as a result of Soviet Premier Khrushchev's bluffs in the second Berlin crisis.[55] In late 1958 Khrushchev stated that the time had arrived for the Western powers to renounce their "occupation regime" in Berlin. Because of Western violations, he said, the Soviet Government no longer considered itself bound by the Four Power Agreements on occupation. At an appropriate time the Soviet Union would transfer its functions to the German Democratic Republic. The solution to the problem should be to convert West Berlin into an independent political unit, a free city, and the Western states would have up to a half a year to make such changes. If this did not occur then the Soviet Government would automatically transfer its powers over Berlin to East Germany and would terminate its contacts with the Western governments. Thereafter if the Western governments wanted to go to West Berlin they would have to deal with the East Germans. Furthermore, the Soviets would consider any Western "aggression" against East Germany as if the Soviet Union herself had been attacked.

All of this was a bluff. Khrushchev had no idea of turning over his functions to the East Germans and signing a separate peace treaty purporting to eliminate Western rights. When the United States and its Allies simply refused to do as the Soviets requested, and in fact resisted stoutly (as they did again in 1961) Khrushchev was forced to back down. This humiliation reduced the credibility of later Soviet threats.[56]

Once in a while, if conditions are right, an unsuccessful bluff can later be turned to one's advantage. On numerous occasions in the last half of 1971 Egypt's President Sadat stridently proclaimed that 1971 would be the "year of decision;" one way or another, he said, the dispute with Israel would be settled. Nothing of the sort occurred, of course, with the result that Sadat's credibility was severely damaged; the Egyptian leader had been bluffing, and when his bluff had been called and he could not act he looked foolish. This, along with his expulsion of Soviet advisers in 1972, the Arabs' obvious military weakness in comparison to Israel, and the history of Israeli successes in the three previous wars, helped produce a perception in Israel to the effect that it would be totally irrational for Sadat to attack; therefore, he would not. In consequence, in 1973 he was able to make a number of moves that under other circumstances might have been regarded as clear signals of impending attack, and the Israelis thought he

[55]For a succinct, perceptive analysis see Frederick H. Hartmann, *Germany Between East and West: The Reunification Problem,* Prentice-Hall, Englewood Cliffs, New Jersey, 1965, Ch. 6.

[56]A difficulty in this regard is knowing when a policymaker intended to bluff and had his bluff called, and when he did not set out to bluff but changed his mind in light of an unanticipated response.

was bluffing.[57] Of course, they were wrong, and in October Egypt launched a limited war.[58]

Concluding Remarks

As the preceding analysis demonstrates, the instrument of negotiation is multifaceted and complex; it is used in many different ways for a variety of purposes. Sometimes it is effective, sometimes not. And as is true with respect to all of the policy tools, a policymaker has no guarantee of success just because he picks the right instrument (or combination of instruments); he can only analyze each situation as rationally as possible, make his choice, and hope for the best.

The first five chapters of this book have provided an analysis of the international environment within which the policymaker operates, a discussion of the formulation of policy, an examination of the foundation of capability, and an analysis of the instruments of policy implementation. Throughout one point has been evident: policymakers have an extremely difficult job. Unfortunately, things are even more complicated than these chapters have indicated. In the first place, all policymakers operate within a vortex of domestic pressures; they are not free to just act in whatever manner they believe would be best. Such domestic problems provide the subject matter for Chapter 7. In addition, there are policymaking problems that occur with amazing regularity, problems that present obstacles to the formulation and implementation of an effective policy. It is to these that we now turn.

SELECTED BIBLIOGRAPHY

Barghoorn, Frederick C., *Soviet Foreign Propaganda*, Princeton University Press, Princeton, New Jersey, 1964.

Brown, J.A.C., *Techniques of Persuasion: From Propaganda to Brainwashing*, Penguin Books, Middlesex, England, 1963.

Burton, John W., "Resolution of Conflict," *International Studies Quarterly*, March, 1972, pp. 5–29.

Davison, W. Phillips, *International Political Communication*, Praeger, New York, 1965.

Deutsch, Karl W., *Nationalism and Social Communication*, Wiley, New York, 1953.

Eubank, Keith, *The Summit Conferences, 1919–1960*, University of Oklahoma Press, Norman, Oklahoma, 1966.

Fagen, Richard N., *Politics and Communication*, Little, Brown, Boston, 1966.

Fisher, Roger, *International Conflict for Beginners*, Harper & Row, New York, 1969.

Frank, Thomas M., and Edward Weisband, *Word Politics: Verbal Strategy Among the Superpowers*, Oxford University Press, New York, 1972.

George, Alexander, David K. Hall, and William R. Simons, *The Limits of Coercive Diplomacy: Laos, Cuba, Vietnam*, Little, Brown, Boston, 1971.

[57]See Chapter 7, footnote 47 for some useful citations.
[58]See Chapter 4, pp. 153–154.

Harr, John E., *The Professional Diplomat*, Princeton University Press, Princeton, New Jersey, 1969.

Hoffman, Arthur P., *International Communication and the New Diplomacy*, Indiana University Press, Bloomington, Indiana, 1968.

Horelick, Arnold L., and Myron Rush, *Strategic Power and Soviet Foreign Policy*, University of Chicago Press, Chicago, 1966.

Ikle, Fred Charles, *How Nations Negotiate*, Praeger, New York, 1967.

Joy, C. Turner, *How Communists Negotiate*, Macmillan, New York, 1955.

Kaufman, John, *Conference Diplomacy: An Introductory Analysis*, Oceana Publications, New York, 1968.

Lall, Arthur, *How Communist China Negotiates*, Columbia University Press, New York, 1968.

Lall, Arthur, *The U.N. and the Middle East Crisis of 1967*, Columbia University Press, New York, 1968.

Merritt, Richard L., *Communication in International Politics*, University of Illinois Press, Urbana, Illinois, 1972.

Mosely, Phillip E., *The Kremlin and World Politics: Studies in Soviet Policy and Action*, Vintage Books, New York, 1960.

Newhouse, John, *Cold Dawn: The Story of SALT*, Holt, Rinehart and Winston, New York, 1973.

Nicolson, Sir Harold George, *Diplomacy*, Third Edition, Oxford University Press, New York, 1964.

Padelford, Norman J., and George A. Lincoln, *The Dynamics of International Politics*, Third Edition, Macmillan, New York, 1976.

Phillips, Warren R., "International Communications," in Michael Haas, ed., *International Systems: A Behavioral Approach*, Chandler, New York, 1974, pp. 177–201.

Qualter, Terence H., *Propaganda and Psychological Warfare*, Random House, New York, 1962.

Schelling, Thomas C., *Strategy of Conflict*, Oxford University Press, London and New York, 1960.

Sheehan, Edward R. F., *The Arabs, Israelis, and Kissinger: A Secret History of American Diplomacy in the Middle East*, Reader's Digest Press, New York, 1976.

Spanier, John W., and Joseph L. Nogee, *The Politics of Disarmament: A Study in Soviet-American Gamesmanship*, Praeger, New York, 1962.

Thayer, Charles W., *Diplomat*, Harper & Row, New York, 1959.

Whitaker, Urban G., Jr., ed. and comp., *Propaganda and International Relations*, Chandler, San Francisco, 1963.

Young, Kenneth T., *Negotiating with the Chinese Communists: The United States Experience, 1953–1967*, McGraw-Hill, New York, 1968.

CHAPTER **Six**

Common
Policymaking
Problems

Certain problems seem to plague policymakers with startling frequency, problems that defy precise categorization. There are intellectual errors such as overabstraction and excess generalization, formulating and attempting to achieve
incompatible objectives, acting on the basis of distorted preconceptions, failure
to foresee the differential impact of decisions, and not putting oneself in the other
fellow's shoes; there are implementation problems such as policy inconsistency
and information distortion that flow from such intellectual mistakes; and there are
some very practical difficulties such as historical limitations, insufficient time,
unanticipated developments, the snowballing phenomenon, and the interrelationship of events. These difficulties are the subject matter of this chapter.

ABSTRACT GENERALIZATION

The first obstacle a policymaker needs to avoid is the formulation of objectives in
terms that are too abstract and/or generalized. It is emotionally satisfying, of
course, to employ broad concepts and the type of sloganeering that prevails in
democratic political campaigns. In the United States it has been popular since
World War II to speak in terms of defending "democracy," protecting the "Free
World," opposing "communism," supporting "peace," opposing "aggression," opposing "colonialism," and so on.

Unfortunately, this deceptively simple approach has many defects. In the
first place, the concepts are of such a generalized nature that they hide as much as
they reveal. When speaking of defending democracy, for example, how does one
define "democracy?" There are any number of definitions but people would be
hard put to reach one that was universally acceptable. Even if this could be done,
it is highly unlikely that one could find a nation-state in the real world to which it
would apply. Even if this should occur, could a policymaker develop a meaningful definition that would apply to all of those states he or she wished to defend? It

is doubtful. And beyond this, could policymakers of different governments agree on a precise definition of "democracy" and also agree which countries deserve that appellation? Probably not. The point is that such abstract generalization provides the policymaker with no specifically applicable basis for handling the concrete problems with which he must deal daily. His world is one of practical specifics, not abstract generalities.

A second basic difficulty with this approach is that it drastically over-simplifies reality, categorizing and compartmentalizing factors of great complexity and obliterating significant distinctions. Formulas become a substitute for thought, and the hard thinking necessary to make discriminating judgments is avoided. This often leads to an extremely rigid situation in which the status quo is seen as permanent. For example, for years after World War II American policymakers perceived all Communists to be basically alike, as interchangable parts of an expansionist monolithic bloc directed by Moscow. Washington accepted the world's division into two hostile camps as unalterable fact, and sought to develop policies to contain "the other side."[1] Because this was assumed to be a permanent situation, seldom was any thought given to devising policy options that might aid and encourage Communist bloc fragmentation. A policymaker must have the capacity to discern the differences and nuances in and between situations, and the ability to refine his or her policies accordingly. This is nearly impossible if abstract generalizations provide the policy foundation.

A third defect with overabstraction concerns the tendency to include within such concepts a sense of moral imperative.[2] If a policymaker considers the problem before him or her to be primarily an ethical issue it inevitably becomes emotion laden. The practical problem is transformed into a question of "Good" and "Evil," and naturally each party tends to feel that it has "Right" on its side.[3] When this occurs negotiation and compromise are nearly impossible. How does one negotiate concerning an absolute moral principle? If a policymaker compromises in this situation it is considered a "sellout," or "appeasement." The practical impact of this fact is that a great element of rigidity is introduced into the situation, making resolution of a conflict via mutual agreement extremely difficult.

---

[1] In this connection the student would be well-advised to read the famous article proclaiming "Containment" (actually written by George Kennan, Director of the Policy Planning Staff of the State Department, under the initial "X"), "Sources of Soviet Conduct," *Foreign Affairs,* July, 1947, pp. 566–582. For an excellent discussion of the question of whether the United States had any real alternative to containment in the immediate post-war world, see Charles Gati, ed., *Caging the Bear: Containment and the Cold War,* Bobbs-Merrill, New York, 1974, Part Two.

[2] For more discussion of the role of ethics see Chapter 1, pp. 11–16. Also pertinent is the discussion of the American Liberal Ideology, Chapter 1, pp. 22–24.

[3] It can be argued that this is not *always* bad. If one believes that there are standards of Right and Wrong, then clearly he can say that there have been "good" and "bad" nations, policymakers, actions, and so on. It could further be stated that there are limits to compromise and certain principles *must* be defended if there is to be any civilized order in the world. Thus, perhaps "rigidity" and conflict may be "good" in certain circumstances.

The practical results of a policy based on generalized abstraction can be demonstrated by briefly considering some of the implications of one of the major bases for American policy for nearly two decades after World War II, "anticommunism." When American policymakers analyzed the events of the immediate postwar period they perceived a major Communist threat. Developments such as the establishment of Soviet domination in Eastern Europe and the Balkans, the deepening division of Germany and the Berlin Blockade, the coup in Czechoslovakia, the "fall" of China to the Red Chinese (assumed to be controlled by Moscow), the North Korean attack on South Korea (assumed to have been ordered by the Russians), these and many other factors all seemed to point to this conclusion.[4] The situation seemed clear enough: these events were part of an attempt by a monolithic Communist bloc to conquer the world.[5] Gone were the unity and hopes of World War II. In their place were disillusionment, anger, and conflict. Thus it was "obvious" that anti-communism had to be one of the foundations of policy.

This belief had considerable practical impact. It led policymakers to assume that American relations with Russia were totally conflictual.[6] Because of this little effort was expended to determine whether or not there might be common interests (such as the creation of a unified, neutralized Germany). Every issue was a matter of the triumph of Right; there could be no compromises, no agreements with the Devil.

Another effect, since the Soviets were Evil and were presumed to control all communists, was that American relations with other Communist states also "had to be" adversarial.[7] Thus there was little consideration given to the possibility that various Communist states might have different objectives and that these differences might yield opportunities to exert American influence (let alone the

---

[4]This is not to say that such perceptions were inevitable, however. As is now known, and a more discriminating analysis then might have ascertained, both the Chinese and North Koreans possessed considerable independence of Moscow. Also, the Soviet tactics in Europe could have been viewed as defensive in nature, a means to protect their vulnerable Western approaches. The point is, however, that the American perception was understandable.

[5]It should be pointed out that, to many Americans, this was not only an instance of yet another power-hungry state attempting to conquer its neighbors but also an attack on the very way of life of Western man by a centrally directed, monolithic, atheistic ideology committed to world revolution.

[6]Particularly useful for this discussion are Hartmann, *The New Age of American Foreign Policy*, Chs. 10–12; Spanier, *American Foreign Policy Since World War II*, Sixth Edition, Chs. 2–6; and Ulam, *The Rivals: America and Russia Since World War II*.

[7]An interesting exception occurred, however, with respect to Yugoslavia. The one Balkan state in the Communist bloc not "liberated" by the Red Army, she refused to accept Soviet dictation. In 1948 Yugoslavia broke with Moscow (without renouncing communism) and American policymakers responded with economic and military assistance. In this case Washington *was* able to discern the advantages of helping an anti-Russian Communist state. One should note the significant situational difference here between Communist states under tight Soviet control and Yugoslavia, which was outside Moscow's sphere. Whereas American policymakers made some distinctions in the Yugoslavian case, they assumed that all states within the Soviet bloc were unreachable (and it was assumed that all other Communists *were within this bloc*).

possibility that a degree of cooperation might develop). Instead there was undifferentiating hostility, and this put pressure on all Communists to sublimate any potential differences in favor of the common interest of opposing the United States.

It is clear that the generalization of undiscriminating anticommunism has ceased to provide the primary basis for American policy. This does not mean that it no longer has any role in policy calculations, but it certainly is less important than it used to be. Most policymakers are opposed to communism in principle and believe that any conflicts exist, but they tend to be rather pragmatic in their analysis of the concrete problems of the day. They have witnessed the fragmentation of the Communist bloc and the bitter Sino-Soviet dispute, and realize that monolithic communism does not exist (and never did).[8] They have seen that it is possible for common interests to exist between potential adversaries; the wide range of agreements coming from the May 1972 Summit Meetings provided ample evidence of this.[9] Generally speaking one can say that most policymakers have learned that all states have a variety of objectives, and although some of these are in conflict, some are common or complementary.[10]

INCOMPATIBLE OBJECTIVES AND INCONSISTENT POLICIES

The problems of overabstraction and overgeneralization are often tied in with two other common errors, namely, formulating objectives that are incompatible with each other and following inconsistent policies. Unfortunately, it is often the case that to the extent one objective is achievable another is not. The crippling effect that the simultaneous pursuance of incompatible objectives can have on policy is magnified when the objectives are formulated on a generalized abstract basis. Inconsistency in policy itself is often the result of trying to achieve incompatible objectives.

Before examining a case in which all of these elements were present, it should be pointed out that there are many instances in which objectives of a very concrete nature are incompatible. In this situation, even if policy is consistent it cannot be more than partially successful because some of the objectives simply cannot be achieved.

The policies of West Germany's first Chancellor, Dr. Konrad Adenauer, provide us with a good example. When World War II ended Germany lay in utter devastation. She was temporarily divided into four military occupation zones, the

---

[8]For further analysis of the Sino-Soviet dispute see Chapter 2, pp. 76–78.

[9]The Soviet-American meetings of May 22–29, 1972, yielded a broad range of bilateral agreements in various technical and scientific spheres, a series of economic agreements designed to invigorate trade and reform the entire pattern of US-Soviet economic relationships, two agreements partially limiting strategic weapons, and agreement on twelve basic principles of conduct for future actions. For some other examples see Chapter 1, p. 34.

[10]Also see Chapter 1, p. 33.

United States, Britain and France sharing what later became West Germany, the Soviet Union occupying what became East Germany. In addition, vast territories traditionally German came under direct Polish and/or Russian administration, and have remained outside the "Fatherland" to this day.

In 1949 an all-West German government was created and Dr. Adenauer was elected Chancellor. A strong nationalist, he believed that reunification was an objective of fundamental importance. He also recognized the absolute necessity of rebuilding his country politically and economically, however, and felt that this had to occur first. He knew outside assistance was necessary and shared American perceptions of the Soviet threat; thus an alignment with the West seemed the logical orientation to adopt, so he did. Much economic assistance was received, particularly through the Marshall Plan, and the economy boomed.[11] With American blessings a limited rearmament was undertaken and West Germany joined NATO in 1955.

Dr. Adenauer also believed, however, that the alliance with the West could help achieve the fundamental objective of the restoration of territorial integrity, that is, German reunification. His idea was that when Russian policymakers saw what became known as a "position of strength," the combined power of the United States and Western Europe, they could be induced to make concessions that would allow progress toward reunification. Thus, to Adenauer, alignment with the West meant a reunified Germany.[12]

The problem was that these objectives were in conflict. The Soviets, of course, would have preferred a united Germany in their bloc above all else. Failing that, they had hoped to hold East Germany and keep West Germany unarmed. In this situation they might have considered a disarmed, neutral Germany with a "favorable" internal governmental structure and limited territorial base. A source of friction could have been removed and there might be the possibility of peaceful conquest via subversion.

But a powerful, rearmed Western-oriented Germany, given the history of twentieth century German-Russian relations, could be perceived as nothing but a threat in the Kremlin. Adenauer's belief that a Western alignment would induce Russian concessions ignored the Soviet fear of possible German desires for revenge. The simple geographical fact that now there would be German troops facing Russian troops on German territory, and that no free German regime was willing to acquiesce in the permanent occupation and subjugation of fellow Germans and their lands, inevitably heightened tension. Furthermore, Moscow believed that its military strength was sufficient to deter any military attack; control of this area would provide geographical defense-in-depth against any assault. Thus, once the Federal Republic was rearmed and aligned with the West,

[11]From the vast devastation of World War II West Germany has risen to become one of the four or five most economically powerful nations in the world. See Tables 3 to 6, Chapter 3.

[12]See Hartmann, *Germany Between East and West: The Reunification Problem,* p. 159.

the Soviets decided to dig in permanently. Adenauer's objectives of recovery and protection via an alignment with the West were simply incompatible with reunification. *The closer he came to achieving the one, the less chance he had of achieving the other.*

Now let's turn to a case in which abstract overgeneralization, inconsistent policies, and incompatible objectives were all apparent: the 1956 Suez Crisis. Before analyzing the crisis *per se* some background information would be helpful. With the exception of Soviet pressure on Turkey and Iran at the end of World War II, until the mid-1950s the Middle East had been an area characterized by disputes that were largely extraneous to the Cold War. In 1955, however, Turkey, Iraq, and Great Britain signed military agreements that eventually culminated in the Baghdad Pact, thus "filling" the West's alliance gap between NATO and SEATO.[13] This development, plus a massive Israeli raid against the Egyptian-controlled Gaza Strip on February 28, impelled Egypt's President Nasser to intensify his existing quest for military assistance. Unable to obtain the types and quantities of arms he wanted from the West on terms he considered to be acceptable, he turned to communist sources. On September 27, 1955 he announced the signing of an arms agreement with Czechoslovakia, irreparably shattering the Western arms monopoly and allowing the Russians to leapfrog the Baghdad Pact into the heart of the Arab world. In one bold stroke Nasser did more to break Arab dependence on the West than had any Arab leader in history.[14]

The United States, which had been on reasonably good terms with Nasser since the Free Officers' overthrow of King Farouk in 1952, sought to counter further Soviet penetration and in December of 1955 announced it would help Egypt finance the construction of a High Dam at Aswan, a project of immense political, economic, and psychological importance.[15] Great Britain and the World Bank also made offers to participate in the financing, but their offers were contingent upon Washington's.

Negotiations about the precise conditions of the American loan dragged on through early 1956. True to his orientation of participatory nonalignment, Nasser continued to deal with any and all who would help him irrespective of their problems with each other. In May he granted diplomatic recognition to Communist China, at that time the bogeyman of the United States, and made it quite clear that he was dickering for more aid from the Russians, including assistance

---

[13]Iran and Pakistan also became members, and the United States a very interested observer and unofficial participant.

[14]An American diplomat said, "If Nasser ran for President in Lebanon, Syria or Jordan today, he would be elected unanimously." Quoted in Wilton Wynn, *Nasser of Egypt: The Search for Dignity,* Arlington Books, Cambridge, 1959, p. 120.

[15]In its announcement, the U.S. Department of State used the phrase "inestimable importance." See U.S., Department of State, *American Foreign Policy, 1950–1955: Basic Documents,* Vol. II, p. 2230.

in financing the High Dam. The American Secretary of State, John Foster Dulles, deeply resented the fact that Nasser was negotiating with Moscow, feeling that this playing of East against West really amounted to no more than simple blackmail. On July 17, 1956 Nasser publicly announced that Egypt would accept the American offer, but on July 19 Mr. Dulles brusquely withdrew it.[16] On the next day the British and the World Bank followed suit.

Secretary Dulles was correct in his assumption that the Soviets would not immediately move in to pick up the tab (although they did a couple of years later), but he made a gross miscalculation in not anticipating a strong reaction from Nasser. On July 26, 1956 Nasser nationalized the Universal Suez Maritime Canal Company, and the Suez crisis proper began.

Washington immediately received a cable from British Prime Minister Eden stating that Britain would not allow Nasser to succeed and would use force to "bring Nasser to his senses" if necessary.[17] Now America's generalized abstract objectives made it extremely difficult, because some indicated one line of policy and some another. Policymakers naturally wanted to support those countries who supported or furthered the achievement of the underlying policy principles, and oppose those who opposed or hindered the achievement of said principles. The United States was anti-communist, pro-democracy and pro-West (i.e. Free World), but also pro-international law, anti-military aggression and anti-colonial. Britain was clearly anti-Communist, democratic, and a bastion of the Free World, but she was an ex-colonial power considering violating international law via military aggression. To the extent that Washington tried to support one set of principles, it inevitably could not support the other. As long as a final decision could be avoided this inherent inconsistency might not cause trouble. But suppose a full-scale showdown should occur; what standards could policymakers use to determine which abstractions were most worthy of support, and what would this mean in terms of specific policies?

With no coherent guidelines to follow Washington erratically sought a middle course, hoping to dissuade the British from any type of aggressive action, trying to develop a plan for international control of the canal, and yet making it clear that it did not agree with Nasser's action.[18]

An international conference was called. Nasser said he would not attend since the conclusion was foreordained and no real negotiations would occur.[19] The result of the conference was a plan for international control of the canal by a

---

[16]An interesting discussion may be found in Herman Finer, *Dulles Over Suez:The Theory and Practice of His Diplomacy,* Quadrangle Books, Chicago, 1964, pp. 47–48.

[17]For complete text see Anthony Eden, *Memoirs: Full Circle,* Houghton Mifflin, Boston, 1960, pp. 476–477.

[18]In fact, the American Ambassador to Egypt, Henry Byroade, "was instructed . . . to make clear to Nasser some possible consequences of his act of force." Finer, p. 89.

[19]See Egypt, Ministry for Foreign Affairs, *White Paper on the Nationalization of the Suez Maritime Canal Company,* August 12, 1956.

nonpolitical board. This was immediately rejected by Nasser, who considered it to be collective colonialism. A mission to convince him to consider otherwise ended in failure.[20]

Dulles developed another plan for international control, the Suez Canal Users Association. This was designed to create an international organization of primary countries using the canal, which would "insulate" the canal from the politics of "any country" (i.e., Egypt). Mr. Eden had been leery of this approach, but gave in to the importuning of Dulles and officially announced it on September 12, 1956. The very next day Dulles said the United States did not plan to shoot its way through, thus cutting the rug out from under him.[21] Naturally Egypt did not accept SCUA, and said its implementation would mean war.

The United States, caught in the web of its contradictory generalizations, continued to flounder erratically as the scene shifted to the United Nations Security Council. Although a set of six principles were agreed upon, they were so ambiguous that each party could "interpret" them to its own satisfaction.[22] The British and French had made up their mind that force would be necessary, and began to implement a plan for a collusive action with the Israelis. On October 29 the Israelis struck, and on October 31 the British and French joined in.

American policymakers were now in a very difficult situation, because the showdown had come. The pro-democracy, anti-Communist, anti-neutral and pro-"free world" principles indicated that they should at least adopt a policy of neutrality, and certainly should not oppose the attack. But they were also pro-international law, anti-aggression, and anti-colonial. Obviously these abstractions dictated opposition to the attack.

A decision had to be made, however, and Washington opted for the pro-international law principles and the like, pressing the case with evangelical fervor.[23] It led the fight for adoption of a cease-fire and withdrawal resolution by the General Assembly, and this was followed by the creation of the United Nations Emergency Force. Under intense pressure from Washington and amid threats of rocket warfare by the Soviets to "crush the aggressors," the British agreed to a cease-fire on November 6.[24] The French and Israelis reluctantly concurred and the worst was over.

---

[20]Given his political gains from the nationalization, and the obvious losses that such a plan would entail, it is hard to see how anyone could have expected him to do anything different. See John C. Campbell, *Defense of the Middle East: Problems of American Policy,* Second Edition, Praeger, New York, 1960, p. 101.

[21]Eden was extremely bitter. See Eden, pp. 539–540.

[22]For text, see U.N. Security Council, *Official Records, Supplement for October, November and December, 1956,* Document S/3671, pp. 19–20.

[23]See Noble Frankland, ed., *Documents on International Affairs, 1956,* Royal Institute of International Affairs, London, 1959, p. 269; U.N., General Assembly, *Official Records,* First Emergency Special Session, Plenary Meetings, pp. 10–12; Beal, p. 288; Murphy, p. 381.

[24]Many, including top United States officials, were surprised at the British action. See Murphy, p. 391.

No one can guarantee success in international relations. The Suez Crisis was very complex and any policy undertaken would have involved a large element of risk. Had one formulated policy in accordance with the steps outlined in Chapter 2, however, and made wise choices at each point, and then chosen the most appropriate combination of implementation instruments and used them wisely, the chances of achieving the particular objectives would have been maximized. Certainly one would not have angered friend and foe alike, as Mr. Dulles was able to do. Here the generalized principles were incompatible, there was no basis on which to make a rational selection, and the resulting inconsistency achieved a remarkable degree of alienation on all fronts. The policymakers simply had no sense of direction, operating much like a ship without a rudder.

UNANTICIPATED EVENTS AND SNOWBALLING

The policymaker's job is even more difficult because no one can possibly be aware of everything that is going on, know everything about each issue, or accurately anticipate all future developments.[25] Things are made even worse because of the fact that no state has absolute power and much occurs outside of its control. Many times events take place that are largely unanticipated and about which one can do little; things "just happen" and seem to develop a momentum of their own.[26] The problem is compounded by the fact that the process is often cumulative and a kind of "snowballing" effect develops. Let's take an in-depth look at a case in which these elements were present: the factors leading to the 1967 Arab-Israeli War.

From the time of the Suez Crisis until the mid-1960s the Arab-Israeli conflict had been relatively dormant. The majority of Middle Eastern political activity had revolved around a variety of inter-Arab disputes and attempts by the United States and the Soviet Union to consolidate their positions with their respective client states.

Egypt's President Nasser had become too involved in inter-Arab problems to consider challenging the Israelis, and had also recognized the fact that his military machine was simply no match for theirs.[27] He said many times that he did not want another round with the Israelis unless and until the Arabs were unified and they had drastically increased their military capabilities. The Israelis, relatively content with the existing territorial situation and recognizing their

[25]The problem of distorted information due to preconceptions will be dealt with later. See pp. 210–213.

[26]One noted ex-diplomat calls this "the most potent of all factors—the chain of circumstance." See Harold Nicolson, *The Congress of Vienna*, Harcourt Brace, New York, 1946, pp. 19–20.

[27]In addition, by the end of 1963 he had committed 40,000 Egyptian troops to the cause of revolution in the Yemen Civil War, the number growing to perhaps 70,000 by the mid-1960s. Most of these troops were still there (and remained there) when the new Arab-Israeli crisis developed. See Malcom H. Kerr, *The Arab Cold War: Gamal 'Abd al-Nasir and His Rivals, 1958–1970*, Third Edition, Oxford University Press, London, 1971, pp. 96–97, 106–114. Also useful is John S. Badeau, *The American Approach to the Arab World*, Harper, New York, 1968, Ch. 7.

military superiority over the Arabs, also had adopted a policy based largely on the status quo.

It is difficult to know precisely when the dispute began to heat up again but it appears as if it may have begun with a coup in Syria in February of 1966. The new Syrian leaders, a leftist faction of the Ba'ath party, called for the liberation of Palestine via military means and began to take operational steps to bring this about. They began to assume more and more control over the Palestinian guerilla organization El-Fatah and to encourage its raids via Jordanian territory into Israel.[28] The Israelis knew full well that these raids were originating in Syria, but they also held Jordan partially culpable for allowing the guerillas to use Jordanian territory. These developments obviously were outside of the control of the United States. Most of the raids occurred without Washington's prior knowledge, and they were certainly contrary to the American interest of maintaining stability without conflict.

Following two particularly serious incidents in the late fall of 1966, the Israelis launched a major retaliatory attack against the Jordanian village of Samu; the stated purpose was to destroy a guerilla base. This unanticipated Israeli response was a key factor in the development of the crisis. It demonstrated Jordan's vulnerability, putting extreme pressure on King Hussein to be "ready" next time. It did not soothe Israeli public opinion because the citizenry knew that the guerillas were based in Syria. It led Hussein to castigate Nasser for Egypt's involvement in the Yemen Civil War where it was killing Arabs instead of Israelis. It encouraged the Syrians to continue their incitement since they had gotten away unscathed. And it contributed to Egyptian and Syrian boldness since it occurred shortly after their signature of a mutual defense pact and made them feel that the pact had had a deterrent effect on the Israelis (since the attack had not been directed at Syria).

Throughout early 1967 terrorist activity increased. In April a small scale incident escalated into an exchange of fire between Syrian and Israeli tanks, and this in turn led to an aerial clash in which six Syrian MIGS were downed by Israeli Mirages. Although in retrospect one can see that momentum was building toward another Arab-Israeli clash, this was not at all clear to the participants or to interested observers. As late as May 1 Nasser accused Hussein and King Feisal of Saudi Arabia of being in league with the United States and Israel against Egypt, clearly demonstrating his unawareness of the impending war with Israel.

As things continued to deteriorate the Israelis began to take a harder and harder line. On May 11 Prime Minister Eshkol spoke of "drastic measures" if things got worse. Two days later he once more said that Israel knew full well that the terrorists were primarily based in Syria, and indicated that Tel Aviv would choose the appropriate time and place to retaliate. American policymakers to this

---

[28] See Walter Laqueur, *The Road to War: The Origin and Aftermath of the Arab-Israeli Conflict 1967–8*, Penguin Books, Middlesex, England, 1969, pp. 67–72. This was also published as *The Road to Jerusalem*.

point had been concerned but they did not really feel that the dispute would explode into armed conflict. Then on May 13 the Egyptians received messages from the Syrians and from the Soviet Union to the effect that the Israelis were massing troops on the Syrian border and that an attack was very likely.

Events seemed to be snowballing. Nasser ordered a partial mobilization and, with great fanfare, sent a small force into the Sinai.[29] Stung to the quick by the many Arab comments concerning his unwillingness to help his Arab brothers and his "hiding behind the skirts" of the United Nations Emergency Forces (which had been established along his borders with Israel after the 1956 Suez War), angered by the constant accusations concerning his willingness to kill Arabs in Yemen but not Israelis, Nasser apparently felt that he had no choice but to at least make some type of move in this regard.

By now it seemed evident that the Israelis were planning to take *some* type of action against Syria if the raids did not cease, but it was not clear precisely what kind of operation was envisaged. It appears as if (with the advantage of hindsight) one can see that Israel did not at this point have troops mobilized for a massive attack. However, Egypt felt that it must never again be unprepared as it was in the 1956 Suez War, and also felt that it had no choice, given the nature of inter-Arab politics, but to be ready.[30]

What happened next is another example of unanticipated events. The Egyptian field commander, moving his troops to the Sinai border, asked the commander-in-chief of the United Nations Emergency Forces to withdraw his men. As Nadav Safran has accurately stated, "there is absolutely no doubt that the Egyptian Government wanted the U.N. troops to be removed only from the Egyptian border with Israel."[31] Thus, only the UNEF forces along the Sinai front were to be involved, not those at Sharm al-Sheikh or in the Gaza Strip. The field commander immediately informed Secretary General U Thant, who in turn immediately contacted the Egyptian Representative. The secretary in essence said that only *he* could make such a decision, and that a temporary or partial withdrawal was unacceptable. He went on to say that the UAR (Egypt) had the right to request a *general* withdrawal of *all* UNEF forces because the UNEF was there only with Egypt's consent. If it so requested then he would order a withdrawal of all troops, not only from the Sinai *but also from Gaza and Sharm al-Sheikh*.[32]

---

[29]For a very interesting analysis of both the contents of the messages and the reasons for Nasser's reactions, see Nadav Safran, *From War to War: The Arab-Israeli Confrontation, 1948–1967*, Pegasus, New York, 1969, pp. 272–285.

[30]Prior to the Israeli attack in 1956 Nasser had thought that Israel was preparing to attack Jordan, and his forces had been unprepared for the Sinai assault.

[31]Safran, p. 285.

[32]It is not very clear why U Thant posed the alternatives in this all-or-nothing fashion, especially since the Egyptian request had been so limited. The most commonly accepted explanation is that he thought Nasser would back down when confronted with this choice, although Thant himself explained it on legal grounds. See *"Special Report of the Secretary-General of the United Nations, U Thant, to the General Assembly, May 18, 1967, on the United Nations Emergency Force,"* Document A/6669, May 18, 1967.

But this was not what the request had been. This certainly was an unanticipated development and a tragically significant one. Sharm al-Sheikh, commanding the Straits of Tiran at the entrance of the Gulf of Aqaba, the passage through which the Israelis must go to reach their only southern port, Elath, was of immense strategic importance. This was the last location from which the Israelis had withdrawn in 1957 following the Suez attack, and they had withdrawn then only on the condition, as they understood it, that there would be guaranteed freedom of navigation. They had time and again stated their position, that if the Straits were ever closed it would mean war. If the UNEF forces were withdrawn from this point, the psychological pressure on Nasser to reoccupy it would be immense. Confronted with this choice of alternatives from U Thant, however, Nasser felt that it was necessary, once again to a great extent for reasons of inter-Arab politics, to take up the challenge. He requested that all UNEF troops be removed, and Egyptian forces then moved in to Sharm al-Sheikh. On May 22 Nasser announced the reinstitution of the blockade of the Straits.

In retrospect it seems that from this point on the die was cast; it was only a question of time before some type of war occurred. Even at the time most parties believed that there would be some kind of military response. What amazed people, however, was the fact that Israel did not strike immediately. Prime Minister Eshkol, in fact, delivered a very moderate speech calling for a mutual withdrawal of UAR and Israeli troops to prevent conflagration, and suggested negotiations. All this did was to contribute to Nasser's prestige among the Arabs, and his speeches became more bellicose.

By this time both American and Soviet policymakers recognized the extreme danger and both sought to prevent the outbreak of violence; they soon discovered how powerless they really were, however, how "uncontrollable" events had become.[33] Both parties talked to the Israelis and the Egyptians urging negotiations, almost pleading that there be no resort to violence. Yet the situation continued to deteriorate. On May 26 Hussein signed a defense treaty with Egypt, contributing to Israeli fears of military encirclement. Nasser stated that the situation was no longer a question of the Gulf of Aqaba but was now the rights of the people of Palestine; if a battle were launched it would be total, and its result would be the destruction of Israel. Apparently the Soviet Union had convinced Nasser that it would at least neutralize the United States if war should occur, and this contributed to his confidence.

Israeli policymakers had become quite confused because they "knew" of their military superiority, or at least they thought they knew, and also "knew" of Nasser's previous moderation on the issue of another war. When Nasser became more and more bellicose, given the fact that he had been so moderate and given

---

[33]The illusion of omnipotence dies hard. An excellent discussion of the general topic may be found in Dennis W. Brogan, "The Illusion of Omnipotence," *Harper's*, December 1952, pp. 21–28.

the fact he had said he would not reach a point of conflict unless the Arabs were united and superior, it made the Israelis think twice. After considerable reassessment, however, and some domestic political infighting, Moshe Dayan was appointed Minister of Defense (June 2, 1967). And, of course, on June 5, 1967 Israeli aircraft took off and the Six Day War began.

With the advantages of hindsight it is possible to identify several key events that contributed to, and were a part of, the snowballing process that culminated in war: the Syrian coup and the ensuing raids by El-Fatah; the unexpected Israeli retaliation on Samu; the reciprocal escalation of early 1967; the Soviet and Syrian intelligence received by Nasser and Nasser's resultant movement of forces; U Thant's totally unanticipated response to Nasser's request for troop removals; and the imposition of the blockade.

This case provides a prime example of the impact that unanticipated events can have, as well as demonstrating the development of a kind of "snowballing" effect. Of course, there were key points at which decisions *could* have been made differently and they might have stopped this "chain-of-circumstances," but the simple fact is that they were not, and it is plain that many of the participants felt themselves to be "swept along by the current of events."[34] Nasser did not seek war but the pressures of inter-Arab politics and specific events made him feel as if he had no choice but to take certain actions (mobilization, seizure of Sharm al-Sheikh, blockade, etc.). Israeli policymakers did not seek war but certain actions (the removal of UNEF forces and the blockade) made them feel as if they had no choice. And so the list goes on. As the American Diplomat, Charles Yost, remarked, though "no government plotted or intended to start a war in the Middle East in the spring of 1967," war did occur.[35]

What "lessons" can one learn from this episode? How does it help to know that not all events can be anticipated, that many things occur that seem to be beyond one's control, and that events can develop a snowballing "uncontrollability" of their own? First, it helps the policymaker keep things in their proper perspective; sometimes things will not work out no matter how hard one tries. Second, it makes one emphasize flexibility and adaptability in his approach. A policymaker must be able to adjust to changing conditions, to unanticipated developments. Third, it illustrates the need for preparing for a variety of contingencies so that one has a range of options from which to choose. Hopefully one of them will be appropriate (or at least close). Fourth, it makes one cognizant of the dangers that may develop if things do get out of control and points up the necessity of making a concerted effort to prevent this from happening.[36] And fifth, it underlines the importance of obtaining accurate information, correctly

[34]Badeau, p. 168.

[35]Yost's analysis of the entire sequence of events leading to the war supports this author's thesis. See Charles W. Yost, "The Arab-Israeli War: How it Began," *Foreign Affairs,* January, 1968, pp. 304–320.

[36]See the discussion of the Cuban Missile Crisis, pp. 219–221.

interpreting it, and anticipating as accurately as possible; one should not be caught unaware any more than is absolutely unavoidable.

INFLUENCE OF THE PAST

Another major practical difficulty policymakers often encounter is the fact that the feasible alternatives are limited by the past and one usually has only a narrow range of options from which to choose. This unpleasant truth seldom receives sufficient emphasis with the result that observers tend to exaggerate the number of *realistic* choices a policymaker actually has.

There are several facets to this concept. First, a nation's historical experience influences the content of its policymakers' perceptions of various features of the international environment such as ethics, law, and ideology. The fact that the United States is the only major state in the world "whose historical experience occurred so predominantly in the rather unusual—even peculiar—century between 1815–1914," for example, is a matter of immense significance.[37] This was an era of peace and Americans came to assume that peace was the normal state of affairs, that the policies they followed in that era "must" be correct, and that things would just get better and better.[38]

A second point is that one's perception of the past significantly influences the content of objectives, and his choice of policy implementation instruments as well. Certain options will be eliminated from consideration and certain objectives just taken as "givens."[39] Soviet attempts to develop defense in depth along her western frontiers by assuring that Central European regimes are "friendly," for example, must be assumed as a constant because of the number of times she has been attacked through that area. Israeli policymakers could not even consider the option of reducing their military forces unilaterally, given what has happened to the Jews throughout the centuries. Third, once a particular policy has existed for a while a degree of inertia seems to set in. Operations become routinized and the underlying assumptions are not questioned. The fundamental American assumptions underlying the containment policy went for nearly two decades without being challenged. Fourth, once a policy is undertaken those policymakers responsible for its formulation and implementation have a vested interest in its success.[40] Thus they would prefer to have the present policy succeed rather than consider other options, and will make every effort to see that it does. Fifth, the execution of any policy inevitably brings about commitment of some of the state's resources for its success. These may be economic, military, and psycho-

---

[37]Hartmann, *The New Age of American Foreign Policy*, p. 27.

[38]See Chapter 1, pp. 21–23, for further discussion. Hartmann's analysis, *ibid*, Chs. 1–3, provides an excellent examination of this subject.

[39]See Chapter 2, pp. 46–47.

[40]See Chapter 7 for a discussion of bureaucratic politics in connection with the third and fourth points.

logical, as well as political in the broadest sense. It is not easy to suddenly rearrange the allocations of resources. Sixth, once a policy is undertaken the state inevitably has invested some of its prestige. It is not only the individual policymakers who may lose by failure, but also the nation itself.[41] Finally, it is often assumed that there is some value in having a degree of certainty and stability in foreign policy; sudden changes would tend to produce just the reverse.

These influences from the past often combine to produce what has been termed a policy of incrementalism.[42] Roger Hilsman puts it this way:

> Rather than through grand decisions on grand alternatives, policy changes seem to come through a series of slight modifications of existing policy, with the new policy emerging slowly and haltingly by small and usually tentative steps, a process of trial and error in which policy zigs and zags, reverses itself, and then moves forward in a series of incremental steps.[43]

A critically important point to remember is that the policymaker must deal with *the situation as it is today, not as it might have been.* For the policymaker, for example, if he or she is in charge of American policy toward Vietnam the general wisdom of past policy in terms of his or her value judgments is less important than a knowledge of what that policy *actually has been* and the recognition that *he or she can not change what has occurred.* The policymaker must act on the basis of what *has* happened, whether it was wise or not; one does not start with a blank sheet of paper.

This is a fundamental difference between the position of the policymaker and the position of all those who are not forced to take the responsibility of making the decision. The latter have the luxury of discussing the wisdom or lack thereof of particular previous decisions and can totally reject the past. The policymaker is forced in the very nature of things to accept the fact that certain decisions were made, and he or she must now proceed from there.

Let's take a specific practical example. It is not a feasible option for an American policymaker today to consider whether or not it is wise for the United States to commit itself to the existence of the country of Israel. Even though there is no formal treaty commitment to such existence it is absolutely clear that the United States would fight to prevent Israel's destruction.[44] This has been deter-

---

[41]See pp. 219–221 for a discussion of the Cuban Missile Crisis. Both Khrushchev and the U.S.S.R. suffered as a result of the outcome.

[42]For more on incrementalism see Charles E. Lindblom, "The Science of Muddling Through," *Public Administration Review,* Spring, 1959, pp. 79–88.

[43]Roger Hilsman, *The Politics of Policy Making in Defense and Foreign Affairs,* Harper, New York, 1971, p. 5.

[44]The precautionary alert of American armed forces to the perceived threat of unilateral Soviet intervention in Arab-Israeli War No. 4, October 25, 1973 provided eloquent testimony to this commitment. The issue of whether the response itself was appropriate and solely the result of the perceived threat is a different question.

mined to be an objective of fundamental importance. Thus it really is an exercise in irrelevance for a policymaker to speculate concerning the wisdom of such a decision and whether this decision *should* be made, because in fact it is already a generally accepted axiom of policy. This being so it is one of the bases from which the policymaker must act, regardless of his personal evaluation. One result, of course, is that an option has been eliminated because of what has gone on in the past.

Although most observers fail to give sufficient weight to the influence of the past, it is possible to give too much; the point also can be overstressed. One should not automatically assume that there is *no* room for change and that policymakers are *inevitably* restricted to specific courses of action no matter what. Commitment to Israel's *existence* does not necessarily mean humble American acquiescence in all the policy decisions made in Jerusalem. In fact, it does not *necessarily* even mean (although it may) that the United States is committed to the existence of the country of Israel with regard to any specific geographical boundaries.[45] All it really says is that the United States will not allow the country of Israel, within certain unspecified boundaries, to be eliminated from the face of the earth.[46] This point needs to be mentioned as a caution against assuming that because of the past nothing can ever be changed. One should interpret the options of the future accurately but give them as much leeway as possible.

An example of the degree to which flexibility may ensue despite past policy is provided by the change in American policy toward the People's Republic of China with the advent of the Nixon Administration. The new leadership could not, of course, eliminate what had gone on before. Previous policy had been based mainly on the concepts of military containment and diplomatic isolation; the Chinese were an enemy and had to be dealt with accordingly.[47]

Actually, feelings of suspicion and distrust had dominated policymakers on *both* sides.[48] Each viewed the other as the incarnation and epitome of Evil, and each policymaker automatically interpreted the actions of his counterparts in the most unfavorable way. For over two decades relations remained rigidly adversarial and neither side seemed particularly interested in changing.

---

[45]In the light of Arab oil wealth and the American energy crisis this is a particularly significant point, because it does not exclude significant United States pressure on Israel for boundary adjustments.

[46]One can, of course, question the extent of *any* commitment and postulate extreme circumstances in which a state may not fulfill its obligations. States have even "acquiesced" in their *own* partition as the Czechs did at Munich in 1938, and in their complete elimination as Poland did (in three stages) in 1772, 1793, and 1795. Basically, however, it means that if the United States will fight to protect the independence of anyone besides Uncle Sam, it will fight to protect Israel.

[47]One should keep in mind the pertinent points in several topics discussed earlier including the discussion of ideology, the role of abstract principles and anticommunism, the assumptions of containment, American views on who was involved in Vietnam, and so on. Also useful in this regard is Stoessinger, *Nations in Darkness: China, Russia, and America,* Third Edition, Chs. 3–6.

[48]Also see p. 210.

President Nixon and Dr. Kissinger, however, felt change was necessary. The People's Republic of China was potentially very powerful, and would just have to be dealt with if there was to be any hope of real peace in the world. Of course, changes would take some time. Mutual perceptions would have to be altered, public opinion conditioned, and some feeling of American-Chinese trust would have to be developed. But the effort had to be made.

The process began in late 1969 when American officials told the Chinese that they were ready to resume Ambassadorial discussions at Warsaw. The Chinese responded and a meeting was held in early 1970.[49] President Nixon also undertook a series of unilateral actions. Trade and travel restrictions were eased on July 21, 1969, and some items were taken off the embargo list in December. Controls on oil companies were lifted in August 1970, and restrictions on the visits of PRC citizens to the United States were relaxed by April 1971. Coupled with these actions were speeches of American officials that now called China by its correct name, the People's Republic, instead of Red China or something much less flattering. Washington also worked through a series of third parties to let Peking know it really meant what it said: it wanted better relations.

In early 1971 the Chinese finally responded, the invitation to the American table tennis team to come to China being one of the manifestations of change. In July and again in October of 1971 Dr. Kissinger visited Peking and had extensive discussions with Premier Chou En Lai, one of the major purposes being to pave the way for President Nixon's visit. From February 21 to February 28, 1972 an American President for the first time was welcomed to the People's Republic of China.

This was clearly a watershed in international politics, even though the immediate objectives for the talks were simply a sharing of perspectives rather than concrete agreements (which clearly would not have been possible yet). A statement of principles (generalized and abstract admittedly, but nevertheless constructive in their import) was agreed upon. And it was agreed that various bilateral personnel exchanges should be increased, there should be more trade, and continuing efforts should be made through cultural and diplomatic channels to normalize relationships. Throughout the remainder of the year trade did in fact increase as did these personnel exchanges, and there were additional movements toward normalization. Today the process continues, with full diplomatic relations having been established in 1979.

The fact that such an innovative approach could develop underlines a critical point: despite the fact that one's options are limited by the past, there still may be sufficient latitude for an immediate incremental change, and over a lengthy

[49]In 1955 the United States and the People's Republic of China had begun talks at the Ambassadorial level, first in Geneva and then in Warsaw. Since neither government officially "recognized" the other, these were, for all practical purposes, their only direct contacts. From 1955 to 1969 one hundred thirty-four talks were held. In February 1969 the Chinese cancelled the 135th session and no direct communication occurred again until late in the year.

period this incremental change may culminate in a substantially different policy.[50]

The question of the degree to which one's options are limited by the past is also related to the question of generalized abstractions as a basis for policy. If one states objectives in specific terms he or she is much more able to be flexible than when generalizations are used because it is much easier to change a concrete alternative than a policy based on abstract principle; after all, the People's Republic of China is still a Communist system. When one concerns oneself with the possibility of specific mutual objectives and carefully defines what those objectives might be, there is some possibility of a significant alteration of policy.

FAILURE TO EMPATHIZE

Another problem develops if the policymaker sees things only in terms of his or her own perspective, if he does not empathize and put himself in the other fellow's shoes. It is absolutely necessary when attempting to "understand" a problem that one try and see it from the point of view of each of the parties.[51] One must analyze the situation as *they* would in light of *their* perceptions. This requires a concerted effort to "role play," to really "be" someone else for a while. It requires the development of what has been called "tough-minded empathy;" one must see things from the other fellow's perspective but also have the strength to independently evaluate that point of view.[52]

The failure to empathize can lead to extremely harmful policies. Let's take an example, the Eisenhower Doctrine of 1957. The Suez crisis had effectively destroyed British and French influence in the Middle East. Viewing the world through the Cold War prism of containing the Communist bloc, American policymakers were distressed. The Middle East was an important region in this struggle and now the ramparts of the West had been breached. This left a power vacuum, at least in terms of non-Middle Eastern states. It was believed that it was inevitable that someone would fill this vacuum; if the West did not do it the Communists would. Washington's response was the Eisenhower Doctrine.

The wheels were officially set in motion on January 5, 1957 in a Presidential message to Congress. Stating that it was essential that the United States manifest through the joint action of Congress and the President its determination to assist nations desiring that assistance, the President requested authorization to provide military assistance, including the use of American armed forces, to secure and protect the territorial integrity and political independence of nations requesting such aid. What would be the purpose of this aid? To protect the asking nation

---

[50]It should also be pointed out that sudden crises may force (or allow) one to substantially change his policy. The Japanese attack on Pearl Harbor "allowed" a major change in American policy.

[51]Such "understanding" implies nothing in the way of agreement or disagreement.

[52]Ralph K. White, *Nobody Wanted War: Misperception in Vietnam and Other Wars*, Doubleday, New York, 1968, pp. 32–33.

"against overt armed aggression from any nation controlled by International Communism."[53]

American policymakers felt that the situation was critical and wanted Moscow to know that they would fight if necessary. Secretary of State Dulles indicated that unless the President's proposal was passed immediately the chances of war would be greater than they had been at the time of the Berlin airlift; any major delay in Congressional action would mean that the area would "be in a short time dominated by international communism."[54] With this as the context Congress quickly passed the President's proposal and the Eisenhower Doctrine was born.

Now, just suppose you were an Arab. It is true that there had just been an overt armed attack against an Arab country, but by whom? Certainly not a nation controlled by international communism. The attack had been by Great Britain, France, and Israel, and the Soviet Union had been one of the strongest political defenders of Egypt and, along with the United States, had led the United Nations effort to condemn the aggressors. From the Arab point of view, nothing could have been more remote from their experience, not only in the Suez crisis but throughout their history, than the possibility of an overt armed attack by a nation controlled by international communism.[55]

The Arabs thus felt that the Eisenhower Doctrine "had" to be an attempt by the United States to fill the void left by the departure of the British and French via the use of American armed forces. After all it is not too difficult to arrange a call for military assistance. And since no nation in the Middle East could conceivably be considered controlled by international communism, outside perhaps of Syria if one were to stretch rationality all out of proportion, it also looked like a direct thrust at those Arab nations who were neutral or somewhat left of neutral, and a possible warning that American military forces might be used against them. It looked like a naked exercise of power.[56]

The American response to the Middle East situation following Suez can be aptly characterized as monumentally inappropriate, and it did much to eliminate

---

[53]U.S., Department of State, *U.S. Policy in the Middle East, September 1956–June 1957: Documents,* p. 20.

[54]U.S., House of Representatives, Committee on Foreign Affairs, *Hearings on H.J. Res. 117, A Joint Resolution to Authorize the President to Undertake Economic and Military Cooperation with Nations in the General Area of the Middle East in Order to Assist in the Strengthening and Defense of Their Independence,* 85th Cong., 1st Sess., 1957, p. 34.

[55]Mohammed Heikal, one of Nasser's most influential and trusted advisers, put it this way: "It has seen imaginary Russian plans of aggression even before they take shape but has completely failed to see the sinister plans of Britain, France and Israel, which are not based on conjecture but have actually taken the shape of bloodshed, devastation and arson." *New York Times,* January 10, 1957, p. 7.

[56]The only Arab state to formally accept the Eisenhower Doctrine was Lebanon. However, Jordan, although never formally accepting it, did not hesitate to invoke its protection in the 1957 crisis. See Chapter 4, p. 148, for further discussion.

whatever potential for better relations the stance against the invasion might have brought. As has so often been true, a failure to empathize had extremely harmful effects. A policymaker just must make a concerted effort in this regard.

PRECONCEPTIONS

One of the most dangerous pitfalls a policymaker must avoid is distortion due to preconception. To put it somewhat differently, he must be very careful to avoid prejudgments based on preconceived ideas about the sources of information one would believe, its interpretation, about the intention and objectives of various parties, their capabilities, even about the identification of who is involved and what the issues may be.

Examples of misperception due to preconceived ideas are legion. John Stoessinger, in his excellent book, *Nations in Darkness: China, Russia and America,* gives us a detailed analysis of several flagrant examples. One of the most interesting examples concerns the American view of Red China and Peking's view of Washington during the Korean War.[57] Given the self image each nation had, namely, the American view that it was the defender of the free world, the nation destined to protect the world against the scourge of communism, and the Chinese view that Peking was the proper and natural leader of all Asia and a leading Communist power, and given the fact that each side viewed the very existence of the other system as a threat to itself, it was inevitable that each would misperceive the objectives of the other. This, indeed, was precisely what occurred.

The Chinese, assuming that the United States was inherently hostile and aggressively imperialistic toward all Communist states, assumed that the objectives of the United States included not only the protection of the hated Nationalist regime on Formosa (Taiwan) and the rehabilitation and rearming of China's arch enemy Japan, but also preparation for an invasion of China. Thus all assurances to the contrary were dismissed out of hand. The United States, assuming the People's Republic of China to be part of a monolithic Soviet directed Communist bloc whose basic objective was the eventual domination of the world, assumed that the attack on South Korea by the North Koreans, and the later entrance into the war by "volunteers" from the People's Republic of China, were simply a part of this overall program. Therefore, Washington believed that Peking's professions of concern about American intentions were misunderstandings at best, and more likely were fabrications. As Stoessinger points out, these misperceptions influenced the policy alternatives chosen for implementation.

Preconception may lead to either a refusal to consider certain information that does not conform to one's preconceived mental images, or to an "interpretation" that distorts the information to make it fit. To the extent that the mental

---

[57]John G. Stoessinger, *Nations in Darkness: China, Russia, and America,* Ch. 4.

image the policymaker possesses is "closed," unable to adjust to new or conflicting information, he or she will have a distorted view of reality as conditions change. If one's preconception is inaccurate to begin with, the distortion is magnified.[58]

Let's look at another case in more depth: the early stages of the 1958 Lebanese crisis. Our analysis earlier has examined the developments at Suez, the Eisenhower Doctrine, and the 1957 crises in Jordan and Syria. These provide the background. The next major development in the Middle East occurred on February 1, 1958 when Egypt and Syria merged into the United Arab Republic (UAR). As indicated many times, the United States had been hostile to President Nasser of Egypt because of the belief that he was willingly or unwittingly a tool of the Communists. Washington's conception of the significance of Nasser's dedicated pan-Arabism was that he intended to be the leader of a unified Arab world, and he was actively pursuing this goal with a policy that was designed to create instability and perhaps even rebellion throughout the area. Therefore, American policymakers assumed that much if not all of the unrest in the Middle East was due to the active instigation of Nasser in the furtherance of his own particular objectives. Naturally, this being the preconception, it was assumed that the formation of the United Arab Republic was part and parcel of his plan.

In point of fact, the Syrians had taken the initiative in the formation of the UAR and Nasser had been very cool to the idea. Early in the negotiations he laid down a number of highly restrictive conditions for his assent, conditions of such a demanding nature that it seemed very unlikely the Syrians would accept. Somewhat surprisingly they did, however, and soon thereafter the merger was consummated.[59] Because of its relatively closed image, Washington peremptorily dismissed the possibility that Nasser was the pursued and not the pursuer, that the Syrians had taken the initiative and come to him.

Shortly after the UAR was formed disturbances erupted in Lebanon, a country which was approximately half Muslim and half Christian and split by loyalties to the West and to its Arab brothers. Throughout late 1957 and early 1958 there had been a series of civil disturbances that often found the factions divided along religious lines. When President Chamoun, a Christian, became the only Arab leader to formally accept the Eisenhower Doctrine, for example, he was generally supported by the Christians but opposed by the Muslims. It also was clear that the mid-1957 elections had been rigged, resulting in a sweeping victory for the Christian government.

The announcement of the formation of the UAR had considerable impact,

---

[58]A very interesting if somewhat complex analysis of the connection between John Foster Dulles' belief system and his perceptions of the Soviet Union is Ole R. Holsti, "The Belief System and National Images: A Case Study," *The Journal of Conflict Resolution*, September, 1962, pp. 244–252.

[59]See Kerr, Chapter 1. Also useful is Patrick Seale, *The Struggle for Syria: A Study of Post-war Arab Politics, 1945–1958*, Oxford University Press, New York, 1965, Ch. 22.

and pan-Arabist feeling was evident in the Muslim community. Chamoun added fuel to the fire by giving indications that he was going to have the country's Covenant (Constitution) amended to allow him to succeed himself. The assassination of an antigovernment newspaper editor provided the spark that brought about a full-fledged crisis, and soon armed rebellion was in full swing.

The Western reaction, given its preconception of Nasser, was swift, horrified, and one sided. It was automatically assumed that Nasser and the Communists were causing the problem. On May 13, 1958 Lebanon's foreign minister, Charles Malik, specifically accused the UAR of instigating the rebellion. Nasser charged that the Lebanese rulers had to create this impression so they could ask for Western assistance to maintain their internal political position. The United States contributed to the unrest on May 20 by emphasizing that there was a provision of the Eisenhower Doctrine which provided that the independence of the Middle Eastern countries was *vital* to the peace and national interests of the United States. And as discussed earlier, another basic clause provided for United States military assistance against overt armed attack by a nation controlled by international communism if the authorities requested this assistance, a "request" that could be easily arranged. This American reaction, resulting from its preconception of Nasser, reciprocally increased Nasser's suspicions that it was a pretext for a possible invasion.

Lebanon then took the issue to the United Nations Security Council charging that the UAR was intervening in Lebanon's internal affairs. The United States echoed this charge. The fact is that there was no substantial *hard* evidence at this point to support this conclusion. On the contrary, many sources indicated that this was *not* the case but American policymakers assumed that Nasser "must" be behind the problem and convinced themselves that *their* sources were the more trustworthy.[60]

The Swedish representative, Gunnar Jarring, developed the concept which the Security Council adopted. A United Nations Observer Group (UNOGIL) was created to go to Lebanon and report on the charges of infiltration of personnel and equipment. The United States was pleased with this since it assumed that the report would validate Washington's position. What actually happened, however, was that UNOGIL determined that the affair was primarily an internal dispute. The report minimized outside support for the rebellion, stating that the vast majority of those involved in the fighting were Lebanese. A second UNOGIL report had basically the same import. American information was incorrect.

---

[60]One is reminded of events in the fall of 1950 in the Korean War. As U.N. forces under the command of General Douglas MacArthur penetrated far into North Korea and approached the Chinese border, the Communist Chinese and many neutral nations (especially India) warned that Peking would not tolerate the approach of U.N. forces to the frontier. MacArthur, however, said his sources indicated otherwise and kept on. Shortly thereafter Chinese "volunteers" entered the war. And for a fascinating account of Stalin's unwillingness to believe reports of Germany's impending World War II attack because they came from capitalists, see Stoessinger, *Why Nations Go To War,* pp. 48–60.

Changing one's image is difficult. It is difficult to admit one has been wrong, and the problem is compounded by the fact that policymakers often have an investment in being right once they are on the public record. In such a case contrary information may not be wanted because it is a threat. To President Eisenhower's credit, however, he began to accept the fact that this was primarily a domestic power struggle; he began to recognize that his preconceptions had prevented him from accurately assessing the situation.[61]

INTERRELATED EVENTS

Another difficulty for policymakers is that seldom is an event the result of a single cause, and each policy affects more than one party (even if not so intended). Like it or not, events are interrelated.

Let's continue the analysis of the 1958 Lebanon crisis since it illustrates this point nicely. Because American policymakers had finally realized that the crisis was primarily a domestic affair they had tentatively decided to shelve any ideas of armed participation. Instead it was decided to adopt the orientation option of limited support for Chamoun. Then on July 14 a coup occurred in nearby Iraq. The pro-western government of King Feisal and Nuri Said was deposed by a leftist military regime headed by General Kasim and his followers, men who had previously made known their sympathies to Egypt's President Nasser. When this occurred Washington "reinterpreted its reinterpretation." With the most pro-western government in the area overthrown by "pro-Nasser" elements, it was felt that the existing framework of American Middle Eastern policy was in danger of being completely destroyed, and because of the interrelationship of events in the Middle East and the preconceived generalization that President Nasser was out to subvert the entire Arab world in his quest for Pan-Arab leadership, the United States responded to a call from the President of Lebanon for military assistance. Thus American Marines landed in Lebanon.

Clearly the dispatch of these Marines was not primarily due to events in Lebanon but rather was the result of developments in Iraq and the perceived interrelationship of these factors. The point here is that all calculations of policy with respect to Lebanon, if viewed only in that narrow perspective, would not have (and indeed previously had not) required the deployment of American Marines. It was only the perceived relationship of events in one country to those in another that brought about this decision.

Let's look at a more current example. For most of the 1950s and 1960s the Soviet Union had sought to convene an all-embracing European Security Conference. The United States and its NATO allies had balked, fearing that such a gathering would probably yield no substantive agreement and would simply provide a forum for Communist propaganda. Washington's position had been

---

[61]See White, pp. 231–233, for a fascinating example of what he called Washington's "selective inattention" to events that failed to fit its "black-and-white" picture in the Vietnam conflict.

that it was wiser to negotiate on specific issues. Once some measure of success could be shown, then, with the hope that more progress might be forthcoming, a general conference might have some value.

Due, in considerable measure, to the efforts of West German Chancellor Willy Brandt and his predecessor Kurt Kiesinger, conditions were eventually created that allowed this to come to pass. Breaking with the Adenauer "position of strength" approach, the West German leaders sought a relaxation of tensions with the Eastern European countries and the Soviet Union. The first steps involved the establishment of diplomatic relations with Rumania and Yugoslavia. By late 1969 Brandt began speaking of two German states within one German nation, and suggested various areas of potential cooperation. Clearly his words were directed to Moscow. In March and in May of 1970 he broke precedent by meeting with Willi Stoph, the East German Chairman of the Council of Ministers. In August of 1970 West Germany signed a treaty with the Soviets "normalizing" relations with Moscow and recognizing the "inviolability" of existing frontiers, and in December a similar treaty was signed with Poland.[62]

The various West German initiatives were concrete signs of progress and this contributed to much greater flexibility in European relations. This led to some optimism that other issues in conflict might receive the benefit of this momentum. But the treaties, although signed, were not ratified immediately. West German policymakers made it clear that Bonn would not act so unless the Four Powers could achieve an agreement on freer access to Berlin, and freer movement and communication between the sectors.[63] The clear relationship between these events, however, gave impetus to Four Power negotiations, and a Quadripartite Agreement was signed in September of 1971. Once this occurred many West Germans felt that the normalization treaties could be ratified without injuring German interests, and on May 17, 1972 this was accomplished by a very narrow margin.

[62]The eastern borders of post-World War II Germany have never been definitively delimited. Approximately 40 percent of present Polish territory was obtained as a result of World War II. Much of this land was historically German, and until these treaties were signed and ratified no West German regime had given any credence whatever to Poland's western frontier. The Polish-West German Treaty binds the Federal Republic and the Polish Government on this issue but does not substitute for the definitive delimitation a peace treaty would provide. That is the responsibility of the Four Powers who defeated Germany in World War II. The present treaty would not be binding on a reunified German state either. Useful on this point is the statement of West Germany's Foreign Minister, Walter Scheel, reprinted in *The Treaty between the Federal Republic of Germany and the People's Republic of Poland*, Bonn, Press and Information Office of the (West German) Federal Government, 1971, pp. 41–53. It should also be pointed out that the Final Act of the Conference on Security and Cooperation in Europe (the 1975 Helsinki Agreements), whose signatories declared that they regarded the frontiers of all the states in Europe as inviolable, was only a political statement of intent; it was neither a treaty nor a legally binding agreement.

[63]Berlin was located deep inside the Soviet occupation zone at the end of the Second World War, and there were no written provisions for Western access thereto. It soon became a focal point in the Cold War.

While these Germany-focused agreements had been in the process of negotiation, the United States had been engaged in an extensive and intensive series of bilateral negotiations with the Soviet Union. As mentioned above, the Moscow Summit meetings of May 1972 yielded a wide range of United States-Soviet Union agreements including two limiting strategic armaments. The willingness to sign these agreements had been greatly influenced by the fact of the reduction in tensions due to the German treaties and the Quadripartite Agreement over Berlin.

All of these agreements were interrelated, and their conclusion met the American demand that concrete progress had to be demonstrated before a European Security Conference could be held. Now that this condition had been fulfilled preparatory work could be commenced, and it was in November 1972. The Conference on Security and Cooperation in Europe opened at the foreign minister level in July 1973, and began its working operations in Geneva in September.

The policymaker must always attempt to ascertain and anticipate the interrelationship of events. What happens to A will affect B, and perhaps it is only after B acts that C can be influenced. Thus the route to influencing C may begin with one's relations with A.

DIFFERENTIAL EFFECTS

Another point that can be beneficially illustrated by the ever-present Lebanese crisis is that all decisions have differential effects. This really means two things. *First, it means that all decisions have both costs and benefits.* The presumed benefits of the American decision to land the Marines were that this would prevent the subversion of the Middle East by President Nasser, maintain a certain element of stability in the area, and therefore prevent a further degree of penetration by the Soviet Union. It was designed to show Nasser that there were limits to what the United States would tolerate, and it was felt that it demonstrated to the Russians that the United States would act whenever and wherever it considered its fundamental objectives threatened. Finally, it was also believed that it would show the Arabs that the Soviets would *not* come to their aid in each and every case. These were the perceived benefits of the decision.

There were many costs, however. First, the decision gave the illusion of validity to the charges made by Nasser and the Soviets earlier in the year to the effect that the crisis was all a pretext for the intervention of Western military forces. Second, the landing of troops inevitably gave rise to suspicions about ultimate Western intentions in the area. As soon as the British and French were gone (because of Suez) another Western Power intervened militarily. The landings also did much to reunite the Arab world behind Nasser, certainly a development Washington did not desire. It also angered the Arabs because it demonstrated Washington's doubts over the Arabs' ability to solve their own problems.

And finally, this was the first time the *United States* had landed its forces on Arab soil and it raised the specter of specifically *American* colonialism. Perhaps the charges against the Eisenhower Doctrine were correct. Obviously there were many disadvantages as well as advantages to this particular move.

The fact that all options have both advantages and disadvantages has also plagued the effort to develop strategic principles for NATOs defense posture.[64] For most of the 1950s the United States Strategic Air Command provided the major deterrent for all of the "Free World" via a strategy known as "massive retaliation." In essence this concept postulated that the Communist bloc would be deterred from all acts of aggression by the knowledge that, if aggression occurred, there might be a devastating nuclear response on military targets and urban centers within the Soviet Union itself. The perceived advantages of this approach were its apparent simplicity and certainty. But there was an offsetting disadvantage, namely, what if the threat's credibility was questionable? Suppose, in other words, one's adversary just did not believe him. If he acted on that basis and one had no other options he would be forced either to acquiesce in aggression or initiate a nuclear war, neither of which were pleasant alternatives.

By the latter 1950s the logic of this dilemma had permeated official thinking. This had been reinforced by two basic situational changes. First, the Soviets had developed considerable operational nuclear capacity of their own, eliminating the possibility that a nuclear war would be a one-way street.[65] Second, there had in fact been a wide variety of ambiguous, low level military conflict situations, which obviously the threat of massive retaliation had not deterred and to which its use seemed totally inappropriate.

One way to mitigate the dilemma was to give NATO forces a wider range of possible options so that a differentiated series of flexible, graduated responses would be available.[66] The West would not be forced to risk national survival or capitulate on every issue. Thus, by a kind of cost-benefit analysis, each act of aggression would be met with a response of appropriate severity; the punishment would fit the crime.

Unfortunately this concept too has some offsetting disadvantages. The idea of minimum threat with maximum credibility assumes a high degree of rational-

[64]This is a continuing problem. An excellent (if somewhat technical) work is Steven Canby, *The Alliance and Europe: Part IV, Military Doctrine and Technology,* International Institute for Strategic Studies, Adelphi Papers No. 109, 1975.

[65]This development led the French to conclude that there were circumstances in which the United States might not be willing to use its nuclear forces to defend Europe. Therefore, the French decided to develop an independent nuclear force.

[66]Another proposed remedy was a nuclear sharing program, some procedure by which NATO members would participate in the decisional and operational aspects of strategic warfare. Suggested by many in the early 1960s, this concept never was satisfactorily implemented. For an excellent, very brief discussion see Cecil V. Crabb, Jr., *American Foreign Policy in the Nuclear Age,* Third Edition, Harper, New York, 1973, pp. 257–258.

ity on both sides, certainly a dubious assumption for a warfare situation. It assumes acceptance by all parties of a limited warfare "game" and the concept of a limited nuclear war in Europe strains credulity. It assumes the capacity to determine what punishment is appropriate to the crime. To put all of this a different way, graduated deterrence and flexible response demand a cool rational analysis by all parties, the avoidance of emotion, precise calculation, and a conscious refusal to escalate no matter what the circumstance or provocation.

The second basic meaning of the term differential effects is that each decision has an impact on more than one party, and each affects each party differently. The impact of the Israeli attack on Samu (see above) provided us with an excellent illustration.[67] This can also be seen in the continuing saga of the Lebanese crisis. The advantages and disadvantages of the American decision to deploy Marine units as related to United States relations with Egypt and the Russians were discussed above.

But this decision also had an impact on American relations with Great Britain, France, and Israel. Washington's action was compared with its refusal to assist, or even be neutral toward, these countries in the Suez crisis. Clearly the differential impact of Suez had been immense: the weakening of United States ties with its major allies and closest friend, the deterioration in NATO cohesion, the elimination of British and French influence in the Arab world and the corresponding decline in the capacity of the British-supported states of Iraq and Jordan to combat "Nasserism," the increase in Soviet influence, and the increase in Nasser's political prestige despite a military debacle. Despite all of this, Washington had led the opposition. Yet in Lebanon it had responded unilaterally with the deployment of Marines. A major but often overlooked effect of this decision was its reinforcement of a growing European belief that the United States was only willing to use force unilaterally to protect narrowly defined American objectives, and that therefore the NATO nations had better begin to look out for themselves a little more.

Before closing this section one more comment is in order. Because of the increasing power of the People's Republic of China and the development of the Sino-Soviet dispute, it has become common to speak in terms of a diplomatic triangle involving the United States, Russia, and China. In a sense, this triangle involves a series of bilateral relationships, United States-Russia, United States-China, and Sino-Soviet, varying in the degree of common, complementary, and opposed objectives. As the United States has directed its policies toward a "normalization" and "betterment" of relations with each of the other two, and as the Sino-Soviet breach has deepened and intensified, a highly flexible and uncertain situation has developed. The United States has received the benefit of a split among its adversaries, and China and Russia have each gained a new enemy. Each party has two potential opponents, and each is constantly faced

---

[67]See p. 200.

with the possibility of collusion by its potential adversaries against itself. A primary objective of each party is to prevent such collusion. At the same time, there tends to be a primary adversary for each party, either generally or on a given issue, and this inevitably brings about pressure for collusion.

In this situation every decision has a differential impact. Each party must watch the other two very closely. Each movement toward a Soviet-American détente must also be evaluated in terms of its effect on Peking. As Washington and Moscow work more closely together it inevitably increases Chinese fears of collusion. Similarly, as Washington proceeds to "normalize" relations with Peking it inevitably makes a Soviet-American détente more problematical. Obviously the policymaker in this case must proceed with extreme care and caution, constantly guarding against an over-aggressive act that would drive the other two parties in the triangle together.

As a policymaker analyzes each situation then, he or she must consider the potential differential effects of each choice. The policymaker must recognize that all alternatives have both advantages and disadvantages, and choose the one with the best ratio. But he or she must do this within the confines of the second facet of differential effects, namely, the fact that every choice has an impact on several parties and the effect is different for each. Thus the alternative the policymaker is seeking is the one that yields the best *net* cost-benefit ratio when calculated in terms of the anticipated impact on *all* the parties affected.

INSUFFICIENT TIME

The final difficulty is that often the policymaker does not have enough time to analyze the problem thoroughly; things just happen too fast. Developments at the beginning of the Korean War illustrate this point well.

When World War II ended the allies occupied Korea to take over from the Japanese (who had annexed Korea, and renamed it Chosen, in 1910). The United States took over south of the 38th parallel, the Russians to the north. All attempts at peaceful unification failed as Korea became a victim of the Cold War. By the end of 1948 two separate governments were set up, the Republic of Korea in the south and the Democratic People's Republic of Korea in the north. Shortly thereafter an American withdrawal began, and by mid-June 1950 only a few advisers remained.[68] On June 25 North Korean armies swept across the 38th parallel into South Korea in an all-out attack. A U.N. Commission on the scene verified the effectiveness of the surprise invasion, and it was clear that unless

---

[68]For a concise, highly readable account of the background factors see Carl Berger, *The Korea Knot: A Military-Political History,* Revised Edition, University of Pennsylvania Press, Philadelphia, 1968, Chs. 1−7.

something were done to halt the Communists' advance, and done quickly, all of Korea would be in their hands.

The pace of military events demanded that something be done immediately. One would either have to stick with the earlier decision or, because of changed circumstances (or perceptions thereof), try to stop the assault. The purpose here is not to analyze all of the various considerations and factors that influenced the American decision to intervene.[69] Instead, the point is simply this: there was not time to go through carefully all of the steps discussed in Chapter 2, because by the time one finished doing that the North Koreans would have conquered the whole peninsula and the ballgame would have been over. Thus there was no way policymakers could be very confident that they had made the optimum choice because they simply had to act before considering all facets of the problem.

Let's look at a contrasting situation, an example of the controlled step by step management of a crisis in order to provide sufficient time for all parties to analyze the significance of information and act accordingly: President Kennedy and the Cuban Missile Crisis.[70] In the summer and early fall of 1962 American policymakers received considerable soft evidence indicating the Soviets might be installing intermediate and medium range ballistic missiles in Cuba. Because the Kremlin had never before placed such weapons outside Russia, because the possibility of discovery was high, and because the risks such action would produce were enormous, United States officials were skeptical of the incoming soft evidence. Since there was always a chance they were wrong though, via a wide range of public statements and private messages Washington made its position abundantly clear: such action would not be tolerated. Any number of times Moscow stated there was no reason for concern; the Soviet Union had no need to deploy missiles outside its frontiers. In light of all these facts policymakers considered it highly unlikely that missiles actually were being emplaced. Therefore, when the National Security Council's Executive Committee met on the morning of October 16 and was confronted with unmistakable evidence that, in fact, that was exactly what was happening, "the dominant feeling was one of shocked incredulity."[71]

Once it was clear that Soviet missiles *were* being emplaced President Kennedy felt compelled to act. After assessing the options with the Executive Committee, the President selected an approach with as low a level of violence as

---

[69]For a fascinating and highly perceptive analysis of decision-making in the first few days of the crisis, see Glenn D. Paige, *The Korean Decision, June 24–30, 1950*, The Free Press, New York, 1968.

[70]"Information" is used here in the broadest sense, referring to all messages, signals, and cues of a transnational nature, including the impact of actions.

[71]Robert F. Kennedy, *Thirteen Days: A Memoir of the Cuban Missile Crisis*, Norton, New York, 1969, p. 8.

possible so that the Russians would have the time to consider the real impact of each step by the United States, and the consequences that would flow from each projected response.[72] Even then Kennedy sought to avoid a confrontation. On October 18 he met with Soviet Foreign Minister Gromyko, a conference arranged prior to his knowledge of the Russian action. Gromyko, unaware of Kennedy's knowledge, assured the President again that there were no offensive weapons being delivered.[73] For Kennedy this was the last straw.

The President announced the American quarantine on all offensive military equipment under shipment to Cuba in the evening of Monday, October 22, 1962.[74] In the same speech he evidenced his ultimate resolve when he stated that any nuclear missile launched from Cuba against any nation in the Western Hemisphere would be considered as an attack by the Soviet Union on the United States, and would require a full retaliatory response directly on the Soviet Union. This determination to pace and manage events so as to give the Soviets time to think out the consequences of each move illustrated Kennedy's fear of the situation getting out of control, and the possibility that an incorrect assessment of the information being received might lead to that. He worried that the Soviets might feel pushed into a corner and have a spasm reaction. Although the quarantine was announced on Monday, he waited until Tuesday, until after he had received approval of the Organization of American States, to issue the actual proclamation, and it was not to become effective for another 24 hours. He ordered the Navy not to intercept a Soviet ship until absolutely necessary, and did so publicly so that the Soviets would be fully aware of what was going to happen. The first ship intercepted obviously carried no arms, and it was hailed but not boarded. The first boarding occurred the next day, and the ship was not a Soviet ship but rather a Lebanese freighter under Russian charter.

Meanwhile the Administration had been taking steps to demonstrate that this was not a bluff. Troops and ships were deployed, B-52s with nuclear weapons were put on airborne alert, and the Polaris fleet was moved into operational range. Diplomatically, Washington asked for and received unanimous support from the Organization of American States for the quarantine, a rare occurrence indeed, and in the United Nations Ambassador Adlai Stevenson had pressed the United States case with unusual vigor and decisiveness.

The President clearly hoped that Moscow would "get the message." On

---

[72]One of the questions that the Executive Committee had to consider, of course, was "why" did the Soviets put the missiles into Cuba. In a brilliant study Graham Allison indicates that one's answer is highly dependent on his analytical model. See Graham T. Allison, *Essence of Decision: Explaining the Cuban Missile Crisis,* Little, Brown, Boston, 1971.

[73]Several times in the preceding months Moscow had assured Washington that no offensive weapons were being delivered. Kennedy had publicly indicated that were it to be otherwise the "gravest consequences" would arise.

[74]In actuality, of course, this was a naval blockade. The term "quarantine" was used because a blockade could be considered an act of war under International Law.

October 26 he received a private communication from Soviet Premier Khrushchev suggesting a removal of the missiles under international supervision in exchange for an American no-invasion pledge.[75] On the following morning, however, the Russians publicly presented a much more uncompromising position, suggesting a removal of the missiles in exchange for removal of United States missiles from Turkey.

Kennedy's crisis management had been designed to allow the Soviets time to think, but it also had involved the concept of gradual escalation. Now the time had come to give the screw another turn. The President ignored the uncompromising Soviet proposal of October 27 and responded favorably to Friday evening's private message. He then sent his brother Robert, the Attorney-General, to meet Soviet Ambassador Dobrynin. Robert emphasized the Soviet deception, made it clear that "if they did not remove those bases, we would remove them," and stated that Washington had to have a commitment to this effect by Sunday morning.[76] The next morning such a commitment was received. Moscow had "gotten the message." [77]

As the Korean example shows, there are situations in which policymakers have to act rapidly and simply do not have sufficient time to analyze all the relevant information, logically consider each alternative, and so forth. In these cases hopefully contingency plans have been developed that can be applied, the foreign-policy machinery functions efficiently, and the parties exert every effort to keep things as logically controlled as possible. As President Kennedy's actions in the Missile Crisis demonstrate, even under severe stress a policymaker can often do much to manage and pace the tempo of developments. Such an effort can maximize the efficiency with which time is utilized and some of the debilitating effects that insufficient time often creates can be lessened (or even eliminated).

ASSESSMENT

In this chapter a number of rather common policymaking problems have been analyzed. Each of these can constitute an obstacle to effective policy and the policymaker must try to avoid or overcome them in order to optimize his chances of success. Each broad consideration and each specific option must be carefully

---

[75]Also, on this same day, John Scali, diplomatic correspondent of the American Broadcasting Co., received a similar message from Alexander Fomin, purportedly a counselor at the Soviet Embassy but actually a KGB colonel. Scali communicated this to the State Department. See Elie Abel, *The Missile Crisis,* Bantam, New York, 1966, pp. 155−164. The Russians had claimed that there were only defensive weapons being given to Cuba to protect them against an American attack. Because the Central Intelligence Agency had helped to plan and execute the ill-fated Bay of Pigs assault in April 1961 a plausible case could be made.

[76]Kennedy, p. 86.

[77]See Allison, pp. 62−66.

thought out so that (1) its formulation is neither overabstract nor overgeneralized, (2) it is compatible with the rest of one's policy, (3) the actions of implementation are consistent, (4) the policy is sufficiently flexible to allow for unanticipated contingencies yet it allows one to manage events as much as possible, (5) recognizes the limitations of one's knowledge and influence, (6) it takes into account the realistic limitations on future choice given the dead hand of the past and yet is not limited to the status quo, (7) it avoids the distortions of action and information which preconceptions provide, (8) as much as possible it allows for sufficient time to analyze the significance of information and action, (9) it recognizes the interrelated nature of the causation of specific policies, (10) it allows for the differential impact which decisions may have, and (11) it is based on a true "understanding" of all parties in the situation.

SELECTED BIBLIOGRAPHY

Abel, Elie, *The Missile Crisis,* Bantam, New York, 1966.

Brogan, Dennis W., "The Illusion of Omnipotence," *Harper's,* December, 1952, pp. 21−28.

Campbell, John C., *Defense of the Middle East: Problems of American Policy,* Second Edition, Praeger, New York, 1960.

Ellis, Harry B., *Challenge in the Middle East: Communist Influence and American Policy,* Ronald Press, New York, 1960.

Farrell, John C., and Asa P. Smith, eds., *Image and Reality in World Politics,* Columbia University Press, New York, 1968.

Finer, Herman, *Dulles over Suez: The Theory and Practice of his Diplomacy,* Quadrangle Books, Chicago, 1964.

Hammer, Ellen, *The Struggle for Indochina, 1940−1955,* Stanford University Press, Stanford, California, 1966.

Hartmann, Frederick H., *Germany Between East and West: The Reunification Problem,* Prentice-Hall, Englewood Cliffs, New Jersey, 1965.

Hilsman, Roger, *To Move A Nation: The Politics of Foreign Policy in the Administration of John F. Kennedy,* A Delta Book, New York, 1967.

Holsti, Ole R., "The Belief System and National Images: A Case Study," *Journal of Conflict Resolution,* September, 1962, pp. 244−252.

Hoopes, Townsend, *The Limits of Intervention: An Inside Account of How the Johnson Policy of Escalation in Vietnam Was Reversed,* Revised Edition, David McKay, New York, 1973.

Jervis, Robert, *The Logic of Images in International Relations,* Princeton University Press, Princeton, New Jersey, 1971.

Kennan, George, *American Diplomacy, 1900−1950,* University of Chicago Press, Chicago, 1951.

Klineberg, Otto, *The Human Dimension in International Relations,* Holt, Rinehart and Winston, New York, 1964.

Laqueur, Walter, *The Road to War: The Origin and Aftermath of the Arab-Israeli Conflict 1967−8,* Penguin Books, Middlesex, England, 1969.

Love, Kenneth, *Suez: The Twice-Fought War,* McGraw-Hill, New York, 1969.

Morgenthau, Hans J., *In Defense of the National Interest,* Alfred A. Knopf, New York, 1951.

Pachter, Henry M., *Collision Course: The Cuban Missile Crisis and Coexistence,* Praeger, New York, 1963.

Paige, Glenn D., *The Korean Decision, June 24–30, 1950,* The Free Press, New York, 1968.

Qubain, Fahim I., *Crisis in Lebanon,* Middle East Institute, Washington, 1961.

Safran, Nadav, *From War to War: The Arab-Israeli Confrontation, 1948–1967,* Pegasus, New York, 1969.

Sorensen, Theodore C., *Kennedy,* Harper & Row, New York, 1965.

Spanier, John, *American Foreign Policy Since World War II,* Sixth Edition, Praeger, New York, 1973.

Spanier, John W., *The Truman-MacArthur Controversy and the Korean War,* W. W. Norton, New York, 1965.

Stoessinger, John G., *Henry Kissinger: The Anguish of Power,* W. W. Norton, New York, 1976.

Stoessinger, John G., *Nations in Darkness: China, Russia and America,* Third Edition, Random House, New York, 1978.

Stoessinger, John G., *Why Nations Go to War,* Second Edition, St. Martin's Press, New York, 1978.

Sullivan, Michael P., "Vietnam: Calculation or Quicksand? An Evaluation of Competing Decision-Making Models," Research Series No. 13, Institute of Government Research, University of Arizona, October, 1972.

Truman, Harry S., *Memoirs, Volume II. Years of Trial and Hope,* Doubleday, New York, 1956.

Tuchman, Barbara, *The Guns of August,* Dell, New York, 1962.

Wohlstetter, Albert, and Roberta Wohlstetter, *Controlling the Risks in Cuba,* International Institute for Strategic Studies, Adelphi Papers No. 17, London, 1965.

White, Ralph K., *Nobody Wanted War: Misperception in Vietnam and Other Wars,* Doubleday, New York, 1968.

X, "Sources of Soviet Conduct," *Foreign Affairs,* July, 1947, pp. 566–582.

Yost, Charles W., "The Arab-Israeli War: How it Began," *Foreign Affairs,* January, 1968, pp. 304–320.

Seven

Domestic Influences

In the first six chapters our analysis has proceeded as if the policymaker were able to act without regard to domestic pressures and considerations, as if international relations and domestic politics could be separated into watertight compartments and neither would affect the other.[1] Unfortunately things are not this simple; nearly all decisions are taken within a vortex of internal pressures and policymakers often do not have the freedom to just go ahead and make whatever decisions they feel would be best.

In most situations the "official" policymaker is only one of the participants in the policymaking process. A variety of other parties also are involved, each attempting to influence the course of action.[2] As a result the policymaking process usually is much more complicated than even the admitted complexities of international relations would dictate. A staggering quantity and variety of mutual interactions occur yielding a very hazy web of complex, reciprocal relationships.

Because in all political systems the leadership needs some degree of domestic support, policymakers often attempt to build a coalition that will provide a consensual base for themselves and their policies.[3] The major groups and individuals who are needed and who are in a position to provide the requisite support thus become the target of a wide range of requests, promises, threats, and demands.

At the same time that policymakers are wooing these elements they are returning the favor. Each "policy-influencer" makes certain demands and expects a certain amount of satisfaction as the price for its support.[4] If a particular policymaker is unwilling or unable to provide this satisfaction the policy-influencer may not give him the support he seeks.

---

[1]For years international relations was studied with little regard for domestic pressures and this is still the approach in many courses and textbooks today.

[2]As Hilsman pointed out when analyzing the Cuban Missile Crisis there was "an appalling array of rival interests and competing factions." Roger Hilsman, *To Move A Nation: The Politics of Foreign Policy in the Administration of John F. Kennedy,* A Delta Book, New York, 1967, p. 196.

[3]Also see Chapter 3, pp. 123–124.

[4]See William D. Coplin, *Introduction to International Politics: A Theoretical Overview,* Second Edition, Rand McNally, Chicago, 1974, Ch. 3, from which the term "policy-influencer" is taken.

Of course, there may be specific situations in which the policymaker does not have to respond positively. Perhaps the party in question is very weak, or maybe offsetting pressures are more powerful. Maybe he or she can convince it that the demands cannot be filled or another course of action is better. In some systems there are such tight restrictions on group and individual activity that they may have no choice but to support him or her much of the time, or maybe there is no alternative. Perhaps the party is willing to give in this time in the hope of making a gain on another issue or to pave the way for more influence in the future. Despite all these qualifications, however, the policymaker eventually will find that there is a certain core or minimum level of demands that must be met if one is to succeed. If they are not, one will at some point become ineffective (and perhaps even be removed from power).

POLICY-INFLUENCER: PUBLIC OPINION

What are the major types of policy-influencers? The first is public opinion. In many states policymakers profess that they are significantly influenced by the public. Is this really the case or is it just a pretense? If public opinion does have an impact, what is it?[5]

Before beginning this analysis directly it is necessary to make the distinction between the general public, what has been termed the "attentive" public, and opinion elites.[6] When one speaks of the "general public" he or she is referring to all of the people within a society. The term "attentive public" refers to a much smaller group and is defined as that body of informed citizenry that constitutes the primary nongovernmental audience for foreign policy discussions. The "opinion-elites" are the articulate policy-influencing *core* of the population that gives some kind of structure to policymaking discussions and provides the effective means of access to those in charge.

In analyzing the influence of public opinion a very important consideration is the nature of the political system. Although a wide variety of classification schemes are possible, for the purposes of this analysis the basic distinction between authoritarian and democratic systems is sufficient. In every situation one who is seeking to ascertain the impact of public opinion should seek to determine the location of the system in question on the continuum from authoritarian to democratic.

What are the fundamental differences? Basically, authoritarian systems are characterized by the vast and stringent control of society by the government, very

---

[5]Unfortunately there are no definitive answers that apply to all cases; each situation is different and has to be handled separately. Therefore the analysis that follows can only be treated as tentative, hopefully yielding some preliminary generalizations that can provide the foundation for the requisite separate examination one must make in each specific case.

[6]See Gabriel Almond, *The American People and Foreign Policy,* Praeger, New York, 1960.

little competition, low levels of popular participation, either a single political party or none at all, usually a very powerful and influential internal police force, intensive and extensive controls of the activities of individuals by the policymakers, and control of the structures of society by a relatively small number of people. In a system that is more democratic the government does not control everything, competition and popular participation are fairly extensive, political parties are allowed to operate with relative freedom, police forces are limited by laws, individual rights are protected and there are relatively few restrictions on individual activities, power tends to be somewhat diffused, and the governors themselves operate under certain limitations.

Authoritarian Systems

In authoritarian political systems, such as exist in the Soviet Union and the People's Republic of China, public opinion plays almost no role in policy determination. Usually, in fact, the general public is just a tool in the hands of the policymakers. Because the government controls the media of communication the people hear and see primarily what the government wants them to; seldom do they make any serious demands. To the extent that the general public is involved at all in policy its participation is largely reactive or responsive. And in many cases, of course, it is simply unaware of the policies undertaken (a phenomenon not unknown in democratic countries).

The attentive public in these systems is either nonexistent or terribly small and uninfluential. If there *is* a real foreign policy audience, it acts only as a sounding board on relatively unimportant issues. On major issues decisions are made by the policymakers; the public, including the attentive public, is expected to do as it is told. Similarly, in authoritarian systems nongovernmental opinion-elites are of little significance (except, as is seen below, as they may be leaders of important interest groups). In many cases there may not even *be* any opinion-elites because there just is not any policy-influencing core of the population.

This does not mean that the public *never* exercises any influence, however. Because of the fact that all states today are much more permeable than was the case a few years ago, and because knowledge of other countries continually increases (even if policymakers seek to prevent it), the various publics in authoritarian states are becoming somewhat more aware of international realities. Because people's awareness is increasing, consistent or massive reverses in foreign policy may lead to real pressure on policymakers as general disenchantment or antagonism develops. Also, on a few occasions there may be certain deeply held specific opinions that operate at least vaguely as constraints. The Syrian general public's antipathy to Israel certainly places limitations on the policymaker's freedom of choice, for example. Despite these considerations, however, as a generalization one can still say that usually public opinion has very little effect on the policymaker in an authoritarian country.

Democratic Systems

In more democratic systems public opinion *sometimes* is more significant. In what ways can it have an impact? First, usually the general public has some notion about what policies, methods, and objectives it will tolerate. Although these notions are usually vague and amorphous they do exist; at some point they will *provide a set of boundaries* which a policymaker will transgress only at considerable risk.[7] For example, although since World War II the American public had usually supported its President in national security-related affairs, it eventually became disenchanted with American policy in Vietnam. After it became clear that the war was not being "won," there were certain limits established beyond which governmental action would not be tolerated (e.g., a permanent reescalation of the conflict). In a similar vein, the general public in the United States simply would not allow its government to follow a policy that would permit the destruction of Israel. And the consistently high level of pacifism demonstrated by Japanese public opinion since World War II has limited that government's discretion with regard to building a formidable military machine.

The general public can also be influential in *positively marking out at least the general direction that policy should take*.[8] This delineation too is usually imprecise and vague, but that does not detract from the reality of its existence. Once again referring to the Vietnam situation, general public sentiment in the United States placed considerable pressure on the government to change its policy from one of confrontation and staying power to one of conciliation and compromise leading to withdrawal. And the Japanese emphasis on pacifism referred to above also had a direct influence on the course of policy by the support it gave to the government's resistance to American pressure to expand Japanese military capability.

There are other examples of influencing the general direction of policy. The reaction of the American public to the "loss" of China and the stalemate that developed in the Korean War were important factors in the major electoral reverses the Democratic Party suffered in the 1950 mid-term elections. This setback indicated that those who had advocated a more vigorous anti-Communist policy would be more influential in future policymaking. The resulting "hardening" of American policy toward the People's Republic of China was at least partially due to this manifestation of public displeasure. And in both 1956 and 1967 Israeli public opinion put pressure on the government to adopt very bellicose policies.[9]

---

[7]Obviously some of this "risk" is the risk of electoral reverses.

[8]The word "general" needs to be emphasized. Seldom is public opinion sufficiently coherent, informed, and precise to delineate specific policy directions.

[9]Samuel J. Roberts, *Survival or Hegemony? The Foundations of Israeli Foreign Policy*, Johns Hopkins Press, Baltimore, 1973.

The general public plays another role to the extent that it provides *support for governmental actions.* Often this support is most pronounced in a crisis situation.[10] In noncrisis times people become involved in the joys and frustrations of daily living and neither strongly support nor oppose particular policies, but in time of crisis the general public often rallies behind its leaders. Witness the immense support for their government by the people of England during the Battle of Britain, and the high morale and support of the government of the United States by its people during the Second World War.

But, there are times when the general public does *not* give its government support in a crisis. Although one cannot be certain, it seems that the level of support is related to the attributes of the crisis' perceived importance and its duration.[11] For example, in short crises of high importance the American public seems to rally behind its President. The positive reactions to President Nixon's mining of Haiphong Harbor in 1972, President Johnson's massive increase of the bombing of North Vietnam in 1965, President Kennedy's actions in the Cuban Missile Crisis, and President Truman's decisions at the beginning of the Korean War, provide us with just a few examples.

But if a crisis is long lasting and if the objective is perceived to be out of proportion to the time, effort, and resources expended, public support seems to decrease. World War II was a long crisis but there the obvious importance of the struggle plus the fact that positive results were forthcoming led the American public to give strong support. When stalemates developed in the Korean and Vietnam conflicts and they dragged on and on the public eventually began to turn away; it just was not worth it.

Policymakers thus must remember that there is at least a danger that unless a crisis is resolved swiftly, or at least considerable progress can be shown towards its resolution, the public may withdraw its support. Obviously this fact places pressure on policymakers to at least give the appearance of success, and this in turn often leads them to attempt to deceive the public, a point mentioned earlier.[12]

In each of the cases discussed above the attentive public and the opinion-elites successively summarized and articulated the feelings of the mass society. In these situations what seems to exist is a two step, two-way process.[13] Attitudes flow from the general public to the community and opinion leaders and then to the policymakers, and vice versa. Information is filtered, interpreted, and trans-

---

[10]See John Spanier and Eric M. Uslaner, *How American Foreign Policy is Made,* Praeger, New York, 1974, pp. 91–101. Also see Barry B. Hughes, *The Domestic Context of American Foreign Policy,* W. H. Freeman, San Francisco, 1978, Ch. 2.

[11]See William D. Coplin, Patrick J. McGowan and Michael K. O'Leary, *American Foreign Policy: An Introduction to Analysis and Evaluation,* Duxbury Press, North Scituate, Mass., 1974, pp. 27–32.

[12]See Chapter 3, p. 119.

[13]See Elihu Katz and Paul Lazarsfeld, *Personal Influence,* Free Press, New York, 1955.

mitted in both directions with key elites, including the mass media, acting as the conduit and mediator between policymakers and the public at large.

Despite the fact that public opinion *can* have considerable impact in relatively democratic systems, *as a general rule it is not very important.*[14] Most of the time people are primarily concerned with domestic matters and are ill-informed about foreign policy issues.[15] To put it very bluntly, most people don't know much about foreign policy matters and don't care (unless they feel it affects them directly). Furthermore, inconsistency of views, contradictory ideas, and lack of coherence and direction abound. Actually, *instead of influencing the policymaker the general public usually looks to him or her for guidance.* In most cases the public is more of a *follower* than an *influencer.* Although there are the kinds of exceptions discussed earlier, usually the policymaker has pretty much of a free hand.

This public dependence on the policymaker (rather than vice versa) often leads him to attempt to manipulate the public mood instead of being guided by it. In democratic as well as authoritarian systems public opinion is often "used as an active and manipulable resource."[16]

POLICY-INFLUENCER: POLITICAL PARTY

The second major type of policy-influencer is the *political party.* As used here the concept of political party includes all party members, those who have obtained official political office as well as those who have not.[17] To what extent are policymakers influenced by political parties?

Authoritarian Systems

Once again the distinction between authoritarian and democratic systems is relevant. In authoritarian systems there is usually just one political party, and it supplies all (or nearly all) policymaking personnel. One may wonder whether the

[14]This fact is not, of course, restricted to the United States. In his study of the politics of the British military Kenneth Waltz states that a former British Minister in the Foreign Office felt that there was *no* occasion on which he or his superiors had been significantly affected on important decisions by public opinion. See Kenneth Waltz, "The Politics of the British Military," in Roy C. Macridis, ed., *Modern European Governments: Cases in Comparative Policy Making,* Prentice-Hall, Englewood Cliffs, New Jersey, 1968, p. 40.

[15]See James N. Rosenau, "Foreign Policy as an Issue Area," in James N. Rosenau, ed., *Domestic Sources of Foreign Policy,* Free Press, New York, 1967, pp. 24–36; also see Almond, p. 54.

[16]Milton J. Rosenberg, "American Public Opinion on Cold-War Issues," in Herbert C. Kelman, ed., *International Behavior,* Holt Rinehart, New York, 1965, p. 279. Although the phrase is Rosenberg's, he was not specifically referring to democratic systems. One should also add that public opinion is sometimes manipulated as a means of increasing international capability; it is not always manipulated for domestic reasons.

[17]Obviously there is some overlapping of categories here since some individuals are both party members and policymakers. Nevertheless the distinction is analytically valid for most situations.

idea of a policy-influencer is even appropriate in such cases since the key policymakers are also party members. It *is* relevant, however, because most of these parties have a number of factions within them (each with its own power base, interests, and commitments) and each *faction* acts as an influencer.

A useful example of party influence in an authoritarian system is provided by the Communist Party in the Soviet Union (CPSU). The CPSU is the only political party in Russia and it controls the entire policymaking process. All general policy guidelines and specific blueprints are formulated within various Party organs (with the Politburo usually being dominant), and implementation is similarly concentrated. Although two parallel hierarchies exist, the Party and the governmental, only the former is really significant. All key government figures are Party members and it is to the Party that they owe first allegiance. For this reason the major governmental organs have little independent importance. The legislative body, the Supreme Soviet, acts primarily as a sounding board and rubber stamp for Party leadership. The executive, the Council of Ministers, supposedly has wide authority, but it too is run by Party elites; its Chairman (Premier) is always one of the two or three most powerful Party leaders. Similarly, although various administrative personnel may have some role in policy execution, they also must operate within the guidelines and under the watchful eye of the Party faithful. Thus Soviet foreign policy is CPSU policy.

Although the CPSU's control is complete, it is not always unified. Indeed, there has been *much* intra-Party factionalism as various individuals and groups have competed for control of the Party apparatus. Following Khrushchev's denunciation of Stalin at the Twentieth Party Congress in 1956, for example, those who were threatened such as Molotov, Malenkov, and Kaganovich, combined with men who sought greater power in their own right, like Bulganin, and battled Khrushchev for control.[18] And from the time of the beginning of the Second Berlin Crisis of the late 1950s until Khrushchev's fall in 1964 there were serious factional differences within the Politburo.[19] Despite the continuing internal struggles, however, there was little public awareness of the various disputes until later (if then), and Party officials continually sought to maintain the facade of unity; although there actually was a good deal of conflict it occurred behind closed doors and was denied or minimized in public.

Obviously, in authoritarian states such as the Soviet Union the political party is very influential. In some authoritarian systems, however, it means much less. In Egypt, for example, for years there was only one political party, the Arab Socialist Union, and all key policymakers belonged just as they did in the Soviet Union. But in contrast to the Russian situation the ASU had little importance.

[18]In the struggle for control in the 1956–1957 period the Central Committee actually "overruled" the Politburo (at that time called the Presidium), a majority of which had voted to oust Khrushchev. This was a highly unusual occurrence, however, since major decisions are usually made by the Politburo. For an analysis of this interesting period see Robert Conquest, *Power and Policy in the USSR*, Macmillan, London, 1959.

[19]See Tatu, Parts 1–4.

Egypt's single party functioned primarily as an arm of the leadership instead of as a determiner of policy, and usually was little more than a facade behind which decisions were made (and power struggles occurred). What went on in the ASU, therefore, had little immediate influence on Egyptian policymakers.

Thus, when one is seeking to ascertain the influence of political parties in authoritarian systems he once again is faced with the necessity of becoming specific. There are few generalizations of any value. It is clear that conditions in these systems allow room for a great deal of party influence and that sometimes such a degree of influence exists. In some cases it does not, however, and whether or not it actually does in a given situation can be determined only by means of considerable specific analysis.

Democratic Systems

With respect to more democratic systems it is also difficult to generalize. This can be usefully illustrated through some comments about the influence of parties in Japan, West Germany, and the United States.

In post-World War II Japanese politics, the impact of political parties on the foreign policy process has been considerable. In fact, it has been said that "the most important domestic determinant of Japanese foreign policy is the intra-party decision making process of the Liberal-Democrats. All other components of the political system . . . reach the major foreign policy decisions primarily through access to this process."[20]

The Liberal-Democrats were a parliamentary party without a strong popular base. Party leadership was recruited from various distinct factions, each faction having its own independent sources of finance, promoting its own candidates, and regularly caucusing on matters of strategy and policy. These factions existed primarily for the purpose of gaining and using power, and no policymaker could remain in a position of authority without responding to their demands. Reciprocal self-interest was the glue holding them together.

Within the Liberal-Democratic Party there was a continuing process of bargaining, the result being that policy usually was a compromise based on the accommodation of factional demands. This often led to a stifling of initiative and support of the status quo. This was reinforced because of the traditional Japanese notion that decision making should be based on a consensus and not be simply the result of a majority vote.

Due to the fact that though the factions of the Liberal-Democrats often achieved consensus such consensus usually was vigorously opposed by opposition parties, policymakers frequently sought to minimize public discussion of

---

[20]Hellman, p. 50. In addition to Hellman's work, very useful is I. M. Destler, Hideo Sato, Priscilla Clapp, and Haruhiro Fukui, *Managing an Alliance: The Politics of U.S.-Japanese Relations,* Brookings, Washington, D.C., 1976, Ch. 2.

foreign policy and defense issues. When this tactic was not successful the opposition occasionally was able to take advantage of the belief in consensus and influence both political debate and the substance of policy. Generally, however, policy was the product of the Liberal-Democrats intraparty factional struggles.

It is important to point out that this policymaking process has been significant not just in the sense of providing the context for decisions, although it has done that, but also in producing specific policy choices. For example, the 1956 decision to normalize diplomatic relations with the Soviet Union was preceded by two years of factional maneuvering and bargaining; domestic political victory was the prize and the intraparty power struggle was the prime element in determining the outcome.[21]

In the Japanese case policymakers definitely were influenced by the political party, particularly the faction(s) from which they drew their support. In the West German system parties have often had less of a policy-determining influence but they still have been important. Let's briefly examine one aspect of the role of the party system during the reign of Chancellor Konrad Adenauer. The leader of the Christian Democrats, Adenauer was the dominant force in West German politics for well over the first decade of his government's existence. As noted in Chapter 6, he sought West German recovery via an alliance with the West. Adenauer was seeking to develop a European political order that would tie the direction and structure of German society to the cultural and political forces of Western Europe.[22] It was his assumption that once these purposes were accomplished German reunification would follow.

The opposition, mainly the Social Democrats, had foreign policy priorities that were almost exactly the opposite. While they agreed that both recovery and unification were desirable, they believed that Adenauer's commitment to the West would eliminate any possibilities of German unity. They therefore advocated reunification as the first step with recovery and alliance with the West following to whatever extent possible.

The opposition was not very successful because Adenauer's policy recognized the political essentiality of attaching first priority to German recovery. With the country so war-devastated it simply was not feasible to focus on any other objective in the early years of government, and if alliance with the West was necessary to achieve this goal then that is what the majority of the people would support. Of course, as discussed in Chapter 6, the Social Democrats were correct in their contention that this recovery and Western orientation would prevent unification. The problem for them, however, was that their policy was not domestically realistic.

The political parties in this case did not determine or even significantly

[21]Hellman, p. 52.
[22]Wolfram Hanrieder, *The Stable Crisis: Two Decades of German Foreign Policy,* Harper, New York, 1970, p. 131.

influence the policymakers with respect to their choice of policies; Adenauer's positions were not the result of party pressure, from either the Christian Democrats or the opposition. But the party system was important in a less direct way. Because the Social Democrats provided a viable coherent opposition with a program of reasonable alternatives the policymakers in power were compelled to defend their positions publicly, make clear what their priorities were, and be answerable in case their policies failed. To this extent the party system fulfilled a valuable function for a democratic system in that it helped make the policymaker answerable to the public. The specific content of the policies, their anticipated results, and their actual consequences all were kept in the public eye through the process of debate over the various strategic alternatives.

The United States provides us with a third variation. The American party system is characterized by moderation, decentralization, and pragmatism.[23] In a sense there are no truly national parties but rather congeries of local and state parties that combine once every four years in an attempt to elect a President. Party discipline is very weak. Individual members often have their own organizations and independent bases of power. Party leaders possess little formal authority and almost no sanctions; whatever influence they have is a result of nonparty powers. In terms of influence there really is no hierarchy. A system of decision-making *layers* exists with as much power running from the local to the national level as vice versa.

Because of these facts a large variety of political views are expressed within and between the parties. Intraparty conflicts abound and interparty coalitions form and reform. Because party discipline is so weak there seldom is a "party line" (although this is not always the case); even when there is it cannot be enforced. Although Congress is organized on a party basis most of its conflicts with the President are not primarily *party* struggles.[24]

The net result of all this is that American policymakers are seldom influenced significantly by the political parties per se. Because they owe little of their success or failure to party officials they seldom pay much attention to them in the normal processes of policy formulation and implementation.[25]

In each of the three examples of democratic systems described above the political party policy-influencer had a different impact. In the Japanese case it

---

[23]There are any number of useful analyses of this topic. I would recommend that the introductory student begin with a traditional text such as Robert K. Carr, Marver H. Bernstein, Walter F. Murphy and Michael N. Danielson, *Essentials of American Democracy,* Eighth Edition, Dryden Press, Hinsdale, Illinois, 1977, Ch. 7.

[24]Sometimes the features of governmental structure have a significant impact on the policymaking process, as noted in Chapter 3, pp. 118−121. Today the United States Congress is attempting to enlarge its role vis-à-vis the President, for example. As stated in the text, however, this is not primarily a *political party* issue.

[25]For a thoughtful, concise analysis see Gene E. Rainey, *Patterns of American Foreign Policy,* Allyn Bacon, Boston, 1975, Ch. 8.

was quite influential in policy determination; in the West German situation it did not directly influence policy choices but was indirectly important as an agent to keep the policymaker "on his toes" and publicly accountable; in the American case parties had almost no significance.

What conclusions can be drawn from this? Perhaps the only sure one is that no generalizations are possible (as was true with respect to authoritarian systems). The mere fact that a system is democratic gives one little clue as to how important a policy-influencer the political parties in that system will be. In some they are very significant, in some moderately so, and in some they hardly matter. When attempting to ascertain their influence one must proceed on a case by case basis, carefully analyzing the specific facts and reaching conclusions only on the basis of those facts.

POLICY-INFLUENCER: INTEREST GROUPS

Interest groups are another major category of policy-influencer. An interest group is (1) an association of individuals; (2) external to major policymaking positions; (3) who are "tied" together by a more or less common set of interests and (4) one of whose objectives is to influence the policymaker with regard to specific policies that would advance these particular interests.[26] These associations are often economic in nature, but this is not a requisite and various professional, ethnic, social, and occupational groups exist.

Authoritarian Systems

The distinction made earlier between relatively democratic and authoritarian systems is important here. Fewer independent groups are allowed to exist in most authoritarian states than in their democratic counterparts. For this reason one can say that generally interest groups tend to be less important. But although fundamentally correct, this "obvious" conclusion is to some extent misleading. Even though formal independent associations are fewer, a myriad of informal "groupings" exist and people with common interests *do* work together to achieve common objectives.

In an authoritarian system the policymaking apparatus is centrally controlled and directed, and thus in many ways it is relatively impervious to pressure. Nevertheless, policymakers are sometimes forced to depend on outside sources for certain kinds of specialized information, a certain degree of expertise, and some cooperation in the implementation of decisions. Because often there are groups (or "groupings") that possess these special characteristics, they may have an opportunity to exercise some influence. Generally speaking, the degree of influence will be proportional to the policymaker's *dependence* for informa-

---

[26]Bureaucratic factors that could be considered here will be analyzed in succeeding sections.

tion and advice on such outside sources, his or her *need* for their expertise in handling various matters, and the *extent* to which their cooperation is necessary for the effective implementation of his decisions. Because policymakers in all systems sometimes have such needs, in all systems policymakers are sometimes influenced by interest groups. Certainly there are differences from system to system but basically they are differences in degree, not kind.

There is another aspect of interest group activity to be considered with respect to authoritarian systems, namely, the fact that various groups often struggle to advance their special interests by taking control of the policymaking apparatus. In this situation the objective is not to influence certain specific policies but rather to attain decisive influence within the policymaking organs themselves.

In the Soviet Union, for example, there are several factions competing for control of the Party and governmental machinery.[27] Although Soviet ideology officially allows no room for competing interest groups (which could only be "hostile classes"), these groups do exist. Economic managers, technocrats, the cultural intelligentsia, the scientific community, the police, and the ever-present armed forces compete for supremacy along with the Party and governmental bureaucrats. Instead of a process of competition and accommodation such as occurs in many democratic systems, however, the objective in this case sometimes is the attainment of dominance and the elimination of rivals. Because of this the composition of the various Party and governmental organs often tends to reflect the mosaic of power relationships in existence at a given time.

The policymaker in an authoritarian system thus may find himself subject to two kinds of interest group stimuli. The first is the traditional demands-supports relationship based on reciprocal need and advantage. When the need factor is minimal he will be little influenced *if* the group is not too powerful. But the second impinging factor concerns the matter of competition for control of the policymaking apparatus, and in these situations he must always be aware of the power dynamics of group politics.

Democratic Systems

With respect to more democratic systems it is useful to distinguish between those in which policymaking is relatively centralized and those in which it is not. Great Britain provides us with an example of considerable centralization. With its parliamentary system and fusion of powers, policy is made primarily by the governing political party rather than via any kind of interparty bargaining and compromise. The parties organize and operate the governmental system on a

---

[27]See especially Vernon V. Aspaturian, *Process and Power in Soviet Foreign Policy,* Little, Brown, Boston, 1971, Chs. 15–16. Also see Philip D. Stewart, "Soviet Interest Groups and the Policy Process," *World Politics,* October, 1969, pp. 29–50.

straight, party-line basis. They are highly disciplined and centralized, with sanctions and authority flowing from top to bottom through a well-defined hierarchy. Members seldom depart from the leadership's positions, and when they do they may be risking their political careers. In this kind of a situation there is precious little room for interest group influence external to the party structure. A wide variety of groups *do* seek to influence policymakers at both the executive and parliamentary level, *but they do so primarily by working through and in connection with the parties themselves.*

Because the parties have different although somewhat overlapping bases of support, some groups are much more influential with one party than another. But even with respect to important supportive groups the key point remains: seldom can a group compel a policymaker to depart from the accepted party line. A group's influence exists primarily within the confines of the party structure and is limited to attempting to persuade the party leadership that what is good for the particular group is good for party and country.

In some democratic systems decision making is much more diffused. Because of the system of separate institutions with an intermingling, checking, and balancing of functions and powers, decentralized political parties, federalism, and a variety of other structural features, American policymaking is extremely fragmented.[28] Decisions are made in a wide variety of places and circumstances by a number of different individuals, groups, and coalitions. This means that there are a multitude of points at which one may gain access to the policymaking process. Interest groups investigate these, constantly seeking access to the "key" policymaker. Because these groups sometimes have significant financial resources, occasionally can be important in an electoral contest, sometimes can provide valuable information and assistance, and sometimes are in a position to apply coercive pressure, policymakers on certain issues may be very sensitive to group viewpoints. Various Zionist organizations, for example, have played a significant role in influencing American policy toward Israel.[29] Similarly, for years the notorious China lobby was influential in preventing reconsideration of American policy toward the People's Republic of China.[30]

These examples are the exception rather than the rule, however. Generally interest groups are not very influential with respect to foreign policy issues. Why is this so? In the first place, most major groups such as the AFL-CIO and Chamber of Commerce are large organizations composed of many members who

---

[28]This analysis owes an intellectual debt to the classic and ever valuable work of David Truman, *The Governmental Process,* Knopf, New York, 1951.

[29]Jewish groups are among the most active and the most successful. See Bernard C. Cohen, *The Public's Impact on Foreign Policy,* Little, Brown, Boston, 1973, pp. 104–105. Also see Earl Huff, "A Study of a Successful Interest Group: The American Zionist Movement" *Western Political Quarterly,* March, 1972, pp. 109–124.

[30]See A. T. Steele, *The American People and China,* McGraw-Hill, New York, 1966. Also useful is Ross Y. Koen, *The China Lobby in American Politics,* Macmillan, New York, 1960.

are also members of other groups. Because of this overlapping membership individuals have competing loyalties and most of the time the group's leaders cannot possibly influence their membership sufficiently to have them act as a cohesive body.

A second point is that usually there are a myriad of groups lined up on opposite sides of various issues. For example, with respect to foreign trade bills there are certain groups that tend to be protectionists and others that tend to be oriented toward freer trade. Many times this competition has an offsetting effect as the groups neutralize each other.[31] This allows the policymaker to pick and choose.

Another point is that most interest groups are concerned with only a few problems and are not really operational a good share of the time. Thus policymakers are simply relatively free of interest group pressures on many issues. Also, there are so many competing elements within the policymaking process that even if interest groups should happen to be united and cohesive on some issue they might well be offset or relegated to subsidiary importance by other factors. Furthermore, whereas interest groups are often important in domestic politics because of their capacity to provide critical information, on foreign policy questions they simply do not have such information to provide.[32] Finally, on some issues perceived to have a significant relationship to national security, interest groups sublimate their special needs to the national good; in certain cases politics "stops at the water's edge."

The net result of all of this for the policymaker is that usually he or she is able to act without much regard to interest group pressures. Although there are occasional exceptions, most of the time interest groups are not important policy-influencers on international issues.

Before concluding this analysis it is necessary to deal with what has been called the military-industrial complex, that conglomeration of industries, bureaucratic agencies, Congressmen, interest groups, communities, and states that are concerned with and purportedly influential in the development of defense policy. With the annual American defense budget now over the $115 billion mark it is easy to understand why various organizations seek to influence the policymaking process in their favor. More and more groups are becoming involved, not only because of the size of the pie but also as a result of two other factors (1) the distinction between foreign and domestic policy is becoming increasingly obscure (and meaningless?), and (2) more and more sectors of the economy are being geared specifically to defense and defense-related activities. In recent years completely new industries have developed that depend almost totally on military expenditures, for example, and basic research and develop-

---

[31]Raymond A. Bauer, Ithiel de Sola Pool, and Lewis Anthony Dexter, *American Business and Public Policy,* Second Edition, Aldine-Atherton, Chicago, 1972.
[32]Spanier and Uslaner, pp. 83–84.

ment have been closely tied to military requirements. Decisions such as whether or not to develop a new weapons system or whether to maintain, expand, or close a particular military installation can have an immense impact.

Policymakers expect to be the targets of activity in defense-related areas, and they are. Sometimes the pressures are immense and occasionally a policymaker's decision is definitely influenced. *This is the exception rather than the rule, however, despite misconceptions to the contrary.* The basic reason is that the "complex" is both less coherent and less powerful than is sometimes supposed. There are several reasons for this. In the first place, specific industrial representatives, interest groups, contractors, and whatever usually align with the specific armed service they feel will do them the most good. Different ones choose different services and the services often are in competition. This contributes to an intensification of natural interservice rivalries with the result that the President and his advisers are able to play one against the other, to pick and choose. Second, more times than is recognized the military is simply overruled by the civilians in control.[33] And third, very often there is intense infighting over the plums in the budgetary process; instead of a unified "complex" exercising control one sees a bitter conflict. Much of the time, instead of the policymaker being compelled to do something in particular, he is able to choose from the maelstrom of contending forces.[34]

None of this is to gainsay the fact that the military-industrial complex has a role in American policymaking. It has sometimes been important before and will occasionally be so in the future. But the matter should be kept in perspective: this "complex" certainly is not dominant, much of the time it is not unified, and usually policymakers are not significantly influenced by it.

Our analysis of the significance of the three types of policy-influencers (public opinion, political parties, and interest groups) has led to the general conclusion that most of the time they really are not very influential in democratic systems. With the notable exception of the importance of political parties in certain authoritarian states, in most authoritarian systems they are similarly insignificant. Very seldom are these policy-influencers able to compel the policymaker to do what he does not want to do, and most of the time they cannot even influence him significantly. But does this mean that policymakers are usually free from meaningful domestic pressures? The answer is "no," and the

---

[33]Ibid., p. 85. President Carter's 1977 decision not to produce the B-1 bomber was just such a case.

[34]For a very useful discussion of the politics of the budgetary process, see Samuel P. Huntington, *The Common Defense,* Columbia University Press, New York, 1961; also Warner R. Schilling, Paul Hammond, Glen Snyder, eds., *Strategy, Politics and Defense Budgets,* Columbia University Press, New York, 1962. A concise, competent analysis and review of Defense Department procedures is Lawrence J. Korb, "The Budget Process in the Department of Defense: 1947–77: The Strengths and Weaknesses of Three Systems," *Public Administration Review,* July-August, 1977, pp. 334–346.

reason is that they often are greatly influenced by bureaucratic politics, the subject of the remainder of this chapter.

BUREAUCRATIC POLITICS

Former President Harry Truman has been quoted as saying, "I make American foreign policy."[35] At another time, however, he said, "I sit here all day trying to persuade people to do things they ought to have enough sense to do without my persuading them," and he said of incoming President Eisenhower's problems, "he'll sit here and he'll say do this, do that, and nothing will happen."[36] These quotations point up the discrepancy between what the chief policymaker occasionally feels able to do and what he is so often prevented from doing because of bureaucratic difficulties.

Every chief policymaker in every country operates within a bureaucratic political context.[37] Because there are simply too many decisions for any one person to make and because such a wide variety of expertise is required, an organization exists the purported purpose of which is to help the chief policymaker rationally formulate and efficiently implement his optimum foreign policy. These organizations will be studied here from four related and somewhat overlapping perspectives. First, we will view the bureaucratic political process in terms of the standard operating procedures that exist within most large organizations. Second, we will examine the significance of bureaucratic fragmentation and the competition between organizations. Third, we will analyze the role of small groups in policymaking. And fourth, we will comment on the bureaucratic process as a whole, emphasizing in particular the relationship of the chief policymaker to his bureaucracy.

What is a bureaucracy? Although there are a wide variety of definitions, for the purposes of this analysis it is useful to define it as a large, formal organization that possesses the following characteristics: first, a hierarchical pattern of authority and communication with specific superior-subordinate relationships; second, a specialization of both role and function; third, a complex division of labor; and fourth, internal operations conducted via set procedures that emphasize formal rules and regulations. An example of such an organization would be the U.S. Department of State.

As mentioned above, the presumed purpose of a foreign policy bureaucracy

---

[35]Louis E. Koenig, *The Chief Executive,* Third Edition, Harcourt Brace, New York, 1975, p. 213.

[36]Richard Neustadt, *Presidential Power: The Politics of Leadership,* Wiley, New York, 1960, pp. 9–10.

[37]Naturally the size, complexity, and specific features differ from state to state, and thus the impact of the bureaucratic politics also varies. Although this is a fact and policymaking styles are dissimilar in some ways, the general trend in nearly all states is toward the development of a fairly extensive bureaucracy.

is to aid the chief policymaker in formulating and implementing the optimum policy. It is designed to reflect the need for specialization and expertise in the conduct of foreign affairs, and to provide for the gathering, interpreting, and transmitting of accurate information as swiftly as possible to the correct people. It is also supposed to ensure a certain degree of stability and regularity in the policymaking process. Finally, it is supposed to provide records of what has been done so that one has a basis on which to make intelligent judgments concerning the future.

Few would deny the necessity of having such an organization, and foreign policy bureaucracies exist in all modern nations. But despite these facts the character of the operational procedures that exist within most bureaucracies is such that a great many problems can develop, and it is to these procedures and problems that we now turn.

BUREAUCRATIC POLITICS: OPERATING PROCEDURES

The first point to remember is that the vast majority of foreign policy decisions are made in accordance with standardized procedures set up well in advance of the particular situation. Such procedures are designed to anticipate a wide variety of contingencies, and responses are preprogramed according to specific routines. Policymaking often becomes a matter of selecting the appropriate routine and implementing it according to prescribed rules and regulations. The vast majority of these activities involve relatively low echelon bureaucrats who act within the framework of the procedures and general policies established by their superiors.

Because of the immense volume of issues confronting any state these routinized procedures are necessary. *But the consequence for the chief policymaker is that the vast majority of the "decisions" that are made, although presumably being within the prescribed policy and procedural framework, occur without his or her specific knowledge.* This means that the chief policymaker is removed from the day to day operation of most policy and often wakes up to a *fait accompli.*[38]

Sometimes these low-level decisions have immense significance. For example, in the Eisenhower Administration specific decisions concerning U-2 overflights (spy flights) were taken as a matter of course by the Central Intelligence Agency in accordance with guidelines set down by the President. In the early summer of 1960 such an aircraft was shot down over the Soviet Union shortly before a scheduled Summit Conference. This led to a series of events that

---

[38]A useful study in this regard is Vincent Davis, "The Development of a Capability to Deliver Nuclear Weapons by Carrier-Based Aircraft," in Morton H. Halperin and Arnold Kanter, eds., *Readings in American Foreign Policy: A Bureaucratic Perspective,* Little, Brown, Boston, 1973, pp. 216–275.

culminated in the Russians torpedoing of that Conference, and the spy-plane incident provided the rationale. The decisions had been taken on a routine basis without any direct guidance from above and apparently without sufficient awareness of what embarassment a failure could cause.[39]

Not all decisions, of course, are made so routinely. Although there is not sufficient data to warrant any all-embracing conclusions, generally speaking one can say that the more unanticipated the problem the less routinely it can be handled, and the more complex and important the issue the more likely decisions will be made at higher and higher levels within the bureaucracy.

There is no guarantee that this will be the case, however, because the very judgments concerning whether or not a problem is highly important and complicated are often made by the person with whom the problem first comes in contact, namely, a low level bureaucrat. If this person perceives the problem to be relatively simple or believes that it can be handled within a prearranged framework *he* or *she* may make a decision that has far reaching operational consequences (when he or she should refer it to a higher level). Decisions that tend to be primarily supportive of existing policy or that seem to be neutral with regard to change, and decisions that tend to be perceived as perhaps somewhat different but not particularly important, also tend to be made at lower levels.

A major difficulty that often arises in a bureaucratic setting is the *stifling of initiative and innovation*. Decisions tend to be made that are considered safe, that conform to existing procedures, and that will not require significant judgment concerning whether or not departures from established rules are required. Because procedures are set up on the basis of the results of *past* policy, decisions based on such experience involve very few radical departures. To the extent that these factors operate, the policymaker may never even get the chance to consider new ideas.

There are several other factors that tend to inhibit innovation within a bureaucratic setting. First, the individual whose views or actions differ widely from organizational policy tends to adjust his or her views or be rejected.[40] If that individual cannot be convinced to change those views his or her ideas will have very little influence. Second, there is a rather natural tendency on the part of subordinates to advocate policies that they perceive to be in accord with the views of their superiors. It is usually safe for one to propose alternatives that he or she knows will not "rock the boat" and that will reinforce his or her superior's power and policies.[41] To the extent that superior-subordinate relationships prevent the consideration of new ideas, either because of formal sanctions or informal coercion, innovation is repressed.

[39]See David Wise and Thomas B. Ross, *The U-2 Affair*, Random House, New York, 1962.

[40]Joseph De Rivera, *The Psychological Dimension in Foreign Policy*, Charles E. Merrill, Columbus, Ohio, 1968, pp. 209–211.

[41]This would be especially true in authoritarian states, of course. No low-level Soviet bureaucrat is going to make proposals that differ significantly from the Party line.

A third reason that new policies tend to be eliminated is the mere fact that many decisions must ascend several horizontal layers within the organization. As proposals traverse their hazardous way up the administrative hierarchy the more extreme ideas tend to be weeded out at each level. By the time a proposal reaches the top it very often can be described as the least common denominator, the least innovative and most compromised point of view.

And there is another reason. A bureaucracy contains a wide variety of specialists with differing perspectives, sources of information, and points of view. Because many people take part in a given policymaking situation, in order for a common policy to be developed compromise is necessary. And compromise itself usually involves a rejection of extremes or radical departures from established policy. This too contributes to a lack of innovation.

This discussion of the pressure toward caution and conformity has raised several other important points. As mentioned above, within a bureaucracy there is immense task specialization. While this is necessary because of the detailed expertise required to formulate an effective policy, it also poses certain problems. For example, the *further one is down the hierarchy, the narrower one's perspective becomes.*[42]

All people quite naturally tend to view a problem in terms of their particular position. Within the U.S. State Department, for example, it is quite natural for the Country Director for Egypt to view the Arab-Israeli conflict with particular emphasis on the role of the Egyptians and the impact of various policies on Cairo. However, there are other considerations which people at higher levels with broader responsibility will need to take into account. The Assistant Secretary for the Near East would have to consider the possible impact and importance of all the various factors within that geographical region (many of which will have been presented to him by the various Country Directors). Even his perspective is not sufficiently broad, however, because there are a wide variety of ramifications for international organization, economic development and, of course, for the international organization, economic development and, of course, for the interrelationships from one geographical region to another. The Secretary of State will need to coordinate all of the specialized inputs, and the process continues this way right up to the top.[43]

The problem of parochialism requires that compromises be effected but this must be done in such a way that the specialists do not react too negatively, and in such a fashion that high level coordination of various recommendations can occur. This is often easier said than done, and the many compromises tend to

---

[42]I. M. Destler, *Presidents, Bureaucrats and Foreign Policy: The Politics of Organizational Reform*, Princeton University Press, Princeton, New Jersey, 1974, p. 57.

[43]Another problem sometimes crops up in this regard. Because of their differences in perspective and objectives lower level bureaucrats may refuse to comply with established policy or procedure. In some cases they may even go beyond this and sabotage the leadership's positions, trying to impose their own solutions to problems.

inhibit major policy changes. But the only way to avoid this is to not consider certain points of view and simply make whatever decisions one feels appropriate. This would both fail to take advantage of all relevant information and expertise and lead to a low level of morale and intraorganizational efficiency. So there is no perfect answer to this one.

The myriad of factors that contribute to the stifling of initiative, the parochialism and compromise, and the problem of ''layering,'' lead to another troublesome problem: *often it takes forever and a day to get anything done.* So many clearances are required, there are so many ''bases to be touched,'' that the policymaker sometimes just cannot seem to get started. President Kennedy was continually frustrated by what he felt was a kind of ''built-in inertia.''[44] This kind of difficulty often leads policymakers to bypass the foreign policy bureaucracy in matters of critical importance.

Another major factor indicated by the discussion of the inhibition of innovation is the *problem of obtaining sufficient accurate information and communicating it to the appropriate parties.* As indicated earlier, communication of information will be affected by a subordinate's perception of the rewards or costs that will accrue to him or her as a result of the communication. If he insists on communicating information his superior feels is incorrect or unimportant there may be excessive costs.[45] Therefore certain kinds of information simply may not be communicated.

To some extent, of course, information *must* be selected, evaluated, and filtered from one level to another. There are too many decisions for all of them to be made at the top level, and there is simply too much information for any one party to digest. Therefore, synthesis and summarization must occur, and judgments made as to what should and should not be communicated.

Lower echelon bureaucrats are critically important in this regard. They are the ones through whom most information is funnelled and the ones who make the judgments concerning the kind, frequency, direction, and content of communication. Because of this role it is they who often ''really'' make policy and the individuals at the top, reputedly the chief policymakers, are sometimes relatively powerless.[46]

It was noted in Chapter Six how information can be distorted by preconception or perceptual bias. But even that which is communicated without such handicaps may receive insufficient consideration or be lost in the mass of data that threatens to inundate all bureaucracies. Because of this problem there seems to be an increasing tendency on the part of top level policymakers to

[44]Theodore Sorensen, *Kennedy,* Harper, New York, 1965, p. 287.

[45]See Ellis O. Briggs, ''The Staffing and Operations of Our Diplomatic Missions,'' in Henry M. Jackson, ed., *The Secretary of State and the Ambassador,* Praeger, New York, 1964, pp. 134–135.

[46]See John C. Ries, *The Management of Defense,* Johns Hopkins Press, Baltimore, 1964, pp. 49–50.

consider only a small fraction of that which is directed to their attention and to place more emphasis on the source of the information than on the informational content.

If information is not interpreted correctly or one does not get the attention of the right people (or they do not pay sufficient attention), the result can be disastrous. As Roberta Wohlstetter has so effectively demonstrated, the Pearl Harbor disaster simply would not have occurred if intelligence had been interpreted correctly.[47] And with respect to getting the right people to pay attention, a May 1960 poll indicated that the Cuban majority was heavily supportive of the Castro regime. Obviously in such a situation any attempt at an invasion in the hope of a mass revolution would be very unwise. The poll was distributed widely both inside and outside of government but apparently no one paid much attention since the Bay of Pigs episode occurred early the next year.[48]

Part of the reason that many of these problems are so noticeable is the fact that *policymakers operate under immense time pressure.*[49] Unfortunately the problem is getting worse. One reason is the greatly increased number of nations in the world as compared with 20 years ago and the resulting increase in the number of interactions. Also, there seem to be more problems to deal with and in many ways they seem to possess greater urgency. Policymakers are also under time pressure because as the bureaucracy grows larger there are simply more and more different interests to be taken into account.[50]

In Chapter Six an example of the lack of sufficient time to make decisions and also some attempts to overcome this in a particular crisis were analyzed, but it should be recognized that these are pervasive, continuing problems. There is simply too much to do and not enough time to do it. The problems of too much size and insufficient time contribute to the policymaker's search for informal

[47]Roberta Wohlstetter, *Pearl Harbor: Warning and Decision,* Stanford University Press, Stanford, California, 1962. A more recent failure to interpret intelligence information correctly occurred before the October 1973 Arab-Israeli War when Israeli policymakers failed to anticipate the Egyptian-Syrian attack. See Chaim Herzog, *The War of Atonement: October, 1973.* Little, Brown, Boston, 1975, Chs. 1−4, and Michael I. Handel, ''The Yom Kippur War and the Inevitability of Surprise,'' *International Studies Quarterly,* September, 1977, pp. 461−502. Also see Chapter 5 above, pp. 187−188.

[48]Hadley Cantril, *The Human Dimension: Experiences in Policy Research,* Rutgers University Press, Brunswick, New Jersey, 1967, Ch. 1. Before the October 1973 Middle East War most American intelligence officials did not believe hostilities would occur; those with differing views could not get either Kissinger or Nixon to pay attention. See Ray S. Cline, ''Policy Without Intelligence,'' *Foreign Policy,* Winter, 1974−75, pp. 121−135.

[49]Although the piece is somewhat dated, the student can still get a ''feel'' for this problem by reading Charlton Ogburn, Jr., ''The Flow of Policymaking in the Department of State,'' in H. Field Haviland, Jr., ed., *The Formulation and Administration of United States Foreign Policy,* Brookings, Washington, 1960, Appendix C. Also see Chapter 6, pp. 218−221.

[50]Sometimes efficiency may be hampered because organizations are just too big. See John Franklin Campbell, *The Foreign Affairs Fudge Factory,* Basic Books, New York, 1971.

means of policymaking outside of the foreign policy bureaucracy, and to the stifling of new ideas and policies within the formal structure.

Before concluding this section one other factor must be mentioned. To this point, with minor exceptions, the analysis has proceded as if each of the individuals within the bureaucracy was primarily concerned with developing the optimum foreign policy. Unfortunately this characterization is both over-simplified and inaccurate.[51] Bureaucrats are human beings who have careers and seek personal advancement. Naturally they hope to advance up the hierarchy of influence and/or to maximize their influence at any given level.

Because of this their perceptions and goals may be substantially determined by bureaucratic factors, and their attention may be directed away from international problems to intrabureaucratic concerns.[52] Since they want to succeed, they bargain, manipulate, and attempt to persuade in an effort to achieve their *personal* objectives. Because this is so it obviously is inaccurate to view them as homogeneous unselfish lumps; they are particular human beings with particular interests and perspectives who desire to advance their own careers, and the policymaker *must* evaluate them accordingly.

The logical implication of these facts is that *the process of interaction within an organization is eminently political.* There are a wide range of actions based on interpersonal rivalry, the various processes are characterized by bargaining in both formal and informal settings, and personal gain is often as much a determinant of the decisions made (or not made) as concern for the "best" policy.

Although these statements are true, it should also be pointed out that people often believe that what is best for them and a maximization of their own power *is* the "best" policy, and that their actions are not all cynical manipulations. Furthermore, it is obvious that a great many people *do* legitimately concern themselves with developing the "best" policy at any particular time, and personal influence and prestige are not all that count. Also, as should be evident by now, the substantive problems are so terribly complex that differences among policymakers are inevitable even when they are seeking the optimum decision. Nevertheless, the fact remains that it would be unwise of the policymaker to assume that the maximization of personal power and prestige is not a significant part of the bureaucratic process.

BUREAUCRATIC POLITICS: FRAGMENTATION AND COMPETITION

Another series of problems that the policymaker must face arises largely because of the fact that the bureaucratic policymaking machinery is terribly fragmented. Although there is a difference in degree depending on the system, circumstances,

---

[51] Allison, p. 146, says "The gap between academic literature and the experience of participants in government is nowhere wider than at this point. For those who participate in government the terms of daily employment cannot be ignored."

[52] Halperin and Kanter, p. 3.

issues, and personalities involved, it is almost always true that several organizations or factions participate in the policymaking process. Whereas previously this analysis has been concerned with problems that arise *within* a given bureaucratic organization, now our attention is directed to the fact that there are several such organizations and/or factions interacting.

The United States represents perhaps the extreme in bureaucratic policymaking fragmentation.[53] The President, of course, is the chief policymaker. In his Executive Office the members of his White House Staff and the Office of Management and Budget often play important roles, and in recent administrations the Special Assistant for National Security Affairs has been extremely influential.[54] In addition, the National Security Council, created in 1947 and consisting of the President, Vice-President, Secretaries of State and Defense, and having as statutory advisors the Director of the CIA and the Chairman of the Joint Chiefs of Staff, also may play a major role.

The Department of State, of course, is also a primary participant. Headed by the Secretary of State, the senior member of the President's cabinet, it tends to be at the center of routine policymaking activities. It is organized on both a geographical and functional basis in recognition of the fact that both kinds of expertise are needed for effective decision-making.[55] As noted earlier, this leads to certain problems of coordination, specialization, parochialism, compromise and so forth.

There are many other agencies. The Department of Defense obviously is concerned with matters of military and defense posture, the development of strategic concepts, the allocation of resources, preparation for the most likely military contingencies, and the management of alliance military policies. Headed by a civilian, the Secretary of Defense, it incorporates within it the branches of the armed services and the Joint Chiefs of Staff. There are several intelligence agencies (of which the CIA is the most important), and they have a significant impact on a variety of security-related matters. The Arms Control and Disarmament Agency plays an important role in the sphere of arms limitations. On some kinds of problems an agency whose functions are primarily domestic may have a meaningful input. For example, when dealing with issues of world hunger the

---

[53]This analysis focuses on the American system. Obviously the policymaker (and the student) would need to adjust his or her views to whatever level of fragmentation was characteristic of the particular system under study.

[54]This was especially true when Henry Kissinger held that position. One of the most fascinating statesmen of modern times, Dr. Kissinger has been the subject of many analyses (and legends). Very useful in understanding his approach, in addition to his own *American Foreign Policy*, Expanded Edition, Norton, New York, 1974, are Stephen R. Graubard, *Kissinger: Portrait of a Mind*, Norton, New York, 1974, and John G. Stoessinger, *Henry Kissinger: The Anguish of Power*, Norton, New York, 1976.

[55]Such a breakdown is typical. The headquarters staff of the Soviet Ministry of Foreign Affairs, for example, consists of several functional divisions and "about sixteen geographic divisions or desks." Morton Schwartz, *The Foreign Policy of the USSR: Domestic Factors*, Dickenson, Encino and Belmont, California, 1975, pp. 174–175.

Department of Agriculture is deeply involved. The Treasury and Commerce Departments are major participants in decisions concerning international finance and trade. If oil imports are the issue the Energy Department will play a major role. Of course, the list could be extended even further.

Fragmentation such as this can have harmful effects. One of these may be the lack of policy coordination. The right hand may not know what the left is doing with the result that each faction may develop its own particular approach to a problem. At best this leads to duplication and waste, to an overlapping of jurisdictions with several agencies attempting to do the same thing. But sometimes things are not even this "good." If the right hand does not know what the left is doing, perhaps the job simply will not get done. Each organization assumes that the particular task is someone else's responsibility, so no one undertakes it. Sometimes one unit will act in such a way (unintentionally) to undercut the effectiveness of another. For example, in March 1978 President Carter gave a major speech on defense policy. The speech, written by an aide to National Security Adviser Zbigniew Brzezinski and reflecting the latter's rather "hardline" approach, was designed to dispel any Soviet doubts about Washington's "firmness" and signal Moscow that a continued Russian military buildup might jeopardize U.S.-Soviet cooperation. Shortly before the address was given, however, a high-ranking State Department official telephoned the Soviet Embassy in Washington and urged that the complete text of the speech be transmitted to Moscow so Russian leaders could read the *conciliatory portions.*[56] Obviously, this diminished the speech's impact on the Soviets.

The supposed "solution" for these problems is to establish clear lines of authority and give the appropriate officials "authority" commensurate with their "responsibility." Hopefully by now the student is aware of the substantive complexity of international relations and realizes how difficult this "answer" is to put into practice. Problems are just too large, interrelated, and complex for such a simple solution to work.[57] As Destler has put it:

> More generally, who in the broader government should have "authority" on the issue of possible U.S. troop withdrawals from Europe? The Secretary of State and his European Affairs Bureau? His Politico-Military Affairs Bureau? The Secretary of Defense? The Secretary of the Treasury, given his role as protector of the balance of payments? The Director of the Arms Control and Disarmament Agency, given the relation of troop withdrawals to the military balance? For each of them, "responsibility" on this issue far outruns the "authority" to deal with it.[58]

[56]*New York Times,* April 17, 1978, p. 3. It has been hypothesized that unintentional undercutting occurred when the Russians took great care to deceive the United States with respect to the clandestine shipment of missiles but their installation proceeded with almost no efforts at camouflage. Traditionally, Soviet arms shipments were the province of Soviet military intelligence whose work emphasized secrecy and deception; missiles were usually installed by the Strategic Rocket Forces who seldom were concerned with such things. See Allison, pp. 109–111.

[57]Of course, this does not mean that one should not try to come as close to this goal as possible.

[58]Destler, p. 24.

A second major difficulty develops because *organizations tend to develop interests of their own.*[59] Just as is true with respect to states and their leaders, organizational leaders seek to develop the capabilities necessary to protect their interests. Generally this involves acquiring and preserving a certain structural, personnel, and financial base, and some degree of policymaking autonomy; in some ways it is as if they were seeking bureaucratic "territory" and the right to exert primary influence over its future.[60]

As noted in the preceding section, bureaucratic officials are motivated at least partially by their own self-interests. Since an individual works within an organization, how that organization fares will affect his or her personal welfare. If it gains influence, becomes widely respected, is assigned new and better programs, and receives economic, political, and psychological rewards, then its members will usually benefit. If not, or if the reverse is true, the members will tend to suffer.

Within each organization there are certain patterns of communication and authority and certain rules and regulations that define the expectations of those in various positions. Career advancement is often dependent on serving the organization's interests and it obviously is much safer to promote what seems to be best for the organization than to "cross" the organization in favor of policies that might benefit others.

It is important to note, however, that much of the time these acts are not perceived as "selfish" by their perpetrators.[61] Generally speaking, the representatives of a given organization, while advocating policies that benefit that organization, honestly believe that these policies are also the "best policy" for the resolution of the problem. For example, whereas the Joint Chiefs of Staff generally advocate a high level of spending for the military services, which presumably would have the result of increasing the power and prestige of the armed services, they also genuinely believe that this is essential for the security of the United States. Similarly, when representatives of the Agency for International Development advocate more foreign aid, a result of which would be a greater role for their organization, they also believe this is what is best for the country. It should not automatically be assumed that what is occurring is a cynical manipulation in the interest of organizational influence *at the expense* of the interests of state; one needs to understand that various policies are often advocated in the

---

[59]It has been persuasively argued that certain organizations in the Soviet Union have a stake in maintaining an atmosphere of tension. Because of this they automatically oppose a policy of détente with the West because any real relaxation would cause their role to be reduced. For a perceptive yet concise analysis see Schwartz, pp. 182–188.

[60]This concept is developed in Anthony Downs, *Inside Bureaucracy*, Little, Brown, Boston, 1967.

[61]Of course, in many situations motives are mixed. See ibid., p. 88 and the classification scheme of Robert Presthus, *The Organizational Society*, Knopf, New York, 1962. In fact, in some cases one may even support policies whose impact is at least partially counter to increased organizational influence. See Hilsman, *To Move a Nation*, p. 112.

belief that the interests of the organization are coincident with the interests of the country.

The product of acting in terms of organizational interests is bureaucratic competition.[62] The parochialism generated by the specialization required to solve complex problems is combined with the desire to accomplish organizational objectives, and the result is a process of competitive bargaining. When this occurs the "policy" that emerges is less the result of rational choice than simply the product of bureaucratic interaction. This outcome may provide an effective policy but there is no guarantee that this will occur. It may yield a stalemate, a compromise, an ineffective policy, or no policy at all.

Before leaving this topic one final point should be made. As mentioned many times, it is flesh and blood human beings with all of their qualities and frailties who make decisions. Therefore *interpersonal conflict also can be a very important element in a policymaking situation.* This is true in any context, of course, but it is likely to be exacerbated in this setting because of the fact that the particular individuals represent different interest constituencies when they are members of different organizations; this may aggravate whatever existing tendencies there may have been toward personal conflict.

In the discussions concerning the appropriate policies to be undertaken with regard to the Korean War, for example, there were genuine differences of opinion, to some extent based on organizational interests, between the Department of Defense and the Department of State. But these differences were made much worse by the personal conflicts that existed. It was quite clear that the President had a closer relationship with the Secretary of State than he did with the Secretary of Defense, and in addition to "the tension created by various interdepartmental conflicts, the two Secretaries obviously disliked and distrusted each other personally. Reportedly the Secretary of Defense undercut the Secretary of State whenever he could."[63]

BUREAUCRATIC POLITICS: SMALL GROUPS

There is another phenomenon apparent in much of the policymaking process, namely, that a significant part of the daily activity occurs within the framework of various small groups. The membership of such groups usually transverses organizational lines, and the units are held together by a wide range of professional and/or personal ties.

Sometimes groups develop on a relatively informal basis. If there are suffi-

---

[62]Allison, Chs. 3–4, is excellent on this topic. Also very useful is Matthew Holden, Jr., " 'Imperialism' in Bureaucracy," *American Political Science Review*, December, 1966, pp. 943–951.

[63]de Rivera, p. 215.

cient common interests, meetings may be held over an extended period of time and the group may take on some degree of permanence. If the group is composed of high level leaders and increased trust develops a kind of policymaking "inner circle" may result.[64] When Lyndon Johnson was President there was a small group known as the "Tuesday Lunch Bunch," which constituted an inner circle.[65] Made up of Secretaries Rusk (State) and McNamara (Defense), the Special Assistant, Director of the CIA, Chairman of the Joint Chiefs of Staff, and Johnson, this group provided the "real" policymaking forum for years.

On some occasions a small group may be created specifically to deal with a particular problem or crisis (and the assumption is that it will disappear when its job is finished). These groups may be variable in membership and meet intermittently. In the Korean War, for example, there were six critical meetings during the first week of the crisis, four involving groups of 12 to 14 members, two with six.[66] Sometimes groups are created that meet more or less continuously for the duration of the problem. In the Cuban Missile Crisis President Kennedy appointed a small group known as "ExComm," a group of about 15 trusted advisers whose advice he considered significant, and this group was important throughout the dispute. As was the case in the other examples, a small group made critical decisions outside of the formal policymaking machinery.[67]

Small groups have certain advantageous features. In the first place, other things being equal there will be relatively little conflict because presumably there will be comparatively few viewpoints to reconcile. Second, these "extracurricular" organizations have no organizational interest to protect and are free to deal directly with the substantive issues. Third, usually the group's members can subordinate the interests of the organizations from which they come to the purposes of the informal group and thus organizational parochialism can be avoided. Fourth, the members are not prevented from a free and frank interchange by organizational rules and procedures; there are no artificial barriers to open communication. Fifth, action often can be taken swiftly and decisively. Sixth, innovation and experimentation are not stifled by various bureaucratic devices. And seventh, secrecy is much more probable than in larger organizations.

But there are also disadvantages. In fact, some of the supposed "advantages" can be problems. Secrecy is sometimes harmful, for example. Also, as discussed in Chapter Two sometimes an orientation of avoidance is the best approach.[68] Few small groups recommend doing nothing.

There are other problems. Members of small groups tend to rely on their own memories and perceptions rather than on organizational data (stored, inter-

[64]See Hilsman, *The Politics of Policymaking in Defense and Foreign Affairs,* pp. 118–120.
[65]See Hartmann, *The New Age of American Foreign Policy,* p. 80.
[66]See Paige, *The Korean Decision,* for a discussion of these meetings.
[67]It was recognized that in this setting the members represented the President, not various organizational interests. Sorensen, *Kennedy,* p. 679.
[68]See Chapter 2, pp. 53–54.

preted, and coded information that exists within the policymaking bureaucracy). Often personal recollections are seriously incomplete and/or distorted. Furthermore, as Eden's likening of Nasser to Hitler in the 1956 Suez crisis demonstrates, personal perceptions can be terribly inaccurate.

Another difficulty arises because the particular group members may not be experts in the specific matters under consideration. The inordinate complexity of international relations requires that a variety of specialists be heard on most issues of significance; although a small group could make an effort in this regard, in practice it often fails to do so.

Another difficulty with small groups is that many times the unorthodox personality either is rejected quickly or is required to subordinate his or her viewpoint. Unusual ideas are very noticeable when only a few people are involved, and there is much pressure to conform. Because of the fear that unpopular or unorthodox views may lead to face-to-face humiliation or reprisal such ideas may not even be suggested.

Because personal relationships have paramount importance there is always the danger that agreement will occur because of perceived personal pressure.[69] In some cases one individual may be (or become) dominant and the others just "go through the motions." Also, personality conflicts may occur and very destructive relationships develop.

Finally, the characteristics and procedures of a small group's leadership are very important. The relationship of leader (or leaders) and followers, the degree to which the meetings can be efficiently and effectively run with regard to the objectives at hand, and the procedures themselves can have a critical impact. One must remember that the absence of the regularized procedures that exist in an organized bureaucracy means that the procedures for a small group are set by the group itself, and they may either inhibit or facilitate efficient policymaking.[70]

BUREAUCRATIC POLITICS: THE POLICYMAKING PROCESS

To this point the analysis of bureaucratic politics has examined the impact of bureaucratic procedures, analyzed the results of bureaucratic fragmentation and interorganizational competition, and discussed the role of small groups. It remains for us to look at the policymaking process as a whole, make some comments as to its overall characteristics, and discuss the relationship of the chief policymaker to the bureaucratic organization.

Perhaps the first point one should note is that *it is misleading to think in terms of a single "decision." In reality policymaking is the product of many bits*

---

[69]de Rivera, pp. 218–219.

[70]To keep the "ExComm" discussions from being inhibited or biased during the Cuban Missile Crisis President Kennedy often did not attend.

of decisions emerging and interacting continuously over time. Ideas and information flow into the process from a variety of official and unofficial sources, actions are taken by people at various levels in different organizations, and information is transmitted and communicated laterally and hierarchically to other people in positions of authority. Each "piece of the action" is the result of many different factors and in turn shapes and influences the succeeding ones. Rather than single discrete decisions there is really a stream or flow of decisional fragments.

Because of this process the policymaker often has his or her "decision" already largely determined by actions taken as a result of bureaucratic bargaining, fragmentation, or operating procedure. Whatever one speaks of as a person's "decision" in such a case is actually a part of the entire chain rather than a self contained individual choice.

Because of this fact the chief policymaker is frequently just another participant in the process.[71] Of course the chief policymaker possesses certain attributes and advantages that others do not have, but in many cases he or she is not in a position of "command" even with respect to his or her own policymaking organization. Instead, the "boss" finds that his or her "power" is essentially a power of persuasion, a capability that is exercised primarily via a bargaining process. As Neustadt has effectively demonstrated, this is true even of the President of the United States. He, too, often finds that his power is primarily just a power to persuade, and that "the power to persuade is the power to bargain."[72]

These comments illustrate a third characteristic: *the pervasiveness of bargaining*. Instead of participating in a rational planning and implementing process as one might assume, all participants in the policymaking process negotiate in order to attain maximum influence. This occurs within organizations, between organizations, and between the chief policymaker and all of the other organizational and individual participants. Thus the entire process in many ways consists of a gigantic contest in which the stakes are influence and the outcome is what is sometimes called the policymaking "decision."

This activity occurs in all political systems although it is much more obvious and open, and is extended to a wider variety of participants, in more democratic structures. Nevertheless, for reasons mentioned earlier (the information required, insufficient time, the necessity of expertise, specialization of function, and so forth) in all situations there is some degree of bargaining and bargaining occurs to some extent in all political systems (even though in some cases it may be tacit rather than explicit).

---

[71]Though this is an accurate statement, the word "frequently" is critical here because this is *not always* the case; sometimes the chief policymaker is *not* "just another participant." In other words, while one needs to understand the point being made he or she should not jump to the invalid conclusion that a chief policymaker never is highly important; in certain situations, particularly crises perceived to affect fundamental objectives, the chief policymaker may in fact be preeminent.

[72]Neustadt, Ch. 3.

A related feature is what has been called a *"strain toward agreement."*[73] All of the participants are involved in an effort to build a consensus, to "push" for an accomodation or compromise that all participants eventually can support. Sometimes this leads to a tendency to "oversell" particular policies.[74] In the effort to build a consensus the various participants naturally try to present their case in the most favorable light. As a result they often exaggerate the merits of their particular position. This process of overselling may continue once a decision is reached and policymakers oversell the policy both to the public and to other states. This sometimes leads to self-deception on the part of the very policymakers who made the decisions.

Another danger in this process is that since, as noted earlier, policy may just be the outcome of bargaining, the capacity to achieve consensus may become the test of whether or not a particular policy "should" be adopted. Furthermore, once a consensus is reached people may automatically assume that it is the *appropriate* policy, when in fact it may well not be. The achieved consensus may actually have little or no relationship to the optimum policy; it may be simply a reflection of the power and skill of the participants.[75]

Because of this effort and the myriad of factors discussed in the preceding sections, certain other characteristics abound (some of which are simply a magnification of problems that exist within and between organizations). Because so many different views must be accommodated, radically different proposals tend to be eliminated and innovative ideas stifled. Because so many actors participate the process is time-consuming and prone to excessive delay, and much conflict is generated. Policies once established acquire an immense momentum, inertia sets in, and change is extremely difficult. The participants become so enmeshed in the daily routines and interactions that long range projects receive little attention. Individuals act in terms of personal interest, sometimes even to the point of not complying with existing procedures or policies.

Finally, sometimes a consensus cannot be achieved and the result is just "minimal decisions," the avoidance of deciding any more than absolutely necessary. For example, because of interorganizational disputes American officials could not reach a consensus on the development of a hydrogen bomb in 1950. As a result President Truman made only a very limited commitment, ordering only continued research and the development of a few prototypes. It seems that, for him, the major "issue" was minimizing conflict and building consensus within

[73]Warner R. Schilling, "The Politics of National Defense: Fiscal 1950," in Warner R. Schilling, Paul Hammond and Glenn Snyder, eds., *Strategy, Politics and Defense Budgets,* Columbia University Press, New York, 1962, p. 23.

[74]See Theodore Lowi, "Making Democracy Safe for the World: National Politics and Foreign Policy," in James N. Rosenau, ed., *Domestic Sources of Foreign Policy,* Free Press, New York, 1967, pp. 295–332.

[75]See Roger Hilsman, "The Foreign Policy Consensus: An Interim Research Report," *Journal of Conflict Resolution,* December, 1959, pp. 361–382.

the bureaucracy, and the minimal decision was the method he deemed appropriate.[76] In 1967 President Johnson followed a similar course of action in his decision on the development of an antiballistic missile system (ABM).[77] Here too different organizational actors viewed the stakes differently, bargaining was pervasive, and consensus appeared unachievable. In a fashion reminiscent of Mr. Truman, Johnson opted to decide as little as possible, hoping to avoid antagonizing any of the conflicting elements. Consequently, he neither rejected nor supported ABM deployment. Instead, the President asked Congress to fund the acquisition of certain ABM components, and allowed Secretary of Defense Robert McNamara to state that the administration believed in the concept of a small, anti-Chinese system. But concerning deployment, the "decision" was to postpone any decision.

As the analysis in this chapter has clearly demonstrated, the policymaker usually operates within a maelstrom of divergent domestic forces; the policymaking process is far removed from the calm orderly deliberation presumed in many rational policymaking models. Because of this the policymaker often does not really seek to make optimum choices. Instead, much of the time he is content to examine alternatives until he finds one that meets a minimum standard of acceptability, and once this occurs he acts. This "satisficing" behavior may not appeal to the purist, but to the harried policymaker it is often the best he or she can do.[78]

IN LIEU OF CONCLUSION

There is really no appropriate conclusion for this book. To provide an in-depth summation would be both repetitious and an insult to the reader's intelligence. In lieu of any conclusion I will close with just a few personal remarks.

First, throughout my research and writing I could not help but be struck by the extraordinary difficulty of the policymaker's task. The international arena is such a dynamic mosaic of interactions that sometimes it is a wonder that anyone ever knows what is going on. Situations are so varied that often it seems as if there is no precedent that is useful. Problems are terribly complex and sometimes seem to defy resolution. Each actor has his own interests to protect and a great range of genuine disputes occur regularly. There are few commonly accepted "rules of the game" except trying to ensure one's survival. Because all actors

---

[76]See Warner R. Schilling, "The H-Bomb Decision: How to Decide Without Actually Choosing," *Political Science Quarterly,* March, 1961, pp. 24–46.

[77]See Morton H. Halperin, "The Decision to Deploy the ABM: Bureaucratic and Domestic Politics in the Johnson Administration," *World Politics,* October, 1972, pp. 62ff. Also see Spanier and Uslaner, pp. 115–126.

[78]See Herbert A. Simon, *Administrative Behavior,* Macmillan, New York, 1959, in which the concept of "satisficing" behavior is fully developed. Some have indicated that such "satisficing" behavior has been very evident in Washington's failure to develop an overall energy policy. See Joseph S. Szyliowicz, "The Embargo and U.S. Foreign Policy," in Szyliowicz and O'Neill, p. 214.

operate from different perspectives they perceive things differently, and these perceptual differences and distortions often magnify the many substantive differences that occur. Individual policymakers operate from within different systems and cultures and possess any number of differences in personality, role perception, and so forth. The only real certainty is uncertainty, and change is constant: and on . . . and on . . . and on.

Even the most basic concepts are controversial. Not only is there disagreement about their content, very often even when there is substantive agreement it is not clear how such concepts should be applied to particular practical circumstances. Very few generalizations have much validity for the policymaker, and an immense amount of specific, concrete analysis is necessary in every case.

Recognition of the difficulty of the policymaker's task leads to my second comment—the necessity for policymakers and observers alike to have only modest expectations. When one recognizes the immense uncertainties, complexities, limitations, and disparities that exist one realizes that the most that can be reasonably hoped for is a moderate degree of effectiveness. There will be both gains and losses. No policymaker can always "do everything right," and even if he or she could success would not always be achieved.

Third, it is my hope that this analysis has made the reader highly cognizant of and interested in both the basic and specific nature of many of the most important facets of contemporary international relations. Further, it is hoped that the student now has some understanding of the types of options realistically available to policymakers as they confront the concrete complexities of real world situations, as well as some ideas as to how one ought to try to proceed in certain cases, what he should at least try to do, and so forth. Finally, it has been my intent to provide the student with an enduring analytical framework; complexities and uncertainties exist, yes, but there are also significant means to and degrees of comprehension. It is my fervent prayer that this comprehension will be obtained and that it will be used to bring about a better quality of life for all humankind.

SELECTED BIBLIOGRAPHY

Allison, Graham T., *Essence of Decision: Explaining the Cuban Missile Crisis,* Little, Brown, Boston, 1971.

Almond, Gabriel, *The American People and Foreign Policy,* Praeger, New York, 1960.

Aspaturian, Vernon V., *Process and Power in Soviet Foreign Policy,* Little, Brown, Boston, 1971.

Bauer, Raymond A., Ithiel de Sola Pool, and Lewis Anthony Dexter, *American Business and Public Policy,* Second Edition, Aldine-Atherton, Chicago, 1972.

Berkowitz, Morton, P. G. Bock, and Vincent J. Fuccillo, *The Politics of American Foreign Policy: The Social Context of Decisions,* Prentice-Hall, Englewood Cliffs, New Jersey, 1977.

Brecher, Michael, *Decisions in Israel's Foreign Policy,* Yale University Press, New Haven, Connecticut, 1975.

Cline, Ray S., "Policy Without Intelligence," *Foreign Policy,* Winter, 1974–75, pp. 121–135.

Cohen, Bernard C., *The Public's Impact on Foreign Policy,* Little, Brown, Boston, 1973.

Conquest, Robert, *Power and Policy in the USSR,* Macmillan, London, 1959.

Coplin, William D., *Introduction to International Politics: A Theoretical Overview,* Second Edition, Rand McNally, Chicago, 1974.

De Rivera, Joseph, *The Psychological Dimension in Foreign Policy,* Charles E. Merrill, Columbus, Ohio, 1968.

Destler, I. M., *Presidents, Bureaucrats and Foreign Policy: The Politics of Organizational Reform,* Princeton University Press, Princeton, New Jersey, 1974.

Destler, I. M., Hideo Sato, Priscilla Clapp, and Haruhiro Fukui, *Managing an Alliance: The Politics of U.S.-Japanese Relations,* Brookings, Washington, D.C., 1976.

Deutsch, Karl W., *The Analysis of International Relations,* Prentice-Hall, Englewood Cliffs, New Jersey, 1968.

Deutsch, Karl W., *The Nerves of Government,* Free Press, New York, 1963.

Elowitz, Larry, and John W. Spanier, "Korea and Vietnam: Limited War and the American Political System," *Orbis,* Summer, 1974, pp. 510–534.

Esterline, John H., and Robert B. Black, *Inside Foreign Policy: The Department of State Political System and Its Subsystems,* Mayfield, Palo Alto, California, 1975.

Feld, Werner, "National Economic Interest Groups and Policy Formation in the EEC," *Political Science Quarterly,* September, 1966, pp. 392–411.

Fox, Douglas M., ed., *The Politics of U.S. Foreign Policy Making,* Goodyear, Pacific Palisades, California, 1971.

Halperin, Morton H., *Bureaucratic Politics and Foreign Policy,* Brookings, Washington, 1974.

Halperin, Morton H., and Arnold Kanter, eds., *Readings in American Foreign Policy: A Bureaucratic Perspective,* Little, Brown, Boston, 1973.

Hanrieder, Wolfram, *The Stable Crisis: Two Decades of German Foreign Policy,* Harper & Row, New York, 1970.

Hilsman, Roger, *The Politics of Policy Making in Defense and Foreign Affairs,* Harper & Row, New York, 1971.

Hoopes, Townsend, *The Limits of Intervention: An Inside Account of How the Johnson Policy of Escalation in Vietnam Was Reversed,* Revised Edition, David McKay, New York, 1973.

Huff, Earl, "A Study of a Successful Interest Group: The American Zionist Movement," *Western Political Quarterly,* March, 1972, pp. 109–124.

Huntington, Samuel P., *The Common Defense,* Columbia University Press, New York, 1961.

Kelman, Herbert C., ed., *International Behavior,* Holt, Rinehart and Winston, New York, 1965.

Koen, Ross Y., *The China Lobby in American Politics,* Macmillan, New York, 1960.

Lindblom, Charles E., "The Science of Muddling Through," *Public Administration Review,* Spring, 1959, pp. 79–88.

Macridis, Roy C., ed., *Modern European Government: Cases in Comparative Policy Making,* Prentice-Hall, Englewood Cliffs, New Jersey, 1968.

Mueller, John E., *War, Presidents and Public Opinion,* Wiley, New York, 1973.

Neustadt, Richard, *Presidential Power: The Politics of Leadership,* Wiley, New York, 1960.

Rainey, Gene E., *Patterns of American Foreign Policy*, Allyn Bacon, Boston, 1975.

Rosenau, James N., ed., *Domestic Sources of Foreign Policy*, Free Press, New York, 1967.

Rosenau, James, *The Scientific Study of Foreign Policy*, Free Press, New York, 1971.

Rourke, Francis E., *Bureaucracy and Foreign Policy*, Johns Hopkins Press, Baltimore, 1972.

Schilling, Warner R., Paul Hammond, and Glen Snyder, eds., *Strategy, Politics and Defense Budgets*, Columbia University Press, New York, 1962.

Schwartz, Morton, *The Foreign Policy of the USSR: Domestic Factors*, Dickenson, Encino and Belmont, California, 1975.

Simon, Herbert A., *Administrative Behavior*, Macmillan, New York, 1959.

Simon, Richard C., H. W. Bruck, and Burton Sapin, eds., *Foreign Policy Decision-Making*, Free Press, New York, 1962.

Spanier, John, and Eric M. Uslaner, *How American Foreign Policy is Made*, Praeger, New York, 1974.

Stewart, Philip D., "Soviet Interest Groups and the Policy Process," *World Politics*, October, 1969, pp. 29–50.

Waltz, Kenneth M., *Foreign Policy and Democratic Politics*, Little, Brown, Boston, 1967.

Wohlstetter, Roberta, *Pearl Harbor: Warning and Decision*, Stanford University Press, Stanford, California, 1962.

Index

DATE DUE
